OLD ALBEMARLE
AND ITS ABSENTEE LANDLORDS

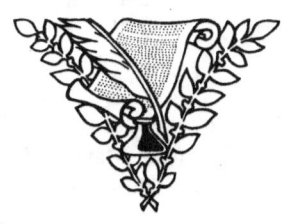

By
Worth S. Ray

CLEARFIELD

Originally published as
The Lost Tribes of North Carolina, Part IV
Austin, Texas
1947

Reprinted by Genealogical Publishing Co., Inc.
Baltimore, Maryland
1960, 1968, 1976

Library of Congress Catalog Card Number 67-9767

Reprinted for Clearfield Company by
Genealogical Publishing Co., Inc.
Baltimore, Maryland
1993, 1994, 1998, 2001, 2004, 2007, 2012

ISBN 978-0-8063-0287-4

NOTICE
This work was reproduced from the original 1947 edition.
The uneven image evident in the reprint is characteristic
of the original typography. This shortcoming not withstanding,
our printer has made every effort to produce as fine a reprint
of the original edition as possible.

Made in the United States of America

OLD ALBEMARLE
AND ITS ABSENTEE LANDLORDS

REV. ROGER GREEN'S grant to a thousand acres of land between the mouth of the Chowan and Roanoke rivers on the West end of Albemarle Sound in 1653, at the instance of WILLIAM BERKELEY, was made by the VIRGINIA ASSEMBLY. At that time there was no dividing line between Virginia and what later became the Province of North Carolina, and Green's grant was issued perhaps on the theory that the land was in VIRGINIA, and not in that somewhat uncertain and undefined area that lay along ALBEMARLE SOUND, South of the Old Dominion.

It was not until ten years later, March 24, 1663, when King Charles Second, restored to the throne of England after the Cromwell regime, exercising the Divine Right of Kings, assembled a little coterie of favorites around him and bestowed upon them as his Royal gift, the vast domain lying between the Atlantic and the "Western Waters", thus making them "Proprietors" of all Carolina.

Who were these men? They were:

1. GEN. GEORGE MONCK.
2. EDWARD HYDE.
3. ANTHONY ASHLEY COOPER.
4. GEORGE CARTERET.
5. JOHN COLLETON.
6. JOHN BERKELEY
7. WILLIAM BERKELEY.
8. WILLIAM, EARL OF CRAVEN.

By historical courtesy these ENGLISH POLITICIANS have been designated as the "PROPRIETORS" of the CAROLINAS. In the simple terms of plain English they were the ABSENTEE LANDLORDS of the vast domain now shown on the maps of the country as North and South Carolina. Each one of them, at the time of the "restoration" had so connived with the "powers that be" as to ingratiate himself into the good graces of the new 31 year old Sovereign on the English throne, who, restored from his exile while the Cromwells were in power, distributed his largess with a lavish hand. It seems doubtful whether any, save WILLIAM BERKELEY, ever set foot on Carolina soil.

"OLD ALBEMARLE" bears the name in perpetuation of GEN. GEORGE MONCK, who afterwards became DUKE OF ALBEMARLE, who is No. 1 among the absentee landlords on the above list. To say the least of it General George Monck was no Saint. When Cromwell was in power Monck was one of his trusted lieutenants, but when the House of Stuart was restored to ascendency, it was Monck's letter which furnished evidence on which some former adherents of Cromwell were meted out punishment, and at least one of them - the Duke of Argyle - was hung higher than Haman. Thus by "carrying water on both shoulders" Monck was given a Dukedom, and an eighth part of all the great Province of Carolina.

EDWARD HYDE (No. 2 on the list) became the Earl of CLARENDON. In the nature of things it was not the Earl of Clarendon who was Governor of the Carolinas in 1712. That was evidently another and different EDWARD HYDE, since it is unlikely that Governor Hyde of 1712 could have been an octogenarian who was prominent in Courts of England a half century before he succeeded THOMAS CARY as Governor. ANNE HYDE, a daughter of the Earl of Clarendon, was seduced by the Duke of York, a younger brother of Charles II, and forced to marry her, and a son of the old Earl, LAWRENCE HYDE was contemporaneous with FRANCIS LORD WILLOUGHBY and with him was given the Governorship of one of the British Islands in the West Indies.

ANTHONY ASHLEY COOPER became the Earl of Shaftsbury. He had vast interests in what is now South Carolina, where two rivers bear his name. His sons came to the Barbadoes and perhaps reached the Carolinas in the South, but LORD ASHLEY COOPER for political reasons, sought an asylum in Holland, where he died in 1683. It is not the province of this work to detail the ventures in what is now SOUTH CAROLINA.

GEORGE CARTERET (Absentee Landlord No. 4). Known as Sir George Carteret, he was one of the wealthiest men in all England. That he became one of the overlords of North and South Carolina is not surprising in view of the fact that during a tense financial crisis in England he dug up a loan of some £280,000 for Charles II, the embarrassed King. In 1669 Carteret was condemned by the House of Commons for corrupt practices and was expelled therefrom. Although we have found no positive record that Sir George Carteret ever came to the Carolinas, PETER CARTERET, known to be his "kinsman" (possibly a brother, or a son), succeeded SAMUEL STEVENS as Governor of Albemarle in 1669, and served until 1673 in that office.

JOHN COLLETON, known as Sir John Colleton, had vast interests in the BARBADOES and in Carolina, but conducted his business by "remote control" as did most of the other absentee landlords. His son JAMES COLLETON became Governor at Charleston.

JOHN BERKELEY was a brother of SIR WILLIAM BERKELEY, and it was he who escorted Charles II back to the English throne from his enforced exile in Holland at the restoration.

WILLIAM EARL CRAVEN, says Wheeler, "was a brave cavalier, an old soldier of the German discipline and supposed husband to the Queen of Bolivia."

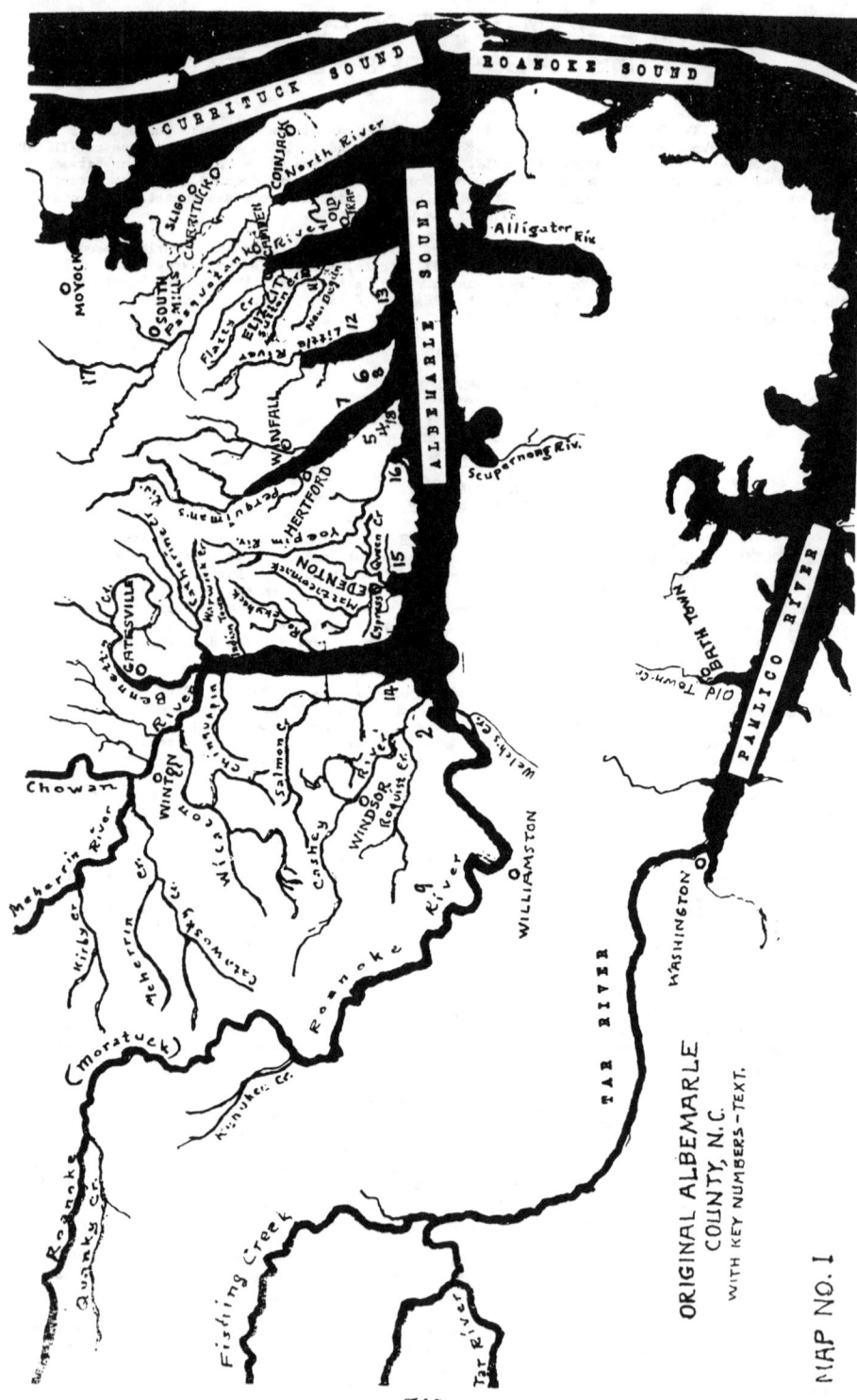

ORIGINAL ALBEMARLE COUNTY, N.C.
WITH KEY NUMBERS - TEXT.

MAP NO. 1

OLD ALBEMARLE, THE GRANDFATHER

By means of the map on page 580, the writer has attempted to delineate a crude outline of ALBEMARLE COUNTY or PRECINCT, the original gateway to the present NORTH CAROLINA and the home of its first settlers. At the time of ROGER GREEN'S GRANT in 1653 there were, of course, no towns, except Indian Towns and even the rivers and streams were without fixed or settled names, and such names as they had were unpronouncible Indian names, to be superseded by others, some of which are not much better, even today. The names of several present day towns, with their locations, and the names of streams, later adopted, have been inserted on the map to enable the writer to designate places, distances and the more important locations, and in order that readers may more easily understand the area sought to be described.

This map and others that may appear herein are not drawn to any particular scale, nor has absolute accuracy been even attempted. By reference to some of the places named and some of the present day towns mentioned, a fairly good idea of the distances and scale of the map may be gained. For instance:

ELIZABETH CITY is approximately 22 miles South of the line between the present NORTH CAROLINA and VIRGINIA. In the days of ROGER GREEN (1653) and GEORGE DURANT (1661) there was no Elizabeth City, no Edenton, Hertford or Windsor, but the distances between these places as afterwards established and named, were the same as they are today.

From the mouth of CHOWAN RIVER to the present day towns of SLIGO and CURRITUCK is approximately 55 miles, as one traverses the modern highways. Windsor, present county seat of BERTIE COUNTY, on the Cashey River is some 14 miles West of the mouth of Chowan, and 21 miles West of EDENTON. Between HERTFORD and EDENTON is 13 miles, and from Edenton West it is seven miles to the bridge across the Chowan to what is called EDENHOUSE POINT. From Hertford, southward to ALBEMARLE SOUND along Harvey's Neck is about 12 or 14 miles, while ELIZABETH CITY is higher up and about 20 miles North of the Sound.

CURRITUCK, the county seat of the County of that name, is about 16 miles South of the Virginia line. COINJACK, in Currituck, is 10 miles South of the town of Currituck, and OLD TAP, low down in Pasquotank County is 16 miles South of the town of Camden, which is four miles East of Elizabeth City, across the long causeway.

POINTS OF HISTORIC INTEREST NUMBERED

Several points of historic interest have been designated on the map by numbers, and those numbers correspond to the numbered items which follow:

(4) This number appears approximately at the site of the old home of COL. THOMAS HARVEY (1694) who was Deputy Governor of what was then called the CAROLINAS. (See p. 61, this volume), after whom this area of Perquiman's County is named "Harvey's Neck".

(2) Between the mouth of the CHOWAN RIVER and the ROANOKE (sometimes then called MORATUCK) is believed to have been the site of the grant of land made to ROGER GREEN in 1653. At that time, from the wording of the grant itself, it appears there were already white settlers living along that section of the Chowan and Roanoke rivers. Who they were, where they came from, and what became of them are questions the answers to which will never be known. It is contended by several writers that Roger Green's colony was never planted, but there are evidences that indicate this conclusion is without foundation. (See p. 289 this book).

(5) Some ten miles South of the town of HERTFORD, county seat of PERQUIMANS COUNTY on the West side of the River of that name, and not far from the old home of Col. Thomas Harvey, is the site of the old home of JOHN SKINNER, a noted character in the early colonial days of old ALBEMARLE. (See p. 153 for Skinner Family notes). "Skinner's Point" is No. 1B.

(6) This number is used to designate the narrow pointed peninsula between LITTLE RIVER and PERQUIMANS RIVER, in the present Perquimans County, which is and has from earliest days been designated as "DURANT'S NECK". It was named for GEORGE DURANT. (See p. 38, this volume). For the deeds from KILCOCANEN, King of the YEOPIM TRIBES to GEORGE DURANT, as copied from the early records to the land on this neck in 1661, see pages 423 and 434, Vol. 3, of Hathaway's N. C. Historical & Genealogical Register.

(7) Almost directly across the Perquimans River from the old home of Col. Thomas Harvey, on the East side of the river, and approximately ten miles South of the present town of Winfall is what is known as the old HECKELFIELD FARM, home of the noted JOHN HECKELFIELD, in whose house the ALBEMARLE COURTS were often held, and where the General Assembly met many times when the affairs of the little colony were hanging in the balance. (See p. 63).

(8) Six miles below the "Heckelfield Farm" is another historic spot, known as the old Leigh home. At this place, in some unidentified spot one is told that SETH SOTHELL is buried. (See p. 156 this volume). He served as Governor from 1683 to 1689. He was finally seized and banished by the colonists. It is also asserted that GEORGE DURANT was also buried here.

(9) From the town of WINDSOR, now in Bertie County, to WILLIAMSTON in Martin County, South of the Roanoke is about 13 miles. The old Tuscarora Indian lands were located about five miles West of this road, along the Roanoke (Moratuck) river.

(10) Two miles below ELIZABETH CITY, on the outskirts of the present thriving little city on the West shore of the Pasquotank river is the old THOMAS RELFE place. Thomas Relfe, Sr. was Surveyor General of North Carolina in 1763, and his father THOMAS RELFE was 93 years of age in 1707. (See p. 140). THOMAS MILLER was Governor of the Colony or Province in 1677, about the time of the advent of JOHN CULPEPPER, and this old RELFE home was the central rallying point during the famous CULPEPPER REBELLION. The place is now known as "Enfield Farm" at "Cobb's Point" on the Pasquotank.

(11) About a mile distant from Enfield Farm is the old home of JOHN HOLLOWELL (see page 68) which dates back of 1800.

(12) This represents approximately the location of NEW BEGUN CREEK, on which or near which is the town of Weeksville of the present day. New Begun Creek is often mentioned in the old North Carolina Records, during the early provincial activities, and in many land grants. In this neighborhood, on the Eastern shore of LITTLE RIVER, but some eleven miles South of ELIZABETH CITY is the location or site of the first school established in Old Albemarle, which was taught by CHARLES GRIFFIN, mentioned in the famous narratives of COL. WILLIAM BYRD who helped run the line between Albemarle and Virginia. Charles Griffin afterwards was in charge of the Indian School at William & Mary College in Virginia. Here also was located the QUAKER SETTLEMENT said to have been the first Quaker Meeting House in North Carolina. NIXONVILLE was some fourteen miles below ELIZABETH CITY, and was called "OLD TOWN". For a long time it was the County seat of Pasquotank County.

(13) Here there is a tablet near the old Hall's Creek Church, on the Creek of that name which is supposed to mark the site of the first Grand Assembly of OLD ALBEMARLE, North Carolina, which was convened by Governor William Drummond in 1665. Governor Drummond was appointed the first Governor of the Province of North Carolina by WILLIAM BERKELEY, and was succeeded by SAMUEL STEVENS in 1667. (See p. 87). For his participation in Bacon's rebellion, Berkeley afterwards had Drummond hung at Jamestown.

(14) CHARLES EDEN, who was Governor of the Province, and for whom the town of EDENTON was named, is said to have had his home on the West Bank of the Chowan river near the end of the bridge, now called EDENHOUSE POINT. He died in 1722.

(15) This is said to be about the location of the first church in the Province of North Carolina. For an account of its location and the full history of the ownership of the lands on which it is said to have stood, see Vol. 1, pp. 256 to 267 of Hathaway's N. C. Historical and Genealogical Register. The place is now called HAYES and is on the East side of Edenton Bay about a mile below town. The property was bought in 1765 by Governor Samuel Johnston (See page 79).

(16) This number marks approximately the location of DRUMMONDS POINT at the mouth of the Yeopim River. It was also perhaps the same as SKINNER'S POINT. On a small island near this point, which is now almost lost by the wash of the tides, was what is called "Batt's Grave". At one time it contained about thirty acres of land, and the tradition is that it was the home of Nathaniel Batts, who died there at an unknown date. Batts may have been among those persons who left Virginia and sought solace in the solitudes of the Roanoke River areas before the coming of Roger Green and his "lost colonists". There is a tradition that Batts may have been "Governor " of that part of Albemarle West of the Chowan River at the same time William Drummond was Governor of the Province, mostly on the East.

(17) This number inadequately locates the Great Dismal Swamp, through which General George Washington and his associates built the great canal, from Norfolk to connect with the Pasquotank River in Albemarle. The swamp extended far inland in both Virginia and North Carolina, and is, to a large extent impassible to this day, though modern engineers have succeeded in reclaiming a large part of the area, and highways traverse some sections of it. Stock in this project, which became valuable, was bequeathed by General Washington towards an endowment of the present Washington & Lee College in Virginia, in his will.

OTHER FACTS IN REGARD TO MAPPED AREA

Until about 1729-30 the location of the line between Virginia and Albemarle was unsettled. There was always doubt whether lands acquired were in one colony or the other.

BENNETT'S CREEK was a navigable stream, as least as far up as the site of the present Gatesville, and fishing was quite an industry along the stream and on the Chowan river.

Yeopim river was the line between Chowan and Perquimans Precincts, after the precincts were established and designated in 1671.

CATHERINE'S CREEK was the line between Gates County and Chowan after the establishment of Gates County. Catherine's Creek was sometimes called OLD TOWN CREEK.

ROANOKE RIVER is called "MORATUCK RIVER" on many of the old abstracts and deeds, which was probably its Indian name. MEHERRIN CREEK was called "MAHARIE", and sometimes referred to as SOUTH MEHERRIN RIVER.

The names of many streams are omitted, since there is doubt about what they were called in the first instance, and the present names were unknown in these earlier periods.

LIST OF EARLY GOVERNORS OF OLD ALBEMARLE UNDER THE PROPRIETORS

Following herewith is a list of the persons who served as Governor of North Carolina, when it was known principally as old ALBEMARLE COUNTY:

1. WILLIAM DRUMMOND, who was appointed by SIR WILLIAM BERKELEY at the request of the Proprietors of the Province. He served from an indefinite date beginning about 1663-4 and until about October, 1667. He was subsequently hung as a traitor by Berkeley, without a trial, as a punishment for having taken part in Bacon's Rebellion in Virginia.
2. SAMUEL STEPHENS, who was appointed by the Lords Proprietors, and who died while in office. He was dead by July 15, 1670, when the General Court met at the house of SAMUEL DAVIS when JOHN CULPEPPER appeared as the attorney for Lord Berkeley, as administrator of his estate. Hon. Peter Carteret had succeeded to the office of Governor and was present at this meeting. (N. C. Hist. & Gen. Reg. Vol. 1 p. 135-6.)
3. PETER CARTERET was appointed by the Proprietors to succeed Stephens, and served until May 1673.
4. JOHN JENKINS was acting Governor of Albemarle from May, 1673 until November, 1676.
5. THOMAS EASTCHURCH was appointed Deputy Governor about the time the Proprietors undertook to govern ALBEMARLE from Charlestown, a scheme that did not appeal favorably the people, who resisted the change. This newly designated Governor failed to show up, because death overtook him, and THOMAS MILLER in 1677, assumed the Governorship, with one TIMOTHY BIGGS as his assistant: (See page 10). It was about this time that the "Culpepper Rebellion" arose (p. 32) and Miller and Biggs were seized and thrown into jail at the old THOMAS RELFE place about two miles below the present ELIZABETH CITY.
6. SETH SOTHEL began to try to govern Albemarle, following JOHN CULPEPPER'S attempt in 1678, but was captured by pirates before he got hold of the office and detained for some two or three years, until 1682, but in the meantime
7. JOHN JENKINS being then President of the Council, was Acting Governor, until that year (1682).
8. HENRY WILKINSON was selected by the Proprietors as a successor to JENKINS, but before he could make his way to the Carolinas and Albemarle he was thrown into prison and never reached his office in ALBEMARLE.
9. SETH SOTHEL was then selected Governor by the Proprietors, but it was while on the way to take office this time that he was captured by pirates, and it was not until 1684 that he actually took the office, which he held until 1689. It appears from all the records that have been examined that he started out very well at first, but soon became autocratic, having bought out Clarendon's share in the Carolinas. Result, he appears to have been most unpopular as a proprietor and Governor.
10. PHILLIP LUDWELL, of Virginia, succeeded Sothel, and remained Governor until 1691. He had been Secretary of the Virginia Council, and was the third husband of Sir William Berkeley's widow, who had first married SAMUEL STEPHENS, second Sir William Berkeley and third Phillip Ludwell. (The Old South, p. 285). Ludwell remained in Virginia, and appointed the popular
11. THOMAS JARVIS, said to have been in ALBEMARLE since 1659 – a remarkable statement, if true – and who was one of the active supporters of the administration under JOHN JENKINS as the acting Governor, in the previous interim.
12. JOHN ARCHDALE was Governor from 1694 to 1696. He was Governor of all the Carolinas, North and South, and made use of a Deputy in Albemarle. Archdale's administration was popular.
13. JOHN HARVEY was Governor from 1694 to 1695. He was the "Harvey's Neck" Harvey.
14. HENDERSON WALKER was acting Governor by virtue of his office as President of the Albemarle Council, from 1699 to 1704. He was succeeded by
15. ROBERT DANIEL, who became Deputy Governor in August 1704, which he held until 1705.
16. THOMAS CARY was Deputy Governor, succeeding ROBERT DANIEL, from 1705 to 1708. He was appointed by Sir Nathaniel Johnston. (See p. 31 of this volume).
17. WILLIAM GLOVER, president of the Council, was Acting Governor during the stormy period of 1706 to 1708. Glover was from Henrico County, Virginia. Then occurred the "Cary Rebellion".
18. THOMAS CARY again become Governor of Albemarle from 1708 to 1711.
19. EDWARD HYDE succeeded CARY as Governor until May 9, 1712, and again from that date until September 8, 1712.
20. THOMAS POLLOCK was Acting Governor thereafter until May 28, 1714.
21. CHARLES EDEN became Governor in 1714 and served until 1722, and died at the end of his service.
22. THOMAS POLLOCK again became the Acting Governor until the succeedding August.
23. WILLIAM REED became Governor August 30, 1722 and served until Jan. 15, 1724. (See page 139 of this book).
24. GEORGE BURRINGTON was then Governor until July 17, 1725 by appointment.
25. RICHARD EVERARD succeeded BURRINGTON and served until May, 1728.

Then the Proprietors sold out and the King took over, with EVERARD serving as the first Governor under the "CROWN"

For a list of the members of the GRAND ASSEMBLY which met at the home of the celebrated JOHN HECKLEFIELD in the precinct of PERQUIMANS on Monday, October 11, 1708, at which the HON. THOMAS CARY, ESQ., President and Commander in Chief, presided, see Vol. 2, of Hathaway's N. C. Hist. & Gen. Register, page 225.

This list will give the student of the history of this particular era in ALBEMARLE some idea of "who was who" in those days.

THE EARLIEST LAND GRANTS
IN NORTH CAROLINA

The first grants (patents) issued by the Province of North Carolina to lands in Old Albemarle are on file in the office of the Secretary of State at Raleigh.

In Volume 1, of Hathaway's North Carolina Historical and Genealogical Register there is a list of these grants, the oldest one of these having been issued to JOHN VARNHAM covering 250 acres on the River Albemarle (by which is meant Albemarle Sound), November 27, 1879. From the text of this document it appears to be the re-issuance of another and older grant issued on September 25, 1663, but the older patent does not appear among these records; only this reference to it. Mr. Hathaway expresses the opinion that the Varnham grant is the oldest shown in the North Carolina records. All of the grants shown in Mr. Hathaway's list in his first number, were located in Chowan Precinct. On other pages to follow will be found listed the names of the patentees and year the grants were issued, but since contemporaneous records show that "OLD ALBEMARLE" was a "going concern" at least two decades previous to the dates of these grants, one naturally wonders where the settlers of the sixtys and seventies found their titles. There is too wide a gap in the records, to assume that no earlier grants were issued.

At least a partial explanation of this puzzle is to be found in Patent Book No. 4, of the early VIRGINIA RECORDS. Whether the action of the Colony of Virginia in issuing grants and patents to lands along the "Carolina River", "Paspetank River", and on the "Chawanoke", "Carratucks", "New Begin" and other obvious derivities of the present day streams in the Albemarle region, owing to the geographical confusion that existed, or because of the belief that these lands, streams and boundaries were Virginia property, is uncertain. Anyway, the grants were issued, and the Hathaway and other records show that the grantees, most of them at least, took possession and held onto the real estate, and that their children and children's children clung fast to their patrimony and there lived and multiplied.

Not having personal access to these early Virginia records, the compiler acknowledges grateful appreciation to Nell Marian Nugent's masterful compilation Virginia "Cavaliers and Pioneers" as the source from which the following interesting notes are taken:

GEORGE CATCHMAID, 3333 acres on the North Side of Roanoke, abutting southly on said Sound, eastly on Katotin river, westerly on Pequimons river, which issueth out of said Sound, and northly on Owascake Creek, which issueth out of Pequimons river. For the transportation of sixty-seven persons. Dated April 1, 1663. The names of the persons transported (evidently to Virginia) are attached to the patent. Among the names attached are WILLIAM FOIX, HENRY GOODMAN, JOHN WHITE, ZACHARIAH SOUTH, JAMES HARRISON, RICHARD FLEWELLYN and JOHN SHARPE, some of whom, we know afterwards appeared in Old Albemarle.

HENRY PALIN, 450 acres at the mouth of New Begin Creek. This grant is dated September 25, 1663. Written on this patent is the name "CAROLINA", and attached to it are the names of the nine persons transported which entitled the patentee to the land. Even without the notation "New Begin" Creek sufficiently identifies the location of the land. This Henry Palin grant is substantially contemporaneous with that of ROGER GREEN'S and antedates the "farmer" Thomas Jarvis, whom Dodd says settled in Albemarle by 1659, by SIX YEARS. This was probably 1663 instead of 1653.

It is plain from the Cathmaid grant (1663) that Albemarle Sound was known as Roanoke Sound. Other grants show "Chawanoke" was used perhaps for Chowan river or Sound, and the term "Carolina River" doubtless was still another ancient name for Albemarle Sound. Some of the other designations we are unable to identify, but other land-marks mentioned undoubtedly place them in Old Albemarle.

THOMAS HODGKIN 1000 acres in a bay of Carolina River, beginning at a small creek called CANNAUGHSAUGH (?) running up same to a branch of MATTATOMECKE Creek, etc. This patent was dated September 25, 1663, and was issued to Hodgkin for the transportation of 20 persons, whose names are attached thereto. Among the names are those of JOHN PHILPOT, JOHN TYLER, SAMUEL BURTON and NICHOLAS WILLS and JAMES ROGERS.

The name HODGKIN in the above grant was probably HODGSON. For the Hodgson family turn back to page 67 of the LOST TRIBES.

WILLIAM MUNDAY, 380 acres in CARRATUCKS Creek, falling into KECOUGHTANKE RIVER, and which river falls into CAROLINA; beginning at the mouth of a swamp where JOHN HARVEY'S land ends, running East Southeast, etc. Dated September 25, 1663. Granted on account of the transportation of six persons. They were WILLIAM EDMONDS, JOSEPH GIBSON, ROBERT READ, RICHARD SMITH, SAMUEL WARREN and JAMES BARD. (Probably transported to Virginia).

It is obvious that "KECOUGHTANKE RIVER" was the name applied in this grant to PASQUOTANKE, and that its falling into "CAROLINA" meant that it emptied into ALBEMARLE SOUND, as it is known today. A reference the MUNDAY family will be found on page 113.

THOMAS SHERWOOD, 830 acres on the North side of CAROLINA RIVER (Albemarle Sound), running Northwest by trees of SAMUEL DAVIS, then East by North, etc. Dated September 25, 1663 for the transportation of eighteen persons, two of whom were WILLIAM GLOVER and FRANCIS GLOVER.

Thomas Sherwood died in PASQUOTANK COUNTY in 1794. Turn back to page 152 for notes on the SHERWOOD FAMILY.

THOMAS KEELY (KEELE?) 800 acres in a bay of PASPETANKE RIVER. Dated September 25, 1663. Granted for the transportation of sixteen persons, who are named, including RICHARD BULLOCK, DANIEL MERRICK, JOHN SHARPE, RICHARD EVANS and THOMAS MANN.

> This was probably THOMAS KELLY of the Kelly family of PASQUOTANKE PRECINCT. For notes relating to this family turn back to page 84.

JOHN BATTLE, 640 acres on the Westward side of PASPETANKE RIVER, beginning on a point which parts this and the land of Mrs. FORTSON, running Southwest, etc. Dated September 25, 1663, and granted for the transportation of 13 persons, who are named. The grant is labeled "Carolina". Among those persons mentioned are THOMAS MORY, WILLIAM HUTTON and MARY STEVENS.

> Here was probably the original progenitor in North Carolina of the BATTLE FAMILY of BATTLEBORO, of which ELISHA BATTLE was a later representative. A JOHN BATTLE died in Bertie County in 1741. See page 8.

JAMES MURDAH, 420 acres on the West side of CHOWANOKE RIVER, September 25, 1663, for the transportation of NINE persons, including THOMAS CRAFFORD, WILLIAM MORRY, NATHANIEL BRIDGES and others. Patent bears the mark "Carolina".

> The "West side of CHOWANOKE" undoubtedly meant the **West side of Chowan River**. This means somewhere along the Chowan in what is now BERTIE COUNTY. It probably was also near the mouth of the Roanoke, and therefore contiguous to the ROGER GREEN grant, which some writers claim was never settled. Here is the evidence in these several patents -- all issued the same day, September 25, 1663 -- that the Roger Green lands **were** settled.

MR. JOHN LAURENCE, 625 acres on the **West Side of Chawanoke River**, running Southwest along land of MR. ROBERT LAWRENCE, etc., to land lately surveyed by JAMES MURDAH, etc. Date September 25, 1663. Granted for the transportation of 13 persons, and marked "Carolina". Some of the names were GEORGE TEAGUE (Teague family long later in CHATHAM COUNTY), KATHERINE CORNELIUS, WILLIAM SHARPE, WILLIAM HARE and THOMAS HILL.

> John probably spelled his name the same as ROBERT LAWRENCE. For notes on this Lawrence family turn back to page 90. One William Justice of Charles City County, Virginia, either transported to Virginia, or obtained the headrights of William, Mary, Anne, Author and Sarah Lawrence in 1653. Nugent p. 329.

MR. THOMAS STAMPE and JAMES NOAKES, 300 acres on the North side of CAROLINA RIVER (Albemarle Sound), beginning at marked trees dividing this and the land of HENRY WHITE, running East, etc., for the transportation of six persons, including Henry Leonard, Robert Flake, Richard Baker, William Preston and Elizabeth Hancock. Richard Stampe died in 1722 (p. 159).

> In the crazy spelling of names of that period, the writer thinks it not improbable that "NOAKES" was intended for plain old "KNOX".

LT. (Or ST.) MOUNT WELLS, 600 acres on the West side of CHOWANOKE RIVER, running by land lately surveyed for JAMES MURDOH, running East, etc. Dated September 25, 1663, and for the transportation of 12 persons, among whom were THOMAS POORE, JOSEPH HILL, THOMAS HIGH, JAMES WHITE, THOMAS BAYLEY and THOMAS and WILLIAM WOOD.

> Here is another settler on the Roanoke River in BERTIE, who settled on the ROGER GREEN tract, or close by, and a neighbor of JAMES MURDAH and the LAWRENCE family. Both the WELLS and WILLS family came from the York-James City peninsula, and a close study shows they used the same Christian names in both domiciles, and may have been **the same family**. Turn back to pages 178 and 188 for notes relating to BOTH FAMILIES.

MR. ROBERT LAWRENCE, JR., 625 acres on the West Side of CHAWANOKE RIVER, September 25, 1663, for the transportation of 13 persons, including WILLIAM YELDING, WILLIAM HARE, THOMAS TURNER, EDWARD MORGAN, ED. STEPHENS, THOS. STROUD and ED. HAWLEY.

> Here was another tract of land in BERTIE COUNTY territory, located in the neighborhood of the ROGER GREEN grant. The names mentioned appear occasionally on the North Carolina Records, so that some of the transportees or headrights may have settled in Carolina, though transported to VIRGINIA.

PHILLIP EVANS 300 acres in NEW BEGIN Creek, beginning at the mouth of a swamp which parts this and the land of Mr. Jennings, etc. Dated September 25, 1663. For the transportation of six persons, RICHARD WHITTY, HENRY CATCHMAID, DINA FARNS, a negro, JOHN SCOTT and MARY ENGLISH.

> For notes on the **EVANS FAMILY** turn back to page 42.

KATHERINE WOODWARD and PHILARETE WOODWARD, her daughter, 750 acres on the West side of PASPETANKE RIVER, beginning at a point above the mouth of a large creek falling into said River, etc. Dated September 25, 1663. For the transportation of 15 persons, including MARY WELLS, ALICE JEFFERY, JOHN NEWTON, CHRISTIAN GREENE, JOHN BARNWELL, RICHARD HARMAN, THOAS WEST and some others. THOMAS WOODWARD was the wife and father of these two patentees.

THOMAS WOODWARD about this time was the Surveyor General of ALBE- MARLE and patented lands both in his own name and that of members of his family, of which this was one. PHILARETE WOODWARD afterwards married JOHN GILES, from Isle of Wight County, Virginia.

MR. WILLIAM WEST, 2500 acres on the East side of PEQUIMMIN RIVER, about six or seven miles up the same, beginning on a point of land near the great marsh close to an Indian Field, running Northeast, etc., to the mouth of a small creek called CURRITICK and from thence up the said river of PEQUIMMIN. Dated September 25, 1663. For the transportation of 50 persons, only the names of 18 of them being attached to the grant. Among the names given, however, are those of JOHN SHANDS, MARIE WILLIAMS, JOHN SANDERS, WILLIAM CAPP and THOMAS STONE. Turn to page 179.

SAMUELL DAVIS, 950 acres on the North side of CAROLINA RIVER, beginning at the mouth of a swamp, running North by West, etc. Dated September 25, 1663. For the transportation of 19 persons whose names are given, including MORGAN WILLIAMS, THOMAS HOLDER, OLIVE WILLIAMS, ELIZABETH WILLIAM- SON, THOS? CAREW and others. Turn to page 34.

SAMUEL DAVIS came to North Carolina from Isle of Wight County.

MR. THOMAS RELFE, 750 acres on the Southwest side of PASPETANKE RIVER, beginning at the mouth of a swamp and running by the land of THOMAS KEELE (KELLY or KEILE), etc., by Mr. Fortson's marked trees. Dated September 25, 1663. For the transportation of 15 persons whose names are attached to the patent, including STEPHEN HARRIS, JOSEPH ROGERS, JOHN and THOMAS ROUSE, MARY BELSON and others. This patentee Mr. Thomas Relfe, was a physician, according to JOHN BENNETT BODDIE (page 132-133). Turn back to page 140 of this book for Relfe notes.

MR. JOHN HARVEY, 600 acres in a small creek called CARRAWTUCKS falling into the river of KECOUGHTANKE, which river falls into CAROLINA RIVER (Albemarle Sound). Dated September 25, 1663. For the transportation of 12 persons, among them being JAMES HARVEY, HUMPHREY EVANS, ANN WOMBWELL THOMAS ELMES, THOMAS POOLE, WILLIAM BASSE and JOHN DAVIS. Other names doubtful.

Notes on the Harvey family and its history will be found on pages 60 and 61 of this volume.

ROGER WILLIAMS, 350 acres on the North side of CAROLINA RIVER (Albemarle Sound). Patent dated September 25, 1663. For the transportation of 7 persons, whose names are given as MAN. (Perhaps MANUEL) ROGERS, THOMAS JONES, THOMAS JEFFRIES, JOHN ROSSE, CHARLES SEWARD, JOHN DANIEL and JOHN ROPER.

Notes relating to the WILLIAMS FAMILY will be found on pages 185, 186 and 187 of this volume. Roger Williams was perhaps the father of JENKINS WILLIAMS who married JOHANNA and had sons ROGER and JOHN WILLIAMS.

WILLIAM JENNINGS, 550 acres in "New begin Creek", beginning at the mouth of a great swamp, which parts this and the land of ROBERT LAWREY (Lowrey), running up the creek, etc. to the mouth of a swamp which parts this and the land of PHILLIP EVANS. Dated September 25, 1663, which was for the transportation of eleven persons named, among whom were SAMUEL HENRICKE, STEPHEN PIERSON, SAMUEL MOSES, THOMAS RICHMOND, MICHAEL PARRAM (Parham), SARAH MARSHALL and PETER DENNIS.

WILLIAM JENNINGS died in PASQUOTANK in 1686, and his son WILLIAM in Currituck in 1729. Turn back to page 78 for the notes on this family.

MR. JOHN HARVEY, 250 acres on the River of CAROLINA (Albemarle Sound), beginning by the land of ROGER WILLIAMS, running down same to the miles end of said Williams, etc. Dated Septem- ber 25, 1663. For the transportation of 5 persons, as follows: VERGIS SMITH, STEPHEN JOHNSEY, GEORGE MOORE, JANE PARNELL and THOMAS POOLE. (See pages 60 and 61 for notes on Harveys).

ROBERT LAWRY, (LOWREY) 300 acres in a bay at the mouth of NEW BEGUN CREEK, beginning at the mouth of a small swamp which parts this and the land of HENRY PALIN, running Southwest, etc. up the said creek to a marked gum in the midst of the mouth of a great swamp which parts this and the land of MR? JENNINGS, etc. Dated September 25, 1663. For the transportation of six (6) per- sons, including himself, RICHARD WOODART and GEORGE PRESTON.

There are some LOWREY family notes on page 96.

THOMAS WOODWARD, SR. and THOMAS WOODWARD, JR., his son, 2500 acres on the North side of PASPETANKE RIVER, beginning at the head of the eastermost branch of ARENEWS CREEK, etc., towards the head of the North River. Dated September 25, 1663. For the transportation of 50 persons. The names of the 50 emigrants are attached to the grant, and the list is too long to publish in full, but among them are the following: CHRISTOPHER DAVIS, RICHARD MAHR, HENRY GREENE, THOS PAT- MAN, THOMAS ROBINSON, a man named HILLIARD, JOHN HOLLOM (Probably HALLUM), RICHARD WYATT, THOMAS HAMPTON, JOHN BARKER, HUMPHREY CHAPMAN, ALEX FRIZZELL, RICHARD HAMMOND and WILLIAM HAZLEWOOD.

THOMAS WOODWARD SR. and **THOMAS WOODWARD JR.**, (another patent or grant) 2000 acres on the West side of **CHAWANOKE RIVER**, beginning 50 poles below the small creek which is at the lower part of the old Indian Town, running West Southwest, etc. Dated September 25, 1663. This patent was for the transportation of 40 persons, whose names appear on the document. Among this long list of names appears the following: **HUMPHREY PAWLE, THOMAS PRYOR, JOHN STEVENSON, JOHN KELLIE, CHRISTOPHER WOODWARD** (twice), **THOMAS MARSHALL, JOHN BIRD, ROBERT HANCOCK, PETER DENNIS, THOMAS MARSHALL, SARAH MARSHALL, PETER JANSON, THOMAS PARIN** (Meant for PARHAM, I am quite sure), **SAMUEL MOSES, ANN SUTTON, ANTHONY WYN, JACOB BROWN** and **EZEKIEL WILLIAMS**.

Compare the names above with some of those in the William Jennings patent.

These Woodwards were from Isle of Wight County, Virginia, and Thomas Woodward Sr., the N. C. Surveyor, had been Clerk of Isle of Wight County for ten years, immediately preceding the issuance of these North Carolina patents.

A **CHRISTOPHER WOODWARD**, as early as 1629 was a Burgess from Charles City, County, and later settled near the Randolphs at **TURKEY ISLAND**, in Henrico, on the Appomattox River. The relationship between Thomas and Christopher Woodward is not known, but the list of headrights above strongly indicate that it certainly existed.

Turn back to page 190 for notes on these Woodwards in North Carolina.

MRS. MARY FORTSON, 2000 acres on the West side of **PASPETANKE RIVER**, beginning at the mouth of a swamp, etc., and running Northeast by land of **THOMAS KEELE** or **KEILE** (KELLY). Dated September 25, 1663, for the transportation of 20 persons. Among a few of the names on this list is that of **EDWARD BARRETT, ED HAWLEY, MARY ADAMS, THOMAS HARPER, THOMAS BAXTON** (twice) and **HIS TWO WIVES** (Of course, at different times, and different wives), **JOHN ROBINSON, THOMAS ROBERTS** and **STEPHEN BREWER**.

From **BODDIE'S 17TH CENTURY ISLE OF WIGHT**, pa. 132: The oldest will recorded in North Carolina is that of **MRS. MARY FORSTEN**. It is dated January 28, 1663 and was probated November 15, 1665, and reads as follows: "Whereas there is a patent granted unto me **MARY FORSTEN**, wife to **FREDERICK FORSTEN** of 2000 acres lying in **PASPETANK**, of which 900 have been assigned, and I give my said husband such presents as to enable him to give bills of sale for said land. To son **THEOPHILUS** 1100 acres, and if it shall please God to send me safely of the child I go with, it shall share equally with the said **THEOPHILUS**."

HENRY WHITE, SR., 250 acres on the North side of **CAROLINA RIVER** (Albemarle Sound), bounded on the West with **JOHN HARVEY'S** line, East with **THOMAS STAMP** and **JAMES NOAKES**, on the North with the woods and South with the river. Dated September 25, 1663. For the transportation of five persons as follows: **ANN DONKASTER, GEO. JENKINS, EDWARD BARRETT, DANIEL WALKER** and **ANN JENKIN** or **JENKINS**.

HENRY WHITE, JR., 750 acres in a small creek called **CORAWATUCKS** that falls into **KECOUGHTANKE RIVER**, beginning toward the head of the same, running West Northwest, etc. Dated Spetember 25, 1663. For the transportation of 14 persons, including **PERRY GREENE, DANIEL WALKER, EDWARD MORGAN, RICHARD STAPLES, HESTER MORGAN, EDWARD PARRETT** (BARRETT), **JOHN PIKE** and again **DANIEL WALKER**.

HENRY WHITE (either Sr. or JR., probably the latter) before or about 1700, said he was 57 years old and knew **SAMUEL DAVIS**, of **PASQUOTANK** County in Isle of Wight County, County, Virginia, who was an apprentice to his father **HENRY WHITE**, and that **SAMUEL DAVIS** married **ANN**, a servant of **CAPT. JAMES BLOUNT**, also of Isle of Wight, and all now of Pasquotank County, etc.

For other notes on this White family see pages 181, 182 and 183 in the first part of this volume.

MR. RICHARD BULLER, 1200 acres lying in **NEW BEGIN CREEK**, beginning at the mouth of Doctor's Creek, running up the first mentioned creek, etc., together with a small island against the mouth of Doctor's Creek. Dated September 25, 1663. For the transportation of 24 persons, among whom were the following: **MATTHEW SMITH, RICHARD WARD, THOMAS HORNE, HENRY WARNER, JOHN MATTHEWS, ANDREW ARMSTRONG, DOROTHY BANKS, THOMAS RICH, THOMAS READ, JOHN CARY** and **ROBERT MASON**.

The above patentee was perhaps **RICHARD BULLARD**, instead of **BULLER**. The Bullard family came from Nansemond County, Virginia. Or, it is possible the name was **BULLOCK**.

THE FOREGOING PATENTS were all issued in SEPTEMBER, 1663. The lands had been surveyed perhaps a long time, and people had settled upon them perhaps before 1660. Nugent's Cavaliers and Pioneers, from which the data is obtained, stops at 1666. Between 1663 and 1685 the Virginia records, if searched, would perhaps show many later grants issued by that Commonwealth to lands in OLD ALBEMARLE, grants of which there is no record, either in the counties or at the State Capitol at Raleigh. The record is perhaps in existence in VIRGINIA.

PERSONS ATTENDING ALBEMARLE COURT 1670

In 1670, when OLD ALBEMARLE, which then comprised the habitable portion of the OLD NORTH STATE, undivided into precincts or other sub-divisions, the Courts and the Government set up under the direction of the agents of the proprietors had begun to function. SAMUEL STEVENS, the second Governor of the Province had just died and the question of the disposition and management of his estate was among the matters considered at a meeting of the General Court held in 1670 at the home of SAMUEL DAVIS. Thanks to Mr. Hathaway, who rescued valuable fragments of the records and published them in his Volume 1, pages 135, et seq. we are able to list the names of many of those who were living at the time, whose names appear on these records. They are all of great Historical significance and interest. Opposite each name appears the number of the page or pages in this work where other data relating to the name will be found:

JOHN BARROWS 19
ROBERT BONO
PETER CARTERET (Governor).
EDMUND CHANCEY 23
CAPT. CATH. CONE 27,
CAPT. WILLIAM CRAWFORD 29
CAPT. THOMAS CULLEN 30
JOHN CULPEPPER 31
SAMUEL DAVIS 34
JOHN DYE
THOMAS EASTHURT (EASTCHURCH?)
    This man was surely
    the same man appoint-
    ed Governor six years
    later who died before
    taking office.
RICHARD FELTON 44
MAJ. RICHARD FOSTER 46
FRANCIS GODFREY 50
LAWRENCE GUNFALLIS 53
HURTULUS GUN
JOHN HARUDY
EDWARD HASWELL 61
JOHN HAWKINS 62
JOHN HILL 65
THOMAS HOSKINS 70

WILL JACKSON 76
JOHN JENKINS (Lt. Col.)
    This man became
    Governor in May
    1673.
ABRAHAM KIMBERLY
WILLIAM LEWERTON 91
THOMAS MATKIE
ROBERT MINTY 107
JAMES NOKES 87
    I think this is
    intended for
    KNOX.
JOHN OUTLAW 110
    Ancestor of the
    Outlaw family
    in N. C.
ROBERT RISHOD
THOMAS SHARPMAN
JAMES SHREWSBURY
WILLIAM SIMONS 152
THOMAS SIMONS 152
ANTHONY SLOCUM 154
HERMAN SMEWIN
HUGH SMITHWICK 156
NICHOLAS STEVENS 161

KATHERINE WILLIAMS 186
ROGER WILLIAM'S WIDOW 186
JOHN WILLOUGHBY 187
ANDREW WOOLWARD 190
WILLIAM VOSS 172

SOME OLD NEIGHBORS OF THE GEORGE DURANT FAMILY ON "DURANT'S NECK" IN THE YEAR OF 1693:

GEORGE DURANT CAME DOWN OUT OF VIRGINI in 1661 and bought from the King of the YEOPIM INDIANS the neck of land between LITTLE RIVER and PERQUIMANS. There he settled and his tribe increased. Who were his neighbors on this neck of land? Thanks to Mr. Hathaway (vol. 3, p. 143-4) we know who they were just 32 years later, for on a list of TITHABLES "For the South side of Little River and Durant's Neck in 1693" we find the following names:

JOHN ANDERSON 3
ALBERT ANDERSON 3
THOMAS ATTAWAY 4
RICHARD BAILEY 5
WILLIAM BARCLIFT 6
JONATHAN BATEMAN 7
MRS. DURANT (ANNE)
    Widow of the
    original GEORGE
    DURANT. She
    died in 1695,
    two years later.
JOHN DURANT 39
THOMAS DURANT 39
FRANCIS FOSTER 46
WILLIAM GASKINS 49
JOHN GODFREY 50
WILLIAM GODFREY 50
JOHN HALFORD 55
MRS. HARTLEY 60
    Widow of
    Francis Hart-
    ley. She be-
    came Mrs. Wil-
    liam DUKENFIELD

THOMAS HOSEA 69
WILLIAM JACKSON 76
JOHN KING 85
WILLIAM MANN 100
ROBERT MOLINES
RICHARD NOWELL (NOEL?)
JOHN PARISH 123
FRANCIS PENRICE 126
WILLIAM PLATTO
RICHARD ROOKES 143
JOSEPH SUTTON 163
    This man
    was the son in
    law of GEORGE
    DURANT, his
    wife was PAR-
    THENIA DURANT
GEORGE SUTTON 163
CHARLES TAYLOR 165
JOHN TOMLIN 167
JOHN WHEDBEE 180
THOMAS WHITE 182
JENKINS WILLIAMS 185
JOHN WILLOUGHBY 187
    From NORFOLK Va.

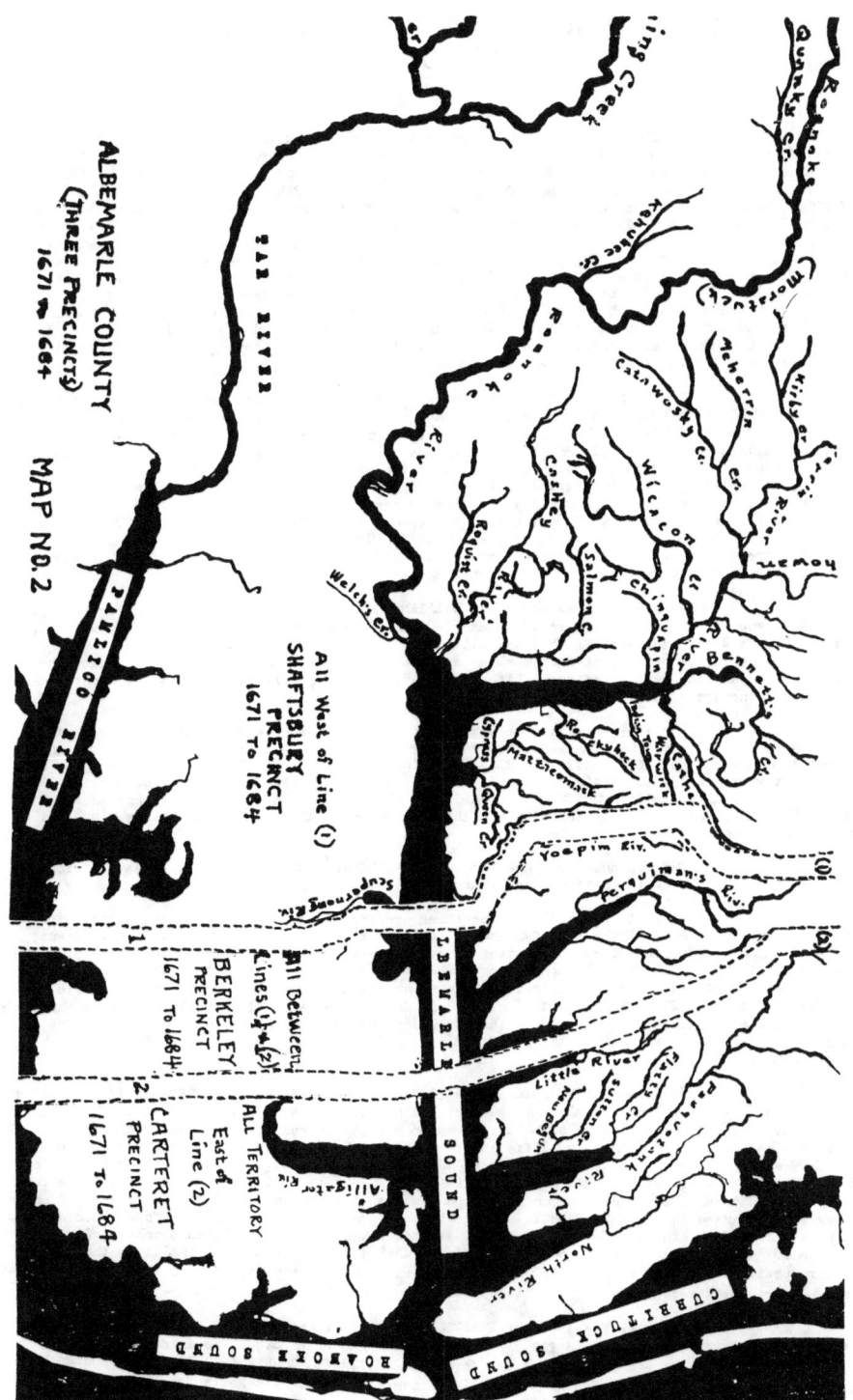

ALBEMARLE AND ITS FIRST THREE DIVISIONS

The LORDS PROPRIETORS (Absentee Landlords) of CAROLINA, as has been stated, were influential politicians who swarmed around the newly-mounted throne of CHARLES II, at the "restoration", viz. GEORGE MONCK, EDWARD HYDE, ANTHONY ASHLEY COOPER, GEORGE CARTERET, JOHN COLLETON, JOHN BERKELEY, WILLIAM BERKELEY and the aged WILLIAM, EARL OF CRAVEN. SIR WILLIAM BERKELEY, being "on the ground" became spokesman. As GOVERNOR OF VIRGINIA, he invoked the laws against dissenters and banished many prominent Quakers who had located South of the James. This policy increased and influenced settlers to seek non-molestation in the new lands on Albemarle Sound, only to find themselves again under the rule of Berkeley as the deputy of the proprietors. We are told that in 1664 Berkeley himself went to the Albemarle regions armed with authority to regulate the affairs of those who had preceded and those who came after him. But it is altogether probable that such men as GEORGE DURANT, NATHANIEL BATTS, JOHN VARNHAM and CATCHMAID and others had already found their way to the banks of Albemarle Sound and the Chowan and Roanoke rivers, had bought or obtained lands from the Indians and were planting corn and exercising the rights of settlers before Berkeley arrived on the scene.

On the North side of the James River in Virginia and the Jamestown settlements lived one WILLIAM DRUMMOND, whom Berkeley selected as Governor of Albemarle. That he was a member of the Drummond family of the "Eastern Shore" of Virginia, related to the Scarburgs and other leading families there is little doubt. In his order issued in 1663 appointing Drummond (Vol. 1, 49 Col. Recs. of N. C.) is the only description of the area which was to comprise Drummon's jurisdiction, and it is almost unintelligible. Whatever the extent of the territory embraced in this proclamation, it is patent that Berkeley was "taking over", in behalf of the proprietors, all habitable parts of the present North Carolina then practical as "settlements". THOMAS WOODWARD, a man of parts, and said to have been personally known at the Court of St. James or Charles II, was appointed surveyor and he and his deputies were dispatched to Albemarle to "step off" or measure the acquisitions of the new comers to that region.

In 1665 the new Governor, WILLIAM DRUMMOND called the first Grand Assembly to meet at a spot near the North shore of Albemarle Sound on the present Hall's Creek, at which George Durant, George Catchmaid, John Varnham and all of the earlier arrivals, were attendants. The only qualifications for membership at that meeting appears to have been that of residence below the Virginia line and the wearing of socks "if not shoes", and the abjurcation of not throwing chicken bones under the trees.

The whole area of the Government at that time appears to have been regarded as a single county, with the usual and necessary officers and a Clerk to keep the records. And it so remained until about 1670, while SAMUEL STEVENS (who had succeeded William Drummond) was acting as Governor. After the death of Samuel Stevens (1. Hathaway No1C. Hist. & Gen. Reg. p. 135) and in about 1671, ALBEMARLE COUNTY was divided into THREE PRECINCTS. The Eastern precinct was called CARTERET, the middle one BERKELEY and the Western one SHAFTSBURY. (See Hathaway's N. C. Hist. & Gen. Register Vol. 3 p. 306-310.).

The map shown on page 565 , shows ALBEMARLE COUNTY, and its three Divisions as it was after 1671 and as it continued until about 1684-5.

It will be noted that the three precincts extended from the general location of the Virginia line ACROSS ALBEMARLE SOUND and at least as far South as the Pamlico River. Deeds, wills and other instruments from the ancient records show that fact, and the proclamation of LORD BERKELEY (Hath pp. 305-6, Vol. 3) appointing DRUMMOND as Governor disclose that the territory over which he was appointed to preside extended at least as far South of Albemarle Sound as it did to the North of it. SHAFTSBURY PRECINCT (afterwards CHOWAN) extended INDEFINITELY WEST of the RIVER CHOWAN and was doubtless limited only by the extent of the original grants to the proprietors, who imagined their domains reached to the Pacific Ocean, a dream subsequently shattered by geographical developments.

In a study of this map it will also be noticed that CARTERET PRECINCT included not only the territory South of Albemarle Sound, but all of the territory North and South of that arm of the sea, later embraced in both Currituck and Pasquotank counties. Later (in 1722) after this area had been divided into two different precincts with different names, STILL ANOTHER CARTERET PRECINCT was established South of the mouth of the NEUSE RIVER, with territory contributed out of BATH PRECINCT. The first CARTERET PRECINCT existed from 1671 to 1684 (approximately) while the second CARTERET PRECINCT, nearly a hundred miles South of the present CURRITUCK began in 1722 and after being changed to CARTERET COUNTY, still exists in practically its original form. Consult maps on page 5 , for details. Deeds and other instruments indicate that ALBEMARLE consisted of these three named precincts until 1684, but the Historian MARTIN gives the date as 1683. In the absence of more positive evidence we can only use dates as being approximate in their application. Statements in deeds are sometimes inaccurate, or miscopied.

That the Precincts of SHAFTSBURY, BERKELEY and CARTERET, into which the original ALBEMARLE COUNTY was divided in 1671, extended across ALBEMARLE SOUND and on down towards the Pamlico River and Pamlico Sound, before the formation of TYRRELL COUNTY in 1729, is evidenced by many recorded statements, particularly one which appears in Hathaway's North Carolina Historical & Genealogical Register, Vol. 3, page 308.

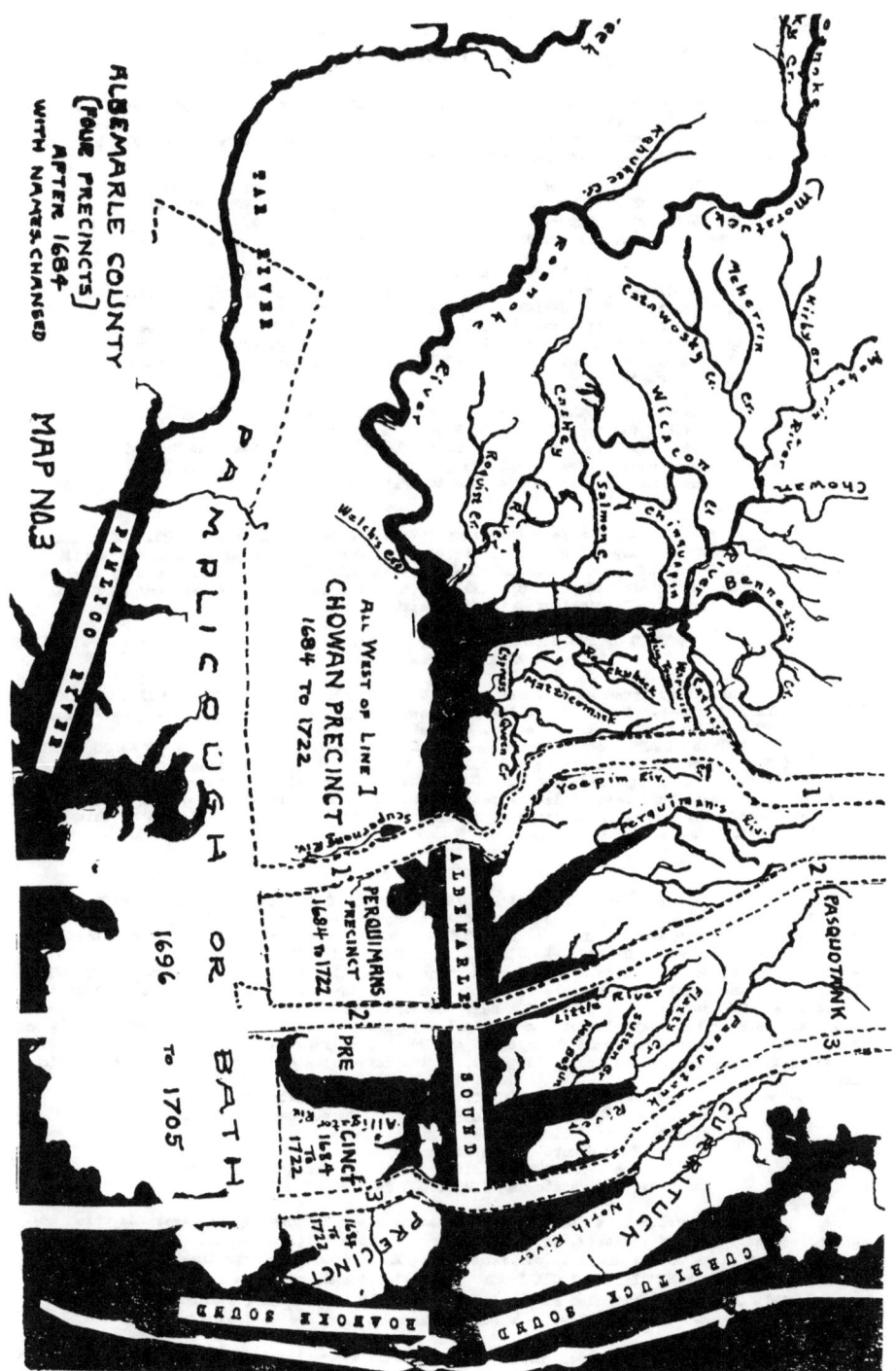

ALBEMARLE DIVIDED INTO FOUR PRECINCTS AND THE NAMES CHANGED IN 1684.

The map shown on page 571 represents ALBEMARLE COUNTY, after 1683-4 (possibly 1685) when the THREE PRECINCTS, Shaftsbury, Berkeley and Carteret were abrogated and the names of the proprietors dropped, and the names of the principal rivers or streams substituted. Mr. Hathaway, in the N. C. Hist. & Gen. Register, page 307, says:

These Precincts retained their names until about the year 1685, when CARTERET PRECINCT was divided into CURRITUCK and PASQUOTANK, and the THREE original precincts appeared thereafter as FOUR. On the same page he quotes Martin, the Historian (Vol 1 p. 176) as saying:

"1683. The FOUR precincts on ALBEMARLE SOUND, which were hitherto designed by the titles or names of some of the Lords Proprietors, viz: SHAFTSBURY, BERKELEY, etc., were now named by the principal streams that water them, CHOWAN, PERQUIMANS, PASQUOTANK and CURRITUCK, appellations which they to this day retain". (Except that after about 1738, they were referred to as "COUNTIES" of those names). Mr. Hathaway continues:

Martin fixes this change of name in 1683, but it was evidently after 1684, for by reference to Book of Land Grants No. 1, pages 104, 105, 144, 145, etc., in the office of the Secretary of State at Raleigh, N. C., it will be found that the grants referred to bear date in 1684, and the land conveyed was located in SHAFTSBURY PRECINCT.

Notwithstanding the fact that from 1671 to 1683-4, or possibly 1685, ALBEMARLE consisted of THREE PRECINCTS named Shaftsbury, Berleley and Carteret, the whole area was still designated as ALBEMARLE COUNTY, and not as CAROLINA or NORTH CAROLINA, as is evidenced by various items that appear on the old records, especially of the General Court. On page 283 of Mr. Hathaways His. & Gen. Register, for instance, there appears a

RECORD of THE GENERAL COURT OF ALBEMARLE COUNTY, HELD FEBRUARY, 1683-4.

This is prefaced as follows: At a Court holden for the COUNTY OF ALBEMARLE, the 6th of FEBRURARY, 1683-4. Present: William Wilkinson, Esq., Thomas Miller, Esq., Mr. Joshua Scott, Mr. Francis Toms, Mr. William Foster, Mr. Patrick Bayley.

THOMAS MILLER, member of the General Court, named above, had been GOVERNOR of ALBEMARLE (Then practically ALL of North Carolina) in 1677, had been imprisoned with his chief assistant Timothy Biggs, superseded by JOHN CULPEPPER, finally had his property, which had been seized and confiscated by irate citizens, restored to him, and in 1683 was a member of the General Court, as stated above. For information as to Miller and his family see page 106 of this book. For William Wilkinson, see page 185.

Whereas the THREE ORIGINAL PRECINCTS of SHAFTSBURY, BERKELEY and CARTERET, as attempted to be delineated on the map on page 565, extended across ALBEMARLE SOUND indefinitely South to the Pamlico river, or further, the FOUR NEW PRECINCTS established in 1683-4, named after the principal streams, CHOWAN, PERQUIMANS, PASQUOTANK and CURRITUCK, at least after 1696 terminated on the Southern line at the somewhat indefinite line of what was called PAMPTICOUGH PRECINCT "Of the County of Albemarle". Whether this precinct had been erected at the same time as the other FOUR North of it, presents a hazy question, which this writer has not found answered. It appears to have been established sometime prior to 1696. This conclusion is arrived at by an examination of a stray note found on page 284 of "North Carolina. A Guide to the Old North State" issued by the Federal Writers Project in 1939, by the University of North Carolina Press, which says:

"PAMTECOUGH PRECINCT of the County of Albemarle, * * in 1696, became the great County of BATH. Pamtecough was the name of a tribe of Indians in the region".
Then occurs this statement:
"In 1705 BATH was divided, the portion North of Pamptecough River constituting PAMTECOUGH PRECINCT."

Considering this statement and numerous other documentary declarations which occur infrequently in deed recitals, no other inference is possible, save that there was an area of country, as shown on the map, cut off from ALBEMARLE at about the same time the Precincts of CHOWAN, PERQUIMANS, PASQUOTANK and CURRITUCK were established, making a FIFTH PRECINCT by the name of PAMTECOUGH, which extended at least far beyond the Pamtecough (Pamlico) River, across the NEUSE to perhaps the Cape Fear, as shown on the maps that are to follow.

After 1705 this area embraced BATH COUNTY (sometimes CLARENDON) the ancestor of that vast area of Country that included most of the present North Carolina, South and West of the water shed of the Neuse and Tar Rivers, even to the line of Virginia near the Western boundary of the original ORANGE COUNTY (See maps to follow).

In 1777 CAMDEN COUNTY (which is properly omitted from these maps, because it was not in existence at this period) was carved out of PASQUOTANK COUNTY, and consisted of all the territory previously comprising PASQUOTANK PRECINCT, which was located North and EAST of PASQUOTANK RIVER.

ALLIGATOR RIVER, as shown on the map of this area, in 1713 was in PASQUOTANK COUNTY, notwithstanding it was on the South shore of ALBEMARLE SOUND. This is verified by a Power of Attorney executed by SARAH EASEWELL on April 13th of that year. (N. C. Hist. & Gen. Register, Vol 3, p. 261. This indicates beyond question that the line between PASQUOTANK and CURRITUCK PRECINCTS, which lay South of Albemarle Sound, ran East of Alligator River, and cut through the territory now comprising the County of DARE. The territory shown in Pasquotank lying West of Alligator River is now in TYRRELL COUNTY, which was established in 1729, from Albemarle.

EARLY RESIDENTS AND TAX PAYERS IN CURRITUCK PRECINCT

The following list of early residents and tithables (tax payers) in CURRITUCK PRECINCT is compiled principally from pages 301 to 304 of Volume 1, of Hathaway's North Carolina Historical & Genealogical Register.

In the study of this very interesting list consideration must be given to the fact that, since the list has been copied several times, many mistakes may have been made in the manner of spelling the names, etc. In some instances this is plainly evident.

The figures set opposite each name is the number of the page of this complete volume and in the first section thereof, containing the Index and Digest of the Hathaway N. C. Hist. & Gen. Register. By turning to the page thus indicated, in many instances, not only the name of the person stated will be found, together with references to pages in the Hathaway Register which gives other information, but which also refers to other citations in the latter work relating to the persons family and historical record. Consult the pages thus given in each instance for not only the personal, but the FAMILY HISTORY of the individual named.

```
JOHN BAKER    -  -      6              JOHN LEWIN
WILLIAM BATEMAN -       8              THOMAS LOYD  - 96
SAMUEL BATES    -       6              DAVID LINDSAY  93
EDMUND BARROW   -       7              ISAAC LITTLE - 94
WILLIAM BASTNETT        7              TIMOTHY MEAD  105
JOHN BENNETT    -       9  (d. 1710)   EDWARD MULLEN  112
EDWARD BONNER   -      12              JOHN NOWELL
JOHN BELL   -   -       8  (d. 1706)   PETER PARKER    123
WILLIAM BELL    -       8              SAM PARSONS     124
JOHN BILLETT    -      10              JOHN PALL (PELL?) 125
DAVID BLAKE     -      10              JACOB PETERSON  127
GEORGE BULLOCK         17  Tull's Crk.    (Father of THOMAS
RICHARD BURTONSHALL    18.                 Peterson who owned
HENRY CASHNALL    ( CASWELL? )             land where EDENTON
DENNIS CASHNALL   (CASWELL ? )             stands now)
MARY COBB   -  -       26              BENJAMIN PETTON  128
THOMAS COBB     -      26              BENJ. REGNAUD
JOHN COBB       -      26              GEORGE RICHARDS  141
NATHANIEL COBB          2              JAMES ROBINSON   142
RICHARD CHURCH         25              RICHARD ROSE     143
RICHARD COMFORT   27 -31               JOHN SANDERSON   149
ANDREW CONSOLL                         RICHARD SANDERSON SR. 149 (d. 1717)
GEORGE COOPER          27              RICH. SANDERSON, JR. 149 (d. 1737)
WILLIAM CORRY          28                 (Sandersons to Craven County)
CHARLES DRAPER         37              THOMAS SCARBOROUGH 150.
WILLIAM FULLER                         RICHARD SIMPSON  152 - 153
ROBERT GARD                            HENRY SLADE   -   154
THOMAS GRANDY                          LEND SMITH    -   155
FOSTER GERVAISE                        WILLIAM STEEL  -  160
RICHARD VESPER                         EDWARD TAYLOR  -  165
RICHARD HARRIS -       58              THOMAS TAYLOR  -  165
WILLIAM HARRIS -       58              JEREMIAH TOCLUSON
JOHN HAWKINS   -       62              MATHIAS TAYLOR -  168.
THOMAS JAMES                           MARKE TULLE
RICHARD JARVIS                         THOMAS TULLE ( Tull's Creek)
EDWARD JELFS                           THOMAS VANDERMERLIN  172
HENRY JOHNSON          78              HUMPHREY VINCE -  172
DAVID JONES    -       72              THOMAS VINCE   -  172
ROBERT JONES   -       21              EDWARD WARREN  - 175 (Tull's Creek)
SAMUEL JONES   -       21              HENRY WOODHOUSE   189
   (Holly Neck Pt).                    JOHN WOODHOUSE    189
ROBERT KITCHING                        THOMAS YOUNG   -  191
```

The compiler is well satisfied that many of the names as shown above, such as "Cashnall" for "Caswell" are mis-spelled, and for that reason unrecognizable.

SOME EARLY RESIDENTS AND TAX PAYERS IN PASQUOTANK

The names of the following early tax payers (tithables) and residents in PASQUOTANK PRECINCT, as shown on the map (p. 5) are culled from pages 301 to 305 of Vol. 1, of the N. C. Hist. & Gen. Register, and other sources from the same work. The pages mentioned do not have a date, but from other record sources it is conclusive that the date of this list is approximately 1697. Again, the numbers opposite the names indicate the pages of this volume, where information about the persons named, and their families may be found, with further references on such pages to where more extended information is available in the Hathaway Register.

DANIEL AKEHURST (d. 1700) 1-4
THOMAS BABCOCK 6
PATRICK BAILEY 5
JOHN BEILMAN . 8
HUMPHREY BOULTON 13
WILLIAM BRAY 14
JOHN BYSHOP 10
CALEB BUNDY 18
SAMUEL BUNDY 18
WILLIAM BUNDY 18
JOHN BURNSBY, JR. 18
URIAH CANNON 21
THOMAS CARTWRIGHT 22
RICHARD CRAIG 29
ELIZABETH COALS (COLE) 26
WILLIAM COLLINS 27
JAMES DAVIS 34
SAMUEL DAVIS 34
FRANCIS DELAMARE 35
ISAAC DELAMARE 35
PHILLIP EVANS 42
PETER FORCE (Flatty Crk)
JAMES GADD
RALPH GARNETT
DENNIS GRAHAM 51
RICHARD GREGORY (d. 1719) 53
GEORGE HARRIS 58
JOHN HAWKINS 62
FRANCIS HENDRICKS 63
CAPT. JOHN HUNT 71
WILLIAM JACKSON 76
THOMAS JAMES 76
WILLIAM JENNINGS 78
DANIEL JOHNSON 78
THOMAS JOHNSON 78
CORNELIUS JONES 79

JOHN JONES 80
THOMAS JONES 81
HENRY KEETON 84 (New Begun Crk)
LAWRENCE KEETON (New Begun Crk) 84
ROBERT LOWREY 96
JOHN LUMBROZIER (Flatty Crk)
THOMAS MACKIE (New Begun Crk) 100
RICHARD MADREW (ANDREW?) 3
ANTHONY MARKHAM (Flatty Crk) 101
JOHN MASON 102
EDWARD MAYO 103
THOMAS MILLER 106 (Governor).
WILLIAM MOWBRAY 112
CHARLES O'NEAL (Flatty Crk) 119
HENRY PALIN, JR. 121
HENRY PENDLETON (New Begun Crk) 125
THOMAS PENDLETON (New Begun Crk) 125
GEORGE PIERCY 129
RICHARD POPE (Court at home) 130
JOHN PORTER 131
DAVID PRITCHARD 133
WILLIAM RAMON
ISAAC ROWDEN 144
ROBERT TAYLOR 165
WILLIAM TEMPLE 166
MORGAN THOMAS 166
JOHN TOMLIN 167
THOMAS TOWERS
AMOS TRUEBLOOD (AREMEUSE CRK) 169
JOHN TRUEBLOOD (AREMEUSE CRK) 169
JOHN UPTON 171.
ROBERT WALLACE 174
BENJAMIN WEST 178
JOHN WEST 178
ROBERT WEST 179
HENRY WHITE 181

EDWARD WILSON (New Begun Crk) 187
WILLIAM WINDBURY (Winburn)
THOMAS WEST (Flatty Crk) 179
ARTHUR WORKMAN

PERSONS LIVING EAST OF HARVEY'S CREEK AND WEST OF FLATTY CREEK IN PASQUOTANK PRECINCT, ABOUT THE YEAR 1695.

FLATTY CREEK is shown on the map on page 5, but the exact location of HARVEY'S CREEK has not been found by the compiler. It was perhaps on the waters of LITTLE RIVER and a tributary of that stream. (See Vol. 3 p. 253 N. C. Hist. & Gen. Register).

WILLIAM BREAD (MEAD?)
JOSEPH COMMANDER 27
JOHN BEILMAN 8
EPHRAIM COSTE
ISAAC DELAMARE 35
JOHN FURBE 47
PETER FURBE 47
JOHN GRIFFIN 53
CAPT. JOHN HUNT 71
JAMES HUNTER 72
CHARLES JONES 79
BENJ. MASSARIEY 102
STEPEN MASSARIEY 102
ANTHONY MARKHAM 101
DANIEL McKIEL 104

STEPHEN MUNDAY 113
THOMAS PALMER 121
WILLIAM RAWLYNSON
ISAAC ROWDEN 144 - 147
JEREMIAH SPROSS
RICHARD STAMP 159
THOMAS WELCH 178
BENJAMIN WEST 178
ROBERT WHITE 182
VINSON WHITE 183
JOHN WEST 178
THOMAS WINGATE 188
JOHN BURNSBY JR. 18
ROBERT WEST 178
JOHN LUMBROZIER
CHARLES O'NEAL 119.

LIST OF EARLY TAX PAYERS IN PERQUIMANS PRECINCT IN 1697.

This list is similar to those shown in CURRITUCK and PASQUOTANK and was obtained from the same source. Refer back to the pages in this volume, the numbers of which appear after most of the names, for further information. Remember, also, that these tax payers (tithables) lived in all parts of PERQUIMANS PRECINCT, both North and South of ALBEMARLE SOUND, as shown on the map.

ALBERT ALBERTSON 2	WILLIAM HALL 55	HENRY SAWYER 150
ALBERT ALBERTSON, JR. 2	THOMAS HARVEY 61	JOHN SAWYER 150
JOHN ARNOLD 3	JOHN HECKLEFIELD 63	ROBERT SAWYER 150
WILLIAM BARCLIFT 6	THOMAS HOLLOWAY 68	THOMAS SAWYER 150
JOHN BARROW 7	EDWARD HOLMES 68	AUGUSTINE SCARBOROUGH 150
JANE BAYARD 8	JOHN HOPKINS 69	STEPHEN SCOTT 150
FRANCIS BEASLEY 8	LAWRENCE HUNT 71 & 72	DAVID SHERWOOD (SHERROD?) 152
ROBERT BEASLEY 8	WILLIAM JOHNSON 78	JESSE SIMMONS 152
ROWLAND BERKELEY 9	MATTHEW KELLEY 84	ROGER SNELL 56
WILLIAM BOGUE 12	BENJAMIN LAKER 88	THOMAS SPEIGHT 158
CALEB CALLAWAY 23	ALEXANDER LILLINGTON 93	CAPT. WILLIAM SPEIGHT 158
PATRICK CANADY 21	JAMES LOADMAN	JOHN SPILLMAN 157
RICHARD CHESSON 24	CORNELIUS LEARY 90	RICHARD STAMP 159
JOHN CHESSON 24	WILLIAM LEARY 90	THOMAS STANTON 160
TIMOTHY CLEARE 25	WILLIAM MAN 100	WILLIAM STEWART 161
JAMES COLE 26	THOMAS MANWARING 100	GEORGE SUTTON 163
JOSEPH COMMANDER 27	GEORGE MATTHEWS 102	GILBERT SMITH 163-5
JOHN COOKE 27	CHARLES McDANIEL 104	CHARLES TAYLOR 165
SAMUEL CRUTCHINGTON	LAWRENCE McGUE 104	JONATHAN TAYLOR 165
JOHN DAVIS 34	JAMES MORGAN 111	JAMES THIGPEN 166
JOHN DEAL	WILLIAM MORGAN 111	FRANCIS TOMES 168
RICHARD EVANS 42	GABRIEL NEWBY 115	JOHN TOMLIN 167
JOHN FENDALL 44	SAMUEL NICHOLSON 116	WILLIAM TURNER 169
RALPH FLETCHER 45	JOHN NORTHCUTT	THOMAS TWEEDY 169
RICHARD FOX 47	RICHARD NOWELL (NOEL)	ANN WALLER 174
WILLIAM GODFREY 50	JOHN OLD 118	ELIZABETH WALLER 174
LAWRENCE GONSALVO 50	JONATHAN PHELPS	JOHN WHITBY
JOHN GOSBY (SUTTON'S CRK)	SAMUEL PHELPS	JENKINS WILLIAMS 185
HANNAH GOSBY	JOHN PIERCE 128	JOHN WILLOUGHBY 187
SARAH GOSBY	THOMAS PIERCE 129	ISAAC WILSON 187
JOHN GODFREY 50	THOMAS ROBERTS 142	RICHARD WOOLARD 190
PETER GRAY 52	ROBERT ROOKS 143	WILLIAM TOMLIN 167 (TOMLING?)

SOME RESIDENTS OF THE UPPER PART OF PERQUIMANS PRECINCT IN THE YEAR 1721.

Prior to the establishment of GATES COUNTY in 1778 PERQUIMANS PRECINCT and COUNTY corresponded to the present boundaries of PERQUIMANS COUNTY except that included a narrow strip of land, a few miles wide, on what is now the extreme eastern border of GATES COUNTY. (Vol 3, N. C. Hist. & Gen. Register, p. 307). This was sometimes referred to as the "Upper Part" of PERQUIMANS, and on May 15, 1721, some of the inhabitants of this section of the then PRECINCT presented a petition or protest to the authorities, to which they signed their names. This petition gives the names, of course, of so many residents of that part of the PRECINCT. They were, as near as can be made out (2 N. C. Hist. & Gen. Reg. p. 196), as follows:

THOMAS BOSELL (BOSWELL?) 18	NATHANIEL ALBERTSON 2
WILLIAM BOSELL (BOSWELL?) 18	CHRISTOPHER NICHOLSON 116
EDWARD MODLIN	ZACHARIAH NIXON 116
ANDREW REED 139	MICHA MORPELL (?)
SAMUEL NICHOLSON 116	THOMAS MONTAGUE 108
JEAMES HIBUINOS (?)	

EARLIEST RECORDS OF PERQUIMANS PRECINCT

HATHAWAY'S N. C. HIST. & GEN. REGISTER contains a most remarkable lot of information about the BERKELEY PRECINCT, PERQUIMANS PRECINCT and PERQUIMANS COUNTY - all of which was the same territory. These are mostly in VOLUME 3 of that work.

The earliest BIRTHS, DEATHS and MARRIAGES in this area will be found on pages 199 to 320, and 363 to 410 of Volume 3. From the year 1740 to 1799 on pages 411 to 422. List of the wills will be found on pages 163 to 198 and 323 to 363. The wills are arranged in alphabetical order, as are some of the marriages, where they occur the same year.

These particular references are worth mentioning, but there are, of course, many other valuable records pertaining to PERQUIMANS throughout the THREE VOLUMES of Hathaway's.

BIRTHS, DEATHS AND MARRIAGES OF
OUR PERQUIMANS ANCESTORS INDEXED

Familiarity with and knowledge of the births, deaths and marriage and intermarriage between the people of a given area and during a long and vital period of time is the key that unlocks the past and explains the history that has been left unwritten.

One of the most remarkable records extant is that which pertains to BERKELEY and PERQUIMANS PRECINCT - now COUNTY - NORTH CAROLINA. We are indebted to JAMES ROBERT BENT HATHAWAY for this record, which appears in the THIRD and unfinished last Volume of his N. C. Historical & Genealogical Register.

The list of BIRTHS, DEATHS and MARRIAGES of this sub-division of OLD ALBEMARLE runs from page 199 to 220, inclusive, then skips and begins again on page 363 and runs uninteruptedly to the bottom of page 422, a total of eighty-one (81) closely printed pages, with several thousand entries painstakingly copied. It is an extraordinary record for any community. This record extends over a period of over 130 years, during which "history was in the making". All it needed was an index.

Following herewith is a sur-name index of this record, which the reader will find of great value, and which has been checked and re-checked for accuracy. EVERY SUB-NAME has been included and none has been omitted. But please remember:

A hyphen between page numbers means that every page in between those numbers contains the name; also that, since the pages on which the name occurs only appear one time for each page, the name may appear several times on many of the pages cited. The names of the SURETIES and WITNESSES are also included in the index as well as both bride and groom in the marriage records.

The page numbers refer to the pages of VOLUME III, of Hathaway, and not this book.

MAP NO. 4

ADKESON 401, 406
AKEHURST 202
ALBERTSON 200, 204, 208, 367, 369, 374, 375, 378, 403, 409, 410, 421, 422
ALEXANDER 371
ALFORD 363
ALLCOCK 422
AMES 217, 403, 408
ANDERSON 204, 368, 369, 370, 377-379, 403, 404
ARMSTRONG 413
ARNOLD 204, 205, 373, 374, 376, 379
ARPS 416, 418
ARRINGTON 414, 416-418, 420
ASHELL 379
ASHLEY 412, 413
ASTIN 200
ATTAWAY 202, 203, 217
ATWOOD 201
AUSTEN 402, 407
AVERY 379, 419

BABB 200
BACKER 420
BAGLEY 379, 413-415, 418, 419, 421
BAGSTER 200, 202, 210
BAILEY (BAILIE, BAYLEY) 199, 201, 202, 218, 219, 363, 371, 374, 417.
BAKER 416, 420
BALL 420
BARBER 379, 414-416, 420
BARBERY 419
BARCLIFT 411, 412, 415-422
BARKER 422
BARNES 376, 379, 399, 410
BARTIE 418
BARROW 199, 204, 206, 207, 211, 215, 216, 364, 370, 379, 380, 404, 405, 408, 413, 417-419
BARTLETT 372, 374, 377, 380
BASS 407.
BATEMAN 204, 205, 210, 216, 220, 363, 370, 375, 380, 408, 409, 412-414, 417, 421, 422.

BAYLESS 411
BEASLEY 203, 207, 220, 374, 375, 377, 403, 407, 409, 419
BEDGOOD 380, 421
BELIOTT 200
BELL 416
BELLMAN 216
BENBURY 415
BENNETT 203, 208, 421
BENTLEY 199, 200, 209, 402, 406, 414
BERRY 373
BIBING 199
BIER 201, 202
BIGGS 220
BIRD 370, 373, 408
BISHOP 380, 405
BLAKE 202, 213, 214, 366
BLAITON 204
BLANK 373
BLITCHENDEN 380
BLOUNT 202, 386, 406, 407, 413-416
BOND 376, 413, 421
BONNE 364, 366
BOSWELL 380, 417
BOUGE 204, 217, 218, 369, 373, 378, 380, 416, 421, 422.
BOUNDS 405
BOUSH 414
BOYD 404
BOYCE 417, 421
BRANCH 417-419, 421
BRATTON 415, 419, 421
BRIGGS 380, 416, 418, 422
BRINKLEY 415, 421
BROOKS 204
BROWN 418, 419
BRYAN 202, 418
BUCKNER 416
BUDGATE 412, 418
BUFFKIN 380, 405
BULLOCK 415
BUNCH 415, 416, 417, 420, 421, 422.
BUNDY 204, 208, 213, 364, 365
BURCH 421
BURKE 418, 420
BURKETT 414, 422.

BURNETT 408
BURNHAM 416, 421
BURROWS 217
BURTONSHALL 409
BUSH 413, 421
BUTLER 369, 417, 420
BUTT 421, 422.

CAIL 417, 418-421
CAIN 421, 422
CALLY 421
CALLAWAY 199, 207, 211, 214,
  216, 220, 363, 364, 380,
  381, 402, 410, 422
CAMLATON 367
CANNADY 214, 216, 406
CANNON 363
CARMON 406, 421
CARUTHERS 412
CARTER 416, 417
CASEY 419
CASSELL 204
CASTELTON 200, 210
CHANCEY 376, 381
CHAPPELL 415, 419, 420, 422
CHARLES 199, 202, 203, 206,
  212, 363, 365, 370, 373,
  375, 376, 381
CHESSON (CHESTON, CHASTAIN,
  CHASTON) 199, 200, 202,
  203, 209, 213, 218, 219,
  364, 365, 368, 370, 381,
  402
CHELSEY 269, 402, 407
CHEW 403, 417, 418
CHOCKE 416
CLAPPER 409
CLARK 402, 413, 421
CLAYTON 405, 414, 417, 418,
  420
CLEARE 201, 213, 219, 402
CIELAND 411
CLEMENS 415
COOK (COOKE) 199, 200, 365,
  368, 402, 408, 421, 422
COFFIELD 422
COFFIN 204, 403
COLES 410
COLLEY 381, 405, 419
COLLYER 408
COLLINS 410-414, 417, 419,
  421
COLESON 413, 417, 419, 420
COLESTON 421
CONNOR 415
COPPAGE 416, 419
COPELAND 411, 421
CORBETT 220
CORKINGIE 364
CORPEW 411, 419
COSAND 381, 382, 406
COTTON 382
COWBOUGH 199
COWILE (CARWILE) 199
COWLEY 199
CREECY 382, 396, 416-418, 420
CRETCHINGTON 375
CREW 366
CROPLEY 407
CROXON 381
CULLER 368
CULPEPPER 203
CULY 210, 363
CUMMINGS 421
CUTLER 364
CUTLET 401

DAIL 420-422
DAMERON 417

DANIEL 422
DAVENPORT 209, 213, 215, 217,376
  382
DAVIES 382
DAVIS 202, 405, 407, 416-418,420
  421, 422
DAWSON 406, 407, 419
DEAL (DEEL, DAIL, DALE) 417, 418,
  419-422
DEDMAN 220
DE CROW 415
DELANO 414, 415
DENES (DEANS) 364
DENWAY 219, 382, 405
DEVATED 408
DICKENSON (DICKERSON) 364, 386
DILLON 422
DIX 374
DOCTON 414
DOE (DOWE) 383, 405, 414, 419, 421
DONALDSON 406, 413, 419, 421
DOREMAN 202, 368
DOWERS 363, 383
DRAKE 200
DUGLAS 418
DUKE 376
DUKENFIELD 407
DUNSTONE 369
DURANT 199, 202, 204, 205, 211,
  212, 215, 218, 365, 370, 372,
  383, 402, 403, 407-410.

EAMES 367
EARLES 413
EASON 415, 416
EDGE 204
EDLING 209
EGGERTON 376, 410
EGLINTINE 211
ELKER 200, 205, 209, 365
ELLIGOOD 414
ELLIOTT 383, 415-422
ELLIS 203, 407
ENNIS 404
EVANS 213, 216, 219, 220, 383,
  403, 406, 421
EVERAGE 420

FANNING 416
FARLEE 411
FENDALL 220, 363, 402, 406, 407
FENOX 403
FISHER 215, 219, 373, 402-404,
  409, 410
FITZPATRICK 422
FIVEASH 418
FLEMING 412, 413
FLETCHER 199, 206, 211, 214-216,
  219, 363, 374, 376, 383, 403,
  407-409, 421
FORBES 420, 422
FORBUSH 415
FOREHAND 417-421
FORKE 366
FOSTER 200, 203, 220, 366, 371,
  383, 402, 407, 409, 411,420
FREEMAN 199
FRENCH 409
FROTHERINGTON 377, 404
FRUGETT 371
FUDDY 408
FULTNER 366
FRUGENY 370, 409
FURRE 204

GALE 220, 410, 411
GARROWAY 201
GARRETT (GARROT) 410, 416, 417
GARRES 412, 420
GIBSON 382

GIDDENS 368, 402
GILBERT 419
GILLIAM 420
GLASGOW 366
GODFREY 200, 202, 214, 219,
  220, 384, 403, 408, 416,
  418, 420, 421
GOODWIN 416-418, 420-422.
GORDON 199-201, 377, 378
GOSBY 200, 201, 215, 216
  407
GOUGH 367, 402
GRAY 214, 373, 409, 410,
  413
GREEN 202
GREENWHITE 413
GREGORY 417, 418
GRIFFIN 415, 422
GUNFALLIS 203, 212, 364
GUY 416

HADDOCK 408
HALL 199, 207, 365, 376,384
  405, 410-415, 420, 421
HALLEM 213, 216, 218
HALSEY 413, 417, 422
HANBY 203, 421
HANCOCK 200, 203, 207, 211,
  215, 218, 363, 403, 416
HARBERT 220
HARDY 410
HARDIN 414
HARE 370, 402, 404, 408
HARLOW (HARLOE) 200, 209,
  218, 220, 365
HARMAN 199, 207, 200-212,
  214, 384, 408, 414,419,
  421, 422.
HARRELL 413, 420.
HARRIS 200, 202, 203, 216,
  365, 370, 373, 374, 407
  413, 414, 416, 420.
HARRISON 404
HASKETT 370, 373, 377, 386,
  415
HASSELL 412
HATCH 386, 411, 412
HATFIELD 418
HATTON 364, 416
HART 411
HARTLEY 201, 204, 407
HARVEY 201-205, 216, 219,
  220, 363, 364, 367, 376
  384-386, 405-407, 409,
  411-417, 419, 422
HAWKIN (HACKINGS) 209,365,
  368, 372, 375, 413
HEARE 371, 373
HEATH 408, 411
HECKELFIELD 403
HEIRES 373
HENBY 413
HENDRICKS 203, 386, 412,413
  418-420
HENLY 363
HERST 375
HILL 386, 407, 413
HIMES 386, 417
HINTON 419
HOBBS 369
HODGES 413, 418, 421
HOFLER 414
HOGG (HOG) 200, 211, 212,
  215, 220, 367
HOLMES 408, 418
HOLLOWAY 386, 387, 404, 417
HOLLOWELL 414, 416-422
HOPKINS 201, 203, 369, 402
  421
HOPPER 203

577

HORNBY 421
HOSEA 415-418, 421, 422
HOSKINS 204, 209
HOUGHTON (HAUGHTON) 217,218
  367, 369, 374, 375, 377,
  403, 411, 414.
HOUSE 204, 411
HOWARD 419
HOWCOTT 413
HOWETT 415, 417, 420
HUBBARD 419
HUDSON 405, 415, 418-421
HUFTON 416
HUGHES 202, 212, 215, 364,
  416
HUMPHREYS (HUMPHREYS) 415
HURDLE 416

INKERSON (INKOSON) 200, 364,
  373.

JACKSON 377, 387, 404, 414,
  418-420, 422
JACOCKS 220
JAMES 199, 412
JAMESTON (JAMESON) 418
JEFFREYS 410
JENKINS 201, 220
JENNET 387, 413, 415
JOHNSON 203, 215, 217, 387,
  401, 403, 406, 408, 411,
  419-421.
JOHNSTON 413, 414, 416, 418,
  419.
JONES 203, 205, 217, 365,
  367, 368, 371, 386, 387,
  403, 405, 409, 411, 413,
  415, 417, 419, 421, 422.
JOOKES 202
JORDAN 202, 204, 403, 421

KEATON 411
KEITH 366
KENT 199, 200, 202, 204,205,
  365, 375
KINKADE (KINKETT, KINCAID)
  201, 203
KING 404, 419
KINGKELE 370
KENDALL 364
KENNEDY (KANNADY, CANADY)218
  220, 367
KINSEY (XINSE) 218, 220, 371
  406
KINYON (KENYON) 387, 419, 421
  422
KNEA 200
KNIGHT 403, 410
KNOX 387, 415

LACY (LACEY) 369, 370, 373,
  387, 402, 404, 416, 419,
  422
LAKER 402, 405, 407, 409.
LANE (LAIN) 417-422.
LAMAR 416
LAMBERT 366
LANDMAN (LANDMAN) 415
LANKER (LAKER) 202, 204, 366
LAYDEN (LATEN) 387, 388, 410
  412, 415, 416, 419, 420
LAWRENCE (LARRANCE) 199, 203
  204, 206, 368, 401-403,
  407
LAWTON 414, 415
LEARY (LURY, LARY) 199, 202,
  210, 213, 216, 220, 366,
  388, 406, 410, 411, 416,
  421, 422.

LEE 416
LEPER (LEEPER) 199
LESLEY (LESLIE) 413, 414
LEWIS 378, 416, 419
LILES 415
LILLINGTON 199-205, 211, 214,
  216, 219, 220, 366, 402,
  406, 407
LILLY 201, 204, 210, 217, 367,
  403, 415-417, 419, 420
LINDSAY 199
LOKEMAN 201
LOFTEN 370, 404
LONG 202, 203, 208, 215, 216,
  219, 364, 365, 368, 370, 375,
  388, 404, 405, 410, 411, 415,
  417, 421
LOWE 415, 419
LOWREY 412
LUNSFORD 418, 420
LUTEN 418

McMILLAN (MACKMILLIN) 363
MALLORY 416
MANERS 204
MANN (MAW) 200, 218, 388
MANSELL 218, 367
MANWARING 217, 402
MARCUM 412
MARCY 203, 204, 212, 402, 412
MARITT (MARIOTT) 219
MARKER 388
MARSON 212
MASSAGNEY 371
MATHIS (MATHES) 369, 402, 407
MAUDLIN 368, 375, 376, 388,389
  404, 411, 412, 416, 419,420
McCARTNEY 414
McCONNELL 414, 417
McCOY 422
McDANIEL 204, 417
McGUIRE 420
McMULLEN 417
McNIDER 417, 421, 422
McSHEEHY 416
MEADES 412
MELTON 410
MERCER 404, 410
MICANTUSH 204
MIDDLETON 389
MILLER 413, 414
MILBURN 419
MING (MINGE?) 415, 417
MINGE 405, 409
MODLIN 370, 372, 418, 422
MOLLTON (MOULTON) 366
MONRO 409
MORGAN 200, 208, 372, 373, 375,
  376, 377, 389, 407-409, 413
  418, 421
MOORE 203, 369, 371, 373, 376,
  377, 389, 410, 413-415,417,
  418, 421
MORLEY 377
MORRIS 419
MARWOOD (MORWOOD) 199
MOSS 417, 420
MULLEN 399, 412, 417, 419, 420,
  422
MUMFORD 201
MUNDEN 415, 422
MUNS (MUNDS) 420
MURDAUGH 389, 390
MURRAY 419

NAILOR 402
NELSON 200
NEWBOLD 414-416, 418, 419
NEWBURN 420

NEWBY 372, 374, 377, 390,
  415, 416, 418,421
NICKELS (NICHOLS) 219
NICHOLSON 200, 203, 204, 209
  211, 213, 216, 218, 364,
  367, 369, 374, 390, 391,
  402, 404, 405, 409, 410
NIXON 390, 405, 408, 414,415
  418
NOGILL 366
NORCUM 368, 370, 376, 410,
  414, 415
NORFLEET 416
NORMAN 363, 372, 373, 416
NORMENT 411, 412
NORRINGTON 408
NORRIS 199
NOWELL (NOEL) 410
NOYS 406

OATS 369, 404
ODEAR (ADAIR?) 213
OLD 376, 387, 406, 410
O'NEAL 421
ORENDALL 412
OSBORNE 204
OVERMAN 391, 416
OVERTON 418, 422
OWEN 202, 214

PAGETT (PADGETT) 391, 392
PAIGE 213
PAINE (PAYNE) 208, 365
PALMER 405, 414
PARK 422
PARKER 409, 419, 421
PARMER (BALMER) 367
PARRIS 392, 405
PARSONS 368
PASSONS 370, 373, 378, 392,
  404, 407
PEAD 419
PEARCE 405, 413, 418
PEARRE 201, 202, 204, 212,
  365
PEARSON 417, 418
PEMBRACE 365
PENRICE 392, 407, 408, 412,
  419
PERDY 403
PERISHO 200, 210, 366, 371,
  372, 375, 392, 411, 412,
  413, 418
PERKINS 368, 402
PERRY 406, 413, 416-420,
  422
PETERSON 369, 403, 407, 408
PETTIT 412
PHELPS 208, 212, 214, 363,
  377, 393, 413,415, 416
PHILLIPS 203, 204
PICKRIN 411
PIDARS 368
PIERCE 208, 217, 219, 368,
  376, 404, 406, 408, 416
  417, 418
POINTER 418
POOL 409, 420
POPE 363
PORTIS 365
PORTLOCK 421
POSISON 410
POWELL 204
PRATT 414, 415, 418, 421-2
PROCTOR 417
PRITLOW (Various Spellings)
  199, 206, 220, 365, 368,
  370, 371, 373, 376, 407,
  410.

RANKHORN (RANKIN) 418
RAPER 417, 418, 421 422
RATLIFFE 410, 417
RAY (REA) 418, 421
READING 422
REDKNAPP 405
REDDICK (See RIDDICK)
REED 370, 403, 412, 414-416, 419, 420
RELPHE (RELFE) 204, 414, 415
RICHARDS 409, 410, 413, 422
RIDDICK 393, 412, 415, 416, 418, 421
RIGGS 412
RIPLEY 414, 420
RIGET (See WRIGHT)
ROBERTS 412, 417-419, 421
ROBINS 413, 419-422
ROBINSON 393
ROE 411, 414
ROGERS 364, 405
ROGERSON 393, 394, 415-417, 420, 421
ROOKES 219
RORUS 402
ROSE 375, 404
ROUNDTREE 419-421
ROWDEN 204
RUSSELL 201, 210
RUTTER 375, 410

SALTER 410, 417, 419
SANDERSON 411, 417
SANDIN 412
SANDERS 394, 418-420, 422
SAUNDERS 394, 412, 415, 419
SAYERS 421
SAWYERS 422
SCARBOROUGH 412
SCOTT 201, 202, 211, 212, 218, 365, 366, 394, 410, 412, 415, 419, 422
SCRINER 373
SCRYMSHOE (SCRYMSHER) 401
SEXTON 409
SHADDOCK 408
SHARBO 394
SHERWOOD (SHERROD, SHEARER) 219, 369, 372, 374, 377, 383, 394, 408
SIBBISTON 413
SIMONS 204, 370, 395, 415
SIMMONS 395
SIMPHER 200
SIMPSON 414, 416, 420, 422
SITTERSON 394, 395, 415-420, 422
SKINNER 395, 396, 405, 406, 411-413, 415-420
SLATER 217
SLOCUM 201
SMALL 418, 420, 421
SMITH 220, 366, 396, 407, 409 411, 413, 414, 416, 419-422.
SNELL 204, 211, 212, 214, 216, 220, 370
SNELLING 203, 216, 403
SNOWDEN 375, 377, 396, 397, 410, 413, 418, 420, 422.
SPEIGHT 422
SPELLMAN 212, 218, 363, 368
SPENCE 369, 371
SPENCER 419
SPRAGUE 204
SPRUILL 414, 420
STACEY 203, 364, 417, 420, 421
STAFFORD 411, 413, 417-422
STALLINGS 405, 416

STAMFORD 214
STANFORD 213
STANDIN 397, 411-417, 421, 422
STANLEY 203, 204
STANTON 417, 418, 419
STARKE 366
STEPNEY 201, 212, 214, 215, 217, 219, 220, 364, 366, 368, 370, 374, 375, 401, 413, 415, 417.
STEVENS (STEPHENS) 205, 220, 368, 375, 397, 410, 414
STEVENSON 411, 412, 415, 416, 418-421
STEWARD 203, 214, 215, 369, 397.
STOKES(STOAKES) 411, 412, 414, 422
STONE 397, 413, 416-419, 421
STANDRIDGE 202
STUART 367
STUCKE (STUCKEY) 406
STURGEON(STERGION) 199, 207
SUMNER 397, 412
SUTTON 199, 201, 207, 208, 211, 214, 365-367, 369, 371, 375-376 377, 397, 398, 400, 402, 403, 404, 405, 407, 409, 411-414, 416-418, 420-422
SWANN 391, 398, 402, 404, 407, 410 413, 414
SWARTOUT 422
SWETTMAN 201
SYLVESTER 420

TARKINGTON 220
TAYLOR (TAILOR) 199, 200, 217, 364, 365, 367, 398, 402, 403, 407, 410, 413-415, 420
TETTERTON 212, 366, 408
THACH 405, 412-414, 417, 421
THERRILL 200, 365
THIGPEN 218, 220, 367, 369, 398
THISEL 402
THOMAS 207, 366, 398
THORNTON 419
THURSTON 199, 204-206, 211, 220
TITMARSH 220
TITTERTON (See TETTERTON) 199, 202
TODDE 371
TOMS 400, 416, 421
TOMES (THOMAS?) 202, 204, 212, 219, 364, 365, 371, 372, 376, 377, 399, 404, 409.
TOMLIN 219
TOMLINSON 217
TOWE (TOW) 414, 420.
TOWNSEND 399, 413
TROWELL 202, 214
TRUEBLOOD 411
TRUELOVE 422
TRUMBULL 372, 417
TULLE (TULL, TULLY) 414
TURNER 399, 406, 412, 413, 416, 417-422.

UPTON 422
URMSTONE 400

VARDEN 420
VILLER 413
VOLLWAY 374, 377
VOSS 200, 203, 207, 210.

WAFF 418
WAITE 202, 203, 205, 212, 215, 364
WALKER 202, 204, 214
WALLACE 414
WALLER 203, 211, 213
WALLIS (See WALLACE) 411, 412
WALTON 413, 415, 421
WARD 204, 412, 414, 419, 421

WARREN 374, 399, 403, 409
WATTSON 202
WEBB 412, 421, 422
WHEELER 422
WEEKS 411, 417, 419, 421, 422
WELCH 199, 421
WELLS 375, 376, 404, 414, 421, 422
WELLWOOD 199, 207
WEST 367
WHEATON 420
WHEDBY (WHEDBEE) 201, 205, 213, 215, 216, 363, 399, 403, 407, 412, 413, 415, 418, 420
WHERRY 373, 408
WHITE 202-204, 364, 399, 400 404, 406, 410, 417, 418, 419-422.
WHITEHALL 366
WHITEMAN 415
WHITLOCK 214, 216
WIGGINS 400
WILCOX 419
WILDER 417
WILEY 412, 419
WILKINS 411, 415
WILLARD 421
WILKINSON 203
WILLIAMS 203, 204, 211, 217, 220, 364, 369, 367, 400, 407, 411, 412, 413, 416, 417-420, 422
WILLIS 203, 363, 366
WILLOUGHBY 213, 403
WILSON 214-218, 220, 363, 367, 369, 374, 403, 408, 409, 417, 421, 422.
WINBU 4, 9
WINGA 417
WOGGELL 202
WOLFINDON 363
WOLLINFOR 406
WOOD 199, 200, 400, 401, 404, 411, 413, 417.
WOODLEY 413, 415, 422
WOODWARD 419
WOOLLARD 216, 374, 376, 400 410
WRIGHT 201, 375, 403, 413, 417, 420
WYATT 208, 401, 405, 415, 416, 418, 420.

...

The foregoing INDEX to the marriage records of BERKELEY (and PERQUIMANS) Precinct and County, includes both bride and groom and also the sureties and witnesses.

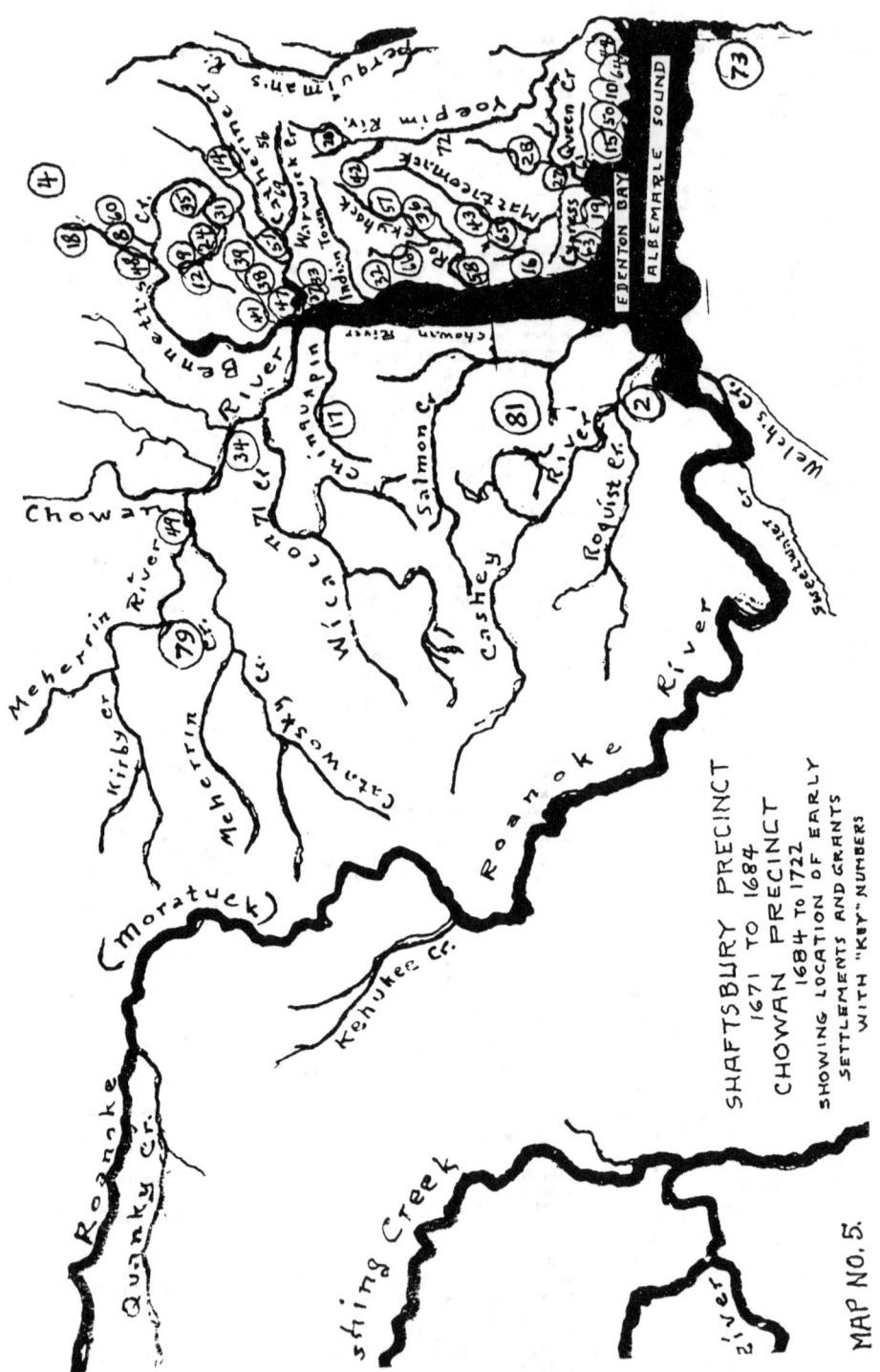

INDEX TO MARRIAGES IN CHOWAN COUNTY
FROM 1740 TO 1840

AS RECORDED AND PUBLISHED IN HATHAWAY'S NORTH CAROLINA HISTORICAL AND GENEALOGICAL REGISTER BETWEEN PAGES NO. 235 TO 567.

(References are to VOL. 1, HATHAWAY'S N. C. REGISTER.)

ADAMS 236, 237
ADDISON 244
AFFORD 294
ALBERTSON 244, 400
ALLEN 237, 239, 394, 400
ALEXANDER 566
ALLUMS 414
ALPHEUS 407, 413, 561
ALSTON 236, 238
AMBROSE 238, 248
ANDERSON 237, 247, 251, 392, 394, 396
ANTHONY 405
ARCHER 402
ARKILL 237
ARMISTEAD 240, 561
ARNALL 259
ARNOLD 251
ARPS 250
ARRINGTON 565
ARTIE 238, 240
ASH 237
ASKELL (ASBELL) 253, 254, 392, 393, 397, 403, 559, 560, 563, 566
ASHBURN 247, 408
ASKEW 244, 398
ASHLEY 245, 247, 249, 250, 252, 254, 393, 395, 397, 399, 400, 401, 403, 405, 406, 407, 409, 411, 412, 414, 561, 563, 564- 567.
ATKINSON 562
AVERY 397, 401, 403, 405, 409, 558, 564, 566.

BACCHUS (BACKUS) 246-249, 252 254, 397, 399, 400, 410, 559, 565
BACOST 252
BADHAM 240, 247, 248, 252, 255, 392, 395, 397, 400, 406, 409, 412, 559, 561, 564
BAGLEY 558, 561
BAILEY 394, 409
BAINES (BAINS) 240, 248, 250, 253, 392, 394, 395, 396, 398, 400, 401, 403-405, 408.
BAKER 239-241, 409, 412, 559, 566.
BALDWIN 398
BALLARD 243, 253
BANKS 248, 252, 408
BANN 244
BARCO 394, 403
BARKER 237, 247, 251, 407, 408.
BARNABY 244, 247
BARNETT 564
BARNEY 411-413, 559, 560
BARNS 393, 403
BARROW 247, 250, 251, 394, 408
BARTEE 253-254, 394, 403, 408 409
BASS 562, 564, 566
BATEMAN 241, 245, 248, 250, 254, 394, 397, 399, 401, 402, 413, 564, 565.

BEASLEY 238, 242-246, 249-255, 394, 396, 399, 400, 407, 411, 412, 413, 559-561, 563, 565.
BELL 560, ..
BEMBURAGE 253
BENBURY 236-238, 240, 245, 393, 396 397, 400-402, 410, 414, 561, 564
BENNETT 239, 244, 253, 254, 395, 402, 409.
BENSON 392, 406
BENT 248, 251, 397, 403
BENTLEY 235, 242, 250, 253
BENTON 237, 241, 250, 409, 562
BERRY 560
BERRYMAN 561
BEST 399, 401, 410, 565
BEVINO 251
BILLINGS 409
BILLUPS 244
BISHOP 240, 247
BISSELL 392, 396, 397, 401, 402, 404, 411
BLACK 241, 243, 254
BLACKALL 237
BLACKBURN 244, 247
BLACKMAN 244
BLAIR 254, 408, 413, 558
BLANCHARD 238, 241-243, 254, 396, 403, 404, 411, 412, 558, 559, 563, 567
BLAND 560
BLATONY 254
BLAXTON 558
BIXATON 249
BLOUNT 236-239, 241-243, 245, 246, 254, 255, 393-395, 397-401, 403 404, 405, 410, 413, 559, 562, 564
BOGGS 244
BOGMAN 402
BOGUE 395, 400, 559, 563
BOHANNON 252, 561
BOLTON 395
BOND 238, 242-244, 246-248, 250-252 393, 395, 396, 398, 399, 402-408 411, 412, 560, 562, 563, 565, 566
BONFIELD 241
BONNER 236-241, 243, 245-247, 249, 250, 252, 402, 404, 407, 564, 566.
BOON 403
BOOTH 558
BORITZ 404, 412, 565
BORY 244
BOSWELL 240, 404
BOTH 253
BOULTON (SEE BOLTON) 243, 254
BOUSHALL 398
BOYCE 244, 249, 251-255, 392, 393 396, 397, 399, 402, 403, 406, 407, 408, 410, 411, 413, 414, 559-563, 566.
BOYD 235, 238, 241, 405, 407, 411
BOZMAN 396, 404, 405, 410, 412
BRADLEY 393
BRANCH 235, 239
BRANTLEY 409
BRATTON 399, 406, 413, 562, 566.
BRICKHOUSE 410, 568

BRICKLE 250
BRIGGS 238, 562
BRINKLEY 250, 255, 401, 410
BRINN 245, 247, 249, 253, 254, 394, 399, 405, 406, 408, 410, 412, 413
BRITAIN 244
BRITT 559
BROCKS 396
BROUGHTON 413, 562, 563
BROWER 407
BROWN 241, 243, 251, 255, 392, 395, 396, 402, 406, 410
BROWRIGG 241, 243, 403, 405, 406, 409, 559, 560, 564
BRUCE 246
BRUER 405, 562
BRYCE 394, 403
BUCHANAN 244, 252, 407
BUCKLEY 245, 246, 250, 251, 254, 394, 395, 401
BUFF 253
BULLOCK 402, 408, 409, 413 414.
BUNCH 237, 240, 241, 245, 246-251, 253-255, 392, 393-396, 398-402, 404, 406-409, 411-414, 558, 559-561, 563-567.
BURBAGE 562
BURDICK 248
BURDOE 396
BURKE (BURK) 244, 245, 397, 401, 404, 406, 559
BURKETT 239, 251, 253, 255, 392
BURN 251
BURNHAM 412
BURNETT 251
BURROUGHS 560, 562
BURRUSS 393, 397-399, 401, 409, 412
BUSH 251, 397, 410, 412, 413, 414, 558, 566.
BUTLER 235, 238, 239, 247, 250, 254, 397, 402.
BYRD 561
BYRUM (BIRUM) 248-252, 255 393-394, 396, 398-403, 406, 408, 409, 411, 413 558, 560, 563, 565, 566

CABARRUS 253, 400, 412, 559
CADDY 410
CAIL 250, 412
CAIN 244
CALLAGAN 247, 248
CAMERON 243, 249, 250
CAMP 249
CAMPBELL 236, 238, 242
CANADY 559
CANNON 560
CARLISLE 241, 562, 563
CARNEY 396
CAROON 244
CARPENTER 395, 407
CARR 244, 245, 247
CARRELL 241

CARTER 243, 245, 246, 251, 560, 564
CARUTHERS 236, 238, 246, 248
CASTELLAW 400
CHAMBERLAIN 252
CHAMBERS 253, 400, 410, 563, 564.
CHAMPION 236, 239, 257, 250, 404
CHAPMAN 241, 243, 244
CHAPPELL (CHAPPIE) 245, 247, 254, 392, 394, 396, 397, 407, 408, 412, 559, 566.
CHARLTON 235, 237, 240, 244, 248, 251, 252, 392, 398, 403, 406-408, 412, 559, 562.
CHARLES 558
CHARRIER 410
CHESHIRE 248, 252, 395, 400, 403, 405, 408, 563.
CHESTER 407
CHEW 248, 250, 255.
CHILDRESS 395
CHINA 382
CHISWELL 242
CHRISTIAN 396, 398, 558, 565
CHRISTOPHER 565
CHURCHILL 412
CHURTEN 255
CITIZEN 398, 559
CLARK 244, 245, 249, 250, 395, 408
CLARKSON 249, 397, 408
CLASTRIX 246
CLAYTON 235
CLELAND 238, 240
CLEVELAND 252
CLEMENTS 248, 403, 405, 409, 410, 413
CLEMMONS 412
COBB 408
COCHRAN (COCHRANE) 394, 399, 401, 404, 567
COFFIELD 240, 244, 247-249, 252-254, 392, 397, 398, 400, 403, 405, 406, 410, 411-413.
COLE 238, 241, 244
COLEMAN 238
COLIES 408
COLLINS 235, 240, 241, 245, 246, 249, 252, 253, 561.
COINER 246
COLSTON 397
COLETRIXXE 236
COMARTE 241
COME 407
COOK 243, 399.
COPELAND 239, 241-243, 246, 248, 253, 397, 401, 402, 403, 413, 560, 561
CORE 255
CORBY (CORBIE) 242, 408
CORPEW 237
COSTAIN 408
COTTON (KOTTEN) 246, 255, 396, 398, 401, 403, 405, 407, 408, 410, 412, 413
COTTREL 243
COURIS 397
COWAN (COWAND) 246, 249
COWPER 244
COX 249, 403, 405, 408, 564
CRAIG 242, 243
CRAVEN 235-239.
CRAWFORD 250
CRAWLEY 401

CREECY 237, 241, 246, 247, 392, 396, 400-403, 406-409, 411, 413, 558, 559, 561, 563, 565
CRICKELL 236
CRIGIZ 392
CRISMAN 246
CROCKER 255
CROMARTEE (See COMARTEE) 245
CROMLIES 240
CROSS 560
CROTHERS 393.
CULLINGTON 236
CULLENS 240, 255, 393, 397, 402
CUNNINGHAM 243, 245, 251, 252, 254, 392, 393
CURRIE 250
CURTIS 392
CUSTIS 244
CURTICE 340
CUTIS 392
CUTEHEL 559

DAIMAN 249
DAIL 399, 408, 409, 412, 562
DAILEY 244, 561
DALLINGS 392
DANIEL 251, 252, 400
DARBY 242
DARE 241
DAVIS 236, 239, 243, 244, 247, 252, 399, 403, 404, 406, 563
DAVIDSON (DAVISON-DAVERSON) 238, 240, 400, 405, 406, 564.
DAWES (LAWS) 246, 255, 407
DEAL (DRALE-DAIL) 247, 393, 402, 405, 408
DEAN 560
DEAR 245
DE CLUGAY 253
DE CROW 392
DE COST 393
DE NARD 253
DENNIS 564
DERMODY 242, 244
DESCHAMPE 250
DICKINSON 395, 397, 398, 403
DIGIN 244
DISHON 246, 250
DITCHBURN 245
DOEBER 249
DOLLY 412
DOMINIQUE 394
DONALDSON 248, 253, 393, 394, 395, 397
DORE 241
DOUGLAS 244, 560, 562
DOWD 241
DOZIER 402, 405
DUCKETT 414
DUFFY 406
DUKE 564
DUNCAN 243, 247
DUNSCOMBE 238, 241, 244, 247, 248
DUNSTON 239
DURHAM 250
DYER 392

EAGLES 408
EARLE (EARL) 241, 245, 246
EASON 243, 246, 249, 400, 563, 565
EASTON 409
EBORN 399
ECCLESTON 244, 246
EDES 405
EDNEY 252
EDWARDS 250, 393
EELBECK 237, 253
EGAN 244, 248, 250.

EHRINGHAUS 41
EILBERSON 239, 241, 42
ELDER 241, 243
ELLIAS 559
ELLIFFE 242, 243
ELLIS 240, 247, 252, 564
ELLIOTT 243, 247-249, 251-255, 394-396, 398-400, 402-404, 406, 409-414, 558-562, 564-567.
ENDLESS 245, 247, 248
ENOS 253
EPPES 564
ESHON 565
ETHERIDGE 247, 250, 254, 255, 564
EVANS 238, 241, 246, 247, 253, 392, 395, 397, 399, 402, 404, 405, 407, 411, 412, 413, 558-561, 563, 564.
EVERETT 403, 405, 408
EVERTON 252, 396, 399.

FALLOW 236, 240, 242, 246, 250, 251
FARIBAULT 404, 407, 410, 416
FARIS 394, 400
FARROW 242, 246, 248, 250.
FELTON 251, 253, 255, 403, 407, 409, 412, 558, 559, 560, 561, 564
FIFE 255, 393, 394, 398, 409, 412
FIGURES 406
FINCH 567
FISHER 247
FITT 392, 407, 413
FLEETWOOD 248, 249
FLETCHER 566
FLOYD 245, 252, 395, 397, 408, 410, 414, 558, 561, 566
FLUHY (FLUHRY-FLEURY) 238, 242, 246, 249, 254, 401, 405, 412, 563
FORBES 245
FORD 240, 394-396, 399, 566, 567.
FOREHAND 393, 405, 408, 410, 560, 562, 566
FOREMAN 565
FOSTER 243, 244, 249, 255, 560
FRAZEL 245, 249
FRAZIER 240, 253, 255
FREEMAN 239, 242-245, 394, 397, 409, 411, 560
FULLER 404
FULLERTON 236, 239
FULLINGTON 249, 392, 402, 410, 412, 559.
FURMAN 403.

GAINER 404
GALE 236, 237, 242, 254
GALLATLY 242, 243, 254.
GALLOP 393
GARDNER 239, 247, 251, 252, 392, 393, 396, 401, 405.
GARRETT 239, 240, 242-244, 246, 250, 254, 396, 408, 410, 412
GASKINS 243, 562, 567
GASSER 246
GATLIN 402
GEAR 236
GEORGE 247, 252.

GHOLSON 401
GIBBONS 243
GIBSON 239
GILBERT 242
GILES 414
GILLIAM 238
GLAUGHAN 246
GLOHORN 252
GODFREY 216, 412
GOELET 561
GOLDSMITH 239
GOODIN 246
GOODWIN 247, 250-252, 254,255
 393, 395, 396, 401, 403,
 407, 408, 410, 411, 558,
 559-561, 564, 565.
GOMAIRE 403
GONZAL 408
GORDON 248, 559
GORHAM 253, 254
GROHAN 408
GRANBERRY 244, 254, 558
GRANDY 247
GRANGER 406
GRANTHAM 405
GRAY 236, 248, 255, 397, 408
GRAYSTOCK 250
GREEN 241, 242, 398, 399, 406
 559, 564
GREGORY 235, 240, 241, 245,
 246, 253-255, 393 - 395
 397, 398, 400, 402, 404
 405, 407-411, 414, 558
 559, 562, 566, 567.
GRIFFIN 244, 254, 396, 399,
 404, 411, 558-562, 567.
GRIMES 397, 402, 404, 559
GROGAN 247
GROSHON 245
GROVES 245
GURLEY 251
GUSSAM 409
GUSTON 236

HACKETT 241
HADDICKS 249
HADLEY 409
HAGARTHY 563, 564
HAINS 562
HALL 235, 237, 245, 247, 250
 251-253, 398, 400-402,
 410, 560, 566
HALSEY 237-242, 244-246, 249
 252, 393, 396, 397, 401,
 402, 405, 409, 410, 412,
 413, 414, 558, 561, 567.
HAMBY 241
HAMMETT 560
HAMILTON 243, 248, 250, 252,
 253, 409, 560
HANDSEY 252
HANKINS 247, 252, 253, 401,
 408, 411, 412
HARDCASTLE 566
HARDY 240, 245, 404, 406
HARDISON 245
HARE 237, 239, 245, 249, 393
HARFORD 245
HARLOWE (HARLOE) 236, 239,244
HARMAN 399, 407
HARPER 244
HARRELL 242, 250, 253, 393,
 399, 401, 402, 414, 561
 562, 565, 567
HARRINGTON 564
HARRIS 249, 254, 255, 393,
 394, 396, 404, 406, 409,
 411, 413, 414, 560, 561,
 567.

HARRISON 241, 243, 397, 398, 405
 406, 560, 563, 566
HARROD 245, 246, 250, 252, 254,
 395, 407
HARRON 235
HARTMUS 403, 405, 407
HARTSON 236
HARVEY 245, 246, 252, 399, 407,414
HARRELL 400
HASSELL 241 248, 250, 251, 255,
 392, 395, 399, 407, 408
HASTE 403, 558, 560-562, 564, 566
HATCH 236, 237, 238
HATHAWAY 251-253, 255, 395, 406,
 411, 566
HAUGHTON 237-239, 243, 245, 246,
 248-251, 253, 255, 392 - 399,
 405-407, 410, 412-414, 358,
 359, 360, 562-564.
HAWKS 410
HAYES 247
HAYWOOD 239
HAZARD 235
HEARALD 252
HEATH 561
HEDRICK 397, 404, 405, 412, 558,
 565, 567
HENDERSON 564
HENDRICKS 397, 408, 410, 413, 561,
 562, 567
HERNDON 561, 563
HERRICK 393
HEWES 241
HIBBS 399
HICKS 248, 251, 252, 401, 409, 411
HIGGINS 412
HIGHSMITH 251
HILL 239-241, 253, 392, 398, 403,
 405, 414, 562, 563
HILLMAN 251
HINESLEY 245, 246, 255, 412
HINTON 239, 243-245, 247, 392,393
 405, 561
HIX 253
HOBBS 240, 248, 250, 253-255, 393-
 395, 398, 399, 403,. 405 -409,
 413, 561, 564, 565, 567
HOBDAY 241
HODGES 398
HOFF 249
HOFFLER 240
HOLLEY 404
HOLLINS 253
HOLLOWAY 404
HOLLOWELL 249, 252, 254, 255, 394,
 396, 399, 400, 405, 408-410,
 562, 566.
HOLMES 248, 253, 401, 402, 409
HOOD 236
HOOKER 397
HOOTEN 251
HOPKINS 238, 244, 565
HOPPER 240
HORNE 566
HORNIBLOW 242, 399, 403-408
HOSEA 401
HOSKINS 236, 239-242, 246-254, 392
 393, 398-400, 402-404, 407,
 408, 410, 411, 558, 559, 562,
 563, 565, 566
HOSMER 252
HOUGH 246
HOUGHTON 404, 411
HOUSE 255, 393
HOWARD 236
HOWCOTT 236, 238, 241, 242, 251,
 256, 403, 407, 412, 413, 560
 564.
HOWE 392
HOWELL 239

HOWETT 402, 405, 406
HUBBARD 407
HUBBALL (HUBBIE) 251, 392, 405
 409
HUDGINS 401
HUDSON 396, 399, 405, 565, 566
HUFF 241
HUGHES 405
HUGGINS 403
HULL 236, 244
HUMPHREY 250, 393
HUMPHREYS 248, 258, 254
HUMPHRIES 246, 249, 255, 394
HUNT 243
HUNTER 242-244, 402, 412
HURDLE 240, 248, 249, 253, 392
 393, 396-399, 401-404
 410-412, 414, 559, 561,
 562, 564-566
HURST 239, 241
HUTSON 236, 402

INGHAM 255
IREDELL 408

JACKSON 241, 244-246, 249,
 251, 255, 393, 396, 398,
 400, 405, 407, 410, 412,
 413, 559, 565, 566
JAMES 248, 249, 253, 255,
 395, 401, 403, 406
JAMISON 246, 393, 396, 406
JACOBS 347, 248
JACOCKS 406
JENDERS 393
JENKINS 240
JENNETT 246
JENNY 252
JETHRO 565
JINKER 244
JINSON 250
JOINER 250, 410, 413, 559
JOHNSON 246, 250, 400, 404,
 560, 564
JOHNSTON 248
JOLIFFE 564
JOSEPH 248, 250
JONES 236-248, 250-255, 392,
 394-399, 404-409, 411,
 413-414, 560-567.
JORDAN 244-247, 249-251, 253,
 254, 255, 394-410, 412,
 414, 559-561, 563, 564,
 566, 567.

KAIE (KAIL) 246, 404, 407,408
KEATING 394, 395, 404, 408,
 412, 413
KEEL 248
KEITH 563
KELLEY 253
KEMBALL 565
KENNEDY 243, 393
KENYON 397, 410
KIMSEY 236, 241
KING 236-239, 243, 247, 250
 254, 392, 400, 402, 404
 567
KINGHAM 239
KIRBY 248, 253
KNIGHT 242, 244, 413
KNOWLES 411
KNOX 395, 412, 564
KRAGELIN 392, 393

LACKEY 398
LAFITTE 235
LAFONT 244, 245
LAMB 403, 410, 411, 413,558,
 560, 561, 564.

583

LAIN 413, 414
LANE 247, 251, 252, 395, 397
398, 403, 404, 407, 408,
411, 412, 413, 565
LANGLEY 396
LANK 396
LAQUER 246
LANSTON 412
LASSITER 242, 243, 246, 255,
394, 396, 408, 409, 414,
561, 562, 563
LATEN 240
LATTIMORE (LATTIMER) 401, 414
565
LAUGHINGHOUSE 564
LAVERSAGE 404
LAWRENCE 254, 395, 398, 404,
411
LEARY 235, 239, 244, 245,
248, 255, 394, 402, 404,
405, 406, 412, 559, 560,
561, 562
LEATH 255, 402, 406
LEE 253, 410
LEEMING 240, 247, 248, 250
LEGGETT 407
LEIGH 240
LEIGHTON 245
LEMMENT (LEMMETT) 398, 409,
565
LEONARD 249
LESTER 245, 246, 251, 252
LEATHERBERRY 408, 559
LEWIS 237, 238-240, 250, 563
LILES 236, 238, 240, 246, 248
250, 253, 255, 395, 397,
398-402, 408, 411, 412,
559, 561, 562, 567
LOCKEY 395
LONG 236, 241, 243, 250, 253
404, 406, 414, 561, 564.
LONGGUET 253
LOVE 253, 396, 397
LOVELL 236
LOW (LOWE) 251, 253
LOWTHER 240, 395, 411.
LOYD 236
LUCAS 255.
LUTEN 236-242, 252, 394, 396,
397, 399, 402, 407, 409,
410, 412
LYONS 253, 392, 559, 564

MACKEY 236
MAINES (MEANS) 246, 248
MALLONE 393
MALTBY 253, 396
MALTY 411
MANN 396, 398, 400, 411, 412
566, 566
MANNING 240, 394, 400, 404,
406, 408, 414, 560, 561.
MANSFIELD 242, 250, 564
MARE 397, 398
MARKEL 406
MARTERI 246
MARSH 241
MARSHALL 240, 241, 243, 246
MARTIN 236, 240, 249, 250,
405
MARTINDALE 564
MATHIAS 240, 244, 248, 394,
398, 402, 404, 559, 562
MATHEWS 236, 247, 564
MASSEY 564
MASTERS 393
MASSIN 414, 461
McCABE 253, 392

McCAIN 241
McCLENDEN (McCLENNON) 245
McCOTTER 394, 411
McCOWEN 255
McDERMOTT 401
McDONALD 249, 252, 396, 400, 404
406, 563
McDOWELL 407, 409-412, 414, 562
McCLURE 235
McFARLANE 393
McGUIRE 245, 249, 250, 252, 254
255, 393-398, 402, 405, 412
559, 560, 561
McKAIN 245
McKEEL 246, 247, 249, 250, 252,
255, 404, 561
McKEEN 240
McNEIL 398
McMATH 240
McNIDER 244, 248, 250, 560, 562
McSHEEHEY 244
McTEER (MelTEER) 565
MEAZELLS (MIZELLS) 395
MEEKINGS 254
MELSON 255
MELVIN 398
MEREDITH 240, 243, 403
MESSENGER 238, 239
MEWBORN 250, 398, 402, 409, 412.
MIDDLETON 251, 255, 408, 561, 565
MIERS (MYERS) 248, 394, 400, 401
406, 412, 565
MILES 253, 254.
MILLEN 252
MILLER 239, 241, 242, 245, 251,
255, 393, 399, 403, 407, 413
559, 560, 562
MILLS 251
MINCHEW 247
MINER 396
MINERVA 247
MING (MINGE?) 235, 237, 239, 246,
247-249, 253, 255, 398-401,
403, 408, 566
MISKELL 560
MITCHELL 237, 247, 253, 254, 393,
398, 399, 401, 407, 408, 412,
559, 561-563, 566
MIXON 253, 397, 409, 413, 560,
561, 563, 566
MODE 395
MODELIN 560, 565
MONTFORT 241
MONTGOMERY 244, 245
MOORE 246, 251, 401, 407, 411, 414
558, 561
MORGAN 246, 393, 560, 561, 566
MORRELL 245
MORRIS 248, 250, 254, 402, 414,
564
MOSZLEY 252
MOW 240
MUIR 249
MURRAY 245, 246, 248-250, 392,
393, 394, 397, 398, 565
MURRER 253-255
MUNS (MUNDS) 247, 249, 250, 251,
252, 253, 399, 400, 402, 408
409, 414, 559, 561-563, 565.
MUSE 248, 249, 394, 401.
MUSHROW 244

NASH 398, 400, 401, 403, 406, 407
409
NASRIE 395.
NEIL (NEILL) 237, 246, 251, 253,
255, 398, 409, 410, 560, 566
NELSON 404
NEVIL 237

NEWBY 251, 254, 408, 411, 413,
560
NEWBOLD 247, 566
NEWBORN (NEWBURN) 248, 252, 395
398-400, 402, 407, 409, 411,
558, 559, 561, 562
NEWSOM 254
NICHOLS 236, 245, 246, 398, 404
NICKERSON 401
NIXON 239, 254, 396, 401, 410,
411, 412, 559, 561, 564
NOLAN 559, 563, 565
NORCOM 235-237, 247, 249, 250
252, 253, 393-396, 399,
400-402, 410, 411, 413,
558, 560, 563, 565
NORFLEET 243, 247, 249, 253,
254, 396, 398, 399, 402,
404, 410, 414, 566
NORMAN 255, 393, 401
NORSWORTHY 243
NOXON 395, 410

OLDHAM 240
OLIVER 236
O'MALLEY 248, 249, 252-254,
393, 399, 405
O'NEILL 247, 255, 394, 396,
398, 401 (O'NEAL).
ORMOND 243, 248
OUTLAW 244, 558, 563
OVERTON 403, 404
OWEN 238

PAGE 561
PAGETT 237
PALMER 245
PARKER 238, 245, 246, 249, 250
252, 255, 393-396, 398,
399, 400-402, 404, 406,
407, 409, 410, 412-414,
558-562, 564-566.
PARKS 255, 558, 563, 566
PARISH 248-251, 255, 394, 395
397, 399-402, 404, 407-410,
412, 413, 559, 563, 565
PARRIS 236
PARSONS 406
PATTERSON 242, 247, 393
PATRICK (PADERICK) 406
PAXTON 393, 401, 404
PAYNE (PAINE) 235, 236, 238,
240, 243, 248, 252, 392,
558, 564
PEARSON 242, 248
PELL 398, 413, 565
PENRICE 236, 239, 242
PEPPER 392
PERKINS 246, 248-250, 404, 563
PERRY 240, 252, 253, 255, 393
397-399, 402, 404, 411,
413, 558-561, 564, 565.
PERSON 249
PETERSON 238, 393
PETTIGREW 245
PETTYJOHN 246, 248, 250, 255,
395, 399, 401-403, 405-407
409, 410, 414, 560, 561, 563
PHELPS 242, 247, 248, 408, 414
PHILLIPS 247
PICKARD 412, 559
PIERCE 245, 249, 562, 564
PIPKIN 409, 413
PLUMMER 249
POINTER 250
POLLOCK 246, 410
POPHELSTON 247, 253-255, 392,
400, 402, 558
PORRIE 258

PORTER 413
POTTER 236, 239, 414
POU 247, 248
POWELL 237, 247, 250, 395,
    398, 404
POWERS 244, 245, 247, 401
PRATT 243, 244, 250, 558, 559
    561, 565, 567
PREDY 236, 238
PRITCHARD 402, 559, 563
PRICE 240, 243, 244, 247, 250
    252, 254, 255, 394, 395,
    398, 401, 404
PRIVETT 238, 250, 255, 394,
    398, 410, 413, 559, 560
    566
PROCTOR 248, 255, 392-394, 398
    562, 563, 566
PUGH 237, 254
PURDIE (PURDY) 241-243, 246,
    392, 397, 405, 406
PURRER (PURYEAR?) 392
PURSELL 237
PYE 244
PYLE 248

RABY 237, 240
RANDALL 244, 253
RANDELL 393.
RAUTEN 406
RAY 395
REA 250, 255, 394, 397, 400,
    401, 405, 406, 410, 411,
    413, 561-565
READ 562
READY 243, 245, 247, 249
REDING 237
REED 236, 237, 255, 402, 403,
    411
REEVES 247, 251
REILLY 397
REUBEN 563
REVILL 255
RHODES 240, 245, 247
RHODA 246, 248, 250, 251, 396
RICE 236, 237
RICHARDS 236, 250
RICHEE 564
RICKETTS 237
RIDDICK 242, 244, 252, 255,
    397, 404, 408, 559, 565
RIDDLE 399
RIEUSSET 237
RIGHT (WRIGHT?) 247
RIGHTON 399, 400, 409, 560
RILEY 406
RIMBOUGH 243
ROADY 254
ROBERTS 238, 241, 246, 249,
    251-253, 255, 392-394
    397, 399, 401-403, 406
    407-410, 414, 558, 560
    561, 562, 564
ROBERTSON 241, 243, 414, 564
ROBINSON 237, 239, 243, 245,
    397, 398, 408, 564
RODNEY 250
ROE 255
ROGERS 241, 251
ROGERSON 393, 411
ROMBOUGH 237, 246, 247, 250,
    252, 392, 393, 395, 396,
    404, 406, 411
ROSCOE 410
ROSE 255
ROSS 240, 247, 255, 393
ROUNDTREE 251, 408

ROWER 237
RUDOLPH 565
RUNNELS 241, 402
RUSSELL 243, 245
RYALL 248
RYAN 400

SADDLER 236
SAMPSON 560, 566
SANDERS 244, 253
SANDERLIN 241, 244, 248, 249,
    251, 255, 401, 407, 495.
SANSBURY 405, 413, 562
SATTERFIELD 249, 251-254, 393
    398, 404, 409, 411, 414,
    558, 562, 563, 565
SAUNDERS 247, 254, 397, 402, 558
    559
SAVAGE 247, 248, 251
SAWYER 252, 411, 413, 558, 560
SCARBOROUGH 411
SCHELISTAIN 247
SCOTT 240, 241, 246, 254, 255,
    392, 394, 412, 413, 563
SCHRIMPSHIRE 241
SEWARD 236, 244, 249, 251
SHAW 250
SHERWOOD 407, 409, 562
SIBBALDSON 243
SIMMONS 247, 563, 566
SIMONS 235, 249, 250, 252-255,
    397, 401, 403-405, 409, 411.
SIMPSON 237, 245, 246, 248-250,
    252, 253, 394, 395, 398, 400,
    401, 402, 406, 408, 409, 411,
    559-563, 566.
SINCLAIR 247, 394
SINGLETON 402, 565, 566
SINKLER (SINCLAIR?) 237, 245, 255
SITTERSON 413, 562, 563
SKINNER 246, 252, 255, 394, 395,
    397, 399-403, 405-414, 558,
    559, 561-566.
SKITTLETHORP 563
SLADE 254, 396, 410
SLEEP 248
SLAUGHTER 235, 240
SMALL 246-250, 252, 254, 392, 393
    395, 397, 398, 400-407, 410,
    412, 414, 559-567.
SMILEY 255
SMITH 236, 241, 242, 245-247,
    249-253, 255, 392, 393, 396,
    398-400, 404-406, 408, 410,
    411-414, 558-567.
SNELL 241
SNOWDEN 241
SOWELL 251, 394
SPARKMAN 409
SPEIGHT 238, 240-242, 244, 409
SPENCE 401, 559-563, 565
SPENCER 394, 559
SPINGLEY 248, 249
SPIVEY 248, 249, 252, 392-394,
    397, 398, 400, 404, 560, 562
SPRUILL 394
SQUIRES 248
STACEY 244, 247, 250, 254, 255,
    393, 396-398, 403, 405, 406
    412, 413, 561, 563, 565
STAFFORD 394
STALLINGS 242, 248-250, 252, 254
    395, 396, 398-400, 410, 558,
    562, 563, 567
STAMP 235
STANDIN 237-239, 247, 250, 252, 253
    255, 392, 397, 398, 402, 403,
    405-408, 558.

STANFORD 564
STANLEY 410
STANTON 251, 252
STARNS 250, 255
STARR 241
STEARNS 252, 412
STEELE 236, 559
STEPNEY 241, 403
STEVENS 250
STEWART 237, 244, 245, 248,
    252, 399, 563
STILLWELL 235, 237
STIRON 244
STOCKER 245
STONE 254, 398
STREETER 237, 245
STRONG 399, 402
STUART 241
SULLIVAN 240, 243, 245
SUMMERS 248
SUMNER 243, 244, 401
SUTTON 246, 250, 393, 403, 405
    406, 409, 565
SWAIN 239, 394, 397
SWANN 237, 242, 245, 252
SWEENEY 245, 395
SWIFT 255
SYKES 254
SYLVIA 239

TABOR 560, 562
TALBOT 235
TAYLOR 235, 236, 238, 239, 241
    245, 252, 254, 392, 394,
    395, 397, 401, 403, 406,
    407, 411, 413, 562, 563,
    564, 565
THACH (THEACH) 237, 247, 392
    394, 395, 405, 406, 564
THOMAS 238, 247, 252, 405
THOMPSON 236, 237, 239, 243,
    244, 245, 248, 249, 254,
    255, 394-396, 401, 404,
    406, 407, 409, 411, 412,
    558, 559, 561
THURMAN 400
THURSTON 248
TILLMAN 252
TODD 403, 560
TOLAR 395
TOMS 399
TOPPING 255, 394, 396, 397, 402
    405, 406, 562, 566
TORKSEY 402, 404, 406, 408, 558
TOTTEN 409
TOW 247
TREDWELL 410, 413, 559
TROTMAN 242, 249, 393, 410, 411
    413, 414, 564
TROTTER 236, 237, 238
TRUELOVE 396
TUCKER 244
TURNER 242, 395
TUTHILL 414
TWINE 392, 397, 401, 405, 412
    559, 560, 561, 565

UNDERHILL 239, 392, 403, 560,
    561, 564

VAIL 236, 237, 239, 241, 242,
    344, 247, 396, 398, 561,
    564.
VALENTINE 246, 248, 253
VANN 238, 245
VANDEMON 562
VANDERSLICE 238
VANDEWATER 242, 243
VAN HORN 409.

VAN NUYSE 565
VAN PELT 255
VAUGHAN 562
VERNICE 248
VICK 254
VICKERY 407
VIRDAMON 567
VISHER 250

WADE 243, 394
WAFF 240, 241, 244, 245, 247
    248-251, 253, 395, 398,
    405-407, 409-411, 413,564
    565, 567
WAGGONER 242
WALCH 247
WALKER 240, 241, 245, 254,398
    413
WALLACE 235, 239, 250
WALLIS 242, 251
WALTON 239, 241-243, 246, 250
    251, 396, 398, 400, 411,
    561-563
WARBURTON 239, 254
WARD 237, 239, 243, 245-247,
    249, 251-255, 394-396,398
    400-411, 413, 414,558-560
    562-567
WARNER 249, 251, 413
WARREN 238, 244, 558
WARING 252, 253, 392
WATERO 245
WATERIDGE 239
WATKINS 235, 247, 251
WATSON 243, 246, 248
WEAVER 394

WEBB 244, 245, 247-252, 254,
    392, 394, 396, 398-400,
    402-404, 408, 409, 559,
    562, 563, 564, 566
WEIR 244
WELCH 248, 249, 255, 392, 393
    394, 397, 401, 402, 405,
    407, 409, 412-414, 558,
    559, 562-565, 567
WELLS 241
WELLWOOD 238, 242
WESCOT (WESKETT) 409, 563
WESSON 236
WEST 248, 396
WESTON 239, 558
WHEDBEE 242, 244, 246-248,252
    253, 255, 393, 395, 396,
    398, 400-402, 406, 563,
    566
WHEELER 398
WHIPPLE 410
WHITE 237, 238, 245-247, 249
    250, 251, 253-255, 393, 394
    397-401, 403, 404, 406, 407
    409, 412-414, 558-560, 562
    564, 565, 566
WHITFIELD 560
WHITEMAN 244, 255, 398, 403, 412
    558, 565
WIGGINS 242
WILDARE 248
WILDER 240, 248, 251-253, 255,
    395-397, 402, 403, 405, 406
    408-410, 414, 560, 562,565.
WILEY 248
WILKINS 235, 236, 238, 240, 241,
    249, 251, 252, 406, 411

WILKINSON 243, 248, 249, 251,
    254, 255, 392, 394, 403
WILLIAMS 238-241, 243, 245, 247
    248, 249, 252-254, 392, 398
    401, 403, 407, 413, 414,560
    561, 563-566
WILLIAMSON 246, 393, 394, 397,
    403, 405, 406
WILLS 244, 245, 254, 396, 403,
    404, 406-409, 414, 562,567
WILSON 238-240, 244, 245, 251,
    406.
WITHAM 406
WOLFE 409
WOOD 241, 246-249, 255, 393,396
    399, 400, 403, 407, 409,
    410, 413, 561, 562
WOODARD 400, 403
WOODBINE 241
WOODWARD 237-239, 248, 252, 393,
    395, 398, 399, 402-404, 409,
    410, 411, 566
WORLEY 237, 238
WORMINGTON 397, 405
WORTH 243, 244
WRIGHT 251, 395, 399, 403, 411,
    413, 560, 564, 565
WYATT 241, 243, 245, 250
WYNNE 404, 413, 561
WYNNS 393

YEARGIN 409
YEATTS 236, 405
YEOMANS 394, 564
YOUNG 236, 240, 396, 401, 407, 41_

THE WOODWARD FAMILY OF CHOWAN COUNTY - MARRIAGES

     In order to illustrate the value of the foregoing SUB-NAME INDEX, and to show how by following the index and by reference to the pages in VOLUME III of Hathaway's Historical and Genealogical Register, to which the paging refers, below will be found a reconstruction of the marriages of members of the Woodward family in Chowan, from 1750 to 1837. The index item referring to WOODWARD is as follows: (See above)

              WOODWARD 237-239, 248, 252, 393,
                    395, 398, 399, 402-404, 409,
                    410, 411, 566.

     Turning to HATHAWAY'S VOLUME 1, by a swift appraisal of each page called for, we find the following records:

Page 237. SAMUEL WOODWARD m. MRS. SARAH PURSELL, August 2, 1750. LUKE WHITE, Sec.
Page 238. RICHARD WOODWARD m. ABIGAIL WHITE, Jan. 23, 1752. LUKE WHITE, Sec.
Page 239. SAMUEL WOODWARD m. MARY COPELAND, Sept. 17, 1754. ARTHUR ALLEN, Sec.
Page 248. ZILPHA WOODWARD m. JOSEPH B. POU, Sept. 23, 1788. HARDY HURDLE, Sec.
Page 252. CHARITY WOODWARD m. JOSIAH SMITH, Feb. 16, 1795. RICHARD WOODWARD, Sec.
Page 393. RICHARD WOODWARD m. LYDIA PARKER, Dec. 21, 1802. ISAAC WELCH, Sec.
Page 395. POLLY WOODWARD m. WILLIAM ASHLEY, Jan. 22, 1805. JONATHAN ASHLEY, Sec.
Page 398. MARY WOODWARD m. ANTHONY PRIVETT, Oct. 26, 1808. WILLIAM PRIVETT, Sec.
Page 399. JETHRO WOODWARD m. ELIZABETH FORD, May 7, 1810. WILLIAM FORD, Sec.
Page 399. MILLY WOODWARD m. JOHN GREEN, June 3, 1811. URIAH HUDSON, Sec.
Page 402. RICHARD WOODWARD Security for John Runnels m. Charity McClenny, 1814.
Page 403. MIRIAM WOODWARD m. GEORGE MEREDITH, Nov. 15, 1815. CALEB NASH, Sec.
Page 404. EDWARD WOODWARD m. RACHEL CHAMPION, Ja. 8, 1815. THOS. COCHRANE, Sec.
Page 409. ELIZABETH WOODWARD m. THOMAS JORDAN, Jan. 12, 1820. JOSEPH JORDAN, Sec.
Page 410. DOLLY WOODWARD m. JOHN BOYCE, May 29, 1822. WILLIAM PRIVETT. Sec.
Page 410. RICHARD WOODWARD, Security for AZOR HOLLOWELL m. JINTY WOOD, March 19, 1822
Page 411. JOHN M. WOODWARD m. WINNIFRED M. BOND, Aug. 20, 1822. D. McDOWELL, Sec.
Page 566. SUSAN M. WOODWARD m. JAMES N. FLOYD, Aug. 17, 1837.

     There is a world of information of genealogical value in this list of CHOWAN marriages given above. A casual glance over it suggests intimate relationships between the Woodward family of Chowan and the WHITES, ALLENS, COPELANDS, PARKERS, ASHLEYS, PRIVETTS, GREENS, FORDS, BOYCES, JORDANS, WOODS, HUDSONS, COCHRANES, WELCHES, MEREDITHS, CHAMPIONS, FLOYDS, HURDLES and BONDS. Herein lies the value of the CHOWAN COUNTY MARRIAGE INDEX preceding.

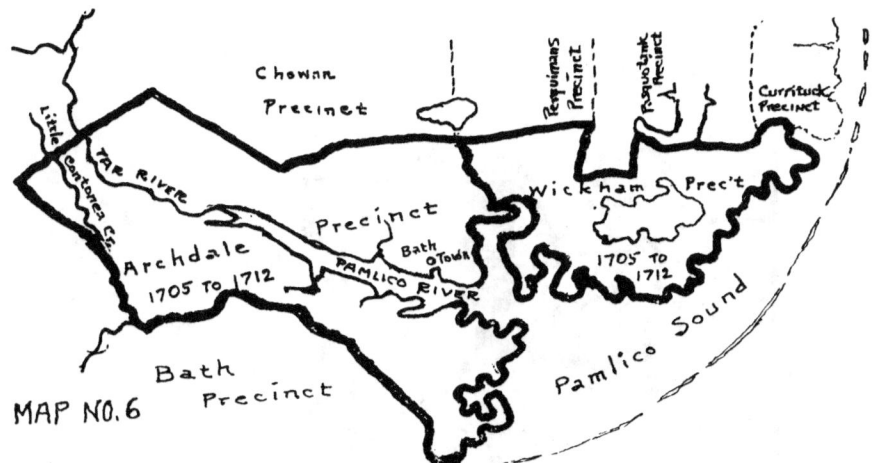

WICKHAM PRECINCT — EARLIEST RESIDENTS

The above map, showing the Precincts of ARCHDALE and WICKHAM, which existed from 1705 until 1712, and comprised the same territory which after 1712 became BEAUFORT and HYDE, respectively. On the list below will be found the names of persons who signed an undated petition addressed to "HON. THOMAS CARY, ESQ., President and COMMANDER IN CHIEF, and the rest of the HONORABLE COUNCIL" for the said Government, seeking the establishment of a Court "as in other Precincts"; as, due to the distances they suffered inconveniences from BATH COURT, to which they were evidently attached at that time. This was probably about the year 1705-6, or 1708-11, the periods covering the THOMAS CARY regime. The signers of the petition were:

WILLIAM ADAMS 1
RICHARD BACHELOR
ROBERT BANKS 6
GEORGE BELL 8
WILLIAM BELL 8
JACOB BODITE 12
WILLIAM BONNER 12
JAMES BRIGHT 15
JOHN BRIGHT 15
THOMAS BRITT 15
EMAN CLEAVES
THOMAS DAVIS 34
NICHOLAS DAW 34
HENRY EBORN 40
HUMPHREY EDWARDS 40-41
CULLUM FLIN
JOHN FOREMAN 46
DANIEL FOX 47
THOMAS GOODIN 51
ROBERT GREEN 52
JOSEPH HALL 55
RICHARD HARVEY 60

ARCHIBALD HOLMES 68
PHILLIP HOWARD 70
JOSEPH HULL
WILLIAM HURSING
ISAAC JACKSON 76
ISAAC JACOB 76
WILLIAM LEWIS 92
FRANCIS LINGFIELD
JOHN MARSHALL 101
IODOVICK MARTIN 101
JOHN MASON 102
ROGER MONTAGUE 108
THOMAS MORRIS 112
SAM NORTON
THOMAS PHILLIPS
HENRY PRICE 132
WILLIAM PRICE 132
JOHN PROCTOR 133
JOHN ROPER 143
RICHARD RUTTMAN
BEN SAUNDERS 149
SIMON SILVERTHORNE 152

HENRY SLADE 154
JOHN SLADE 154
JOSEPH SLADE 154
CHARLES SMITH 155
ROBERT SPRING 159
JOHN SQUIRES
RICHARD STUBS 162
DARBY SULLIVANT 162
JOHN SULLIVANT 162
JOHN TYCE
MATHIAS TYCE
THOMAS TULEY (TULLE?) 169
JONATHAN WATSON 177
THOMAS WAYNE
ABRAHAM WILKINSON 185
RICHARD WILKINSON 185
WILLIAM WINDLEY 188
THOMAS WOLFE
JAMES WOLFE

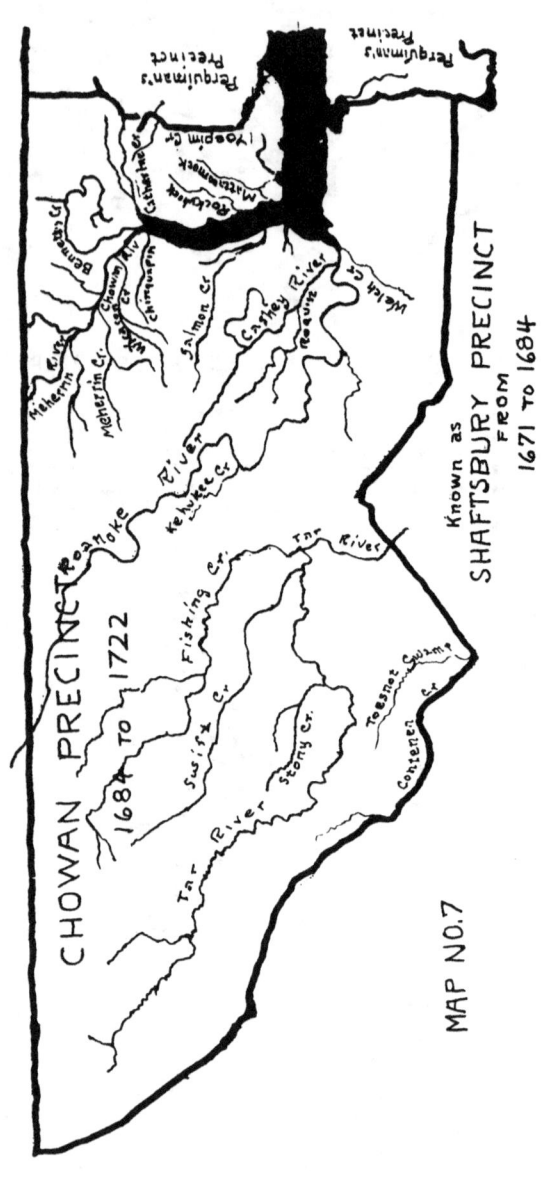

EARLY RECORDS OF CHOWAN PRECINCT

From the old Rent Roll of ALBEMARLE COUNTY (Vol. 1, pp. 301 - 304 Hathaway) are taken the following persons who were then paying taxes in CHOWAN PRECINCT. Figures following each name refer to pages of this work where information can be found about them:

EDWARD BERWICK
JAMES BLOUNT 11-19
JOHN BLOUNT 11-19
HENRY BONNER 12
RICHARD BOOTHE 13
WILLIAM BRANCH 14
EDWARD BRYAN 16
FRANCIS BRANCH 14
WILLIAM CHARLTON 24
THOMAS COOPER 27
NICHOLAS CRISP 30
VINES CROPLEY 30-73
WILLIAM DAWS 34
GEORGE DEAR 35 (Batt's Grave)
JOHN EARLY 40
JAMES FARLOW 44
GEORGE FORDYCE (Albemarle Sound) 46
JOHN FOSTER 46
THOMAS GARRETT 48
THOMAS GILLIAM 50
JOHN GORHAM 56
JOHN HARDING 56
JOHN HEALE 63
ARNOLD HOPKINS 69
THOMAS HOSKINS 70
JOHN JONES 80 - 83
JONATHAN JONES 80 - 83
JOHN KING 85
EPHRAIM LEWERTON 91
LEONARD LOFTIN 94
THOMAS LUTON 99

JOHN ODOM 118 (Rogers' Branch)
FRANCIS PARROTT 123
JOHN PATCHETT 124
COL. THOS. POLLOCK 130
JOHN PORTER, JR. 131
JOHN PLOWMAN 30
COTTON ROBINSON 142
THOMAS SESSIONS 151
ELIAS SESSIONS 151
MATTHEW SIMMONS 152
ANN SIMMONS 152
NICHOLAS SIMMONS 152
ANTHONY SLOCUM 154
JOSEPH SLOCUM 154
EDWARD SMITHWICK 155
THOMAS SPEIGHT 158
THOMAS STACEY 159
WILLIAM TANNER 166
EDWARD TITTMAN 167
HENDERSON WALKER 173
  (Moseley's Point)
JOHN WALKER 173
WILLIAM WALSTON 174
SMITHWICK WARBURTON 175
FRANCIS WELLS 178
JOHN WHEATLEY 180
WILLIAM WILKINSON 185
  (Sandy Point)
LEWIS WILLIAMS 186
WILLIAM WILLIAMS 186
  (Wife was FRANCES)

The map on page 5, is this writer's conception of what, after 1671, was called the **SHAFTSBURY PRECINCT**, and after 1685, **CHOWAN PRECINCT**, and all of which was a part of the original **ALBEMARLE COUNTY**.
The boundaries of BERKELEY PRECINCT (later PERQUIMANS) and CARTERET PRECINCT (later PASQUOTANK and CURRITUCK) were well defined, except on the Southern boundary, but SHAFTSBURY (late Chowan) had no definite line on the West, but extended as far Westward as settlers dared to penetrate, which at those periods was not far. On paper, however, and for practical purposes, SHAFTSBURY PRECINCT, when first named, embraced everything West of the Perquimans line as far as North Carolina extended, or to that mythical domain beyond the blue mountains, sometimes referred to as the "Western Waters".

WHO WERE THE FIRST ARRIVALS IN OLD ALBEMARLE?

1. REV. ROGER GREEN

As early as 1652, according to a statement in William H. Dodd's "The Old South", Sir William Berkeley negotiated with ROGER GREEN, "Clarke", who undertook to seat a hundred men on the banks of the Chowan River, in return for a thousand acres of land.
The location of the Green grant is designated on the accompanying map by the number (2), and it is said to have been between the mouth of the Chowan and Roanoke rivers. The grant was actually issued, and refers in its own text to the presence already of certain settlers in that general vicinity at that time.

2. THOMAS JARVIS

The same authority, Dodd, says on page 285 that Thomas Jarvis, who was the acting Deputy Governor under Phillip Ludwell, had been a farmer in Albemarle since 1659.

3. GEORGE DURANT

Received a deed to lands from the Yeopim Indians to "Durant's Neck" March 1, 1661, and from GEORGE CATCHMAID March 13, 1662.

4. JOHN VARNHAM

patented 250 acres at "Skinner's" (Moseley's) Point on Albemarle Sound Nov. 27, 1679.

EARLY LAND GRANTS IN CHOWAN PRECINCT

The first land grants or patents issued by the proprietary government of North Carolina, and which are filed in the office of the Secretary of State, as heretofore mentioned, were copied by Mr. Hathaway, and those embracing real estate in CHOWAN PRECINCT - now COUNTY - were published in his "Register" beginning on page 1, of his first volume.

The grant issued to JOHN VARNHAM on November 22, 1769, is designated as the oldest of these CHOWAN grants, but it, too, was among those issued, along with the others shown herein, in the OLD ALBEMARLE region, on September 25, 1663, and the one of 1679 was a renewal of the first patent, though the VARNHAM grant of that date does not appear among those published by Nugent in her "Cavaliers and Pioneers" of Virginia.

We find that it would be impractical to publish the abstracts of all these CHOWAN grants in this compilation, due to lack of space. Some - but only a few - of these early grants were issued during the existence of SHAFTSBURY PRECINCT, which was coterminous with CHOWAN as the area was later designated.

In lieu of publishing abstracts of these early CHOWAN GRANTS it has been found expedient and informative to insert hereinafter a list of these patentees, with the date of the grant in each instance following the name - the YEAR ONLY. As an additional source of information subjoined figures, following both the name and the date refer back to the pages on which further information in regard to the patentee may be found in this work. This is preceded by a crude map on which the approximate location of the lands may be visualized, which locations have been marked by RINGED NUMBERS for each LIST of neighbors in particular localities so designated. The compiler believes this information will be helpful to all historical and genealogical researchers.

ON ALBEMARLE SOUND (10)

In Chowan Precinct:

Name	Year	Page	Name	Year	Page
JAMES BLOUNT	(1716)	11-19	EDWARD PORTER	(1722)	131
JOHN BLOUNT	(1696)	11-19	JOHN PORTER	(1696)	131
VINES CROPLEY	(1694)	30-73	WILLIAM PRIVETT	(1714)	133
GEORGE DEAR	(1694)	35	NICHOLAS SIMONS	(1694)	152
GEORGE FORDYCE	(1694)	46	ANN SIMONS	(1694)	152
WILLIAM FARLOW	(1721)	44	JEREMIAH SIMONS	(1716)	152
THOMAS GILBERT	(1717)	49	JOHN TAYLOR	(1719)	165
THOMAS GILLIAM	(1720)	50	JEREMIAH VAIL	(1719)	171
EDWARD MOSELEY	(1720)	112	JOHN VOLWAY	(1714)	172
THOMAS PIERCE	(1722)	129	JOHN BENBURY	(1722)	8
			THOMAS WILLIAMS	(1719)	186

GEORGE DEAR (Mouth of YEOPIM RIVER) 1696 - 35. (11)

BEAR SWAMP (Or Creek, somewhere in the bands of BENNETT'S CREEK in what is now GATES COUNTY). (12)

Name	Year	Page	Name	Year	Page
JOHN EVANS	(1718)	42	LAWRENCE SARSEN	(1714)	149
JOHN HERON	(1720)	64	RICHARD SKINNER	(1718)	153
THOMAS JONES	(1711)	81	FRANCIS THORNTON	(1714)	167
WILLIAM JONES	(1720)	81	GEORGE WALSTON	(1717)	174
JOHN LASSETER	(1723)	39	PHILLIP WALSTON	(1717)	174-214
JOHN MARKS	(1717)	101-113	WILLIAM WALSTON	(1716)	174
GEORGE MOBBY	(1714)	111	JOHN WHITE	(1714)	181
EDWARD PADGETT	(1720)	121	WILLIAM WOODLEY	(1718)	190
SAMUEL PADGETT	(1720)	121	WILLIAM YATES	(1717)	191.

(a) BEAVER DAM SWAMP, COVE (Or Branch) NEAR ABOVE

Name	Year	Page	Name	Year	Page
DAVID ATKINS	(1717)	4	DANIEL McDANIEL	(1717)	104
EDWARD COCKRELL	(1717)	26	PETER PARKER	(1716)	123-135
WILL'M COPELAND	(1712)	28	RICHARD LEWIS	(1717)	92
JAMES FARLOW	(1711)	44	THOMAS LUTEN	(1717)	97
THOMAS HORTON	(1704)	69	JOSEPH WICKER	(1716)	184

---

(24) DEEP RUN (OR BRANCH) SOMEWHERE IN NEIGHBORHOOD OF BEAR SWAMP.

Name	Year	Page	Name	Year	Page
HENRY BONNER	(17...)	12	PHILLIP WALSTON	(1717)	174-214
JAMES FARLOW	(1712)	44	THOMAS WILLIAMS	(1716)	186
MILES HALSEY	(1715)	55	ISAAC WILSON	(1717)	187
ROBERT HICKS	(1715)	64	CHARLES JORDAN	(1719)	81
GEORGE WALSTON	(1717)	174	JOHN JORDON	(1719)	82
WILLIAM NEWLAND?	(1717)		SAMUEL PADGETT	(1719)	121

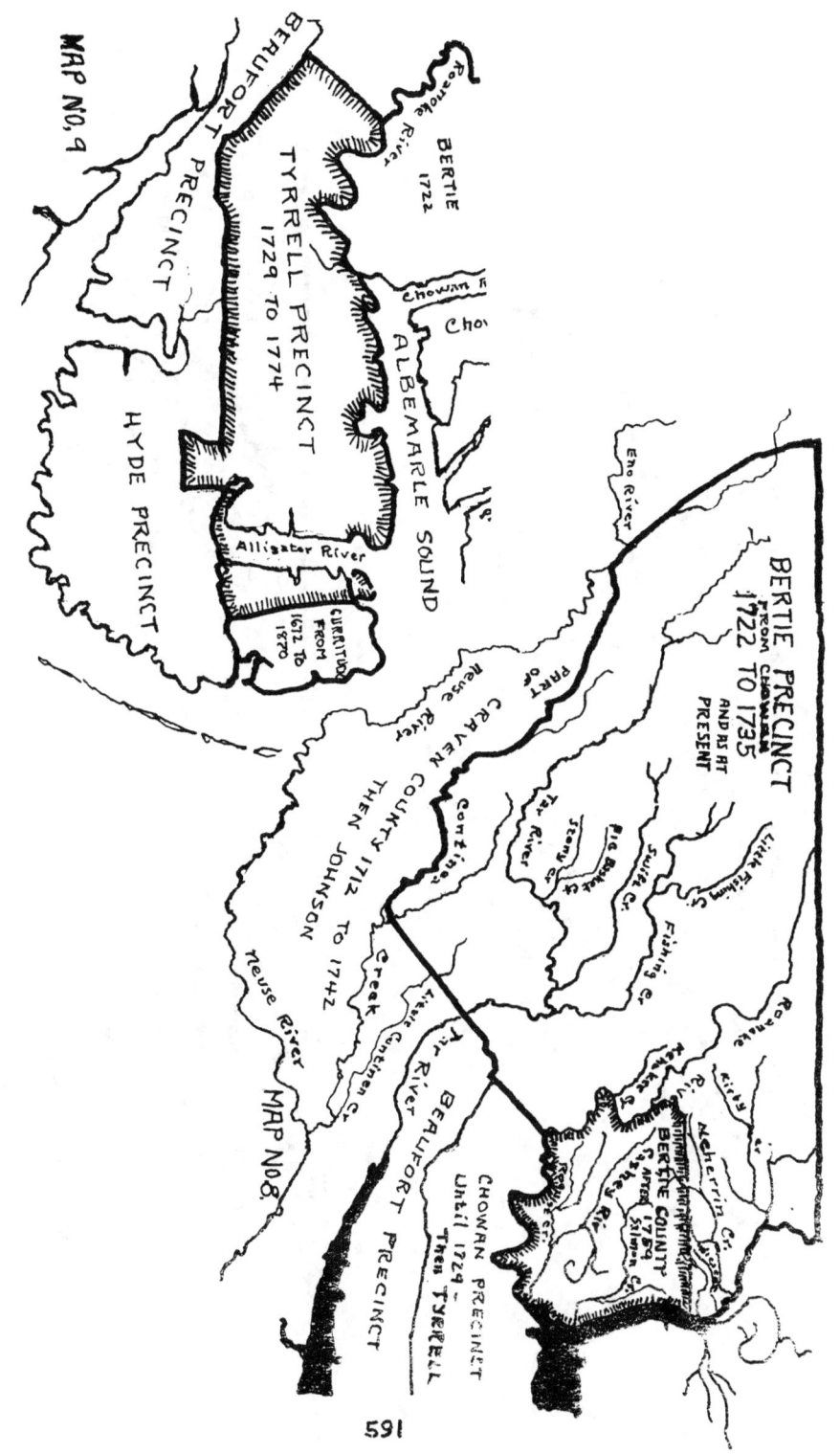

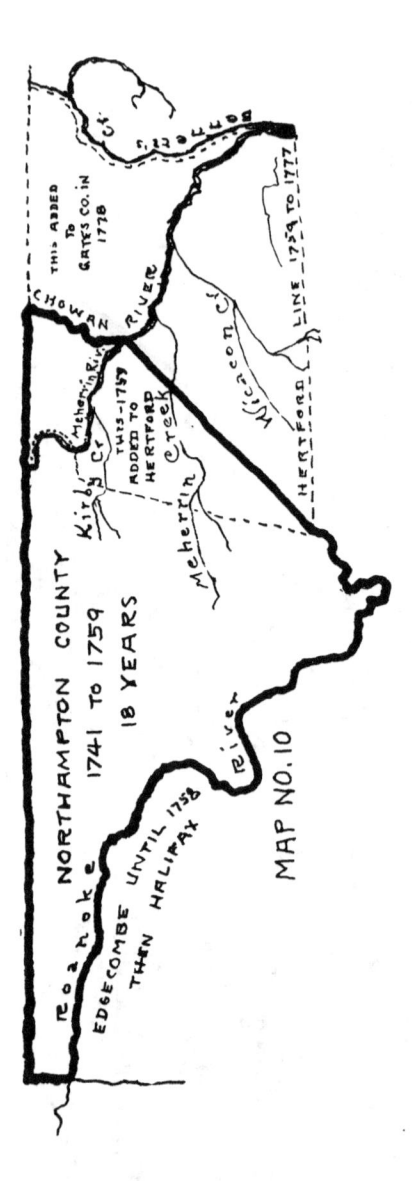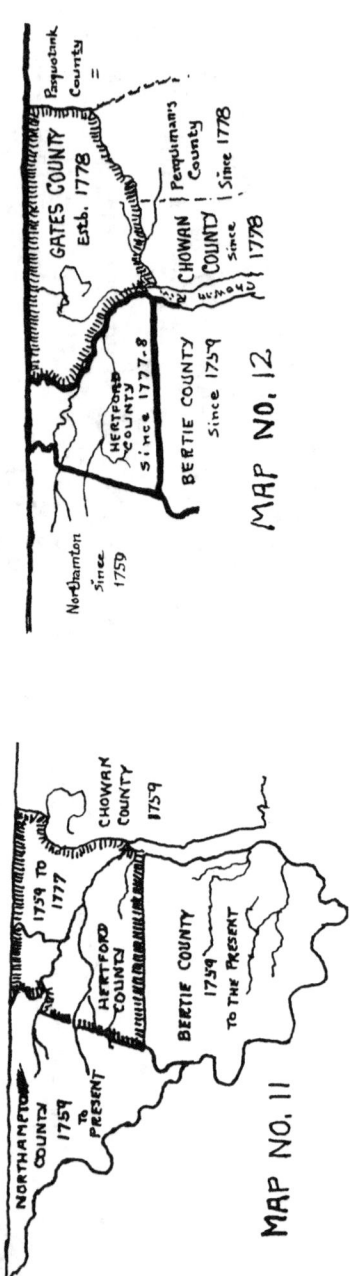

(9) LAND GRANTS ON BENNETT'S CREEK, AND RESIDENTS ON
ROBERT ROGERS' BRANCH.

LAND GRANTS:

JOHN ALSTON (1711) 2
RICHARD BERRYMAN (1719) 9
WILLIAM DANIEL (1721) 33-38
JOHN KING (1697) 85
JOHN LASSATER (1721) 89
PATRICK LAWLER (1712) 90
WILLIAM LEWIS (1720) 92.

(14) LAND GRANTS BETWEEN
CATHERINE CREEK AND
STOPPING CREEK:

THOMAS GARRETT (1701) 48
THOMAS ROUNDTREE (1716) 144.

(21) GRANT ON COW ISLAND, EAST
SIDE OF BENNETT'S CREEK:

HENRY BONNER (17...) 12
....

THESE WERE PERSONS WHO SETTLED IN THE GENERAL NEIGHBORHOOD
OF BENNETT'S CREEK AND ROGERS' BRANCH:

JOHN ALSTON 2
WILLIAM DANIEL 33
JOHN COLLINS 27
EPAPRODITUS JONES 79
LEONARD LANGSTON 89
WILLIAM LANGSTON 89
JOSEPH VANN 172
EPAPRODITUS BOYCE 13
HENRY HACKLEY 55
THOMAS HARRIS 58
EDWARD DAUGHTRY 34
JONATHAN KITTRELL 86
ROBERT HICKS 64
THOMAS HICKS 64
SAMUEL GILLIAM 50
JOHN LANGSTON 89
EDWARD VANN 172
JOHN VANN 172
WILLIAM VANN 172
JESSE VANN 172

WILLIAM DAVIS 89
JOHN LASSITER 89
ROBERT LASSITER 89
JAMES LASSITER 89
JAMES BROWN 89
JOHN LANGSTON 89
ROBERT ROGERS 89
EPHRAIM HUNTER 89
WILLIAM HUNTER 89
MARY BARNES 89
THOMAS ROUNDTREE 144
FRANCIS ROUNDTREE 144
JOHN KING 85
ROBERT ROUNDTREE 144
JOHN BENTON 85
HENRY KING 85
WILLIAM HUGHES 64
JOHN WARD 175
JOHN ODOM 118
THOMAS SPIVEY 89

(16) GRANTS TO LAND ALONG CHOWAN RIVER IN CHOWAN PRECINCT

CONRAD EICHORN (1714) 41
THOMAS MARTIN (1704) 101
DENNIS MacCLENDEN (1704) 103
RICHARD MOORE (1713) 110
EDWARD MOSELEY (1719) 112
WILLIAM PADGETT (1713) 121

FRANCIS PUGH (171..) 134
THOMAS STACEY (1714) 159
ARGALL SIMONS (1714) 152
PETER PARKER (1706) 123-135
FRANCIS WELLS (1696) 178
LEWIS WILLIAMS (1697) 186

(15) Grants on EDENTON BAY:

THOMAS GILLIAM (1697) 50
EDWARD SMITHWICK (1700) 155
JEREMIAH VAIL (1710) 171
MICHAEL BRINKLEY (1713) 15

(18) Grant near the County Line:

WILLIAM BENNETT (1719) 9

(20) Grants on Creek Fork of YEOPIM RIVER:

CATHERINE CARLINTON (1718) 22
WILLIAM EDGERTON (1723) 40
WILLIAM HAUGHTON (1720) 62
JOHN PORTER (1720) 131
JOHN HARLOWE (1721) 57.

(17) Grants on CHINQUAPIN CREEK or SWAMP:

WILLIAM BADHAM (1717) 5
THOMAS BRAY (1717) 14
THOMAS GILBERT (1715) 49
EDWARD STANDING (1722) 159
RICHARD SOWELL (1715) 157
THOMAS ROGERS (1715) 143
WILLIAM CHARLTON (1713) 186-7.

(19) Grants at mouth of CYPRESS BRANCH below EDENTON on the Sound:

DAVID AMBROSE (1720) 2
WILLIAM FARLOW (1720) 44
JOHN HARRIS (1720) 58-289
WILLIAM WOODLEY (1720) 190
JOHN JONES (1720) 80-83
WILLIAM WOODWARD (1719) 190-192

(27) EARLY GRANTS ON LANDS WHERE TOWN OF EDENTON IS NOW LOCATED

NATHANIEL CHEVIN (1707) 24
EPHRAIM LEWERTON (1680) 91
ROGER HALL (1681) 55
THOMAS PETERSON (1714) 127
THOMAS SPEIGHT (1702) 158
ALEXANDER RAY (1702) 138.

RICHARD SKINNER (1702) 153
WILLIAM WHITE (1702) 183
ISAAC WILSON (1702) 187
ANTHONY WHERRY (1702) 181
RICHARD WOOLARD (1702) 190

(28) Grants on FILBERT CREEK, North of the
Present EDENTON:

HENRY BONNER (1715) 12
WILLIAM BONNER (1717) 12

(29) Grants on FORKED SWAMP in CHOWAN PREC'T.

HENRY HALSTED (1716) 55
HENRY LAWLEY (1716) 90

(31) GREEN HALL, NEAR DEEP RUN, BENNETT'S CREEK AREA

HENRY BONNER   (172) 12
EDWARD CHAMPION   (1719) 23
ORLANDO CHAMPION   (1720) 23
THOMAS LUTEN   (1721) 97
THOMAS WEST   (1716) 179
JAMES BLOUNT   (1716) 11-19
WILLIAM WILKINSON (1694) 185

(34) HORSE LANDING on CHOWAN RIVER

DAVID AMBROSE   (1720) 2
THOMAS HARVEY   (1722) 61
CALEB STEVENS   (1720) 161
SAMUEL WOODWARD   (1720) 190
LUKE WHITE   (1718) 182

(33) HORSE POOL BRANCH on CHOWAN RIVER:

THOMAS BRAY   (1717) 14
CHARLES BARBER   (1712) 6
JOHN WILLIAMS   (1714) 186
WILLIAM WOODLEY   (1703) 190

(35) NAW BRANCH and LONG BRANCH
     (Present Gates County)

JAMES HOOPER   (1715) 69
ROBERT HICKS   (17..) 64

(32) HELL'S POCOSIN, EAST OF CHOWAN RIVER:

RALPH BALLARD   (1722) 5
WILLIAM HUNTER   (1722) 72
JOHN PORTER   (1722) 131
JONATHAN ROBERTS   (1722) 144
JOHN WINBORN   (1722)
WILLIAM CHARLTON   (1696) 24

(36) HICKORY CREEK in CHOWAN

ROBERT WARBURTON   (1719) 175
JAMES FROST   (1719) 47
JOHN SMITHWICK   (1720) 156

(37) Indian Swamp, East of the Chowan River:

RALPH BALLARD   (1712) 5
JOHN JORDAN   (1712) 82
RICHARD SOWELL   (1712) 157
JOHN WHITE, JR.   (1712) 181

(38) Indian Town Creek:

JAMES FARLOW   (1717) 44
JOHN JACKSON   (1711) 76
EDWARD MOSELEY   (1719) 112
JOHN PETTIVER   (1716) 128
ROBERT WILSON   (1716) 188

(39) INDIAN LANDS ON SOUTH SIDE OF BENNETT'S CREEK:

JOHN LASSITER   (1721) 39
MARY ROUNDTREE   (17..) 144

------

(43) EARLY GRANTS TO LAND ON MATTICOMACK CREEK AND SWAMPS ON THE EAST SIDE OF CHOWAN RIVER

These land grants lay immediately North of where
the present town of EDENTON is located:

JAMES BLOUNT   (1697) 11-19
FRANCIS BRANCH   (1719) 14
HENRY BONNER   (1718) 12
JOHN CANNON   (1681) 22
ORLANDO CHAMPION   (17..) 23
WILLIAM CHARLTON JR (1719) 24
EDMUND GALE   (172.) 48
JOSEPH GILBERT   (1680) 49
THOMAS HOSKINS   (1712) 70
JONATHAN JONES   (1694) 80

JOHN JONES   (1693) 80
THOMAS LUTEN   (1703) 97
JOHN PADGETT   (1719) 121
SAMUEL PADGETT   (1719) 121
WILLIAM LEWERTON   (1680) 91
JOHN LEWIS   (1720) 92

(It will be noticed that some
of these land grants were issued in SHAFTSBURY PRECINCT.)

COTTON ROBINSON   (1697) 143-146
ELLENER SADLER   (1715) 148
ANTHONY SLOCUM   (1684) 154
JOSEPH SLOCUM   (1684) 154
EDWARD SMITHWICK   (1681) 155
EDWARD SMITHWICK   (1694) 155
ROBERT STACEY   (1719) 159
JOHN TAYLOR   (1681) 165
SMITHWICK WARBURTON (1694) 175
ROBERT WINDLEY   (1680) 188.

------

(50) Land Grants on ALBEMARLE SOUND at MULBERRY HILL below EDENTON

JOHN BLOUNT   (1714) 11-19
JAMES BLOUNT   (1684) 11-19
JOHN BLOUNT   (1721) 11-19
WILLIAM HAUGHTON   (1721) 62
SAMUEL PADGETT   (1721) 121

(51) Land Grants issued on CATHERINE CREEK
     (Sometimes OLD TOWN CREEK)

THOMAS FARLOW   (1702) 44
THOMAS GARRETT   (1697) 48
COL. THOS. POLLOCK (1697) 130
WILLIAM LEWIS   (1706) 92
HENRY WARREN   (1705) 175

------

(57) LAND GRANTS ISSUED TO LANDS LOCATED ON ROCKYHOCK CREEK IN CHOWAN:

DAVID AMBROSE   (1719) 2
JOSEPH BENNETT   (1719) 9
THOMAS BRAY   (1716) 14
MATTHEW BRYAN   (1714) 16-20
MARTIN CHARLES   (1714) 24
WILLIAM FARLOW   (1714) 44
THOMAS GILBERT   (1711) 49
ROBERT HICKS   (1713) 64
EDWARD HOWCOTT   (1716) 71
HENRY LILES   (1714) 92
THOMAS MARKS   (1702) 101-113

LAWRENCE McGUE   (1720) 104
EDWARD MOSELEY   (1720) 112
THOMAS MUNDS   (1714) 113
EDWARD PADGETT   (1716) 121
JOHN PETTIVER   (1711) 128
JOHN ROBINSON   (1714) 143-146
GEORGE SUTTON   (1703) 163
WILLIAM DUKENFIELD (1705) 37 *
THOMAS HARVEY   (1722) 61
RICHARD TAYLOR   (1715) 165
SAMUEL WOODWARD   (1719) 190-192.

*WILLIAM DUKENFIELD's main lands, however, were on the West
side of Chowan River in the Cashey River section of the present
BERTIE COUNTY.

(58) ROCKYHOCK NECK ON CREEK OF THAT
     NAME:

     WILLIAM DUKENFIELD (1705) 37
     THOMAS HARVEY (1722) 61
     JOHN ROBINSON (1715) 142-146
     RICHARD TAYLOR (1715) 165
     SAMUEL WOODWARD (1719) 190-192

(64) SKINNER'S POINT ON ALBEMARLE
     SOUND

     JOHN VANNHAM (1663)
     HENDERSON WALKER (1696) 173

(62) SANDY POINT ON CHOWAN SOUND

     THOMAS POLLOCK (1720) 130
     JOHN PORTER, JR. (1696) 131
     WILLIAM WILKINSON (1684) 185
     ROBERT WEST (1716) 179

(63) SPRING BRANCH AND TOTTERING
     BRIDGE SWAMP

     DANIEL HALSEY (1711) 55
     DANIEL McDANIEL (17..) 104
     JOHN ARTHUR (1720)

(69) WARWICK SWAMP IN UPPER
     CHOWAN

     BENJAMIN BLANCHARD (1701) 10
     THOMAS GARRETT, JR. (1718) 48
     TIMOTHY TAYLOR (1716) 165

(56) ON LINE OF PERQUIMANS AND
     CHOWAN

     THOMAS WOODLEY (1716) 190

(66) TIMBER BRANCH ON ROCKYHOCK
     CREEK

     JOHN JONES (1714) 81
     JOHN JONES (1720) 81-83

(65) TANYARD BRANCH ON MATTACOMACK CR.

     HENRY BONNER (1719) 12
     THOMAS LUTEN (1697) 97
     WILLIAM WALSTON (1711) 174

---

(71) ON WICACON CREEK IN CHOWAN
     PRECINCT

     DENNIS MACLENDEN (1717) 103
     FRANCIS MACLENDEN (1717) 103

---

(72) SOME EARLY GRANTS TO LANDS ON YEOPIM RIVER, CHOWAN PRECINCT
     NEAR THE LINE OF PERQUIMANS

     JAMES BEASLEY (1722) 8
     JOHN CHARLTON (1721) 24
     WILLIAM CHARLTON (1721) 24
     THOMAS CLARK (1701) 25
     HENRY CLAYTON (1716) 25
     PATRICK EDGERTON (1719) 41
     JOHN FALCONER (1720) 44
     JAMES FISHER (1699) 45
     JOHN FOSTER (1694) 46
     WILLIAM HAVET (1718) 62
     JOHN HIBBINS (1694)
     JOHN HOPKINS (1696) 69
     WILLIAM HORTON (1719) 69
     PETER JONES (1716) 80
     LEONARD LOFTIN (1694) 94
     JOHN LOVICK (1719) 96
     JOHN NORCOMB (1714) 116
     MARY PORTER (1717) 131
     JOHN PORTER (1719) 131
     IRA SMITH (1720) 155
     THOMAS SNOWDEN (1704) 156
     JOHN SWAIN (1716) 163
     ARGALL SIMONS (1694) 152
     JAMES WARD (1714) 175
     WILLIAM WILKINSON (1696) 185

(79) RESIDENTS OF THE UPPER PART OF CHOWAN PRECINCT
NOW IN HERTFORD AND NORTHAMPTON
COUNTIES, N. C. IN 1720

ROSTER OF CAPT. ROBERT PATTERSON'S COMPANY

Between MEHERRIN CREEK to
MEHERRIN RIVER and up the
River on BOTH SIDES:

From Vol. 1, p. 443, of Hathaway's N. C. Hist. & Gen. Register, giving a roster of the members of COL. ROBERT PATTERSON'S COMPANY on April 11, 1720, is obtained a list of most of the residents of the then upper parts of CHOWAN PRECINCT, lying West of the CHOWAN RIVER, a most interesting list. Here is a list of the ancestors of many great families who are now scattered throughout the Southern states. The lineal descendants of these men are all probably eligible to join the COLONIAL DAMES and other patriotic organizations. Here is the list:

JAMES ALLINGNOW (?)
WILLIAM ARCHDEACON
JOHN BAILEY 5
JOHN BARDEN
THOMAS BONNER 12
JOSEPH BOON 18
NICHOLAS BOON 18
THOMAS BOON 18
WILLIAM BOON 18
    There are hundreds
    of descendants of
    this BOON family,
    who now mistakenly
    claim relationship
    with DANIEL BOONE,
    while, as a matter
    of fact THIS FAMI-
    LY was of more an-
    cient AMERICAN AN-
    CESTRY. The name
    is now spelled
    BOONE universally.
WILLIAM BROWN 16
JOHN BRASWELL 14
RICHARD BRASWELL 14
ROBERT BRASWELL 14
WILLIAM BRASWELL 14
    These Braswells
    were all from
    Isle of Wight
    County, Va.
SAMUEL CANADAY 21
WILLIAM CARROLL 22
THOMAS CASSEY (Casey?)
JOHN CARSEY (Casey)?
JONATHAN CHRISTMAS 25
    York Co. Va.
    family.
JOHN COLSON 26
MATTHEW COPPS
JOHN CROSBY 104
NICHOLAS CULVER
JAMES DENTON
JOHN DEW 86
JOHN DEW, SR 86
AARON DRAKE 67
JOSEPH DURDEN 33 (DARDEN?)
WILLIAM ELLIOTT 41
FRANCIS FIBUSH
JOHN FOLK 45
WILLIAM FOLK 45
LEWIS FORD
JOHN GAINEY
THOMAS GAINEY
WILLIAM GAINEY
JOHN GARDNER 45
PETER HAYES 62
TIMOTHY HINDS 66
LAWRENCE HOERY 67
RICHARD HORNE 69

RICHARD WASHINGTON 176
SAMUEL WHELEY
WILLIAM WILSON 188
JOSEPH WILLIAMS 186
ARTHUR WILLIAMS 185.

THOMAS HORNE 69
MILES HOWELL 71
ROBERT HOWELL 71
EDWARD HEWES 64
JOHN HUNT 71
JOEL HUTCHESON 72
    This man was con-
    stable of the
    Precinct North of
    Meherrin Creek.
JOHN JACKSON 76
JOHN JARNIKIN 77
THOMAS JARNIKIN 77
    This name was and
    is properly
    spelled JARNIGAN;
    ancestors of the
    famous CHESLEY
    JARNIGAN, of
    Tennessee.
THOMAS JOYNER 79
LEONARD LANGSTON 29
DANIEL MACDONNELL 104
OWEN MACKERAEE
    Now what do you
    suppose that name
    really is?
THOMAS MAYER 106
JOHN MOLTON, JR.
JOHN MOLTON, SR.
GILBERT MONK 108
    The DUKE OF ALBE-
    MARLE was GEORGE
    MONCK, one of
    Cromwell's favor-
    ites. Gilbert
    may have been some
    poor cousin!
WILLIAM MOORE 111
JOHN NELSON
JOHN PAGE 121
NICHOLAS PERRY 127
JOHN PROCTOR 133
WILLIAM REED, SR. 139
    A WILLIAM REED
    was Governor
    from 1722 to 1724.
WILLIAM REED JR. 139
BENJAMIN RICKS 141
WILLIAM RICKS 141
JOHN ROGERS 143.
ROBERT SHERROD
MATTHEW SILVER
JOHN SMITH SR. 155
JOHN SMITH 155
THOMAS STONEHOUSE
JOHN TAYLOR 165
HENRY TURNER 169
DAVID VINSON 172
THOMAS VINSON 108
WILLIAM VINSON 172

(81) SOME RESIDENTS AND LAND OWNERS IN THE LOWER PART
OF CHOWAN - NOW BERTIE
IN 1719.

LIVING BETWEEN SALMON CREEK AND CASHEY RIVER

Following below is a list of the early residents of CHOWAN COUNTY, who lived West of the Chowan River, in the general vicinity of the present WINDSOR, before Bertie County had been established. This list is authentic and is taken from the early records by Mr. Hathaway and published in his Volume 1, at pages 444 and 445.

The numbers opposite each name is that of the page of this volume where additional information may be found in regard to these persons or their families.

THOMAS ASHLEY 4	DAVID HENDERSON 63	WILLIAM HEDITT 139
RICHARD ABEY	JOHN HARDY 56	SAMUEL RATLIFF 137
WILLIAM BURT	WILLIAM HARDY 57	ELIZABETH ROSE 143
THOMAS BALL 5	JOHN HOLBROOK	JAMES ROBERDS 142
REBECCA BYRD 10-19	ARNOLD HOPKINS 69	LAWRENCE SARSEN 149
ROBERT BELL 8	SAMUEL HEARIN 63	THOMAS SUTTON 163
CHARLES BARBER 6	JOHN HEARIN 63	JOSEPH SKITTLETHORPE 154
MATTHEW COATES	JACOB HARDY 56	JONATHAN STANDLEY 160
JOHN COOK 29	RICHARD HINES 66	DAVID STEWART 161
JOHN CROMEY 30	DAVID HEK (?)	ROBERT TURNER 169
JOHN COMES 27	SOLOMON JORDAN 82	CHRIS VANTUSIN 172
WILLIAM DUKENFIELD 37	ABEL JOHNSON 78	THOMAS WILLIAMSON 187
DARBY DENSON 35	JOHN JOHNSON 79	WILLIAM WALSTON 174
MARTHA EDWARDS 41	MICHAEL KING 85	ROBERT WEST 179
SAMUEL EDMONS 40	WILLIAM MAULE 102	THEOPHILUS WILLIAMS 186
JOHN EDWARDS 41	JOHN PLOWMAN	JOHN WILLIAMS 186
JOHN EDWARDS JR. 41	RICHARD PECKERIN	JOHN WALKER 173
RICHARD FRYER 47	JOHN PRICE 132	JOSEPH YOUNG 191
WILLIAM GARDNER 48	CHARLES PATE 124	PHILLIP WALSTON 174
WILLIAM GRIFFIN 58	WILLIAM PATE 124	Constable of Precinct.

-----

(73) CHOWAN PRECINCT SOUTH OF ALBEMARLE SOUND

SETTLERS WEST OF SCUPERNONG IN LOWER CHOWAN

As settlers multiplied in the OLD ALBEMARLE TERRITORY and began to expand their activities many of those who had settled North of Albemarle Sound began to take up lands to the South, as well as on the River. That part of CHOWAN PRECINCT lying South of Albemarle Sound and West of Scupernong river soon absorbed many of the families, or their representatives, that had first settled on Queen Anne's Creek and around the present EDENTON. Notable among these were the BLOUNTS and others. From an old petition, from old deeds and other sources, it is known that among these were the following:

RICHARD ADDISON	MARY LAWSON
RICHARD BURTONSHALL 18	Widow of John Lawson
Wife Priscilla.	the surveyor.
JOSEPH CANINGS (?) 21	MRS. ALICE LONG
LEWIS CONNOR	Widow of James Long.
CHARLES CRADDOCK 29	JOHN NAIRNE
RICHARD CRADDOCK 29	HENRY NORMAN 117
JOHN DAVENPORT 34	CUTHBERT PHELPS 159
ROBERT FEWOX	EDWARD PHELPS
JONATHAN FISHER 45	JONATHAN PHELPS
THOMAS GARLAND 159	SAMUEL PHELPS
THOMAS GAYLORD 34	These are the
WILLIAM HARDY	Phelps Lake
JOHN HASSELL	Phelpses.
THOMAS HAWKING (HAWKINS)	JAMES SINGLETON 159
ROBERT HOLDBROOK	GODFREY SPRUILL JR. 159
JOHN HOPKINS 29	JOSEPH SPRUILL 159

SAMUEL SPRUILL 159
JOHN TARKINGTON
WILLIAM WILKINSON
JOHN WINGATE
JOHN YATES
ALEXANDER FAMILY
WHITE FAMILY.

More than 75 years later, which means a period of two and three or more generations, the First United States census for TYRRELL COUNTY, North Carolina, which in 1729 was established covering this same territory, every name, with one or two exceptions, shown on the above list, is shown also on the 1790 census of TYRRELL COUNTY. It makes an interesting study. Those on the above list clearly appear to have been the ancestors of numerous tribes.

597

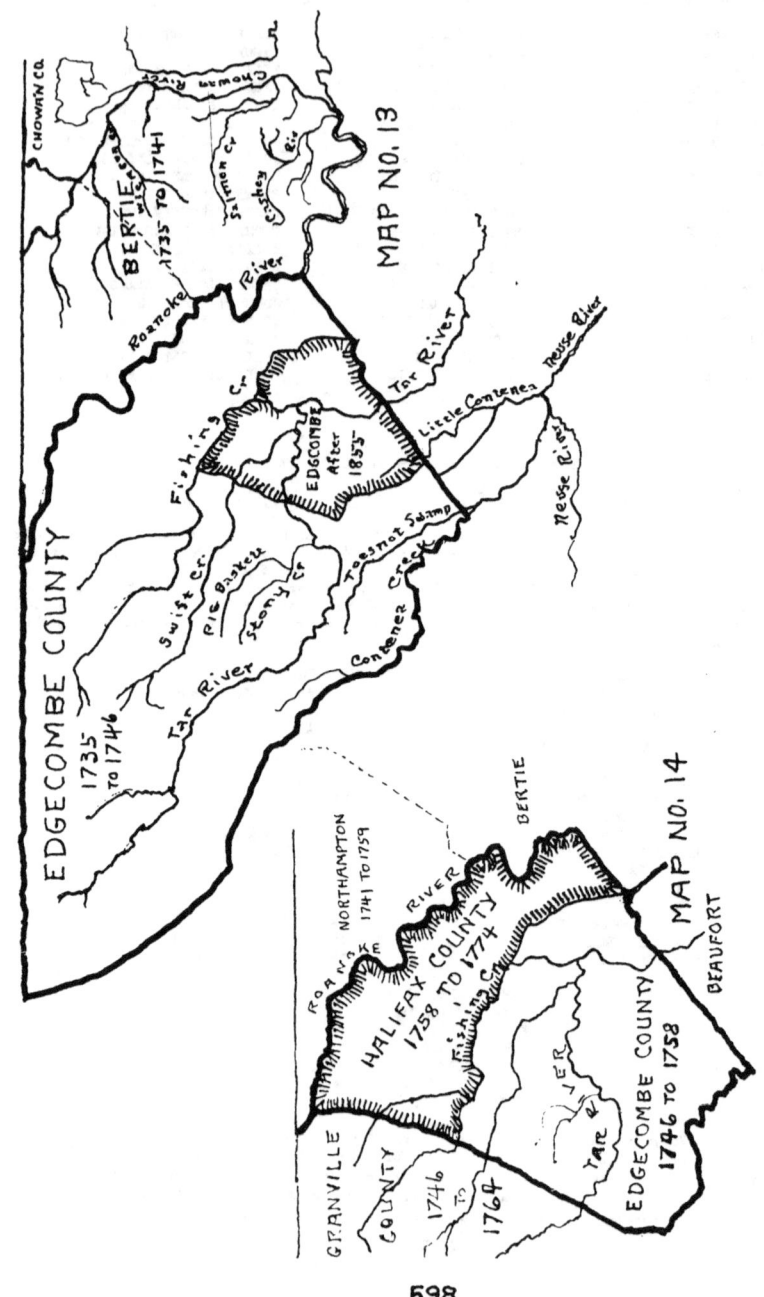

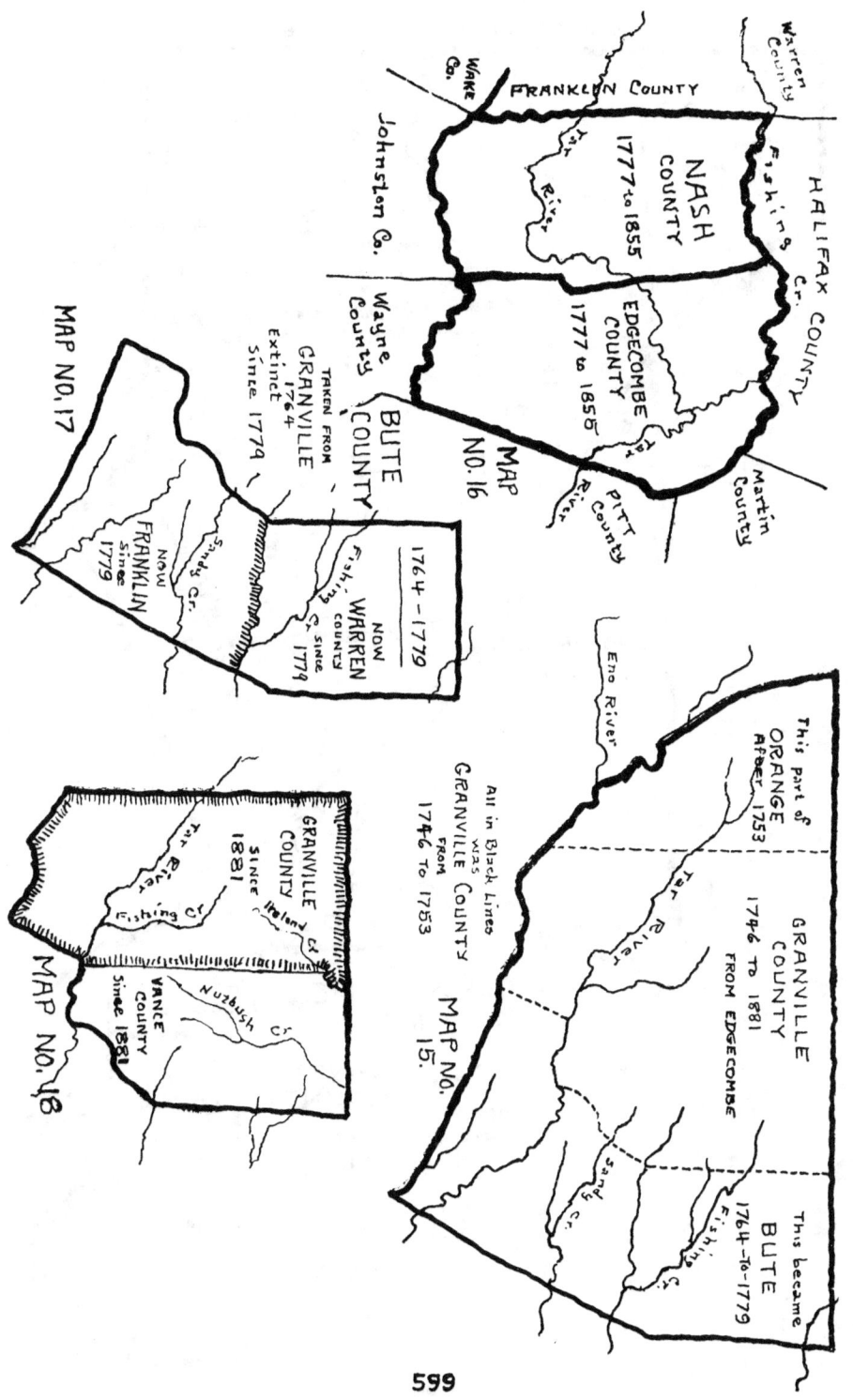

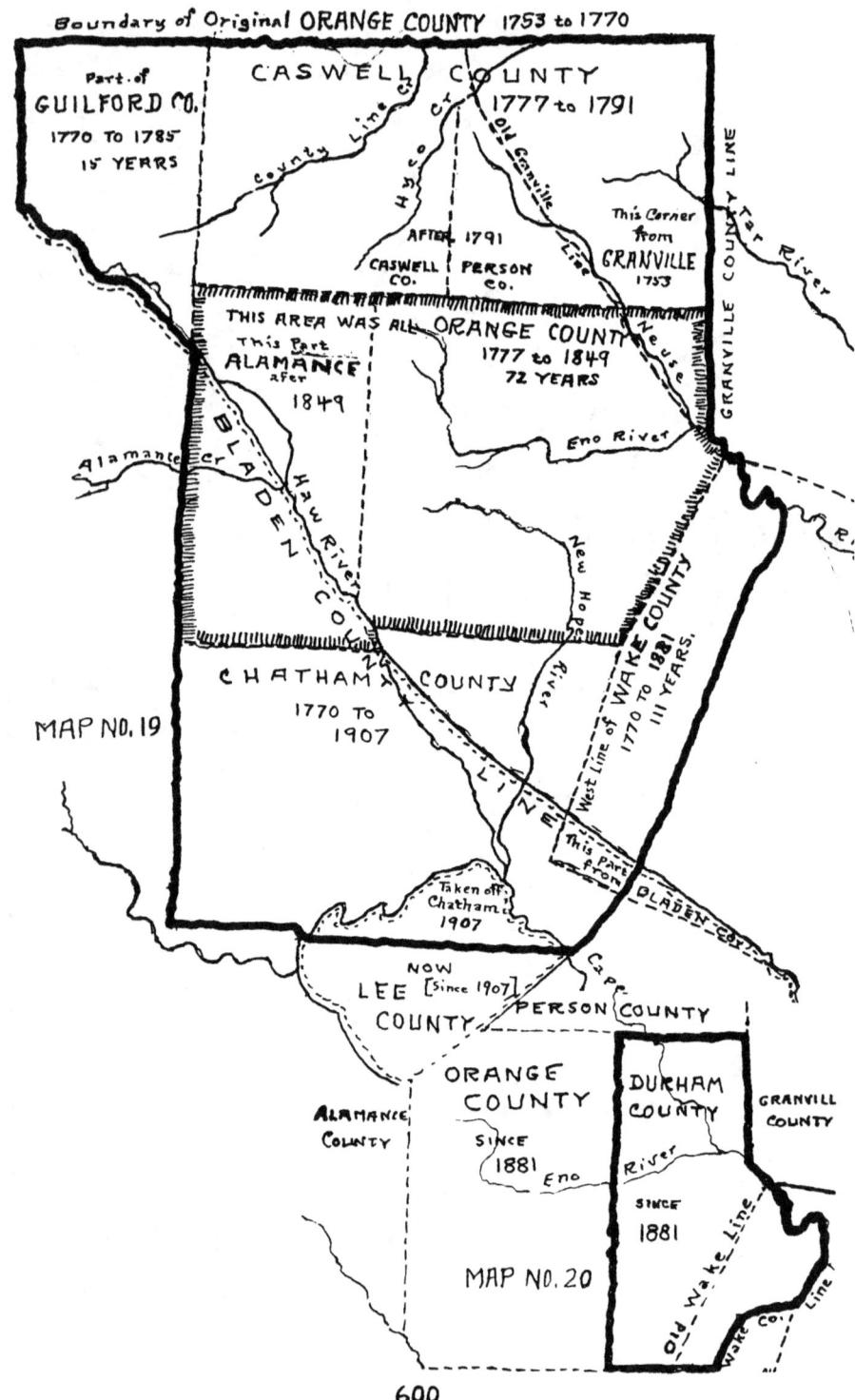

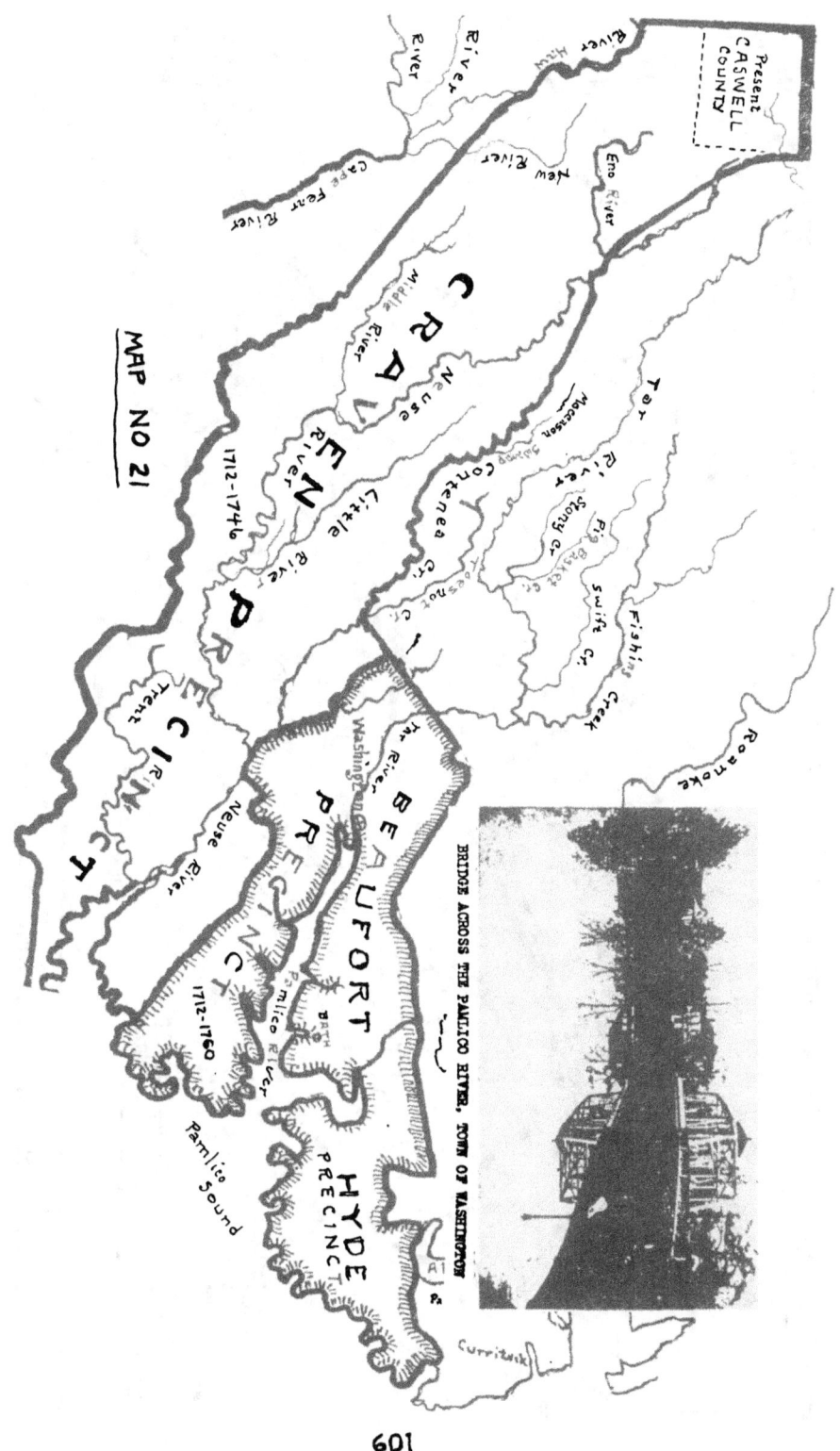

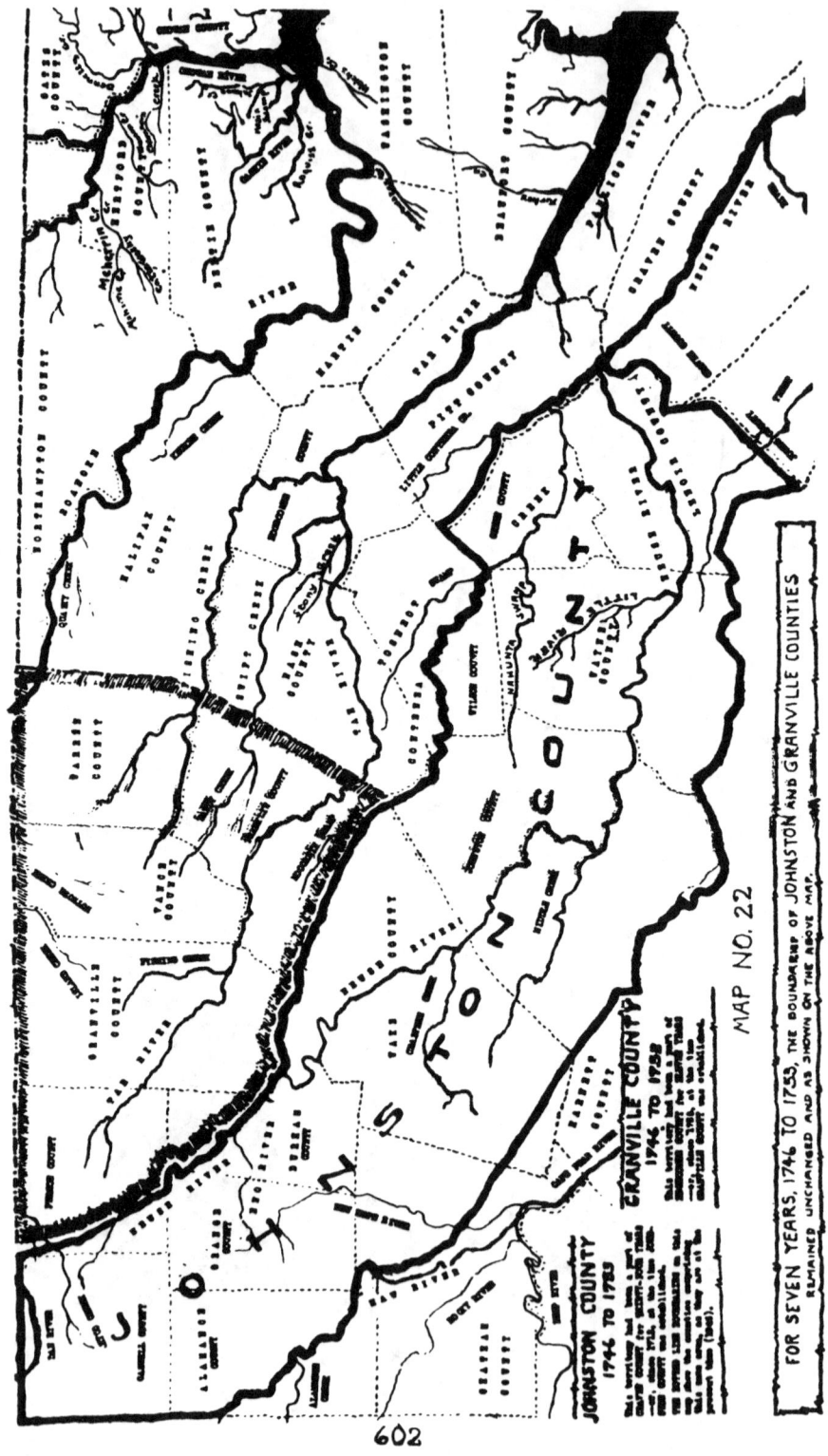

COMPLETE INDEX TO MARRIAGE BONDS OF
OUR BERTIE ANCESTORS, 1755 TO 1834

VOLUME 2, NORTH CAROLINA HISTORICAL AND GENEALOGICAL REGISTER
PAGES 314-320, 364-379 AND 589-593, INC.

ABINGTON 316, 365, 366
ACREE 317, 365, 366, 368, 371, 373, 374, 591
ADAMS 367
ADKERSON 376
ALEXANDER 376, 377
ALLEN 314, 318, 370, 376, 589
ALLENWORTH 318
ALSTON 314
ANDREWS 317, 371, 378, 591
ARMISTEAD 318, 319, 370, 590
ARNOLD 372
ASBELL 318, 367, 372, 590
ASHBURN 314, 316, 371, 374
ASKEW 365, 367, 370, 373, 375, 376, 377, 379, 592, 593
ASHLEY 314
AVENT 367
AVERET 315, 316, 317, 319, 320, 366

BAILEY (BAYLEY) 368, 374, 378, 366, 589
BAINES 374
BAKER 314, 318-320, 365, 367, 369, 370, 373, 375-379, 589-591, 593
BARBER 316, 317, 368, 370, 374, 375, 592
BARFIELD 319
BARKSDALE 364
BARNCASTLE 371, 589, 592
BARNES 319, 365, 372, 373, 376, 377, 591, 592
BARRADALL 366, 367
BARRETT 314, 370, 371
BARRON 371
BARTLETT 364, 589
BASON 364
BAS... 314, 318, 364, 371
BAZE 315, 316, 370, 375, 376, 377, 378
BATEMAN 378
BAZEMORE 319, 320, 367, 368, 372, 373, 376, 377, 591, 592, 593
BECK 591
BEATLEY 370
BELL 315, 316, 374
BELOTE 317-320, 364, 368, 372, 376
BENBURY 317
BENSON 377
BENTLEY 314, 317, 318, 364, 366, 369, 373, 375, 377
BENTON 320, 370, 373
BERTIE 314
BERRY 318, 374
BEST 364
BEVINS 314
BILLUPS 315, 318, 320, 365, 366, 370, 371
BIRCH 317
BIRD (BYRD) 314, 319, 369, 371, 373, 376, 377, 590, 593
BIDDIE 318
BISHOP 590
BITTLE 366, 372
BIZZELL 591

BLACK 314
BLACKSTON 373, 589
BLANCHARD 320, 592
BLOUNT 316, 364, 365, 372, 373, 376
BLUME 590
BOND 315, 317-319, 365, 366, 371, 373, 376, 377, 379, 593
BONNER 315, 374, 375
BOON 317
BOSWELL 365, 366, 371, 377, 379, 591
BOWEN 320, 369, 371, 375, 376, 590, 591, 593
BOYCE 318, 320, 365, 366, 369, 589
BOYDTON 314
BRANCH 364
BRAMPELT 377
BRANTLEY 319, 377, 592
BRASWELL 371
BRAYBOY 374, 376, 379
BRICKELL 589
BRIDGEN 365
BRIDGER 319, 592
BRIDGES 315
BRIGGERS 318
BRIMMAGE 369
BRINKLEY 364
BRITTAIN 367, 375, 377, 592
BRITT 317, 364, 366, 367, 370, 371, 374
BROADWELL 320
BROGDEN 319, 365, 368, 370, 373, 374, 376, 592
BROWN 315, 320, 366, 368, 369, 370, 373, 374, 589, 592, 593
BRUCE 378
BRYAN 314-320, 366, 368, 369, 372, 377
BUCK 367, 372
BUNCH 314, 315, 319, 365-367, 371, 373, 591, 592
BURCH 374
BURDEN 369
BURGESS 317
BURKE 593
BURKETT 366, 371
BURLINGHAM 370
BURN 320, 366, 368, 377
BURRUSS 369
BUTT 378
BUTTERTON 314, 370, 593
BUTLER 318, 319, 364, 365, 367, 370, 371, 374, 377, 378, 591, 593, 589
BRYCE 374
BYNUM 365
BYRUM 366, 367, 369, 372, 373, 590, 592.
CAIL (CAIE) 369, 370, 377
CALLAWAY 368, 372, 590
CALLUM 319
CAMPBELL 367
CANADY 368, 372, 373
CAPEHART 366, 369, 370, 372, 373, 374, 376, 591
CARLASS 318

CARNEY 320, 364
CAPPS 371, 590
CARR 315
CARTER 316, 317, 369, 373, 375, 590
CARY 378
CASTELLAW 316, 319, 366, 367, 375, 589-593
CASWELL 376
CAVEN 375
CHAMBERLAIN 317
CHAMBERS 316
CHAMPION 370, 376, 377, 589
CHAPMAN 316
CHAPPELL (CHAPLE) 369, 375, 376, 377
CHERRY 317, 364-368, 370, 373, 376, 377, 379, 590, 592, 593
CHURCH 319, 368, 373, 374, 379
CHURCHWELL 317, 367, 375, 377.
CIFF 375
CLARK 314, 316, 317
CLIFTON 315, 316, 369, 374
COBB 317, 318, 320, 365-368, 370, 374-377, 589-592
COCHRAN 315, 320, 379
COFFEE 368
COFFIELD 364, 365, 373, 375, 376, 378
COLE 315, 369, 372, 378, 590, 592
COLLINS 314, 316, 317, 320, 366, 367, 369, 375-377.
COMBES (COMBS) 373, 375, 376, 589
CONE 593
CONNOR 376, 592, 593
COOK 315, 316, 318, 320, 367, 369, 370, 371, 591, 593.
COOPER 317, 319, 320, 364, 365, 368-371, 590
COPELAND 377, 378, 590
CORBERT 367
CORBETT 366, 370
CORNEDAY (KORNEGAY) 370
COTTLE 365
COTTON (COTTEN) 316, 318, 372, 374, 589
COWAN 376
COWAND 366, 370, 374, 375, 590
COWARD 375, 591, 593
COWIES 376
COX 377
CRAFT 371, 375
CRANK 364
CRATCH 315, 364, 375
CRICKETT 314
CROOK 373
CROSS 372
CULLEN 318, 364, 366
CULLIFER 319, 366, 368-370, 372, 591-593
CURLE 377
CURRY 317, 318, 366, 368, 375, 376, 377, 590, 592.
DAUGHTRY 375, 376, 592
DAVIDSON 317, 320, 364, 375, 376, 379, 591.

DAVIS 314, 316, 319, 364, 365
368, 369, 371, 372, 590,
592, 593
DAWSON 320, 372, 373, 377 589
DEANE (DEANS) 319, 589, 590
DEMPSEY 320, 377, 378
DICKINSON 320
DOIRIL 320
DOLES 317
DOUGLAS 318, 367, 369
DOUERS (DOWERS) 320, 372, 376, 378
DREW 590, 593
DRISEL (DRIZZLE) 366, 369
DRIVER 316, 371
DRURY 318, 366
DUKE 366
DUNDELOW 372, 375
DUNNING 318, 365, 368, 372, 373, 375, 378

EARLY 365, 366, 369-373, 375, 378, 589, 591
EASON 317, 371, 378, 591
EDWARDS 314, 318-320, 372, 373
ELLENSWORTH 369
ELLYSON 592
EPPERSON 317
ETHERIDGE 590
EUER (EWER) 374
EVANS 318, 319, 365, 377, 379
EVERETT 318

FAILING 375
FARMER 317, 365, 367, 372, 373, 591
FARROW (FARROR) 366, 375
FIFE 590
FLEETWOOD 314, 316, 319, 320, 369, 370, 371
FLOYD 318, 370, 371, 372, 374, 375
FOLK 366, 367, 371, 373, 377.
FORCIT 316
FORD 252
FOREMAN 317
FRAME 591
FRANCIS 375, 379
FRAZIER 316, 317, 365, 371
FREEMAN 319, 366, 367, 370, 372, 376, 378, 591
FRY 315
FRYER 371

GAINES (GANES) 317, 318
GAINER 315
GALE 317
GARDNER 315, 318-320, 364, 368-373
GASLAND 593
GARRETT 319, 366, 367, 370, 373, 375, 376, 378, 589, 590, 593
GASKINS 318, 364, 367, 373, 378, 379, 590, 591, 593.
GIBBONS 314
GIFFORD 319
GILLIAM 367, 374, 376, 378, 593
GILMAN 314, 317
GILSON 317
GLAUHON 369
GLISSON 365, 591
GODFREY 320
GOODWIN 375, 590
GOFF 317
GRANBERRY 365, 369, 372, 375 379, 589

GRAY 314, 317-320, 364-368, 374, 592
GREEN 314, 365, 368, 371, 374, 375, 377, 378, 590, 591, 593
GREGORY 377, 591-593
GRIFFIN 318-320, 366-368, 375, 591-593
GROVER 315, 373
GRYMES (GRIMES) 315, 319, 375.

HAIL (HALE) 315, 370, 378
HALL 318
HALLUM 318, 369
HALSEY 315
HAMBLETON 590
HAMPTON 593
HARDEN 367, 369, 374, 377, 378.
HARDING 316
HARDISON 314
HARDY 314-316, 318-320, 364-370 372-374, 376-379, 589, 592, 593.
HARRIS 320
HARRISON 316, 318, 365, 372, 374
HASTE 318
HATHAWAY 374
HAWKINS 318, 369, 371, 592
HAYES (HAYS, HAZE) 316, 319, 320, 367, 590
HAYWOOD 590
HEDGEPETH 316, 320
HENDRY 315, 366, 367
HENLEY 376
HENRY 372, 590
HERMON 370
HICKS 319, 364, 370, 372
HIGGS 318-320, 364, 368, 369, 371, 374, 377, 591
HILL 316-318, 364, 366, 375, 591.
HINESLEY 378
HINSON 364
HINTON 315, 317, 367
HOBBS 376, 593
HOBDAY 367
HODGE 368
HODGES 366, 375-377, 591
HODUM 367
HOGGARD 319, 320, 367, 372, 373 374, 379, 589, 590-593
HOLDER 314, 365, 366, 369-373 376, 378, 590, 592
HOLLAND 314, 315, 319, 369 592
HOLLEY 317, 318, 320, 370-372, 375, 377
HOLLIDAY 365, 369, 379
HOLLOMAN 369, 372, 592
HOLLOWAY 316, 317
HOLLOWELL 367, 371
HOPKINS 316, 367, 368, 370, 693
HOOK 318, 319
HOOTEN 319
HORNE (HORN) 319, 590
HORNBY (HORNSBY) 364, 590
HORTON 369
HOSKINS 318
HOUSE 315, 317, 319, 367, 368
HOW 314
HOWARD 319, 320, 365, 369 375 378
HOWELL 314, 320, 364, 366 371 375, 378
HUBBARD 365, 369, 374
HUBBELL 365
HUGHES 319, 320, 367, 368, 370 373, 375, 377, 378, 591, 593.

HUMPHRIES 377
HUNDLEY 364
HUNT 590
HUNTER 314, 315, 367, 370, 371 378
HYMAN 315, 316, 317, 320, 371 374, 589, 590, 591

INGS 366
IRWIN 316

JACKSON 366
JACOBS 364, 370, 393
JACOCKS 366, 368, 372
JAMES 317-320, 364, 374, 378, 589
JENKINS 319, 372, 373, 375, 378, 379, 590
JENNISON 320
JERNIGAN (JARNIGAN) 314, 318, 365, 367-369, 374-376, 589-591
JOBE 369
JOHNSON 320, 372, 374, 377, 379, 592
JOHNSTON 315-317, 319, 320, 375, 379, 590-593
JONES 318, 364, 365, 368, 371, 372, 374, 589, 592, 593.
JORDAN 314, 316-319, 366, 367 369, 370, 372, 373, 376, 379, 589
JOSEY 316, 377

KAIE (KAIL) 379, 590
KEANE 377
KEATER 364
KEEN 320, 365, 366, 372, 373 375, 376
KELLEY 318
KENT 314
KERR 366
KEETER 370, 591, 592
KING 314, 315, 317-320, 365, 366-368, 370, 372, 377, 378, 379, 589-591
KINGSTON 366
KINSEY 320
KITTRELL 315, 317, 364, 365, 368, 371, 373, 374, 376, 377.
KNOTT 315-317, 319, 320, 368, 371, 372, 374, 375, 377.

LACKEY 320
LAMB 320
LAMBERT 378
LAND 316, 379
LANDRUM 591
LANE 367, 377, 379
LANGDALE 592
LANGLEY 592
LANGSTON 319
LASSITER 319, 320, 364, 365, 368, 370, 377, 378
LAYTON 366, 371, 373, 378 589
LAUGHTON 372
LAWRENCE 316, 318-320, 368, 370, 372, 376, 377, 378, 592
LEACH 315
LEARY 366, 378
LEATS 370
LEDNUM 590
LEE 317, 320, 366, 370, 372, 376
LEEMING 319
LEGGETT 314, 317, 318, 364 371 373, 375, 377, 379, 591, 593

604

LEICESTER 591
LESTER 373
LEWIS 319, 379, 589
LIGHTFOOT 375
LISCOMB 368
LISTER 318
LINTON 378
LLOYD (LOYD) 315, 317, 319, 367, 590.
LOCKHART 314, 368
LONG 316
LORD 317
LOVE 368, 591
LOWE 317
LOWTHER 320
LUCAS 375
LUTEN 592

MAER 314, 367, 592
MADRA 367
MAGRUDER 593
MALONE 364, 365
MANLEY 591
MANNING 317, 319, 320, 368, 370, 376, 377, 591
MANSFIELD 593
MARDHE 365
MARSHALL 398, 590
MARTIN 365, 374
MASON 371, 592
McCLELLAN 369
McDONALD 318
McDOWELL 367, 371, 372
McFARLANE 375, 376
McGASKETT 315
McGLAUHON 318, 367, 375-377, 589
McHENRY 319, 365
McWELL 378
MEAZLE (MIZELL) 379
MEEZLES(MIZELL) 590
MEREDITH 366
M'HOON 370, 374, 592
MIERS (See MYERS) 316, 367, 370, 371, 374-376, 379, 590.
MILBURN 318, 365, 369, 370, 371, 374, 376.
MILLEN 318
MILLER 318, 365, 369, 372, 375-379, 589, 592,593.
MINTON 365, 591, 592
MITCHELL 317-319, 364-366, 368-370, 373-375, 377, 378, 379, 589-593
MYERS (See MIERS) 314, 590, 591
MIWARD 369
MIZELL 318, 319, 364-366, 368, 370, 371, 373, 375, 376, 378, 589, 591, 593
MODLIN 377, 379
MONK 318, 320, 364, 366, 378, 379
MONTGOMERY 319, 320, 366
MOORE 314-320, 365-373, 375, 376, 378, 590, 593
MORGAN 315, 364, 371, 359, 590
MORING 593
MORRIS 318-320, 364-367, 370-373, 375-376, 589, 590, 593
MOTT 319.
MULLEN 375, 376
MURDAUGH 377
MURRAY 317, 376
MYLES 590
MYRICK 593

NAZARY 316
NEIL 592
NEWCOM 369
NEWBORN 319, 364
NEWSOM 367
NICHOLS 315, 319, 368, 371, 372 375, 591
NIXON 368
NOBLES 369
NORFLEET 315, 366, 371, 373,591
NORTH 372
NOWELL 373

OLIVER 315, 364, 366, 372, 373, 378
O'NEAL 375
OUTERBRIDGE 320
OUTHOUSE 364, 369
OUTLAND 369
OUTLAW 314-317, 367, 368, 370-379, 589, 590, 592.
OVERTON 364, 365, 368, 589
OWENS 318, 372, 374, 593
OXLEY 317, 318, 367, 369, 373, 377, 378, 593.

PACE 318
PAGE 318, 320, 365, 368, 372, 373, 590, 592
PALMER 590
PARKER 318, 368, 369, 373, 376, 377-379, 589, 590,592, 593.
PARROTT 318
PATTERSON 589
PEALE (PEELE) 377
PEARCE 319, 377, 378
PEDEN 373, 376
PEELE 369, 374, 376, 379, 589, 591, 592
PENDER 314, 317, 368, 373, 374 376, 378, 590
PENNY (PENNEY) 364, 371, 373, 377, 378
PERRY 315, 316, 318, 364, 367, 379, 592
PETERSON 378
PHELPS 589, 592, 593
PHILLAM 373
PIERCE 364, 366, 367, 369, 591, 592, 593
PIKE 591
PILAND 367, 591
PITTMAN 316
PLUMMER 590
POLLOCK 315
POWELL 316, 318, 319, 369, 370, 372, 374, 376, 378, 590, 591.
POWER 364, 590
POYTHRESS 319
PRITCHARD 317, 367, 371, 374, 376, 589
PRIVOTE (PRIVETT) 365
PRUDEN 320, 367, 369, 373,378
PUGH 314, 315, 318, 367, 376, 377, 589, 591, 592
PULLE 377, 379
PURDY 374
PURNELL 368
PURVIS 368, 374

QUALL 375

RABEY (RABY) 368, 379, 591
RAMSEY 593
RASCOE 317, 318, 320, 366, 370, 374, 376, 377, 378, 590, 591
RAZOR (RAZOR) 315, 316, 364, 370 373.

RAWLS 320, 371, 592
RAY 368, 369, 372-379, 592
RAYNOR 377-379, 590-593
REA 590
REDDITT 315, 369, 374, 378
REED 315, 320, 365, 374, 377, 589, 593
RHEA 591
RHODES 315-320, 365-367, 369, 371, 373-379, 591, 593.
RICE 593
RIGBY 370, 371, 379
ROARK (RUARK) 373
ROBERTS 318
ROBBINS 368, 372
ROBERTSON (ROBINSON) 318, 319, 373, 375, 376
ROGERS 368, 375
ROSCOE 364
ROSE 373
ROSS 366
ROUNDTREE 315, 367
ROWAN 371, 374
ROSE 591
RUFFIN 316, 368, 369, 373, 377, 590
RUTLAND 316, 373, 375, 377, 378, 589, 591
RYAN 314, 365, 591, 593
RYARSON 379

SANDERLIN 377
SANDERSON 365
SASSER 316
SAVAGE 369
SEALS (SEALE) 317, 368, 375, 590
SEAY 316, 364, 366, 376
SEAWELL 592
SESSOMS 378, 591
SHARROCK 367, 371
SHAW 314, 366, 368, 369, 592
SHEHAN 314, 364, 368, 376
SHERLOCK 377
SHOLAR 320, 365-369, 372
SHOULDER 318, 370, 373
SIMONS 320, 364, 367, 372, 378, 589, 593
SKILES 317-320, 367, 370, 373 376, 590, 593
SKINNER 314, 365, 371
SLADE 317
SLATTER 314, 317
SMITH 314-318, 320, 365, 367, 369, 371, 372, 375, 376, 378, 589
SMITHSON 377
SMITHWICK 315, 316, 320, 364, 366, 367, 369, 373-375, 378.
SOUTH 374, 375, 589, 590,591
SOWARD 365
SOWELL 318, 320, 363, 365, 368, 371, 374-378
SPAR 318
SPARKMAN 315, 319, 320,364, 366, 368, 371, 372, 374.
SPEIGHT 365, 366, 368
SPELLER 371, 374
SPENCE 317
SPIERS 314
SPIVEY 314, 315, 317, 367, 368, 369, 370, 371, 373, 376, 590, 592, 593
STAINBACK 366
STALL 592
STALLINGS 314, 318-320, 365, 372-374, 376
STANDLEY 314, 316, 364, 365, 367, 368, 370-373, 593

605

STANDING 370
STANTON 317
STANKE 314, 315
STEEL 369, 371
STEWART (See STUART) 590, 592
STOKES 368
STONE 319, 320, 367-370, 376, 378, 590
STROTHER 371
STUART (See STEWART) 316, 372
STUCKEY 317
SUMNER 364
SURRY 370, 374
SUTTON 317, 318, 320, 364, 369, 370, 371, 374
SWETT 589
SWAIN 320, 364, 367, 370, 372, 373, 376, 378, 590

TADLOCK 318, 376, 593
TART (TARTT) 317, 365, 368, 374, 376
TAYLOE 316, 320, 368-371, 373, 589, 591-593
TAYLOR 314, 318
TEMPLE 376, 590
TODD 318, 365, 368-372, 590, 591, 592
THOMAS 320, 364-366, 368, 372, 373, 374, 377, 590-593
THOMPSON 314-316, 320, 367, 378, 589
THOROUGHGOOD 317
TILLMAN 379
TOMLINSON 314
TOOLE 314
TROTMAN 364
TUCKER 374
TUNSTALL 367
TURNAGE 368
TURNER 315, 316, 318, 320, 365, 367, 371, 373

TYLER 367, 593
TYNER 318, 367

UMFLEET 365
URQUHART 318, 372, 591

VANN 317, 320, 364
VEALE 369, 372, 374, 375, 378, 592
VENTURES 365
VIRGIN 314, 374
VOSS 320

WALKER 590
WALLER 593
WALSTON 370
WARBURTON 315, 316, 364-366, 369, 374, 375
WARD 315, 319, 320, 367, 369, 370, 372, 373, 377, 593
WARE (WAIR) 318, 320, 372
WARREN 364, 368, 373
WATERIDGE 589
WATERMAN 592
WATERS 591
WATFORD 317, 364, 366, 370, 371, 372, 376, 378, 590, 591
WATSON 314, 315-317, 320, 365, 366, 368, 371, 372, 375, 593
WEAVER 364
WEBB 591, 593
WELCH 317
WELLS 315, 317
WEST 314, 315, 320, 366, 368, 371, 373, 375-379
WESTON 314, 318, 364-366, 368, 370, 372, 373, 376, 377, 589, 591-593
WHEELER 315
WHITAKER (WHITEACRE) 316, 317, 365, 367, 372

WHITE 315, 318, 320, 364, 367-370, 372-377, 379, 590-593
WHITFIELD 317, 320, 374
WHITEHEAD 316
WHITLEDGE 320
WHITLEY 593
WHITMELL 314, 315, 377
WIDED 319
WIGGINS 314
WILDER 317, 379
WILFORD 318, 320, 366, 368-373
WILKES 317, 365, 366, 371, 376, 592
WILKINS 375
WILKINSON 318, 364
WILEY 370
WILLIFORD 320, 367, 370, 372, 375, 589-593
WILLIAMS 315-317, 367, 368, 370-373, 375-378, 590-593
WILLIAMSON 373
WILLOUGHBY 367, 589
WILSON 320, 367, 369, 376, 379
WIMBERLY 314, 318, 319, 366, 378.
WINANTS 366, 377
WINBOURNE 593
WOLFENDEN 365, 367
WOOD 319, 320, 365, 366, 369, 374, 379, 589
WORLEY 314, 365, 368, 591, 593
WRIGHT 317, 370
WYNANTS (See WINANTS) 315
WYNN (WYNNE) 378, 379, 589
WYNNS 378, 589

YARBE 314
YATES 320, 366, 368
YEATES 315, 370, 590, 591, 593
YOUNG 315, 317, 366, 373

ZELLEN 369

MODERN BRIDGE SPANNING ALBEMARLE SOUND - LINK BETWEEN BERTIE AND CHOWAN COUNTIES - FROM "GUIDE TO THE OLD NORTH STATE", 1939.

THE THOMAS FAMILY
OF VIRGINIA AND NORTH CAROLINA

CONSIDERED IN CONNECTION WITH OTHER FAMILIES
OF THE SAME PERIOD

BARRETTS - BODDIE - BRIDGERS - BRYAN - COTTEN - CRUDUP - DAWSON - DEW - DIXON - EDWARDS
HARDY - HUNT - LAWRENCE - MARSHALL - MARTIN - McKINNIE - PORTIS - ROBINSON
ROGERS - SHEARER - SHERROD - SHERWOOD - STANDLEY AND WHITFIELD.

Just one of the TRIBES whose members and descendants settled along the CHOWANOKE, the MEHERRIN, MORATUCK, NEUSE and PAMTICOUGH in OLD ALBEMARLE before and after the end of the Seventeenth Century was the THOMAS FAMILY. Its members were perhaps no more numerous or representative than the BRYANS, HILLS, HARDYS, BLOUNTS or WHITFIELDS, any one of whom, together with dozens of other families of that place and time could have been used by this compiler as a vehicle for this study on the LOST TRIBES. Practically all of them came out of VIRGINIA, and they were all more or less kinsmen. These people turned an almost impenetrable wilderness into a land of plenty, with its lucious plantations yielding up the finest tobacco in the world, and its waters turning the wheels of commerce to help supply the needs of a great empire.

Who were these THOMASES?

Where did they come from? Where did they go?

Who were their kinsmen?

And where did *they* come from - and go?

THE FIRST JOHN THOMAS, OF VIRGINIA

The first THOMAS to arrive in VIRGINIA and settle was a certain JOHN THOMAS. In the year 1609 he embarked on the SEA VENTURE in ENGLAND, bound for the new colony over seas, with SIR THOMAS GATES. The "Sea Venture" floundered in a storm off the coast of BERMUDA, but nothing daunted the victims of this disaster rallied and built two pinances capable of withstanding the rough seas and in 1610 came sailing up the JAMES RIVER to the headquarters of the new colony, with all safe on board, save LIEUT. EDWARD WATTERS and one other, who had elected to remain in the BERMUDAS to which they had taken a fancy.

In the contingent that arrived in VIRGINIA in 1610 with SIR THOMAS GATES and SIR GEORGE SOMERS "Admiral of the Fleet" came, among others SERJEANT SAMUEL SHARPE, afterwards prominent in the Colony, and a member of the first Legislative Assembly ever held in America, with SAMUEL JORDAN, of JORDAN'S JOURNEY, in 1619.

NOTE: THOMAS JORDAN, a son of this SAMUEL JORDAN, and JOHN THOMAS, a son of the first JOHN THOMAS patented lands in NANSEMOND COUNTY that adjoined, by the middle of the seventeenth century.

SERJEANT SAMUEL SHARPE married and had children. His wife was ELIZABETH. After the death of SAMUEL SHARPE his widow married THOMAS PARKER. Among the property of value left by SERJEANT SHARPE to his widow was the headright of JOHN THOMAS, whose transportation he had effected, and whose headright he claimed. This headright was used by the widow, ELIZABETH PARKER, in taking out a patent to lands "between CURLES and VARINA," in July, 1636. (Nugent page 45). If this headright had been used before, the land secured had escheated or lapsed, and ELIZABETH here used it again. To further enhance and strengthen these intimate connections, after the death of THOMAS PARKER'S wife ELIZABETH, he had married CICELIE, the widow of SAMUEL JORDAN, and of PETER MONTAGUE, the latter another patentee of lands in NANSEMOND, adjoining young THOMAS JORDAN and young JOHN THOMAS and a HUMPHREY SCOWEN. (Boddie, p. 239). JOHN THOMAS, the first, had sons, JOHN, PHILLIP, WILLIAM, RICHARD and MARKE THOMAS, as shown hereafter. See Nugent p. 173.

The first JOHN THOMAS, if as surmised from the records quoted, he come to VIRGINIA with SIR THOMAS GATES, was born before 1600 - probably by 1590 - in ENGLAND or WALES. He may have been a married man on his arrival in VIRGINIA, leaving his family behind him, or he may have married after he cme to VIRGINIA. That he settled on QUEEN'S CREEK in York County, an adjoining neighbor of JOSEPH CROSHAW, NICOLAS JERNEAU, HENRY MARSHALL, EDWARD MARSHALL, RICHARD MARSHALL is amply verified by numerous records, vis:

Vol. 24, Fleet's Colonial Abs. p. 94.
Vol. 25, Fleet's Colonial Abs. pp. 56, 59.
Vol. 1, Nugent's Cavaliers and Pioneers, pp. 45, 73, 102, 128, 171, 182, 185, 186, 144, 220, 267 and 297.

Some of the notes shown in NUGENT refer to the first JOHN THOMAS, and some have reference to his son, JOHN THOMAS. The descerning worker will be able to segregate them. Other references to his other sons will be cited in the notes that follow.

As before stated, the entire record, considered as a whole, establishes beyond question that the first JOHN THOMAS had at least FIVE SONS, (perhaps some daughters) as follows:

(1) WILLIAM THOMAS
(2) RICHARD THOMAS
(3) PHILLIP THOMAS
(4) JOHN THOMAS
(*) MARK THOMAS (Oldest son, not traced).

Our working notes disclose considerable information about (4) JOHN and (1) WILLIAM THOMAS and their descendants, but not so much about (2) RICHARD and (3) PHILLIP THOMAS. In the sketches that follow for each one they are not taken up in the order set down immediately above, nor have we taken the trouble to identify them in these initial sketches by number, but the reader will have no trouble in identifying each one. * MARKE THOMAS has not been traced. JOHN THOMAS, the first, was deceased by 1753. (Nugent, p. 416.) (Also Mason, Vol. 1, p. 73).

JOHN THOMAS

The name of the wife of JOHN THOMAS (son of the first JOHN THOMAS) was DOROTHY. Her last name before marriage is, of course, unknown. This is evidenced by the following:

JOHN THOMAS, 350 acres YORK COUNTY, October 7, 1649. Upon the North side of QUEEN'S CREEK, N. by West upon the land of JOSEPH CROSHAW, South by East upon QUEEN'S CREEK, West by South upon a little Creek and swamp leading to the Indian cabin and E. by North upon the land of MR. JERNEW, 300 acres formerly granted unto JOHN BROACH and by him assigned to ANTHONY BARCKHURST and purchased of him by said JOHN THOMAS. Also 50 acres for the transportation of DOROTHY wife. (It is assumed this means DOROTHY his wife). Nugent pp. 185-186.

The following notes from reliable sources pertaining to JOHN THOMAS (son of JOHN) are of interest in connection with his history:

PETER MONTAGUE patented 100 acres in NANSEMOND COUNTY NOVEMBER 3, 1647, on the North Side of NEW TOWNE HAVEN RIVER on the Eastward side of the mouth of CROSS CREEK, adjoining THOMAS JORDAN, deceased, and HUMPHREY SCOWEN (Scone). Nugent p. 173.

JOHN THOMAS patented 174 acres in NANSEMOND COUNTY, NOVEMBER 19, 1654, upon the Eastward side of NEW TOWNE HAVEN RIVER; 150 acres at miles end of HUMPHREY SCOWEN and 24 acres adjoining his own lands, MR. JORDAN and THOMAS BEST; 150 acers granted to PETER MONTAGUE, December 18, 1645, and assigned to said JOHN THOMAS; and the residue for the transportation of one person, WILLIAM SEED, SUSAN JACOB, EDWARD POWELL and MARY WATKINS, the "three last Gms". Nugent, page 297.

In the month of MARCH, 1650, a patent was issued to THOMAS PARKER in ISLE OF WIGHT or NANSEMOND COUNTY for 380 acres and 50 acres that had been granted to PETER MONTAGUE, Feb. 25, 1638, and 40 acres for the transportation of a negro Francis. One of these patents recites that THOMAS PARKER had married the widow of PETER MONTAGUE. Boddie p. 239; Va. Mag. 6, 420-424.

It is fairly certain that JOHN THOMAS had the following children:

1. RICHARD THOMAS
2. WILLIAM THOMAS
3. JOHN THOMAS
4. ELIZABETH THOMAS
5. SARAH THOMAS
6. KATHERINE THOMAS.

WILLIAM THOMAS

JOHN BATTS and JOHN DAVIS patented lands at the head of QUEEN'S CREEK in York County, Virginia, April 2, 1639, using the names of WILLIAM THOMAS, RICHARD THOMAS and EDWARD MARSHALL in their list of headrights, while in 1636 CAPT. CHRISTOPHER WORMLEY obtained a patent in York County, using JOHN THOMAS and HENRY MARSHALL. Nugent p. 99. JOHN THOMAS had been living on Queen's Creek for some time when these patents were taken out. Nugent p. 73. WILLIAM THOMAS was living in YORK County in 1648, when by his affidavit evidence the nuncupative will of RICHARD MARSHALL was proven and spread on the court records of YORK COUNTY. Fleet 25 p. 96.

WILLIAM AP THOMAS, who died leaving a will in ELIZABETH CITY COUNTY, immediately below YORK COUNTY at the end of the peninsula, also came to YORK COUNTY, but in 1648 he patented 335 acres in Elizabeth City County, 100 acres of which he had previously purchased from MAJ. NICHOLAS HILL, who had lived there, a close neighbor to THOMAS WATTS and the THOMAS FAMILY before he moved to Isle of Wight County. ELIZABETH HILL married WILLIAM THOMAS. WILLIAM AP THOMAS was perhaps a cousin of JOHN, WILLIAM, RICHARD and PHILLIP THOMAS, and who used the prefix "AP" in signing his name, a throwback to the Welch origin of the THOMAS FAMILY. It was dropped by his children and grandchildren. JOHN ROBINSON, of YORK County was made the overseer of the will of WILLIAM AP THOMAS, and his daughter ANNE THOMAS married into the PARSONS family of York County. He had also purchased lands in York County from WILLIAM HAMPTON, many of whose descendants moved to Isle of Wight and intermarried with the related families of the other THOMAS tribe of QUEEN'S CREEK, who followed in the wake of the MARSHALLS and MAJ. NICHOLAS HILL and others.

WILLIAM THOMAS of QUEEN'S CREEK (above), while some of his sons settled in ISLE of WIGHT and NANSEMOND, moved to the upper Rappahannock section in WESTMORELAND and NORTHUMBERLAND COUNTIES, where his name was frequently used in the headright lists by persons who were previously identified with JAMES CITY and YORK COUNTY life. AMONG those who used the name was JOHN PROSSER, probably a son or relative of ISAAC PROSSER who had been transported by WILLIAM BODDIE before 1665, and ROBERT TALIAFERRO and LAWRENCE SMITH, who used WILLIAM THOMAS' name twice, and the names of HUMPHREY THOMAS, GILES LOVEIL, JAMES HARRISON and ROBERT and JOHN EDWARDS. This was in 1666. Nugent p. 548. In 1648 WILLIAM BARRETT used the names of SYMON and GABRIEL THOMAS in taking up lands on the East side of the CHICKAHOMINY RIVER. These were apparently some of his sons. Barrett also used the name of WILLIAM BATTS, probably a brother or son of JOHN BATTS who patented lands on QUEEN'S CREEK in York County in 1639. WILLIAM THOMAS had:

    10. WILLIAM THOMAS m. ELIZABETH HILL
    11. HUMPHREY THOMAS
    12. SYMON THOMAS
    13. GABRIEL THOMAS
    14. JOHN THOMAS
    15. PRISCILLA THOMAS m. HUMPHREY MARSHALL
    16. REBECCA THOMAS m. WILLIAM HARRISON
    17. ELIZABETH THOMAS m. ROBERT HILL

RICHARD THOMAS

JOHN DAVIS, who with JOHN BATTS in 1639 obtained a patent to certain lands in YORK County, Virginia, used the headrights of WILLIAM and RICHARD THOMAS and EDWARD MARSHALL, the latter perhaps the brother or uncle of RICHARD and HENRY MARSHALL. Nugent 107. But JOHN DAVIS had already used the name of RICHARD THOMAS in obtaining 100 acres of land fronting on ARCHER'S HOPE not far away four years prior to that time. Nugent page 25. He and his partner JOHN BATTS had probably made a tradeof some kind and DAVIS had preserved the RICHARD THOMAS headright in the deal and used it again in 1639, after having used it as his own in 1635 in securing the 100 acres on Archer's Hope. In the first application he stated that he had transported RICHARD THOMAS at his own expense. In the first application DAVIS declared that he himself was a servant of RICHARD PERRY, of LONDON, merchant.

RICHARD PERRY, of London, was the founder of the great mercantile house of PERRY, LANE & COMPANY, of London. His son HENRY was the son in law of the wealthy GEORGE MENIFEE, of Bucklands on the JAMES, and his son MICAJAH PERRY afterwards became the head of the London firm. JOHN DAVIS was perhaps a Sea Captain in charge of one of the PERRY owned vessels that plied between LONDON and Jamestown and brought over many emigrants. Captain DAVIS settled in Isle of Wight as did RICHARD THOMAS, while WILLIAM THOMAS located in Lancaster and Northumberland, though his children lived in Isle of Wight. GEORGE MENIFEE, the "Squire" of "Bucklands", the real show place on the JAMES, was from LONDON and a lawyer, and often represented PERRY, LANE & COMPANY in Virginia, as well as the HARRISONS of Surry County.

RICHARD THOMAS and his wife, whoever she may have been, probably were the parents of several sons and daughters, among whom were:

    38. RICHARD THOMAS
    39. JOHN THOMAS
    40. WILLIAM THOMAS

PHILLIP THOMAS

PHILLIP THOMAS lived on QUEEN'S CREEK in YORK COUNTY, evidently for many years, and was neighbor to JOHN, WILLIAM and RICHARD THOMAS, his brothers. JOHN THOMAS owned lands there before 1637, at the very inception of the actual settlement. Nugent, p. 73. The date of the using of an emigrant's headright is never a criterion of when he arrived in the colony. PHILLIP had already arrived in the colony by 1635, we know, as witness the following:

> WILLIAM HUNT, 800 acres at the head of BEAVERDAM BRANCH, a branch of the Western branch of NANSEMOND RIVER, December 14, 1635, for the transportation of sixteen (16) persons: PHILLIP THOMAS, EVAN THOMAS, SARAH THOMAS, THOMAS BATEMASON, ANNE JACKSON, HENRY MILES, FRANCIS COACH, JONATHAN LONGE, WILLIAM HUNT, MICHAEL MACKEEYE, MARY MATTHEWS, WILLIAM SCOTT and KATHERINE SCOTT. Nugent p. 238.

The foregoing extract from Nell Marion Nugent's CAVALIERS AND PIONEERS (p. 238) is a veritable mine of information, not only on the THOMAS FAMILY, but some of its connecting lines. But in transcribing the names from the old records, regardless of the care exercised, many mistakes have been made, and hidden behind these mistakes are CLUES of great value to the student which are often overlooked.

In ISLE OF WIGHT COUNTY, Virginia, in 1686, there died a very prominent personage, leaving a will whose name is in the list given above, though one would never suspect it were he not familiar with the names. MICHAEL MACKEEYE represents an imperfect transcription of the name of MICHAEL MacKINNIE, sometimes spelled on the old records McQUINNIE. In addition we get from this list the name of the wife of PHILLIP THOMAS, Sarah, who was probably SARAH McKINNIE, a sister of this MICHAEL; also the name of one son, EVAN THOMAS. From other Isle of Wight records, carefully weighed and measured for their significance we conclude that the family set-up of this, the first PHILLIP THOMAS, was as follows:

PHILLIP THOMAS m. SARAH McKINNIE, and had children:

30. EVAN THOMAS
31. JOSEPH THOMAS
32. MICHAEL THOMAS
33. ROBERT THOMAS
34. JOHN THOMAS
35. PHILLIP THOMAS
36. MOURNING THOMAS
37. PRISCILLA THOMAS

HUMPHREY SCOWEN

HUMPHREY SCOWEN was from YORK and ELIZABETH CITY COUNTIES. He perhaps lived near the line between the two counties. An early landmark on BACK RIVER in NEW POQUOSIN about at the line was "SCONE'S DAM" in 1639. (Nugent p. 111). The name is spelled SCONE in some of the older patents. HUMPHREY SCOWEN, or SCONE, retained and used his own headright, along with that of WILLIAM EDWARDS (Nugent p. 47). He was perhaps rather well to do. My conviction is that his daughter married JOHN MARSHALL and that HUMPHREY SCOWEN was the grandfather of HUMPHREY MARSHALL.

> In May, 1637, HUMPHREY SCOWEN sold one hundred acres of land to FRANCIS HOUGH on the South side of the NANSEMOND RIVER. Nugent, p. 55.

> August 29, 1638, HUMPHREY SCOWEN patented 300 acres adjoining MARGARET ROGERS in this same locality. Nugent, p. 96.

> A grant of 100 acres was obtained by HUMPHREY SCOWEN, September 16, 1636, for the transportation of himself and WILLIAM EDWARDS. (Probably the emigrant ancestor or father of ROBERT EDWARDS who married MARY HUNT and later OWEN GRIFFIN and WILLIAM BODDIE. Nugent, p. 47.

> In 1643, HUMPHREY SCOWEN and PETER RAY (One of my own ancestrial flock) owned lands at the head of the main branch of NEW TOWNE HAVEN —in other words that blot on the ancient maps called CHUCKATUCK. He used the headrights of WILLIAM and JOHN BURTON. See the WILLIAM HUNT sketch. Nugent p. 150.

> RICHARD BARTLETT patented lands "at the head of Chuckatuck" next to HUMPHREY SCOWEN and PETER RAY in 1645, and one the headrights used by Bartlett was BRYAN BURTON. Nugent, p. 160.

WILLIAM HUNT

WILLIAM HUNT patented 800 acres of land on the Western Branch of NANSEMOND RIVER in ISLE OF WIGHT COUNTY in 1636 and among the headrights used by him were those of PHILLIP THOMAS, EVAN THOMAS and SARAH THOMAS and MICHAEL MACKINNIE (Nugent p. 238).

JOSEPH CROSHAW, of QUEEN'S CREEK in YORK COUNTY, Virginia, was a neighbor of JOHN, WILLIAM, RICHARD and PHILLIP THOMAS, and on FEBRUARY 27, 1649, had attached to his application for lands he desired to patent "lying on York River, on the South side thereof, about eight miles above the fort", the names of RICHARD HILL, RICHARD SHARPE, JOHN CLARE and WILLIAM HUNT. This was fourteen years after WILLIAM HUNT himself had used the name of PHILLIP THOMAS, EVAN, his son, and SARAH, his wife, as headrights over South of the James River in ISLE OF WIGHT or NANSEMOND COUNTY. Nugent's Cavaliers and Pioneers, in its index and in its abstracts shows NINE persons named WILLIAM HUNT whose names were used as headrights by different persons. A study of those abstracts shows that most of them were the same person.

No authentic and identifiable list of the children of this WILLIAM HUNT has been found by this compiler, but there are items that point unmistakably to persons of the name who were apparently his sons, and we know that he had one daughter MARY HUNT. That WILLIAM HUNT was the father of GODFREY HUNT, who, himself, patented 600 acres of land in NANSEMOND COUNTY, Virginia April 5, 1664, abutting on the lands of one HOPKINS HOWELL and JOHN THOMAS, there is slight doubt in the mind of the writer. More than twenty years before, COEB HOWELL (1638) had used the name of WILLIAM HUNT in taking out a patent in the Lower County of New Norfolk. (Nugent pp. 90 and 492). There are clear references to a younger WILLIAM HUNT in numerous places on the ISLE OF WIGHT records, and found on the same records in after years are the names of DEMPSEY, JAMES, JOSHUA, PRUDENCE, RALF, SAMUEL, WILLIS and other Hunts, of all of whom it may be safely said, WILLIAM HUNT was the emigrant ancestor. The compiler feels safe in assuming that WILLIAM HUNT of this sketch was the father of the following persons of that name:

1. WILLIAM HUNT, JR.
2. COL. JOHN HUNT (Of N. C.)
3. GODFREY HUNT
4. HENRY HUNT
5. MARY HUNT.

DANIEL BOUCHER, Burgess for Isle of Wight in 1653-54, dieed leaving a will in 1667, in which he left lagacies to "kinsmen" ROBERT BOUCHER, HODGES COUNCIL, and WILLIAM and MARY, children of WILLIAM HUNT.

It was this daughter, MARY HUNT, who married (1) ROBERT EDWARDS (2) OWEN GRIFFIN and (3) WILLIAM BODDIE.

WILLIAM HUNT JR. is believed to have been the same person of the name who married TABITHA KILOE, and had GEORGE, JOHN, WILLIAM and MARY HUNT. This younger MARY HUNT married ROBERT MINGE, son of JAMES MINGE, the old Land Surveyor. She was born May 15, 1695, and by this, her first marriage, had two daughters TABITHA and MARTHA MINGE. TABITHA married HUTCHINS BURTON, who was evidently named for RICH'D HUTCHINS, son in law of JOSEPH COBB, and a neighbor on the Western Branch or Cypress Swamp of the HUNTS, BODDIES and COBBS. HUTCHINS BURTON was a son of NOEL HUNT BURTON, and the father of COL. ROBERT BURTON, of Granville County. He hung himself in the well of CEDAR WALK, the old BURTON HOME, on Nutbush in Granville County. He was the ancestor of the BURTONS of Mecklenburg County, Virginia, Granville County, N. C. and LINCOLN COUNTY, North Carolina, including JUDGE ROBERT H. BURTON of the old BUNCOMBE DISTRICT in Western North Carolina. After the death of ROBERT MINGE, the younger MARY HUNT (MRS. MINGE) married WILLIAM ALLEN, and by him had ANN, SAMUEL, WILLIAM HUNT ALLEN, JOHN ALLEN, VALENTINE ALLEN, G. HUNT ALLEN and MARY ALLEN. COL. ARCHER ALLEN, of the American Revolution, was a grandson of this younger MARY HUNT.

For more about the BURTON FAMILY see pp. 241-242, 423-423 of this volume.

HEADRIGHTS AS A SOURCE OF GENEALOGICAL INFORMATION ARE MISLEADING

Students of genealogy who depend upon "headrights" as a source of accurate information about their ancestors will meet with disappointment, for several reasons, unless they have such a keen sense of discernment that they can read between the lines.

When a person came to the colonies (particularly VIRGINIA) his coming entitled somebody to take up FIFTY ACRES OF LAND. If he paid his own passage that right was his own. It was his headright. He could assign or sell it for his fare over, or for a sum of money or tobacco, or for anything else of value. So could the person who acquired it. Headrights were bought and sold as a speculative venture. Some made it a business. Ship owners amassed fortunes that way, and merchants advanced goods and merchandies to obtain them.

Twenty such headrights paid for taking up 1000 acres of land. Often the person who took up the land decided that he wanted some other tract of land, some more land next to it, or land in lieu of it in a different location, shire or county. If so, he allowed the land to forfeit. This did not destroy his "headrights". The lands had reverted, but the headrights were still good. The same names, the same emigrants, even though many years had passed. (See bottom of next page).

HUMPHREY MARSHALL

HUMPHREY MARSHALL was born about 1630. He was the son of JOHN MARSHALL, who may have married a daughter of HUMPHREY SCOWEN. HUMPHREY MARSHALL'S will was proven in ISLE OF WIGHT COUNTY, VIRGINIA, in 1711. Many of his grandchildren moved to NORTH CAROLINA, where his descendants were legion.

JOHN THOMAS, the ancestor of the THOMAS FAMILY, owned lands in York County, Virginia as early as 1637 (Nugent, p. 73). In 1638 the headright of JOHN THOMAS and HENRY MARSHALL were used in taking up lands in YORK COUNTY (Nugent p 102). In 1639, JOHN DAVIS used the headrights of William and Richard Thomas and EDWARD MARSHALL when he patented lands on QUEEN'S CREEK in YORK COUNTY, Virginia. (Nugent, p. 107). In YORK COUNTY, VIRGINIA, in 1648, WILLIAM THOMAS by deposition proved the last will and testament of RICHARD MARSHALL. (Fleet's Abstracts No. 25, p. 96.)

These notes establish the early associations between the THOMAS and MARSHALL families in VIRGINIA. THOMAS HILL, JOHN HILL and NICHOLAS HILL were apparently brothers, (Nugent p. 353) and were kinsmen of the BLANDS and BENNETTS. THOMAS HILL perhaps lived in JAMES CITY or in YORK COUNTY. His brother, NICHOLAS HILL, who married SILVESTER BENNETT, lived in ELIZABETH CITY COUNTY (Nugent p. 175) but later moved to ISLE OF WIGHT, where he died leaving a will in 1674. WILLIAM THOMAS married his daughter, and HUMPHREY MARSHALL married WILLIAM THOMAS' sister, PRISCILLA THOMAS.

JOHN HILL settled in LOWER NORFOLK COUNTY at SEWELL'S POINT, where he was neighbor of CORNELIUS LLOYD, JOHN NORWOOD and the BENNETTS. His son JOHN HILL became Sheriff and was accused of persecuting the Quakers or dissenters. JOHN HILL died about 1647 and his brother THOMAS HILL was his administrator (Nugent p. 172). But among the persons whose headrights had been acquired by JOHN HILL, SR. were those of NICHOLAS SMITH (later Burgess) and JOHN MARSHALL, father of HUMPHREY MARSHALL (Nugent p. 172). JOHN HILL, who used the headright of JOHN MARSHALL, father of HUMPHREY MARSHALL, had a son ROBERT HILL, who married ELIZABETH THOMAS, (daughter of WILLIAM THOMAS) and sister of PRISCILLA, who married HUMPHREY MARSHALL, and ROBERT HILL and his wife ELIZABETH THOMAS had a son THOMAS HILL, who married MARY MARSHALL daughter of HUMPHREY and PRISCILLA (THOMAS) MARSHALL. Then, WIILLAM THOMAS, brother in law of HUMPHREY MARSHALL and ROBERT HILL, became the son in law of NICHOLAS HILL, uncle of ROBERT (m. Elizabeth Thomas) and JOHN HILL, the old Sheriff of LYNHAVEN PARISH in Lower Norfolk, below the BENNETT settlement.

This may all sound rather confusing, but it is comparatively simple, if carefully considered, and when understood will explain many of the complicated relationships that existed between the HILLS, MARSHALLS, THOMASES and other allied families of the CHUCKATUCK SETTLEMENT (OLD NEW TOWNE HAVEN) on the line of ISLE OF WIGHT and NANSEMOND COUNTIES, in early VIRGINIA.

It will be noticed that JOHN HILL, SR. who patented lands in The Tanner's Creek settlement in Lower Norfolk (Nugent 172) used the headrights of both JOHN MARSHALL and NICHOLAS SMITH. The fact that HUMPHREY MARSHALL, son of JOHN, in his old age, married ANNE, the widow of this same NICHOLAS SMITH is ample evidence that HUMPHREY MARSHALL was probably a grown man, or nearly so, at the time of this patent, 1646. He may even have been married then, to PRISCILLA THOMAS, because they had grandchildren by or around 1660, born to their daughter ELIZABETH, who had married RICHARD THOMAS, son of JOHN THOMAS, as hereafter shown.

HUMPHREY MARSHALL had a brother, JOHN MARSHALL, who left will in 1688, and whose son, ROBERT died leaving a will in 1689, ten years later, with surviving children, JOHN, ROBERT and HUMPHREY MARSHALL. The brother JOHN (will 1688) had other sons, among them being THOMAS MARSHALL, carpenter, ancestor of CHIEF JUSTICE JOHN MARSHALL, who moved up the Rappahannock and died leaving a will in 1704. (Fothergill, p. 38.) The MARSHALL FAMILY of KENTUCKY are also descendants of the JOHN, brother of HUMPHREY, of this sketch.

Thus it appears that if a land owner in those days became dissatisfied with his lands, even after many years, or wanted to exchange them for the title to other and more desirable lands in some other part of Virginia that were still open to settlement, he could allow his original patent to lapse and still PRESERVE HIS SAME HEADRIGHTS - the list of emigrants originally used, and if he could trade somebody out of them, or bring more into the colony, he could add these to the first list and enhance his acreage up on the RAPPAHANNOCK, the COROTOMON, or in HENRICO on the James or the appomattox - anywhere. In lieu of this he could sell his original grant to some planter who had a list of his own, preserve his old list, or secure the planter's list to use. Thus, these lists of emigrants were swapped back and forth, first in the hands of one planter, then years later used by another, and so on ad infinitum. This very clearly explains why a lone emigrant or two appear on so many different applications for patents. Thus, also, comes about the strange fact that JOHN THOMAS or HENRY HAMBLIN or some other person appears to have been "brought over" by some shrewd planter, whom he never saw or heard of in his life time, and who in fact had nothing whatever to do with his coming.

IT IS AN EMPTY FALLACY TO BELIEVE that when CAPT. SAMUEL MATTHEWS took up land, for instance, in NORTHUMBERLAND COUNTY, with a long list of headrights that the named headrights settled on that land or in that part of the colony. They may have located somewhere two or three hundred miles away. Anyway, don't waste time and money hunting them there. So called "Early Emigrant Lists" tend

THE LAWRENCE FAMILY

WILLIAM, JOHN, ROBERT and GILES LAWRENCE make their appearance on the ancient records of Colonial Virginia at about the same time and in the same locality. Every indication points to the fact that they were brothers. COL. WILLIAM BERNARD, who in 1642, patented 1200 acres of land at the head of LAYNE'S CREEK, founds his lands abutting on the lands of JUSTINIAN COOPER, ROBERT ELEY and ROBERT LAWRENCE. Two of the headrights, out of the 20 attached to his application for his land, plus FOUR HEADRIGHTS for himself, were JOHN GILES and JOHN LAWRENCE (Nugent p. 131). The 300 acres patented by WILLIAM LAWRENCE in 1643, next to THOMAS STAMP, extended North towards CHIPPOKES CREEK, and then lay in that part of JAMES CITY COUNTY, South of the JAMES in the same general locality (Nugent p. 144). The wife of WILLIAM LAWRENCE was JOANE. In 1647 WILLIAM LAWRENCE sold or assigned his rights to ROBERT WARREN (Nugent 183). In 1656 the names of WILLIAM LAWRENCE, MARY LAWRENCE, SARAH LAWRENCE, ANNE LAWRENCE and ARTHUR LAWRENCE were used as headrights by WILLIAM JUSTICE in CHARLES CITY COUNTY, near Flower de Hundred - still on the South Side of the JAMES RIVER, which circumstance gives us the names of the children of WILLIAM LAWRENCE and his wife JOANE, who was perhaps deceased at that time. (Nugent p. 339). Then in 1665, WILLIAM and JAMES LAWRENCE patented lands together in CHARLES CITY COUNTY adjoining DAVID JONES, thus indicating further that he had another son JAMES LAWRENCE. GILES LAWRENCE patented lands in NANSEMOND in 1651 (Nugent 221) and in 1664 PETER MONTAGUE was his attorney in Nansemond (Nugent p. 479).

Neither the dates of these patents, nor the date their names were used as headrights by others is any criterion whatsoever of the dates of their arrival in VIRGINIA. The record discloses that JOHN LAWRENCE came to VIRGINIA before 1638 (Nugent p. 102) and the others named were perhaps in the colony just as early.

ROBERT LAWRENCE belonged to the QUAKERS, or else was a Quaker sympathizer, because in a deposition or statement by THOMAS JORDAN, the famous Quaker Minister, made in JULY, 1661, he declared he had been persecuted

"by six weeks imprisonment for being taken at a meeting in my owne house and released by the King's proclamation, 2ndly taken at a meeting at ROBERT LAWRENCE and bound over to the court of Nansemond County", and he adds "taken by distress by THOMAS GODWIN, Sheriff, etc."

ROBERT LAWRENCE patented 200 acres in Isle of Wight County Sept. 12, 1644 (Nugent p. 155) next to the "Widow Bennett", and in partnership with ELLIS BROWN another patent in LOWER NORFOLK in 1644 (Nugent p. 156). His headright was used on several other occasions, some of them obviously repetitions, due to the switching of lands and the ownership of the headrights, and possibly, due to the fact that he may have made trips out of the country and returned, thus doubling his rights. The wife of ROBERT LAWRENCE in 1642, was ELIZABETH. No record of his death nor the maiden name of his wife has shown up in any record found. From extant records and deeds the names of FOUR SONS and one daughter have been tentatively if not positively identified. Other documentary evidence seem to make this list conclusive. They were:

1. ROBERT LAWRENCE
2. GEORGE LAWRENCE
3. HENRY LAWRENCE
4. JOHN LAWRENCE
5. ANN LAWRENCE m. JEREMIAH EXUM.

1. ROBERT LAWRENCE was twice married. His second wife was a widow, JANE GAY, her first husband being HENRY GAY, by whom she had at least two sons JOHN GAY and HENRY GAY. ROBERT LAWRENCE was granted lands on the West side of CHOWANOKE RIVER in North Carolina in 1663, at the same time and on the same date with other patents issued as shown in this record. ROBERT LAWRENCE and his first wife had several children, three of whom were:

10. ROBERT LAWRENCE m. SARAH EXUM
11. Daughter LAWRENCE m. HENRY GAY
12. Daughter LAWRENCE m. JOHN GAY.

The following record from ISLE OF WIGHT COUNTY in 1719 (Book 2 p. 291) applies to the relationships that existed between the son, 10. ROBERT LAWRENCE and other families in ISLE OF WIGHT COUNTY at that time: (See next page).

---

to irritate and confuse, instead of helping the student in search of ancestrial data and cause him or her to become discouraged. The object of this note is an attempt to clarify things.

These "Lists" are made up by a religious adherence to the names attached to each patent or grant, followed usually by the name of the person taking out the patent. As, has been explained, these lists were swapped and traded around and the same names often used over and over, sometimes by the person who first used them and sometimes by a different person altogether, who in some way obtained the right to them, after the persons listed had been in this country for maybe twenty-five years or more. The "lists" give no hint of these facts, and one finds the same person on the headright list of different planters in many parts of the Colony, so far as the land patented

"ROBERT LAWRENCE and SARAH, his wife; BARNABY McKINNIE and MARY, his wife; ELIZA EXUM; WILLIAM SCOTT and MOURNING, his wife; WILLIAM OUTLAND and JANE, his wife; CHRISTIAN NORSWORTHY and CATHERINE SCOTT, co-heirs to RICHARD EXUM, deceased, late of NANSEMOND COUNTY. To make an equal division of land of our brother, lately deceased, 200 acres on the head of INDIAN CREEK in the Western Branch of Nansemond, being part of an escheated patent formerly granted to JOHN McKINNIE, for 450 acres, April 20, 1694; the said 200 acres being formerly in the possession of MR. RICHARD EXUM, and adj. Indian Creek, MR. JEREMIAH EXUM'S line and HENRY GAY."

1. ROBERT LAWRENCE owned a plantation in 1704 exactly on the line of ISLE OF WIGHT and NANSEMOND, 400 acres being in one county and 400 in the other. (Quit Rent Rolls). He is said to have died in 1720, part of his will being illegible, so that the names of his children could not be descyphered. (Boddie p. 492.)

2. GEORGE LAWRENCE patented lands in 1680 on the Western Branch of Nansemond, next to his father ROBERT LAWRENCE and his brother JOHN LAWRENCE. Other records pertaining to him and his family have not been found.

3. HENRY LAWRENCE owned 200 acres of land in NANSEMOND COUNTY, Virginia, in 1704, and the records reveal the names of only three of his children:

        13. ISABELLA LAWRENCE m. THOMAS PAGE
        14. MICHAEL LAWRENCE
        15. THOMAS LAWRENCE

It has occurred to the compiler that the wife of 3. HENRY LAWRENCE may have been an ISABELLA PURSELL, sister of ARTHUR PURCELL, and also sister of SUSANNAH PURSELL who married WILLIAM EXUM. In 1710 ARTHUR WHITEHEAD married MARY GODWIN, a sister of MARTHA GODWIN who married JOHN COTTEN, and after her death he appears to have married second ISABELLA PURCELL, whose sister PATIENCE became the wife of the THIRD William Exum. (Boddie p. 453.)

    4. JOHN LAWRENCE patented lands in
       NORTH CAROLINA in 1663.

His North Carolina lands adjoined those of his brother 1. ROBERT LAWRENCE and were on the West side of "Chowanoke" river, which appears to mean in what afterwards became BERTIE COUNTY, West of the Chowan. JOHN LAWRENCE was a QUAKER, and from the Quaker Records it is shown that her name was MARY. This JOHN LAWRENCE and his wife MARY had a most interesting family. From Judge John Bennet Boddie's "Seventeenth Century Isle of Wight" we have the names of all his children (pp. 494-497). They were:

        20. PRISCILLA LAWRENCE m. MATTHEW WHITFIELD (Ancestors of many).
        21. MARY LAWRENCE m. JOHN THOMAS (She his second wife).
        22. JOHN LAWRENCE m. MARGARET MURPHY (Dau. of William Murphy).
        23. ANN LAWRENCE m. RICHARD EXUM (Son of JEREMIAH EXUM and 5. ANN LAWRENCE).
        24. ROBERT LAWRENCE m. ANN COUNCIL (He died in 1744).
        25. Daughter LAWRENCE m. HENRY SANDERS.
        26. Daughter LAWRENCE m. RICHARD TAYLOR.
        27. ELIZABETH LAWRENCE (d. in 1708, left her lands to her sister PRISCILLA).

21. MARY LAWRENCE who married JOHN THOMAS was his second wife, and apparently the marriage was a late one, and there were no children. This John was 100 JOHN THOMAS, grd-son of (4) JOHN THOMAS (See Chart of his family herein). 100. JOHN THOMAS was the son of 1. RICHARD THOMAS and his wife ELIZABETH MARSHALL. 1. RICHARD THOMAS had a brother 3. JOHN THOMAS, who, in turn had a son 105 JOHN THOMAS who married HANNAH (possibly Hannah Exum). By his first wife SUSANNAH PORTIS 100 JOHN THOMAS was the father of JOHN, RICHARD, WILLIAM, JOSEPH, PHILLIP, BARNABY and ELIZABETH THOMAS (She m. (1) JOHN BODDIE (2) JOHN DAWSON).

        Further light will be thrown on the LAWRENCE FAMILY by
        sketches of the EXUM, WHITFIELD, BRYAN, MURPHY and other fam-
        ilies, which will follow.

---

is concerned, and one wonders where on earth so many persons of the same name came from? If you have read what goes before in this note you should begin to see why.

NELL MARION NUGENT'S "Cavaliers and Pioneers", published in 1934, and still obtainable, gives these patent abstracts in full, and much other and additional information that may be gleaned from them. Because your ancestor's name appears on or attached to a patent away up in the NORTHERN NECK of VIRGINIA don't jump at the conclusion that the headrights or names of the persons attached to the patent SETTLED THERE. The owner of the patent may have done so, and sometimes some of the headrights, but never ALWAYS. Another thing to bear in mind is that the person whose name is used as a headright was not always a "servant". He may have paid his own passage in the splendor of the day and time, and lost his "headright" in a friendly poker game.

MICHAEL McKINNIE

DECEMBER 14, 1635, WILLIAM HUNT in taking out a patent to 800 acres of land on the Western Branch of the Nansemond River, claimed to have transported into the Colony of VIRGINIA at some time prior to that date, several persons, including PHILLIP, EVAN and SARAH THOMAS, and one MICHAEL McKINNIE. SARAH THOMAS may have been the wife of PHILLIP and a sister of MICHAEL McKINNIE. This MICHAEL McKINNIE and his wife ELIZABETH were the ancestors of a long line of McKINNIE descendants scattered through NORTH CAROLINA, SOUTH CAROLINA, GEORGIA, TENNESSEE, KENTUCKY, TEXAS and other Southern States. The wife of COL. NICHOLAS LONG, of Halifax County, North Carolina, was one of his grand-daughters, and many of the THOMASES were related to them, as well.

ELIZABETH, the wife of MICHAEL McKINNIE, who after his death in 1686, married second THOMAS REEVES or RIVES was perhaps ELIZABETH DANIEL, possibly a sister of JOHN DANIEL who died in ISLE OF WIGHT COUNTY leaving a will in 1679, with RICHARD REYNOLDS and PHILLIP THOMAS as the witnesses. The will of MICHAEL McKINNIE in 1686 was witnessed by JOHN MOORE, JEREMIAH EXUM and MARY DANIEL. When ELIZABETH REEVES died in BRUNSWICK COUNTY, Virginia, about 1730, her estate was administered by ROGER DANIEL and JOHN DANIEL.

PHARO COBB and OWEN GRIFFIN effected a division of the estate of JOHN DANIEL in ISLE of WIGHT COUNTY in 1680. After the death of this OWEN GRIFFIN his widow MARY HUNT, became the wife of WILLIAM BODDIE, whose son JOHN married ELIZABETH THOMAS. (See THOMAS CHARTS). The will of MICHAEL McKINNIE in 1686, shows that he had only two sons. They were:

    1. JOHN McKINNIE
    2. BARNABY McKINNIE.

DEPOSITION OF THOMAS REEVES, made December 9, 1701, fifteen years after the death of MICHAEL MacKINNIE, reads as follows:

"Declares that he is aged 52 years; that MICHAEL MacKINNIE was possessed of land and by his will gave the main plantation in Isle of Wight to his youngest son BARNABY. After his decease the land was found to escheat, and holding the land in his (THOMAS REEVES') custody by right of possession of his wife ELIZABETH, which her aforesaid husband MICHAEL MacKINNIE gave for her life time; but there was an agreement with JOHN McQUINNY that he should enter an escheat upon his brother's (BARNABY McKINNIE'S) land, in behalf of his brother BARNABY, because BARNABY was not (then) of age. ELIZABETH REEVES, aged 60, testified to the same. BARNABY MCKINNIE and wife MARY, on account of the decease of his brother JOHN, now sells the land to RICHARD EXUM." Witnessed by JAMES WEBB and JOHN COUNCIL. Boddie, pp. 644-645.

2. BARNABY McKINNIE married the widow of WILLIAM MURPHY, who was MARY EXUM, the daughter of JEREMIAH EXUM and his wife ANN LAWRENCE. They moved to BERTIE COUNTY, NORTH CAROLINA. Later their home fell in EDGECOMBE COUNTY, and still later in HALIFAX COUNTY. BARNABY McKINNIE became very wealthy and influential. His children were:

    10. BARNABY McKINNIE JR. (d. 1736)
    11. WILLIAM McKINNIE (d. 1739)
    12. JOHN McKINNIE (d. 1753)
    13. RICHARD McKINNIE (d. 1755)
    14. ROBERT McKINNIE
    15. ANNE McKINNIE m. WILLIAM MURPHY JR.
    16. MOURNING McKINNIE m. JOHN POPE
    17. PATIENCE McKINNIE m. JOSEPH LANE
    18. SARAH McKINNIE m. ISAAC RICKS.
    19. CHRISTIAN McKINNIE m. WILLIAM HURST
    20. MARY JANE McKINNIE m. JOHN BROWNE.

1. JOHN McKINNIE, the older brother of BARNABY married, but the name of his wife is unknown. From this marriage, however, came one son, MICHAEL McKINNIE, who married ROSE....? and on April 10, 1710, after he became of age, he and his wife executed the following deed:

RICHARD EXUM, of NANSEMOND COUNTY, deed from MICHAEL McKINNIE and ROSE, his wife, of Isle of Wight County, 200 acres on the WESTERN BRANCH of NANSEMOND in the County of Isle of Wight, being the land and plantation on which the grantor's grandfather MICHAEL McKINNIE lived, part of an escheated patent for 450 acres granted on April 20, 1692 to JOHN McKINNIE, father of said MICHAEL McKINNIE, part of this instrument. - Witnesses WILLIAM CRUMPLER and WILLIAM SCOTT.

WILLIAM SCOTT married MOURNING EXUM, daughter of JEREMIAH EXUM and his wife ANN LAWRENCE, parents of the wife of 2. BARNABY McKINNIE.

WILLIAM BODDIE

The first patent to lands in Virginia by WILLIAM BODDIE was issued in 1661 and was for 550 acres. This land was located in Isle of Wight County. He had perhaps been in the colony for some years at that time. On July 12, 1665 he obtained and enlarged patent signed by Sir William Berkeley consisting of 3350 acres, to which was attached the names of over fifty persons whose headrights he owned at the time, claiming fifty acres of land "for the transportation" of each person so named. Nugent pp. 475-476. Boddie pp 342-343.

A check of the list of names thus presented clearly indicates that WILLIAM BODDIE did NOT transport into Virginia, all of the persons whose names are on it. Like other well-to-do planters it would be more proper to say that he had "acquired" these headrights here and there, since he had taken out his first patent four years previously. For instance, the list contains the name of HENRY HUNT, whom we have identified as a son of WILLIAM HUNT, whose daughter MARY was the third wife of WILLIAM BODDIE. The Nugent Records show the name of HENRY HUNT's headright on a list presented by COL. WILLIAM CLAIBORNE in obtaining a large grant of land on the YORK RIVER in 1653. On the Claiborne list with HENRY HUNT appears the names of EDWARD BLOUNT, JOHN BENNETT, WILLIAM EDWARDS and JOHN ASKEW, all later prominent in ISLE OF WIGHT history. The name of HENRY HUNT, as well as MARY HUNT appears also in 1662 on a list of headrights presented by EDWARD SANDERS, in securing a patent to lands on the line of Lancaster and Northumberland Counties; and on this list appears also the names of JOHN SANDERS, ABRAHAM SANDERS, JOHN GOODWIN and the same JOHN BENNETT, mentioned above. All these persons were Isle of Wight settlers. In addition the name of HENRY HUNT appears in 1664 on the list of JOHN STOKELEY in Accomac, p 454, Nugent; Randolph Kirk, of Westmoreland 1665, Nugent, p. 546, and HUGH YEO, of Northampton patent (who went to Westmoreland and the Rappahannock) in 1655, and JOHN LEWIS in Gloucester patent 1663, Nugent, 484. Altogether by 1666, Henry Hunt's headright had been used no less than SEVEN TIMES, and his is just one of the more than fifty names on William Boddie's list traced.

There are three persons on the list named BODDIE - WILLIAM BODDIE, ANNE BODDIE and MARY BODDIE. Eleven headrights were used by WILLIAM BODDIE in 1661 in taking out his first patent, (Nugent p. 393), but none of these names were included - not even his own. John Bennett Boddie in his "Seventeenth Century" concludes that MARY BODDIE, named in the second list, was his daughter, who married JOHN BROWNE, and that ANNE was his first wife. This writer does not share in the first conclusion, but thinks that MARY was a sister of WILLIAM BODDIE, shown on page 339 of his own rare volume, and the one who married, first, THOMAS DIXON, and second HENRY MARTIN (Boddie p. 220), and to whose children WILLIAM BODDIE in 1678 deeded certain property. From this THOMAS DIXON family sprang the MOURNING DIXON, who married first, JOHN or JOSHUA CRUDUP, and second MICAJAH THOMAS, SR. (Chapman's Isle of Wight Marriage Records, p. 13.) The names of these DIXONS and MARTINS appear often on the early North Carolina records in conjunction with the THOMAS FAMILY, wherever you find them, as well as the BODDIES.

WILLIAM BODDIE'S first wife was ANNA, his second ELIZABETH and his third, MARY HUNT, daughter of WILLIAM HUNT, who, in 1635, patented lands on the Western Branch of Nansemond River, using the headrights of PHILLIP THOMAS, EVAN THOMAS, SARAH THOMAS and MICHAEL McKINNIE. This MARY hunt's first husband was ROBERT EDWARDS, her second was OWEN GRIFFIN and her third WILLIAM BODDIE.

THE DIXON AND MARTIN FAMILIES

ADAM DIXON and his wife ANN, his daughter ELIZABETH DIXON and his servant JOHN MARTIN all came to VIRGINIA in the MARGARET and JOHN in 1622. (Nugent p. 8). In 1626 ADAM DIXON was granted 100 acres in a patent at "WARRASCOYACK PLANTATION, continuing downward from HOG ISLAND 18 miles by the river side". THOMAS DIXON who died in 1670, married MARIE or MARY BODDIE, the sister of WILLIAM BODDIE. She was born May 18, 1635 (Boddie p. 339) By her first marriage with THOMAS DIXON, MARY BODDIE had THOMAS DIXON and HENRY DIXON. THOMAS DIXON, their father was the son of ADAM DIXON. After the death of THOMAS DIXON, MARY BODDIE became the wife of HENRY MARTIN, and they had at least one son, HENRY MARTIN. In 1678 WILLIAM BODDIE gave certain cattle to HENRY and MARY MARTIN'S three children, THOMAS DIXON, HENRY DIXON and HENRY MARTIN. (Boddie, p. 220). The following deeds are of interest in this connection:

In 1695 HENRY MARTIN and MARY, his wife, sold to HENRY APPLEWHITE 80 acres of land, which divided the land APPLEWHITE bought of EDWARD PALMER and MR. WILLIAM BODDIE. Richard Reynolds and THOMAS JOYNER were witnesses. (HENRY APPLEWHITE was son in law of HUMPHREY MARSHALL, his wife being ANN MARSHALL). (Boddie p. 625).

SEPTEMBER 2, 1697, HENRY MARTIN and his wife MARY sold JOHN THOMAS, of ISLE OF WIGHT COUNTY (L. P.) 100 acres for 99 years, on land of COL. SMITH and THOMAS PARNELL. (Boddie p. 630). (This was JOHN THOMAS who married HANNAH DAWSON, died in 1725).

HENRY MARTIN and his wife MARY March 25, 1797, of the Upper Parish of Isle of Wight sold ANN JONES land in the Lower Parish, next to WILLIAM BODDIE'S land. The witnesses were JOHN THOMAS (m. SUSAN PORTIS) ALEXANDER MATTHEWS (son of ELIZABETH BODDIE) and JOHN PORTIS (father in law of JOHN THOMAS).

THE COTTEN FAMILY

THE COTTEN FAMILY is another tribe that settled originally on QUEEN'S CREEK in YORK COUNTY, VIRGINIA, then shifted to ISLE OF WIGHT and NANSEMOND and finally poured its descendants of the third and fourth generations into the maw of OLD ALBEMARLE in NORTH CAROLINA.

REV. WILLIAM COTTEN, minister of HUNGAR'S PARISH in ACCOMAC COUNTY, if not the ancestor was a close collateral relative to the COTTENS who settled in YORK COUNTY. But for the fact that REV. COTTEN'S chronicler's wholly fail to refer to any children he had, save VERLINDA COTTEN, who married WILLIAM STONE, who became Governor of MARYLAND, we would say that JOHN, THOMAS and WILLIAM COTTEN, of York County, were his sons. REV. COTTEN married ANN GRAVES, daughter of the ancient planter, THOMAS GRAVES, who was without doubt the grandfather of RALPH GRAVES who married the daughter of JOSEPH CROSHAW, of Queen's Creek in York. MARTIN PALMER married the widow of CAPT. BENJ. CROSHAW, and in 1660 EDWARD PALMER, whose name appears often in the Isle of Wight Records, was a member of the Coroner's Jury in YORK COUNTY (D.& W. Book 8 p. 1) and in 1677 MARTIN PALMER served on the jury in YORK COUNTY in the case of JOHN COTTEN v. JOHN HARRIS, et al (Book 6 p. 26). JOSEPH CROWSHAW was the adjoining neighbor of JOHN, WILLIAM, PHILLIP and RICHARD THOMAS on Queen's Creek. (See their sketches). At a much earlier date JOHN COTTEN owned land on KING'S CREEK in ACCOMAC on the Eastern Shore in the immediate neighborhood of the HUNGAR'S PARISH CHURCH, of which REV. WILLIAM COTTEN was minister (Nugent p. 285). As late as 1861, WILLIAM DRUMMOND, afterwards appointed by Sir William Berkeley the first GOVERNOR OF OLD ALBEMARLE, N. C. used the headright of JOHN THOMAS and many prominent and wealthy notables, who are known never to have lived in Westmoreland County in taking up a patent to 4750 acres of land (Nugent pp. 403-4). Then again, on JANUARY 30, 1659, CAPT. FRANCIS WHEELER had died, and his estate was appraised by CHRISTOPHER HARRIS, ROBERT HARRISON, JOHN STAMPE and JOHN COTTEN. Christopher Harris was a wealthy planter, who eventually returned to England, where he died; ROBERT HARRISON married ELIZABETH COMINS, daughter of NICHOLAS COMINS, and was the ancestor of the HARRISONS of South of the James who married into the THOMAS FAMILY, and CAPT FRANCIS WHEELER had married the widow of NICHOLAS COMINS. JOHN STAMPE lived in York County at that time, but his brother or son, THOMAS STAMPE was the head of a prominent neighbor of WILLIAM BODDIE, the JORDANS, LAWRENCES, EXUMS and others, along CHUKKATUCK in Nansemond and Isle of Wight County. All of the appraisers and parties mentioned owned lands on QUEENS CREEK with JOHN THOMAS, NICHOLAS JERNEW, JOSEPH CROSHAW, the BENNETTS and HARRISONS in York, and it follows that JOHN COTTEN was also of that neighborhood. This compiler has no shadow of doubt but that the JOHN COTTEN, who married MARTHA GODWIN and left a will in BERTIE COUNTY, N. C. in 1728, was a son, nephew or other close relative of this QUEEN'S CREEK JOHN COTTEN.

RICHARD EXUM and THOMAS GODWIN, in 1650 patented 550 acres of land in what is now (it is said) ESSEX COUNTY, Virginia, using the headrights of eleven persons, among them being MORGAN THOMAS, RICHARD EXUM and WILLIAM COTTEN. (Nugent 197). In 1664, HENRY CORBIN used the headright of JACOB COTTEN. There was a JACOB COTTEN in North Carolina at the turn of the next century - possibly the same one. (Nugent 432). JOHN PROSSER in 1665 used JOANE COTTEN (Nugent 528) and the mother of REV. WILLIAM COTTEN was named JOANE. DAVID WILLIAMSON in 1666 used nearly everybody in Virginia as a headright in obtaining 6000 acres in Accomac, including THOMAS COTTEN and PETER COTTEN. (Nugent p. 554). Where these people listed by David Williamson settled nobody knows. They were perhaps all over the country. Many of the names are well known and familiar to research workers in Virginia history. As late as 1682 ARTHUR JORDAN used the headright of THOMAS COTTEN (Valentine 704). ANTHONY MATTHEWS in taking up a patent next to lands of EDWARD PALMER (See York notes above) in Isle of Wight County used the headright of a WILLIAM COTTEN (Looks like he just brought him across the JAMES RIVER, from YORK COUNTY). This ANTHONY MATTHEWS was probably the father of the ANTHONY MATTHEWS who married ELIZABETH BODDIE, the daughter of our old friend, WILLIAM BODDIE, of ISLE OF WIGHT COUNTY. (Nugent p 444). To me this WILLIAM COTTEN looks very much like the father of JOHN and THOMAS COTTEN who died in BERTIE COUNTY, NORTH CAROLINA. Their families were:

JOHN COTTEN (Will 1728)
m. (1) MARTHA GODWIN
Children: m. (2) MARTHA JONES

1. JOHN COTTEN
2. WILLIAM COTTEN
3. THOMAS COTTEN
4. SAMUEL COTTEN
5. JAMES COTTEN
6. ARTHUR COTTEN
7. JOSEPH COTTEN
8. ALEXANDER COTTEN
9. PRISCILLA COTTEN
10. SUSANNAH COTTEN
11. MARY COTTEN m. HOLLAND
12. MARTHA COTTEN m. FRANCIS BENTON
    Sons in laws:
    JOHN SPEARS
    CAPT. JOHN THOMAS.

THOMAS COTTEN m. SARAH DEW (d. 1753)
Ch: (Widow of WILLIAM BRIDGERS)

1. CHARLES COTTEN
2. ROBERT COTTEN
3. MARY COTTEN
4. MARTHA COTTEN m. JOHN SCOTT.
5. PATIENCE COTTEN
6. PRISCILLA COTTEN
   m. RICHARD WILLS.

SARAH BRIDGERS a half-sister of the above children, married 5. JAMES COTTEN, son of JOHN COTTEN, who died in 1728. The other BRIDGERS CHILDREN were WILLIAM, JOHN and JOSEPH BRIDGERS. JOHN DAWSON, RICHARD WILLS and JOHN SCOTT, witnessed above will.

CAPT. JOHN THOMAS married ANNE COTTEN, and his brother, 301 RICHARD THOMAS is believed to have married BARSHEBA WILLS sister of RICHARD WILLS who m. PRISCILLA COTTEN as shown above.

COL. JOHN DAWSON

COL. JOHN DAWSON, of BERTIE COUNTY, NORTH CAROLINA, married twice. His first wife was 206. ELIZABETH THOMAS, daughter of 100. JOHN THOMAS who married SUSANNAH PORTIS and MARY LAWRENCE; his second marriage was to CHARITY ALSTON, daughter of JOHN ALSTON.

In 1637 WILLIAM DAWSON was described as a "planter of Isle of Wight County, Virginia" (Nugent, p. 116) and JOHN DAWSON, probably his brother, apparently lived in YORK COUNTY, neighbor to JOHN THOMAS and his brothers, on QUEEN'S CREEK (Nugent, pp. 134 and 204). HENRY DAWSON in 1658 was used as a headright by WILLIAM LITTLE and JOHN HUDNALL. The widow of HUDNALL became the wife of EDWARD SANDERS. (Nugent, p. 372) Also "Early Settlers of Alabama" p. 340.

HENRY DAWSON, of Isle of Wight County, appears to have been a son of either JOHN or WILLIAM DAWSON of the above notes. He married MARTHA, who was heir at law and next of kin of one MARGERY SHEPARD, of WARWICK COUNTY. (Boddie p. 631). HENRY DAWSON was living as late as 1683, when WILLIAM BODDIE, whose son's widow married COL. JOHN DAWSON.

"Lets to HENRY DAWSON all woodland ground formerly let to Ambrose Hadley and with his wife MARTHA DAWSON and their *four* children, for as long as they shall live, to pay to BODDIE'S heirs 2 yards of Indian corn yearly, etc." June 22, 1683. Witnessed by JOHN JACKSON and JOHN BROWNE. (This JOHN BROWNE was the son in law of WILLIAM BODDIE). (Boddie p. 595)

Twenty years later MARTHA DAWSON, widow of HENRY DAWSON was still living, and the Isle of Wight records show that

"WILLIAM BODDIE and wife MARY sell to NICHOLAS CASEY the plantation where a widow woman, MARTHA DAWSON now dwells and woodland - 100 acres - where MARTHA DAWSON and three sons, HENRY DAWSON, JOHN DAWSON and MARTIN DAWSON now live, and will not sell away their rights during their life-time. June 6, 1703." (Boddie p. 650.)

WILLIAM BODDIE was solicitous about these DAWSONS for the reason that MARTHA DAWSON was MARTHA MARTIN, a sister of HENRY MARTIN, who married MARY BODDIE (her second husband) who was a sister of WILLIAM BODDIE. HENRY DAWSON and MARTHA MARTIN, it will be noticed in the first quotation above had FOUR CHILDREN, and in the second quotation only THREE SONS are named. The other child was a daughter, HANNAH DAWSON. HENRY DAWSON and MARTHA MARTIN had children:

1. HENRY DAWSON
2. JOHN DAWSON
3. MARTIN DAWSON
4. HANNAH DAWSON m. JOHN THOMAS.

May 2, 1698, MARTHA DAWSON "sick and weak" appointed her son HENRY DAWSON to be her attorney with respect to the lands received by her from MARGERY SHEPARD, of Warwick County, and this Power of Attorney was witnessed by JOHN PORTIS and JAMES MERCER. (Boddie p. 631). JOHN THOMAS, who married HANNAH DAWSON was a first cousin of the JOHN DAWSON who married SUSANNAH PORTIS, the daughter of this JOHN PORTIS. The JOHN THOMAS who married HANNAH DAWSON was the son of 3. JOHN THOMAS, ESQ., brother of 1. RICHARD THOMAS who married ELIZABETH MARSHALL. THE JOHN THOMAS (100) who married SUSANNAH PORTIS, was the father of ELIZABETH THOMAS who became the first wife of JOHN DAWSON, son of HENRY and MARTHA (MARTIN) DAWSON.

Note this item from Boddie's "17th Century Isle of Wight" p. 609:

APRIL 6, 1693, JOHN PORTIS gives to his daughter SUSANNAH THOMAS, wife of JOHN THOMAS land in the Upper Parish for life. SUSANNAH was the former wife of JOHN FRIZZELL, deceased, and if she dies before her son, WILL FRIZZELL is of the age of 18, then his grandson WILL FRIZZELL is to possess it. If WILL FRIZZELL have no heirs then to JOHN PORTIS' son, JOHN PORTIS, JR. Witnessed by JOHN BELL and JOHN and EDWARD PRIME.

JOHN THOMAS who married HANNAH DAWSON had two sons SAMUEL and RICHARD THOMAS (See Chart) who married ELIZABETH and ELEANOR SHEARER, daughters of JOHN SHEARER JR., and they had a brother JOHN SHEARER (Or Shearod) who died in NORTHAMPTON COUNTY, N. C. in 1751, making JOHN DAWSON his Executor. COL. DAWSON was therefore connected as a kinsman with the descendants of both 1. RICHARD THOMAS and his brother 3. JOHN THOMAS, ESQ., he, himself, having married ELIZABETH THOMAS, Richard's grand-daughter, while his sister, HANNAH married JOHN THOMAS, the son of 3. JOHN THOMAS, all of which is evidenced by the records above quoted. COL. JOHN DAWSON about 1732 or earlier moved to BERTIE COUNTY - later NORTHAMPTON - and served that District in the General Assembly, member of the Governor's Council, as a member of the SUPREME COURT and Colonel of a Regiment in the Spanish Alarm. He died in 1762. His son JOHN DAWSON JR. by his second wife, CHARITY ALSTON, was a member of the House of Commons from both Northampton and Halifax Counties.

SHEARER - PORTIS - DEW - BRIDGERS

GEORGE SHEARER. His headright was claimed by THOMAS HAMPTON, May 19, 1637 when he secured a patent to 700 acres of land on the NANSEMOND RIVER in the Upper Parish of New Norfolk (Nugent, p. 56). He was the father of JOHN SHEARER or SHEARARD who died in ISLE OF WIGHT COUNTY in 1706/7, and who was born about 1630.

WILLIAM PARNELL was a headright of JOHN WEST in 1651, when he patented 1550 acres of land in YORK COUNTY, VIRGINIA. He was the father of THOMAS PARNELL, whose wife may have been a sister of JOHN PORTIS. (Nugent p. 213.)

ALEXANDER PORTIS patented lands in LANCASTER COUNTY in 1654 with THOMAS WILLIAMS (Nugent page 299). He died in BERKELEY PRECINCT, N. C. in 1675 at the home of ANDREW ELLWOOD (See page 131, this Volume). He was probably the father of JOHN PORTIS, who married DEBORAH HARDY, and of the wife of THOMAS PARNELL.

COL. THOMAS DEW was in turn a member and Speaker of the House of Burgesses of the Colony of VIRGINIA, also a member of the Governor's Council from 1642 to 1660. He represented NANSEMOND COUNTY, VIRGINIA, in the House of Burgesses. He was a "planter" and became a QUAKER. He marrie ELIZABETH and died in YORK COUNTY, Virginia, sometime before 1691. He had a son, JOHN DEW, born in NANSEMOND COUNTY, Virginia, who married ELIZABETH SHEARER, daughter of JOHN SHEARER (or Sherrod).

COL. JOSEPH BRIDGER, of ISLE OF WIGHT COUNTY, VIRGINIA, married HESTER PITT, daughter of ROBERT PITT, Burgess with Col. BRIDGER. JOHN PITT, his wife's brother, married OLIVE HARDY, aunt of DEBORAH HARDY who married JOHN PORTIS. COL. JOSEPH BRIDGER disinherited his son JOSEPH BRIDGER, and his descendants changed the spelling to BRIDGERS. JOSEPH BRIDGER JR. died in 1713. WILLIAM BRIDGERS son of JOSEPH JR. (d. 1729 in BERTIE COUNTY, N. C.) had a son WILLIAM BRIDGERS who married SARAH DEW, grand-daughter of JOHN DEW and ELIZABETH SHEARER. After the death of WILLIAM BRIDGERS, SARAH (DEW) BRIDGERS married THOMAS COTTEN, brother of JOHN COTTEN, whose daughter ANNE COTTEN married 300. JOHN THOMAS. (See Chart).

1. JOHN SHEARER married daughter of THOMAS PARNELL
   and had:

   10. ALEXANDER SHEARER
   11. SUSANNAH SHEARER
   12. ROBERT SHEARER (d. 1727)
   13. JOHN SHEARER JR. married ELIZABETH
   14. ELIZABETH SHEARER m. JOHN DEW.

12. ROBERT SHEARER m. ELIZABETH, and had Children:

    20. ROBERT SHEARER
    21. ARTHUR SHEARER
    22. JOHN SHEARER
    23. WILLIAM SHEARER
    24. PRUDENCE SHEARER m. ARTHUR WILLIAMS.
    24. SUSANNAH SHEARER m. JOHN DEW JR.

12. ROBERT SHEARER'S will was witnessed by HENRY GRAY and JOSEPH BOONE.
    Will dated 1727 in CHOWAN PRECINCT, N. C.

13. JOHN SHEARER JR. died in ISLE OF WIGHT COUNTY, Virginia, in 1703.
    His wife was ELIZABETH and they had:

    30. JOHN SHEARER III (D. in NORTHAMPTON CO. N. C. 1752).
    31. ELIZABETH SHEARER married SAMUEL THOMAS.
    32. ELEANOR SHEARER married RICHARD THOMAS.

24. SUSANNAH SHEARER and her husband JOHN DEW, JR. were the parents of SARAH DEW, who married (1) WILLIAM BRIDGERS (2) THOMAS COTTEN, brother of JOHN COTTEN of BERTIE COUNTY, N. C. For their children see "THE COTTEN FAMILY"

SAMUEL THOMAS and RICHARD THOMAS were sons of JOHN THOMAS who married HANNAH DAWSON, and when 30. JOHN SHEARER III, died leaving a will in NORTHAMPTON COUNTY, N. C. in 1752/3, the inventory of the estate was taken by WILLIAM EXUM and FRANCIS EXUM and JOHN WILLIAMS, and he made his wife and COL. JOHN DAWSON the Executors. SAMUEL THOMAS and RICHARD THOMAS had a brother JACOB THOMAS who married MARY HARRISON, of Isle of Wight County.

When 330 JOSEPH THOMAS of BERTIE COUNTY made his will in 1757/8 and mentioned his son, JOSIAH and other children, he made THOMAS WHITMELL and ARTHUR WILLIAMS, son in law of 12. ROBERT SHEARER, his Executors.

JOHN WILLIAMS, who appraised and inventoried the estate of JOHN SHEARER III, the brother in law of SAMUEL and RICHARD THOMAS, was the father of ARTHUR WILLIAMS, the Executor of 330. JOSEPH THOMAS.

THE HARDY FAMILY

Among the flock of people who went down into OLD ALBEMARLE from Isle of Wight County, VIRGINIA, were innumerable members of the HARDY FAMILY.

The ancestor, or first of the name, of this family was a certain GEORGE HARDYE, shipwright who made an assignment of lands to PETER HAYES, planter, in Isle of Wight County on February 11, 1636. He was a Burgess from Isle of Wight County in 1641 until his death about 1654/5. In his will he mentioned a THOMAS and GEORGE HARDY, his "kinsmen". The first GEORGE HARDY, however, acquired the property known as "HARDY'S MILL" on Lawne's Creek, from one EDWARD BRUCE, the ancestor of all the BRUCE FAMILY afterwards found on the records of Isle of Wight and other parts and sections of VIRGINIA.

APRIL 15, 1646. EDWARD BRUCE deeds GEORGE STEVENS, JOHN WATKINS and GEORGE HARDY, for 17,500 pounds of tobacco, one Water Mill at the head of LAWNE'S CREEK, with housing, land, etc. Witnessed by JOHN HAMMOND, JAMES BREWER and STEPHEN WEBB.
--Vol. 7. Wm. & Mary Mag. p. 227.

After the death of the first GEORGE HARDY, one of the grantees in the above deed, this property fell into the hands of the "kinsman" GEORGE HARDY, mentioned in the will, who in 1663, according to Bell's Old Free State, Vol. II p. 218, married MARY JACKSON, daughter of one RICHARD JACKSON and his wife MARY BENNETT. The second GEORGE HARDY was a son of JOHN HARDY, who, according to Bell (p. 216) was born in 1613 and died in 1670, whose family chart is like this:

JOHN HARDY (b. 1613) married OLIVE COUNCIL in 1632, and had children:

    1. JOHN HARDY m. ALICE. (Will in 1676)
    2. OLIVE HARDY m. COL. JOHN PITT of Isle of Wight County.
    3. GEORGE HARDY (1633-1693) m. MARY JACKSON
    4. RICHARD HARDY.

1. JOHN HARDY and his wife ALICE were the parents of:

    10. OLIVE HARDY m. (1) GILES DRIVER (2) JOHN BROMFIELD.
    11. LUCY HARDY m. HODGES COUNCIL
    12. ANN HARDY m. ROBERT BURNETT (He m. (2) JOAN (ALLEN) WILLIAMSON.
    13. ISABEL HARDY m. WILLIAM MAYO.
    14. DEBORAH HARDY m. JOHN PORTIS

11. LUCY HARDY and her husband HODGES COUNCIL were parents of:

    20. CHRISTIAN COUNCIL m. EDWARD BRYAN
    21. LUCY COUNCIL m. RICHARD WOOTEN
    22. ROBERT COUNCIL
    23. HARDY COUNCIL
    24. JOHN COUNCIL m. the widow of RICHARD JEFFREYS.
    25. HODGES COUNCIL, JR.

EDWARD BRYAN and his wife CHRISTIAN COUNCIL were the ancestors of most, if not all of the persons named BRYAN who left ISLE OF WIGHT COUNTY, VIRGINIA, and went down into OLD ALBEMARLE COUNTY, NORTH CAROLINA.

If the reader will turn back to pages 56 and 57, the Index and Digest to Hathaway's section of this volume, he will find considerable information in regard to the HARDYS who went down into North Carolina. Also see Bell's "Old Free State" Vol. II p. 216.

THE EDWARDS FAMILY

ROBERT EDWARDS was the first husband of MARY HUNT, the daughter of WILLIAM HUNT, who obtained lands on the Western Branch of Nansemond River in 1635 with the headrights of PHILLIP, EVAN and SARAH THOMAS and MICHAEL McKINNIE, in 1635 (Nugent, p. 238). Her second husband was OWEN GRIFFIN. Her third husband was WILLIAM BODDIE, which last marriage took place about 1700. JOHN BODDIE, son of WILLIAM, married ELIZABETH THOMAS. ROBERT EDWARDS and MARY HUNT had several daughters. Two of them married JAMES BRAGG. After JAMES BRAGG died she married THOMAS ROBERTS, about 1674/5. Her name was ELIZABETH. Bragg had first married her sister MARY ROBERTS, and after she died he married her sister ELIZABETH EDWARDS. EDWARD PALMER and ELIZABETH ROBERTS in June 1675 witnessed assignment of THOMAS BARNES to WILLIAM BODDIE. WILLIAM THOMAS, brother of ELIZABETH, who married JOHN BODDIE, had a son JOHN THOMAS who married CHRISTIANA ROBERTS, about 1732. CHRISTIANA ROBERTS was born about 1713 in NANSEMOND COUNTY, VIRGINIA. THOMAS ROBERTS and his wife ELIZABETH (EDWARDS) ROBERTS were probably the parents of THOMAS, JOHN and JAMES ROBERTS, one of whom would be the father of CHRISTIANA ROBERTS, who married 324.REV. JOHN THOMAS, in NANSEMOND COUNTY, VIRGINIA, who died in 1788 in EDGECOMBE COUNTY, NORTH CAROLINA. (See Chart of "100. JOHN THOMAS AND HIS FAMILY".)

See also sketch of WILLIAM HUNT.

THE ROBINSON FAMILY

On page 146 of this volume there is quite an extensive note on the ROBERTSON FAMILY and since that was written the compiler has discovered further evidence which is quite convincing that the ROBERTSON FAMILY of that note were of the same family as the ROBINSON FAMILY of this one. The suggestion is made that, after reading this note, it be compared with the one on page 146. JONATHAN ROBINSON, JOHN SANDERS and RICHARD THOMAS patented lands in NANSEMOND COUNTY, Virginia in 1681. The wife of JONATHAN ROBINSON was SARAH THOMAS, sister of RICHARD THOMAS, and this JONATHAN ROBINSON appears to have been still living in 1703, so that it is doubtful if he was the JONATHAN ROBINSON who owned land on the Western Branch of Nansemond River nearly 50 years prior to his death, adjoining lands patented by JOHN SYMONS or SIMMONS. On the Chart of (4) JOHN THOMAS father of RICHARD THOMAS and the father in law of JONATHAN ROBINSON it is shown that the children of JONATHAN ROBINSON and his wife SARAH THOMAS were WILLIAM, JOHN, JONATHAN and ARCHELAUS ROBINSON. This is not conclusive, and there may have been more children. For the first mention of JONATHAN see (Nugent p. 327). On page 142 of this record (volume) will be found several notes in regard to this family from the North Carolina records, including the patent to lands by JOHN ROBINSON in 1714, which he appears to have sold to RICHARD TAYLOR, a brother in law of JOHN THOMAS No. 100. Also deeds to JAMES BLOUNT, HENRY BOND, JOHN SKINNER and others from NANSEMOND and ISLE OF WIGHT which is sufficient to identify him as a son of JONATHAN. In his will in 1720 he mentions MARGARET, GEORGE and ELIZABETH. JONATHAN ROBINSON's wife had an uncle MARK THOMAS, and the name MARK and JONATHAN both appear in the ROBERTSON FAMILY note on page 146. Here was the ancestor perhaps of the JOHN ROBERTSON who lived in BRUNSWICK COUNTY, VIRGINIA, where he married MARY GOWER and became the father of GENERAL JAMES ROBERTSON, (Of Nashville, Tennessee, fame) who had a brother, MARK ROBINSON (killed by Indians) and a son JONATHAN ROBINSON (who met the same tragic fate. Strong color is loaned to this theory by the fact that when JOHN ROBERTSON, father of GENERAL JAMES ROBERTSON died in NORTH CAROLINA, the guardian of his younger children was MICHAEL ROGERS, a son of JOSEPH ROGERS who left will in NORTHAMPTON COUNTY, N. C. in 1752. RICHARD THOMAS, a son of 100 JOHN THOMAS married a daughter of MICHAEL ROGERS (an older one) back in NANSEMOND COUNTY, Virgina, from whence the THOMAS, ROBINSON and ROGERS family came to North Carolina. GEN. JAMES ROBERTSON married CHARLOTTE REEVES, a descendant of THOMAS REEVES, who married ELIZABETH, the widow of MICHAEL McKINNIE. See "The McKinnie Family" herein. The ROBERTSONS who appear on the tythe lists of LUNENBURG COUNTY, I am sure, were of this same tribe.

THE CRUDUP FAMILY

WILLIAM GODWIN, of the LOWER PARISH, acknowledges receipt of legacies left to ELIZABETH WRIGHT by the will of her father, THOMAS WRIGHT, September 6, 1666. Witnesses, JOHN MARSHALL and BARNETT CRUDUP. - Boddie's 17th Century Isle of Wight p. 545.

The WILLIAM GODWIN, of the above note was the father of MARTHA GODWIN, who married JOHN COTTEN, who died in BERTIE COUNTY, N. C. in 1728. The JOHN MARSHALL mentioned was brother of HUMPHREY MARSHALL. BARNETT CRUDUP was perhaps the father of JOHN or JOSHUA CRUDUP who married MOURNING DIXON, who after her first husband died, married MICAJAH THOMAS. MOURNING DIXON was a daughter of THOMAS DIXON, the son of THOMAS DIXON, whose mother was MARY BODDIE, a sister of WILLIAM BODDIE. WILLIAM BODDIE was therefore the brother of the grandmother of MRS. MOURNING CRUDUP who married MICAJAH THOMAS, SR. as her second husband.

MOURNING DIXON was related also to COL. JOHN DAWSON, who married the widow of the only son of WILLIAM BODDIE - ELIZABETH THOMAS. After the death of Mourning Dixon's grandfather, THOMAS DIXON, his widow married HENRY MARTIN, whose sister MARTHA MARTIN married HENRY DAWSON and was the mother of COL. JOHN DAWSON.

It was this MARTIN FAMILY that married into the MARSHALL FAMILY, and whose representative ABRAHAM MARTIN, after marrying a MARSHALL moved to South Carolina, where his descendants became rather prominent. The intermarriage between the Marshalls and the Martins probably occurred in Isle of Wight County, Virginia.

It was this DAWSON FAMILY who furnished the HENRY DAWSON who moved to AMELIA COUNTY, VIRGINIA, and from there, he or his children, to GREENE COUNTY, GEORGIA, where WILLIAM C. DAWSON became UNITED STATES SENATOR. Space prevents a detailed account of this interesting branch of the family at this time. I have stood in the portal of the old WILLIAM C. DAWSON home in the town of Greensboro, owned at one time by a member of the COBB FAMILY (more off-shoots of early Isle of Wightians) and, if I mistake not, also of the TORRENCE FAMILY.

For more information about the DAWSON FAMILY of N. C. see pages 54 and 55.

FOR more information about the MARTIN FAMILY of North Carolina, turn back to pages 101 and 205 of this volume.

DIXON MATERIAL on page 56.

THE BARRETT FAMILY

In 1689 in YORK COUNTY, VIRGINIA, Hon. Nathaniel Bacon received a deed to certain indentured servants, including an Indian boy, from EDWARD THOMAS. This deed was witnessed by WILLIAM BARRETT and WILLIAM DAVIS. In 1648 a WILLIAM BARRETT used the headrights of SIMON and GABRIEL THOMAS in taking up lands East of the CHICKAHOMINY (Nugent). These notations disclose a positive connection between the BARRETT and THOMAS FAMILY in the earliest years of the seventeenth century in VIRGINIA. The fact that in BERTIE COUNTY, and EDGECOMBE, in the next century there was a THOMAS and a BARRETT family, who were in some way related, is therefore not at all surprising. A Barrett family and a THOMAS FAMILY lived on PIGBASKETT Creek (sometimes called Braswell's Creek) in NASH COUNTY. On April 4, 1777, MICAJAH THOMAS, "of Nash County, North Carolina" sold a tract of land to JAMES DANIEL on the North side of PIGBASKETT, or Braswell's Creek. On May 2, 1786, JAMES DANIEL, of Nash County, sold a part of this same land, which he had purchased of MICAJAH THOMAS to JOHN BARRETT. James Daniel also sold some of this land to FREDERICK DANIEL in 1779. In 1787 this James Daniel bought 200 acres of land farther down in Nash County "on the waters of Tosnet Creek. About that time JAMES DANIEL died and left a will. NATHAN BARRETT witnessed the deed of JAMES DANIEL to JOHN BARRETT in 1786. JOHN BARRETT came from Southampton County, Virginia. Some of these BARRETTS probably lived in FRANKLIN COUNTY along the Tar River, and a certain DAVID BARRETT, who moved to Sumner County, Tennessee, and there intermarried with the THOMAS FAMILY, was doubtless from this stock. Space precludes an extended account of these connections, which the interested student will be quick to understand.

WEST FAMILY OF BEAUFORT COUNTY, N. C.

In the Indian uprisings that preceded the rise and fall of young NATHANIEL BACON along the JAMES RIVER in Virginia, a certain HENRY WEST was killed, and his son WILLIAM WEST joined BACON in his so-called "rebellion", after which, to escape the wrath of Sir William Berkeley he was forced to leave the country. About 1668 -before the rebellion - this WILLIAM WEST married REBECCA, the daughter of ROBERT BRASWELL. Evidently he had been pardoned, and settled in NEWPORT PARISH in ISLE OF WIGHT COUNTY (Boddie, p. 263). This WILLIAM WEST, according to JUDGE BODDIE, left will in 1708 in which his wife was mentioned as MARTHA, and his children as RICHARD, WILLIAM, ROBERT, REBECCA and MARY, the wife of WILLIAM GREEN. I think the great number of persons whose names appear on the Isle of Wight records that apparently belonged to this particular West family has confused those who have worked on the problem, and that it is not improbable that the WILLIAM WEST who died and left will in 1708 with wife MARTHA was WILLIAM WEST, JR. who witnessed a deed of Walter Rutten with JOHN BROWNE - William Boddie's son in law - in 1688. More than likely the children of the "Rebel" William West were HENRY, NICHOLAS, WILLIAM and ROBERT. This writer has many abstracts from the Isle of Wight records, but space will not permit their use in this sketch. In 1690 HENRY WEST and JOHN PORTIS - father in law of JOHN THOMAS - patented 900 acres of land in Isle of Wight, and the same year WILLIAM WEST, WILL GODWIN (father in law of JOHN COTTEN) and WALTER and JEREMIAH RUTTER are all mentioned together. Another WILLIAM WEST, probably a son of WILLIAM WEST JR. died leaving a will in Isle of Wight in 1719. Only one son, THOMAS WEST is mentioned, and daughters SARAH, ELIZABETH and MARY and son in law JOHN WILLIAMS. ISAAC and ISRAEL WEST of this family went to NORTHAMPTON and HALIFAX COUNTY, N. C., and ELIZABETH WEST, daughter of ISAAC married JAMES DANIEL, who bought lands on PIGBASKET CREEK in Nash County, from MICAJAH THOMAS. ISRAEL WEST died leaving property to JAMES DANIEL'S children. WILLIAM WEST and HENRY WEST settled in BEAUFORT DISTRICT, NORTH CAROLINA, and in 1741, WILLIAM sold lands on Seacock Swamp in Isle of Wight County, and south side of main Blackwater swamp to THOMAS BROWNE of Isle of Wight. WILLIAM died in Beaufort leaving will in 1744, and HENRY died in BEAUFORT laving will in 1752. In HENRY'S will he mentions sisters MARY SOJOURNER, SARAH PEYTON, CELIA TYNES, nephew JOHN PAYTON and niece HOLLAND APPLEWHITE. HENRY WEST of this last will was the son of WILLIAM WEST, of the first will, and his Executer. The wife of WILLIAM WEST was SUSANNAH.

SOME WEST AND BARRETT MARRIAGES IN SOUTHAPTON COUNTY, VA.

MARTHA WEST m. ETHELRED HOLT. JAMES DAUGHTRY, Sec. June 14, 1781.
WILLIAM WEST m. CRISSEY BARRETT, BURWELL BARRETT, Sec., Nov. 11, 1793.
JESSE J. WEST m. JANE NEWSOM, May 31, 1834.
JAMES C. WEST m. MARTHA DARDEN, JESSE T. WEST and TALBOT G. WEST, Feb. 15, 1830.
SCUTCHIN WEST m. MARTHA FOWLER, July 7, 1831.
SALLY WEST m. HYRAM FAISON. She was the daughter of WILLIAM WEST. Sept. 21, 1829.
JESSE J. WEST m. LAVINNEY BRYANT, WILLIAM BRYANT, Sec. April 19, 1828.
JESSE B. WEST m. MARY B. POPE. ANDERSON POPE, Sec. March 22, 1827.
JESSE J. WEST m. LUCY NEWTON, daughter of WILLIAM NEWTON, March 21, 1823.
MOURNING WEST m. JONAH W. CATHON, Feb. 1, 1795.
JAMES WEST m. LUCY TRAVIS, Nov. 27, 1800.
PATHEY B. WEST m. DANIEL BOYKIN, July 18, 1811.
ELIZABETH WEST m. BENJAMIN TRAVIS, consent of WILLIAM WEST, May 16, 1814.
MARTHA WEST m. SOLOMON BRETT (daughter of JOHN J. WEST) June 2, 1823.
LUCY WEST m. THOMAS DAVIS (daughter of WILLIAM WEST) May 13, 1823.
ELIZABETH BARRETT m. JAMES C. WEST; RICHARD DARDEN and BENJ. B. WEST, Dec. 31, 1829.
BURWELL BARRETT, Sec. for POLLY WEST m. JOSHUA BARNES, Feb. 4, 1818; also for NANCY WEST m. WILEY LANE and JAMES WEST m. DIANA POND; all married in 1818.

CHART OF THE THOMAS FAMILY
OF VIRGINIA AND NORTH CAROLINA

JOHN THOMAS AND WIFE DOROTHY
[Nugent pp. 185-186]

Came to YORK COUNTY VIRGINIA from BERMUDA ISLANDS with SERGEANT SAMUEL SHARPE in 1610. Settled on QUEEN'S CREEK, YORK COUNTY.
Nugent pp. 45, 73, 102, 128, 171, 144, 185, 186, 220 & 267

(As the JOHN THOMAS who came to VIRGINIA with Sergeant SAMUEL SHARPE was probably of age in 1610, he was born perhaps by 1585, and the four THOMASES who settled around h'm later are believed to have been his sons. The JOHN THOMAS who patented lands in NANSEMOND 1654 is believed to have been his son).

Had four sons who also came to YORK COUNTY and settled for a time, and then removed to ISLE of Wight.
Fleet's Va. Abs. Vols 24-25, and Nugent as cited opp.

THE FOUR SONS OF JOHN THOMAS AND THEIR CHILDREN WERE:

(1) WILLIAM THOMAS
10. WILLIAM THOMAS
 m. ELIZABETH HILL
11. HUMPHREY THOMAS
12. SYMON THOMAS
13. GABRIEL THOMAS
14. JOHN THOMAS
15. PRISCILLA THOMAS
 m. HUMPHREY MARSHALL
16. REBECCA THOMAS
 m. WILLIAM HARRISON
17. ELIZABETH THOMAS
 m. THOMAS HILL

(2) RICHARD THOMAS
38. RICHARD THOMAS
39. JOHN THOMAS
40. WILLIAM THOMAS

A FIFTH SON - MARK THOMAS - IS UNTRACED

(3) PHILLIP THOMAS
30. EVAN THOMAS
31. JOSEPH THOMAS
32. MICHAEL THOMAS
33. ROBERT THOMAS
34. JOHN THOMAS
35. PHILLIP THOMAS
36. MOURNING THOMAS
37. PRISCILLA THOMAS

(4) JOHN THOMAS
1. RICHARD THOMAS
 m. ELIZABETH MARSHALL
2. WILLIAM THOMAS
3. JOHN THOMAS
4. ELIZABETH THOMAS
 m. JOHN SAUNDERS
5. SARAH THOMAS
 m. JONATHAN ROBINSON
6. KATHERINE THOMAS
 m. THOMAS OGLETHORPE

DESCENDANTS OF (1) WILLIAM THOMAS

10. WILLIAM THOMAS married ELIZABETH HILL, the daughter of MAJ. NICHOLAS HILL and his wife SILVESTER BENNETT. With the exception of a son JOHN THOMAS their children are unidentified.

11. HUMPHREY THOMAS, 12. SYMON THOMAS and 13. GABRIEL THOMAS. WILLIAM THOMAS, the father and HUMPHREY THOMAS were used as headrights by ROBERT TALIAFERRO and LAWRENCE SMITH in 1666, and SIMON and GABRIEL were used by WILLIAM BARRETT in 1648. Nugent 175 and 548. The BARRETTS intermarried with the THOMAS FAMILY in both Virginia and North Carolina. 14. JOHN THOMAS is unidentified on the various JOHN THOMAS RECORDS at this writing.

15. PRISCILLA THOMAS was the first wife of HUMPHREY MARSHALL who died in 1711 in Isle of WIGHT County, and the mother of all his children. His second wife was MRS. ANN SMITH relict of COL. NICHOLAS SMITH, Burgess from Isle of Wight with MAJ. NICHOLAS HILL in 1660.

16. REBECCA THOMAS married WILLIAM HARRISON, the father of JOHN HARRISON who married MILBOROUGH BRESSIE, daughter of the old Quaker, WILLIAM BRESSIE, who was one of the trustees of the will of MAJ. NICHOLAS HILL in 1674, and whose wife was a sister of REV. ROWLAND JONES, Rector of old BRUTON CHURCH in Williamsburg, grandfather of GIDEON MACON, of North Carolina. These were the ancestors of the mysterious PRINCE GEORGE HARRISONS whose ancestry has been clouded for a century.

17. ELIZABETH THOMAS married THOMAS HILL, and one of their sons, THOMAS HILL, married his cousin MARY MARSHALL, daughter of HUMPHREY MARSHALL and PRISCILLA HILL.

DESCENDANTS of (2) RICHARD THOMAS

At this writing the compiler has been unable to identify any data on the records which can be said to apply with certainty to the descendants of RICHARD THOMAS. They are therefore omitted.

DESCENDANTS OF (3) PHILLIP THOMAS

The writer is convinced that the wife of PHILLIP THOMAS was SARAH McKINNIE, a sister of MICHAEL McKINNIE, as the names MOURNING and PRISCILLA are to be found often in the McKINNIE FAMILY and PHILLIP and EVAN THOMAS and MICHAEL McKINNIE were all used as headrights in 1635 by WILLIAM HUNT, the head of an old ISLE OF WIGHT FAMILY. Nugent p. 238. Innumerable deeds and instruments appearing on the old records of Isle of Wight strongly indicate such relationship, which tendency is augmented by the continuing intimacy that existed between the two families. With sufficient time to expend I feel sure that this relationship and the various details of the PHILLIP THOMAS family could be worked out. Both families drifted to North Carolina.

(4) JOHN THOMAS AND HIS DESCENDANTS

1. RICHARD THOMAS
married
ELIZABETH MARSHALL (Daughter of HUMPHREY MARSHALL, of I. of W. Co.
had

100. JOHN THOMAS m. (1) SUSANNAH PORTIS
     m. (2) MARY LAWRENCE.
101. PHOEBE THOMAS m. JOHN WINBORNE.
102. SARAH THOMAS (Prob. died young).
103. ELIZABETH THOMAS never married.

100. JOHN THOMAS had children:

200. JOHN THOMAS
201. RICHARD THOMAS
202. WILLIAM THOMAS   m. MARTHA ROBINSON
203. JOSEPH THOMAS   m. ALICE....
204. PHILLIP THOMAS   m. ANNE.....
205. BARNABY THOMAS   m. MARY.....
206. ELIZABETH THOMAS
        m. (1) JOHN BODDIE
        m. (2) JOHN DAWSON

2. WILLIAM THOMAS m. (1) CHRISTIAN
had: m. (2) PRISCILLA

115. JOHN THOMAS
116. WILLIAM THOMAS
117. HENRY THOMAS
118. BARSHEBA THOMAS
119. ANN THOMAS
120. JANE THOMAS m. ... LATEN
121. MARY THOMAS

4. ELIZABETH THOMAS who married JOHN SAUNDERS

106. ROBERT SAUNDERS
107. HENRY SAUNDERS m. LAWRENCE
     (Sister of MARY, the wife of
     100. JOHN THOMAS.

107 HENRY SAUNDERS had children:

208. RICHARD SANDERS
209. ISAAC SANDERS

209. ISAAC SANDERS had daughter:

316. ELIZABETH SANDERS m. 327 SAMUEL
     THOMAS, son of 202. WILLIAM THOMAS

SEE EXPLANATORY NOTES THAT FOLLOW

3. JOHN THOMAS, ESQ.
Name of
His wife UNKNOWN.

had

104. LAZARUS THOMAS m. MARY........
105. JOHN THOMAS m. HANNAH DAWSON

105. JOHN THOMAS had children:
will in 1725.

205. RICHARD THOMAS m. ELEANOR SHEARER
     (Or Sherrod).
206. JACOB THOMAS m. MARY HARRISON
207. SAMUEL THOMAS m. ELIZABETH SHEARER.*

205. RICHARD THOMAS had children
will 1761 I. of W Co.
306. JOHN THOMAS
307. WILLIAM THOMAS
308. TABITHA THOMAS m. EDWARD HAILE
309. MARY THOMAS m. THOMAS WHITNEY GALE
310. SARAH THOMAS m. WILLIAM HAYWOOD.

206. JACOB THOMAS had children:
wife's will 1668.

311. JOHN THOMAS
312. ANNE THOMAS
313. HAYWOOD THOMAS
314. TABITHA THOMAS
315. MARY THOMAS

* The will or SAMUEL THOMAS, or a list
  of his children, not found.

6. KATHERINE THOMAS who married THOMAS OGLETHORPE

had

108. MARGARET OGLETHORPE
109. KATHERINE OGLETHORPE m. JOHN ASKEW
110. SARAH OGLETHORPE m. NICHOLAS ASKEW.

1. RICHARD THOMAS was Executor of
the will of THOMAS OGLETHORPE in 1687.
   JOHN and NICHOLAS ASKEW were sons of
JOHN ASKEW who married BRIDGET SMITH, the
daughter of NICHOLAS SMITH.
   The widow of NICHOLAS SMITH, Anne,
became the second wife of HUMPHREY MARSHALL, father in law of RICHARD THOMAS.

5. SARAH THOMAS married JONATHAN ROBINSON - and they had:

111 WILLIAM ROBINSON
112. JOHN ROBINSON
113. JONATHAN ROBINSON
114. ARCHELAUS ROBINSON

100. JOHN THOMAS AND HIS FAMILY

200. JOHN THOMAS
201. RICHARD THOMAS
202. WILLIAM THOMAS
203. JOSEPH THOMAS
204. PHILLIP THOMAS
205. BARNABY THOMAS
206. ELIZABETH THOMAS

---

200. JOHN THOMAS m. ELIZABETH KEARNEY
had:

300. JOHN THOMAS m. (1) ANNE COTTEN (2) ANNA
301. RICHARD THOMAS m. BARSHEBA WILLS
302. ROBERT THOMAS

---

300. JOHN THOMAS (SEE HIS CHART)

---

301. RICHARD THOMAS and wife BARSHE-
BA WILLS, had:

403. MICAJAH THOMAS m. MOURNING (DIXON) CHUDUP

---

403. MICAJAH THOMAS and wife
MOURNING CHUDUP, had:

512. MICAJAH THOMAS, JR.
513. BARSHEBA THOMAS (never married).

---

512 MICAJAH THOMAS, JR.
  m. (1) ANNE HAWKINS
  m. (2) ELIZABETH CRAFFORD
    had:

600. BARSHEBA THOMAS
601. PHILEMON HAWKINS THOMAS
602. MARY CRAFFORD THOMAS

---

302. ROBERT THOMAS

On Jury with his brother 300.
JOHN THOMAS in CHOWAN COUNTY,
in 1739/40.
— N. C. Col. Recs. 4, p. 517.

---

201. RICHARD THOMAS m. MISS ROGERS
had:

320. RICHARD THOMAS
321. JOHN THOMAS
322. MARY THOMAS
323. ELIZABETH THOMAS

The above children are all mentioned
in the will of their grandfather,
MICHAEL ROGERS, in NANSEMOND COUNTY,
VIRGINIA, in 1710.
——BODDIE'S ISLE OF WIGHT, p. 496.

---

202. WILLIAM THOMAS m. MARTHA ROBINSON

324. JOHN THOMAS m. CHRISTIANA ROBERTS
325. MICHAEL THOMAS m. ANN...
326. LEWIS THOMAS
327. WILLIAM THOMAS
328. SAMUEL THOMAS m. ELIZABETH SANDERS
329. ELIZABETH THOMAS.

---

203. JOSEPH THOMAS m. ALICE...
  d. 1735

330. JOSEPH THOMAS m. ANN.....
331. MICHAEL THOMAS
332. LUKE THOMAS
333. JAMES THOMAS
334. JACOB THOMAS
335. MARY THOMAS
336. JONAS THOMAS
337. CHARITY THOMAS

---

204. PHILLIP THOMAS m. ANNE....
  d. 1748.

338. WILLIAM THOMAS
339. MATTHEW THOMAS

---

205. BARNABY THOMAS m. MARY.....
  d. 1735.

340. ELISHA THOMAS

---

206. ELIZABETH THOMAS
  m. (1) JOHN BODDIE
  m. (2) JOHN DAWSON

341. WILLIAM BODDIE m. MARY BENNETT
342. JOHN BODDIE m. ELIZABETH JEFFREYS

343. HENRY DAWSON
344. THOMAS DAWSON
345. ELIZABETH DAWSON m. WILLIAM KINCHEN JR.

After Elizabeth Dawson's
death her second husband
COL. JOHN DAWSON married
CHARITY ALSTON and had:

346. JOHN DAWSON JR.

See NOTES that appear later in
the pages that follow pertaining to the names on this chart.

203. JOSEPH THOMAS AND HIS FAMILY

Will in BERTIE COUNTY, 1735.
His wife was ALICE....
They had:

- 330. JOSEPH THOMAS m. ANN....
- 331. MICHAEL THOMAS
- 332. LUKE THOMAS
- 333. JAMES THOMAS
- 334. JACOB THOMAS
- 335. MARY THOMAS
- 336. JONAS THOMAS
- 337. CHARITY THOMAS

---

330. JOSEPH THOMAS m. ANN.....

Will in BERTIE COUNTY in 1758. They had:

- 410. MICHAEL THOMAS
- 411. JOSIAH THOMAS
- 412. JOSEPH THOMAS
- 413. MARY THOMAS
- 414. ELIZABETH THOMAS

---

411. JOSIAH THOMAS m. SARAH BAZEMORE
and had:

- 560. MICHAEL THOMAS
- 561. JORDAN THOMAS
- 562. JOSIAH THOMAS (b. Sept. 24, 1770.)
- 563. ELIZABETH THOMAS
- 564. SARAH THOMAS

---

562. JOSIAH THOMAS m. TABITHA...
and had: b. 1777.

- 610. ELIZABETH THOMAS (b. March 9, 1799).
- 611. JAMES SHERROD THOMAS (b. March 4, 1801)
- 612. NANCY THOMAS (b. April 28, 1803)
- 613. MARTHA THOMAS (b. Sept. 29, 1805)
- 614. MARY THOMAS (b. May 20, 1808)
- 615. JOSEPH JOHN THOMAS (b. Aug. 30, 1810).
- 616. MATILDA W. THOMAS (b. April 10, 1813).

(From Family Bible).

---

611. JAMES SHERROD THOMAS
m. HENRIETTA ELIZABETH COPPAGE
Ch : (b.1802)

- 700. MARY THOMAS (b. 1816) m. LEMUEL H. LAW
- 701. MARTHA JANE THOMAS m. MARCUS L. BARRETT
- 702. WILLIAM THOMAS (m. 3 times) (b. 1825)
- 703. NANCY THOMAS (b. 1830) m. ELI INGE
- 704. HARRIET THOMAS (b. 1833) m. LEWIS WAHL.
- 705. JOHN THOMAS (b. 1835) m. MARGARET INGE
  m. (2) ELIZ. BURNS.
- 706. MARIA THOMAS (b. 1833) m. DANIEL HASSELL
- 707. TABITHA THOMAS (b. 1841) m. WILLIAM BLACK
- 708. HENRIETTA THOMAS (Never Married)

MARCUS LAFAYETTE BARRETT and 701 MARTHA JANE THOMAS were the parents of MARCUS L. BARRETT, JR. m. SARAH AMELIA BURNS, who settled in TEXAS. (See later).

---

333. JAMES THOMAS m. SARAH BARNES

Will in BERTIE COUNTY Oct. 1780. They had:

- 415. EZEKIEL THOMAS
- 416. LUKE THOMAS
- 417. JAMES THOMAS (b. 1760)
- 418. SELAH THOMAS m. CHARLES DEMENT
- 419. LUNDILL THOMAS
- 420. SARAH THOMAS
- 421. LYDIA THOMAS m. JAMES LAWRENCE.
- 421* LEODICEA THOMAS

421* From the family records and not from the will.

---

415. EZEKIEL THOMAS m. MISS HOLLAND
and had:

- 565. LUKE THOMAS (d. in Tenn.)
- 566. EZEKIEL THOMAS (d. in Tenn.)
- 567. ELI THOMAS (died young).
- 568. SALLY THOMAS m. ROBERT HENRY.

---

565. LUKE THOMAS (of Carroll Co. Tenn)
m. ELIZABETH BARRADELL

- 620. PINCKNEY THOMAS
- 621. EZEKIEL THOMAS
- 622. HAYWOOD THOMAS
- 623. MATTHEW THOMAS
- 624. JAMES THOMAS
- 625. BENNETTIE THOMAS
- 626. EMALINE THOMAS
- 627. MARIE THOMAS
- 628. ALABAMA THOMAS
- 629. FRANCIS THOMAS
- 630. SOPHRONA THOMAS
- 631. PEACHIE THOMAS
- 632. SALLIE THOMAS

---

417. JAMES THOMAS m. MARY STANDLEY
and had:

- 570. CULLEN THOMAS
- 571. TEMPERANCE THOMAS
- 572. PERRY THOMAS
- 573. STARKEY THOMAS
- 574. MARY THOMAS
- 575. JAMES THOMAS
- 576. STANDLEY THOMAS

Ancestors of HON. CULLEN F. THOMAS and MIKE THOMAS, of DALLAS TEXAS.

300. JOHN THOMAS AND HIS DESCENDANTS

Married first, ANNE COTTEN
Married, (2) ANNA......

Great Great Grandson of (4) JOHN THOMAS
Great Grandson of RICHARD THOMAS and ELIZABETH MARSHALL
Grandson of 100. JOHN THOMAS m. (1) SUSAN PORTIS (2) MARY LAWRENCE
Son of 200. JOHN THOMAS
Had only two sons; one by each marriage.

Children:

400. JOSEPH THOMAS married MOURNING CRUDUP.
401. JOHN THOMAS married JULIAN......?

---

400. JOSEPH THOMAS m. MOURNING CRUDUP.

had:

500. MARY THOMAS m. WILLIAM HORN. (1761)
501. PRISCILLA THOMAS m. GEORGE CRUDUP (1761)
502. CHARITY THOMAS m. GEORGE WIMBERLY (1764)
503. MOURNING THOMAS m. WIL'M PRIDGEON (1761)

400. JOSEPH THOMAS died in EDGECOMBE in 1758.

401. JOHN THOMAS m. JULIAN...... EDGECOMBE COUNTY

d. 1777. had:

504. RICHARD THOMAS m. REBECCA....
505. JESSE THOMAS
506. SARAH THOMAS m. ZACHARIAH MELTON
507. JOHN THOMAS
508. ABIGAIL THOMAS m. LANGLEY
509. MARY THOMAS m. SMITH
510. ABISHAG THOMAS (Daughter).
511. CHLOE THOMAS m. ARTHUR BAILEY.

---

504. RICHARD THOMAS m. REBECCA......

had:

603. JETHRO THOMAS
604. MOURNING THOMAS
605. MARY THOMAS m. JOSEPH STRICKLAND

504. RICHARD THOMAS left will in NASH COUNTY, N. C., probated in 1784.

602. MARY THOMAS and her husband JOSEPH STRICKLAND had one daughter CHARITY.

The above were the THOMASES who settled on PIG BASKETT CREEK, a prong of STONY CREEK, which empties into the TAR RIVER not far from the old TAR RIVER PRIMITIVE BAPTIST CHURCH.

300. JOHN THOMAS, immediate ancestor of the above family died in NORTHAMPTON COUNTY, in 1746, leaving a will in which he mentioned his son JOSEPH THOMAS "by present wife ANNA", thus implying that he had been previously married. He was mentioned in the will of JOHN COTTEN in the year 1728, as "Capt. John Thomas, my son in law". The N. C. Colonial Records show that he and his "wife Anne" appeared in Court in 1727. All data pertaining to 400 JOSEPH and 401 JOHN show clearly that they were brothers, and JOSEPH calls him "My brother, John" in his own will in EDGECOMBE COUNTY, probated at the January Court in 1758. No other children of 300 JOHN appear on the records, which leads inevitably to the conclusion that they were half-brothers.

MOURNING CRUDUP, the wife of 400 JOSEPH THOMAS was the daughter of JOHN CRUDUP and his wife MOURNING. GEORGE CRUDUP who married PRISCILLA THOMAS was her cousin. After the death of JOHN CRUDUP, his widow MOURNING married MICAJAH THOMAS, the son of 301. RICHARD THOMAS. MICAJAH THOMAS was a first cousin to 400 JOSEPH THOMAS, who by his marriage to MICAJAH'S step-daughter MOURNING CRUDUP, became MICAJAH THOMAS' step-son in law. The will of 400 JOSEPH THOMAS was witnessed by both MICAJAH THOMAS and MOURNING (CRUDUP) THOMAS, his wife, and to further accentuate the close relationship between these parties, the records show that in 1784, in NASH COUNTY, when the will of 504 RICHARD THOMAS was admitted to probate, MICAJAH THOMAS, JR. was named as the Executor.

One THOMAS DIXON married a sister of the original WILLIAM BODDIE, in Virginia. Thomas Dixon died in 1670, leaving a son THOMAS, the father of THOMAS DIXON JR. who married ELIZABETH MURPHY. ELIZABETH MURPHY was the daughter of MICHAEL MURPHY, son of WILLIAM MURPHY, and a sister of MICHAEL married JOHN LAWRENCE, brother in law of 100 JOHN THOMAS. MOURNING DIXON, daughter of THOMAS DIXON, JR. married JOHN CRUDUP, who after John's death, as stated, married MICAJAH THOMAS.

324. JOHN THOMAS AND HIS FAMILY

324. JOHN THOMAS married **CHRISTIANA ROBERTS**
(b. 1704/5)

Children:
- 404. JOHN THOMAS
- 405. JONATHAN THOMAS
- 406. OBEDIENCE THOMAS
- 407. THEOPHILUS THOMAS
- 408. MILLICENT THOMAS
- 409. TERESA THOMAS m. THEOPHILUS HILL.

404. JOHN THOMAS married perhaps three times. had:	405. JONATHAN THOMAS m. MARY (HILLIARD) NEWSOM and had:	407. THEOPHILUS THOMAS m. MARY ROGERS, and had:
520. MILLICENT THOMAS	542. JONATHAN THOMAS JR.	546. OBEDIENCE THOMAS (b. 1771)
521. TILLIE THOMAS	543. ELIZABETH THOMAS	547. MILLICENT THOMAS
522. ROBERTS THOMAS	544. SARAH THOMAS	548. ICHABOD THOMAS
523. JOHN THOMAS	545. CHARITY THOMAS	549. BENJAMIN THOMAS
524. WILLIAM THOMAS	545* MOURNING THOMAS.	550. TABITHA THOMAS
525. JOSEPH THOMAS		551. THERESA THOMAS
526. THEOPHILUS THOMAS		552. MICAJAH THOMAS
527. BENJAMIN I. THOMAS	**409. TERESA THOMAS**	553. JOHN ROGERS THOMAS
528. JAMES THOMAS	m. THEOPHILUS HILL	554. THEOPHILUS THOMAS, JR.
529. WHITFIELD THOMAS		556. ELIZABETH THOMAS
530. PEYTON THOMAS		557. NANCY THOMAS
531. JOHN G. THOMAS		
532. TRACY HILL THOMAS	558. LODOVICK HILL	
533. POLLY A. McKINNIE THOMAS	was born in 1765.	
534. MARIAH JOHNSTON THOMAS	559. ANN HILL	**406. OBEDIENCE THOMAS**
535. FREDERICK G. THOMAS	was born June 6, 1787	
536. JONATHAN THOMAS	560. Daughter No record	No record found
537. NANCY THOMAS	561. Daughter No record	and identified
538. PATIENCE THOMAS	562. Daughter No record.	on OBEDIENCE.
539. PATSY THOMAS		
540. SALLY THOMAS	LODOVICK HILL died July 27,	
541. ____ THOMAS	1822 in Edgefield Dist. SC.	**408. MILLICENT THOMAS**
	He married SUSAN GRIGSBY...	No record found.

324. JOHN THOMAS (born about 1704/5) is believed to have been a native of NANSEMOND COUNTY, VIRGINIA --- though possibly of ISLE OF WIGHT COUNTY. The following statement from GEORGE W. PASCHAL's "History of North Carolina Baptists" has reference to 324 JOHN THOMAS, head of the above chart, and is self-explanatory: (Pages 180-181)

> To the South of Tar (River) in the present County of WILSON is a church called TOISNOT. It is not known who first preached the Gospel here or organized the congregation. It had no minister until 1748, when DR. JOSIAH HART came on one of his missionary tours and baptised JOHN THOMAS, who soon after was ordained pastor of the Toisnot Church by Elders George Graham and JOHN MOORE.
>
> This JOHN THOMAS was probably the one of that name who in 1749 was appointed a Justice of the Peace for EDGECOMBE COUNTY.
>
> He had two sons who also became ministers, the one named JOHN and the other JONATHAN, the latter being a great man of God, very affable in his address and a great orator.

404. JOHN THOMAS, the son, who was, as stated, a minister, married (according to one of the descendants of this family) about three times, but the names of no one of his wives is known. In his latter years he removed to the State of Georgia, and settled in the upper part of HANCOCK COUNTY, where he was pastor of the SHOULDERBONE BAPTIST CHURCH. At his death in, or about 1807, he had the list of 21 children shown above. (See later notes on the other charted names).

EXPLANATORY NOTES RELATING TO THE NAMES SHOWN ON THE THOMAS
FAMILY CHARTS, WITH NUMBERS AS SHOWN THEREON:

1. RICHARD THOMAS. The name of his wife was ELIZABETH. That she was ELIZABETH MARSHALL, daughter of HUMPHREY MARSHALL is deducible from his own will, dated April 8, 1687, and that of HUMPHREY MARSHALL in 1711, in which Marshall leaves a bequest to his daughter ELIZABETH and to her son JOHN THOMAS. (D. B. 2 p. 533 of Isle of Wight County). RICHARD THOMAS leaves one son, JOHN THOMAS and three daughters, PHOEBE, SARAH and ELIZABETH. The fact that RICHARD THOMAS had a sister KATHERINE THOMAS, who married THOMAS OGLETHORPE, and had two daughters who married two grandsons of COL. NICHOLAS SMITH, whose widow ANNE SMITH, married HUMPHREY MARSHALL, as his second wife. Thus it is shown that RICHARD THOMAS, who was son in law of HUMPHREY MARSHALL had a sister KATHERINE whose daughters were step-grandchildren of HUMPHREY MARSHALL. The latter relationship is established by positive record evidence, and the former by strong deductive proof.

2. WILLIAM THOMAS was a brother of 1. RICHARD THOMAS, preceding. He perhaps went to SURRY COUNTY, for his will was probated there Feb. 17, 1719 (D. B. 2 p. 243) He outlived his brother Richard for many years, and was probably married either two or three times. He had a first cousin 10. WILLIAM THOMAS who married ELIZABETH HILL, who was a brother in law of HUMPHREY MARSHALL, who married 15. PRISCILLA THOMAS, sister of 10. WILLIAM. Due to the common intimacy between these families it is difficult to distinguish one from the other. 2. WILLIAM THOMAS first married CHRISTIAN. (Boddie p. 258), but his second, or last wife, at least, was PRISCILLA, the widow of RIVER JORDAN, of the SURRY COUNTY JORDANS, who in between had married THOMAS BLOUNT and had a son by him named RICHARD BLOUNT. PRISCILLA had been PRISCILLA BROWNE, probably sister of JOHN BROWNE, who married MARY BODDIE, daughter of WILLIAM BODDIE. 2. WILLIAM THOMAS had sons JOHN, WILLIAM and HENRY, and daughters JANE, BAMBLEY (BARSHEBA), ANN and MARY.

3. JOHN THOMAS, brother of 2. WILLIAM THOMAS who married first CHRISTIAN and second PRISCILLA (Boddie p. 258). His wife's name is unkown, and only two sons are tentatively established, 104 LAZARUS and 105 JOHN. LAZARUS THOMAS settled in what is now GATES COUNTY, one time CHOWAN and BERTIE COUNTY. He sold lands to ROBERT ROGERS in NANSEMOND COUNTY, VIRGINIA, and ROGERS afterwards moved to BERTIE COUNTY, where he died. The wife of 104 LAZARUS THOMAS was MARY.

4. ELIZABETH THOMAS, sister of 1, 2 and 3 above, married JOHN SAUNDERS. Her son ROBERT SANDERS died in 1731 and in his will called PHOEBE THOMAS, daughter of 2. RICHARD THOMAS, his "cousin". Another son, HENRY SANDERS, married a sister of MARY LAWRENCE the wife of her nephew, 100. JOHN THOMAS.

5. SARAH THOMAS married JONATHAN ROBINSON. In 1681, 1. RICHARD THOMAS and JOHN SAUNDERS and JONATHAN ROBINSON patented 1650 acres of land in ISLE OF WIGHT COUNTY. JONATHAN ROBINSON and his wife SARAH had a son WILLIAM ROBINSON, whose daughter married 202 WILLIAM THOMAS, grandson of 1. RICHARD THOMAS. MARTHA and WILLIAM THOMAS were living in CHOWAN COUNTY, N. C. on lands patented in 1703 by JONATHAN ROBINSON and sold to 200. JOHN THOMAS in 1726, while he was still living in NANSEMOND COUNTY, VIRGINIA. (D. B. E, p. 332, Chowan County; Henning's Statutes Vol. 5, page 75).

6. KATHERINE THOMAS m. THOMAS OGLETHORPE, and her husband died about 1687 and 1. RICHARD THOMAS was the Executor. Katherine had three daughters, Margaret, Sarah and Katherine. Sarah and Katherine married John and Nicholas Askew, sons of JOHN ASKEW and BRIDGET SMITH, Bridget Smith being a daughter of COL. NICHOLAS SMITH Burgess from Isle of Wight, whose wife, ANNE SMITH became the second wife of HUMPHREY MARSHALL (D. B. 2, p. 292, Isle of Wight County, Va.).

---

100. JOHN THOMAS was the only son of 1. RICHARD THOMAS and his wife ELIZABETH MARSHALL. He was the JOHN THOMAS, son of ELIZABETH, to whom HUMPHREY MARSHALL left a legacy in 1711, and was certainly alive at that time, although it appears that he was deceased three years later, leaving at least seven children, all presumably by his first marriage to SUSANNAH PORTIS. JOHN THOMAS married (1) SUSANNAH PORTIS. DEBORAH EXUM, the mother of SUSANNAH THOMAS, was perhaps a sister of JEREMIAH EXUM, who with his wife ANN, joined in a deed of lands belonging to the LAWRENCE ESTATE to THOMAS POLLOCK of North Carolina in 1704, said lands being in BERTIE COUNTY (then West side of the Chowan in Chowan County) which was also signed by JOHN THOMAS and his "now wife" MARY, the daughter of JOHN LAWRENCE, and DEBORAH was perhaps an aunt of RICHARD EXUM, who married ANNE LAWRENCE, JOHN THOMAS' sister in law. In other words SUSANNAH PORTIS, the first wife of 100. JOHN THOMAS was very likely a cousin of his second wife, MARY LAWRENCE, for that is the way that marriages went in those days. WILLIAM EXUM, who died in ISLE OF WIGHT County, Va. in 1700, had a daughter by the name DEBORAH, who married EDWARD JONES, doubtless named for the first wife of JOHN PORTIS. (Boddie p. 452). JEREMIAH EXUM dates back and shows that he and his wife ANNE were contemporaneous with 1. RICHARD THOMAS and wife ELIZABETH MARSHALL, since in 1687, he and his wife ANN sold 138 acres of land on Mattacomack Crk near the present town of Edenton, N. C.; at that time JEREMIAH and his wife, however, were "of Isle of Wight County, Virginia." DEBORAH (EXUM) PORTIS was alive in 1704.(D. B. 2, p. 38. I. of W.)

104. LAZARUS THOMAS. See note on 3. JOHN THOMAS. He settled in what is now GATES COUNTY near the ROGERS FAMILY, and. SAREM CHAPEL. Notes on LAZARUS THOMAS are few.

105. JOHN THOMAS lived in the LOWER PARISH of ISLE OF WIGHT COUNTY, where in 1707 he bought land from JOSEPH PARNELL, which joined the lands of the SHEARER FAMILY into which two of his sons married. JOSEPH PARNELL was the son of THOMAS PARNELL, whose daughter married JOHN SHEARER. (This name is spelled in all kinds of ways on the records - sometimes SHEARER, sometimes SHERROD and even SHERWOOD). In order to enable the student to understand some of these connections, the SHEARERS are written up under the head of "THE SHEARER FAMILY", on another page. Attention is directed to the fact that ROBERT SHEARER, son of the above JOHN, had a daughter PRUDENCE SHEARER who married one ARTHUR WILLIAMS, and this ARTHUR WILLIAMS was one of the witnesses to the will of 330 JOSEPH THOMAS in BERTIE COUNTY in 1757-8. The wife of ARTHUR WILLIAMS was first cousin of two of the wives of two grandsons - RICHARD and SAMUEL - of 3. JOHN THOMAS, while 330. JOSEPH THOMAS was a great grandson of 1. RICHARD THOMAS and ELIZABETH MARSHALL. Also that JOHN DEW JR. and this ARTHUR WILLIAMS married sisters, and that SARAH DEW, daughter of JOHN DEW, JR. married a brother of JOHN COTTEN, father in law of 300. JOHN THOMAS, another descendand of 1. RICHARD THOMAS. Thus, it appears throughout the entire record that the children and grandchildren of all of the sons of RICHARD, WILLIAM and JOHN THOMAS, sons of (4) JOHN THOMAS, were continually "marrying into" and otherwise intimately connecting themselves with each other, thus fortifying the deductive relationships assumed for them by this compiler.

------

200. JOHN THOMAS was, perhaps and apparently, the oldest grandson of 1. RICHARD THOMAS and ELIZABETH MARSHALL, of NANSEMOND COUNTY, VIRGINIA. He was living in VIRGINIA in 1726, when his father's cousin, WILLIAM ROBINSON deeded to him 200 acres of land in what afterwards became BERTIE COUNTY, N. C. Sometime after 1726, probably the same year, JOHN THOMAS removed to NORTH CAROLINA, but between that time and 1738, this deed was lost or destroyed, and 200. JOHN THOMAS returned to Virginia and appealed to the Virginia Assembly to have the loss rectified in some way, at which time he stated that he then (in 1738) was living in North Carolina. But only two years before he had been living in Virginia again, and while there made a deed to JOHN LAWRENCE JR. the brother of his step-mother, MARY LAWRENCE, to any interest he may have had in 100 acres left to her by her father. This deed was probably one simply to clear title and dispense with any and all claims 200. JOHN THOMAS might have in or to lands that came to his step-mother by will of her father. But the year following (?1739) 200. JOHN THOMAS had again taken up his domicile in Nansemond County, Virginia, and stating that he was then "Of the Upper Parish of Nansemond County, Virginia" he deeded to JOHN DAUGHTEY, JR. 60 acres of land, being part of a former grant to RICHARD THOMAS in the Lower Parish of Isle of Wight County, Joined by JOHN SANDERS and JONATHAN ROBINSON, who had been the partners of RICHARD in the grant, which the deed stated had been left to JOHN THOMAS, Richard's son, and by the death of the said JOHN THOMAS (100) he, 200. JOHN THOMAS, was now the owner. Again in 1751 his name appears on the VIRGINIA records as living there, and it is presumed that there he ever afterwards resided until his death, the date of which is unknown. It is believed that 200. JOHN THOMAS married a daughter of MAJ. BARNABY KEARNEY, who was a Burgess 1684 from NANSEMOND COUNTY, but this, however, is not established as a fact. There are one or two items that indicate it. He appears to have had only three sons, 300. JOHN THOMAS (See his Chart), RICHARD THOMAS and ROBERT THOMAS. 300. JOHN THOMAS was CAPT. JOHN THOMAS, son in law of JOHN COTTEN and his wife MARTHA GODWIN. ELIZABETH GODWIN married CAPT. BARNABY KEARNEY, sister of ELIZABETH KEARNEY, whom we think was the mother of CAPT. JOHN THOMAS. MICAJAH THOMAS, JR. grandson of 301. RICHARD THOMAS, brother of CAPT. JOHN THOMAS married ELIZABETH CRAFFORD, a grand-daughter of CAPT. BARNABY KEARNEY.

201. RICHARD THOMAS married a daughter of MICHAEL ROGERS, in Nansemond County, Virginia. MICHAEL ROGERS died leaving a will in 1710 in which he mentions the names of four THOMAS grandchildren, the oldest of which, ELIZABETH, was under age. RICHARD THOMAS, evidently the father of these children (See Chart) was the Executor of the will. Either this RICHARD THOMAS, or the son RICHARD, mentioned in the will, in 1737, bought lands from JOHN BODDIE, the son of 206 ELIZABETH THOMAS, of North Carolina. RICHARD THOMAS was at that time a resident of ISLE OF WIGHT COUNTY, VA. (Boddie, page 376.) This RICHARD THOMAS, may or may not have settled in North Carolina after 1737, when he is known to have been living in Virginia.

202. WILLIAM THOMAS was the ancestor of all of the persons named THOMAS whose names appear on the Chart of 324 JOHN THOMAS, his son. Reference to that chart will show that one of his grandsons, REV. JOHN THOMAS, of SHOULDERBONE BAPTIST CHURCH in Hancock County, Georgia, had no less than 22 children. Here, too was the father of REV. JOHN THOMAS, pastor of the old TOISNOT CHURCH in what is now WILSON COUNTY, a part of old EDGECOMBE. He had two sons, Rev. John and Rev. JONATHAN THOMAS, noted ministers. It was JOHN who went to GEORGIA. Theophilus, another son, was prominent in the public life of the Edgecombe area and served as an officer in the militia and high sheriff of his county. 202. WILLIAM m. his cousin, MARTHA ROBINSON.

203. **JOSEPH THOMAS.** He moved to BERTIE COUNTY, NORTH CAROLINA, where he died in 1735, leaving a will in which he mentioned his wife, KAIES. Her name is believed to have been ALICE, as a matter of fact. His son MICHEAL and JOHN SPIVEY were named as his executors. ALICE, before her marriage, in all probability, was a SPIVEY, as there are numerous transactions that show close and intimate dealings with the SPIVEY FAMILY by members of the THOMAS family, both in Virginia and North Carolina. 203. JOSEPH THOMAS may have been twice married, his first wife having been ELIZABETH. On January 16, 1714, the record shows that JOSEPH THOMAS and his wife ELIZABETH, and MICHAEL THOMAS and wife, patented lands in the Upper Parish of Nansemond County, Virginia. (Pat. Book 10, page 140). One writer expressed the belief that this was MICHAEL THOMAS, the son of 203 JOSEPH, but the writer here is convinced that the patentee was 325. MICHAEL THOMAS, son of 202 WILLIAM and his wife MARTHA ROBINSON. The descendants of this 203. JOSEPH THOMAS are set out on a chart preceding, but there will be a few additional notes pertaining to later members of this family, to which the readers' attention is called. This is a very interesting family.

204. **PHILLIP THOMAS.** The name of his wife was ANNE. In 1722 a certain WILLIAM THOMAS, of ISLE of WIGHT COUNTY, believed to have been 202. WILLIAM, a brother of PHILLIP, bought from WILLIAM SIMS, a tract of 180 acres of land from one HENRY SIMS, which was located North of the Roanoke River in what was then BERTIE COUNTY (and had been for two years only) Deed Book A p. 2. In 1739, 17 years later, this land evidently belonged to 204. PHILLIP THOMAS, then living in BERTIE COUNTY, a brother of the purchaser from SIMS, who sold it to a WILLIAM THOMAS, then living also in BERTIE. This was evidently Phillip's son 338 WILLIAM THOMAS. (Deed Book E, p.474). This last deed was witnessed by JOHN BODDIE and JOHN DAWSON. This JOHN BODDIE was the son of JOHN DAWSON'S wife who had married first, JOHN BODDIE and second, JOHN DAWSON. Six years later, 1745, 338, WILLIAM THOMAS sold this 180 acres to his brother, 339, MATTHEW THOMAS. In 1749, four years later 204. PHILLIP THOMAS had died and his wife ANNE had married WILLIAM HALL, and 339 MATTHEW THOMAS that year paid WILLIAM HALL and his wife ANNE for their right of dower in the lands of 204. PHILLIP THOMAS. At that time the dower lands purchased were in NORTHAMPTON COUNTY. (D. B. I, p 411) This deed recites that MATTHEW THOMAS was the son of 204 PHILLIP THOMAS. The wife of MATTHEW THOMAS was ELIZABETH, as shown by these deeds. WILLIAM THOMAS (son of PHILLIP) also had a son PHILLIP THOMAS, who in 1762 was living in GRANVILLE COUNTY, N. C. and sold some lands that year to one WILLIAM WINBORNE next to his father, WILLIAM THOMAS, while MATTHEW THOMAS sold finally in 1756, the same old 180 acres to PHILLIP WINBORNE in NORTHAMPTON COUNTY, N. C. Thus the HENRY SIMS 180 acres finally fell into the hands of WILLIAM and PHILLIP WINBORNE, sons, doubtless, of JOHN WINBORNE and 101. PHOEBE THOMAS, or their grandsons. See (4) JOHN THOMAS CHART.

205. **BARNABY THOMAS.** The name of his wife was SARAH. He died in BERTIE COUNTY in 1735, leaving a will in which he left to his son ELISHA THOMAS his plantation and two negroes. He made his brother PHILLIP his Executor, and WILLIAM THOMAS (probably 202 WILLIAM), JOHN DAWSON and JACOB CARR, were the witnesses. In one abstract of this will the testator refers to John Dawson as his brother in law. Grimes p. 374; Boddie, p. 260. The JACOB CARR, one of the witnesses was perhaps a son of ROBERT CARR, who married one of the daughters of JOHN LAWRENCE, brother in law of 100 JOHN THOMAS, father of 205° BARNABY THOMAS. ELISHA THOMAS son of 205. BARNABY THOMAS is probably the ELISHA who settled in Wayne, Johnston and the Cumberland County area and left a son BARNABY and others, ancestors of some whose names are on the 1790 census.

207. RICHARD THOMAS was the son of 105. JOHN THOMAS and his wife HANNAH. The father, 105 JOHN, died leaving a will in ISLE OF WIGHT, probated at the September term of Court in 1725. (Great Book 2, p. 195), in which he named his wife Hannah and three sons, RICHARD, JACOB and SAMUEL. The son, 207. RICHARD THOMAS married ELEANOR SHEARER, daughter of JOHN SHEARER, JR. and his wife ELIZABETH, while 209. SAMUEL married her sister, ELIZABETH SHEARER. JOHN SHEARER JR. was the son of JOHN SHEARER, SR. and his wife, daughter of the ancient planter THOMAS PARNELL of Isle of Wight. The names of the children of 207 RICHARD THOMAS and his wife, mentioned in his will in Isle of Wight in 1761 (Book 7 p.132 and 208) are shown on the (4) JOHN THOMAS CHART. One of his daughters was TABITHA THOMAS who married EDWARD HAIL or HAILE, another, MARY, married THOMAS WHITNEY GALE, while SARAH married WILLIAM HAYWOOD. WILLIAM HAYWOOD was the father of JOHN HAYWOOD who died in North Carolina, leaving three sons, JOHN, WILLIAM and EGBERT, and the last named was the father of JUDGE JOHN HAYWOOD, distinguished lawyer of N. C. and Tennessee, who produced in 1823 the great "CIVIL and POLITICAL HISTORY OF TENNESSEE. One JOHN MARSHALL, probable son of HUMPHREY MARSHALL, had a daughter, who married a son of THOMAS WHITNEY GALE and MARY THOMAS, and had THOMAS, ANN, ELIZABETH, TABITHA and ALICE GALE, all born prior to 1760. (Chapman's Abstracts of I. of W. Co. p. 34). It is not improbable that TABITHA, the wife of 562. JOSIAH THOMAS, was a descendant of either TABITHA THOMAS or MARY THOMAS, daughters of 207. RICHARD.

208. JACOB THOMAS married MARY HARRISON, who was a daughter of MRS. ELIZABETH HARRISON, who in her will in 1774 mentions her grand-daughters ANNE and TABITHA THOMAS. The other children of 208. JACOB THOMAS were MARY, JOHN and HAYWOOD THOMAS. TRISTRAM NORSWORTHY was another son in law of ELIZABETH HARRISON. (Chapman's Wills of I. of Wight County, page 68.)

MAP OF THE OLD BATH AREA ALONG THE NEUSE AND PAMLICO THE NEW BERN SECTION

MAP NO. 23

ST. JOHN'S EPISCOPAL CHURCH at Williamsboro, oldest church in Vance county, started in 1754 as Nutbush Community House.

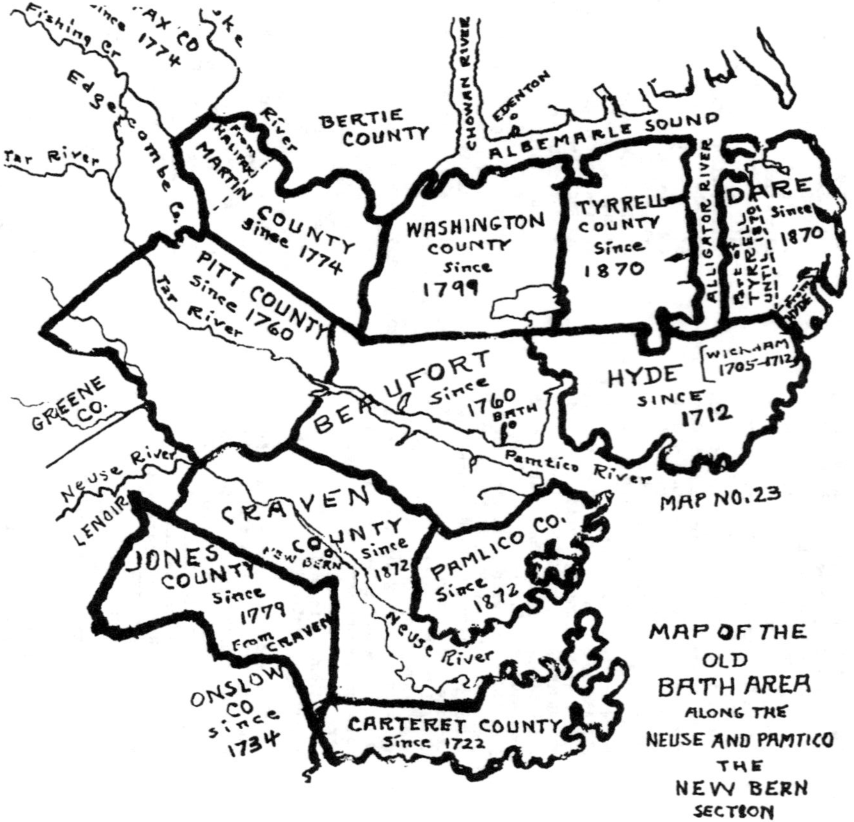

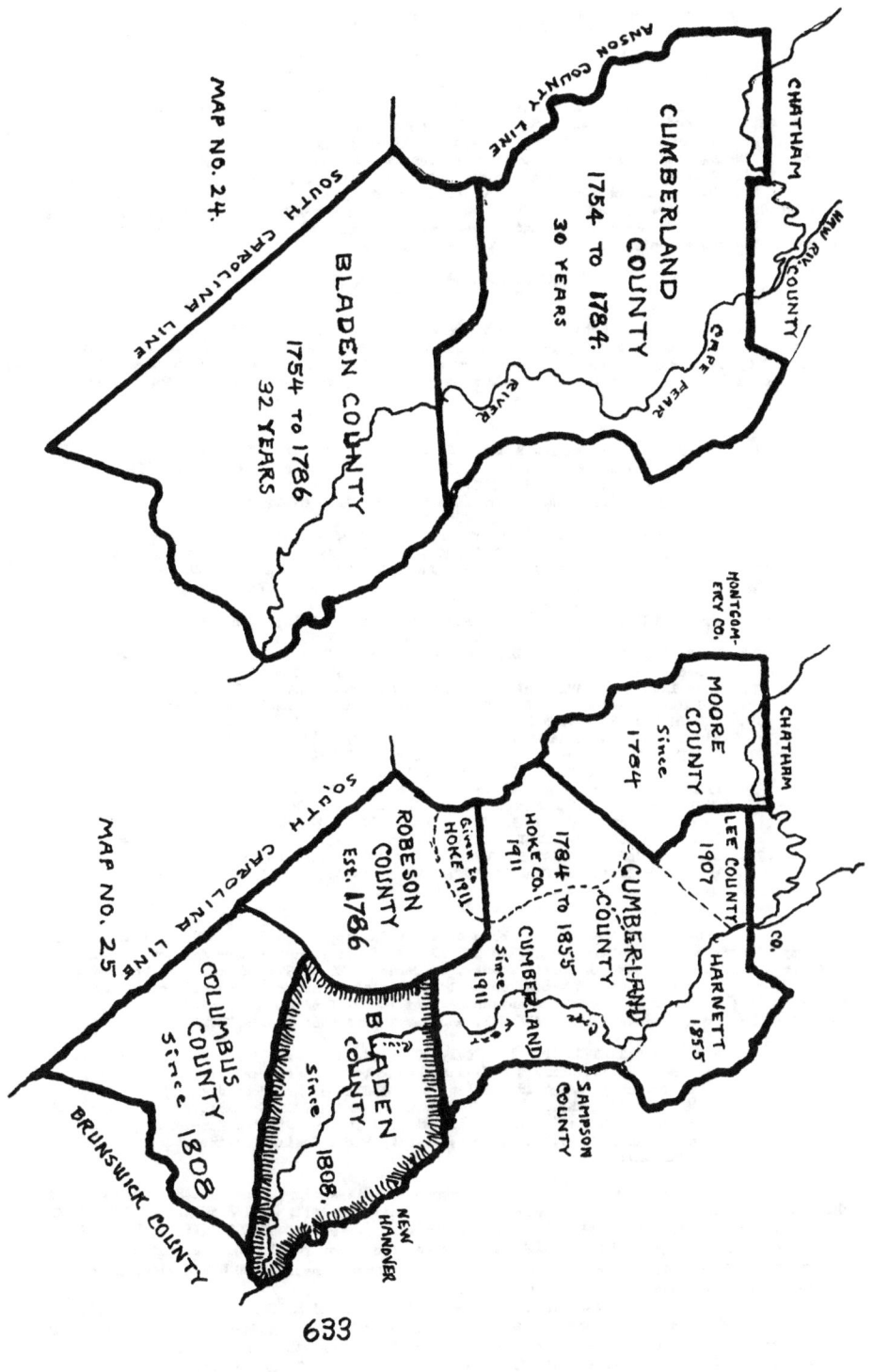

NORTH CAROLINA THOMAS DESCENDANTS
IN OTHER STATES

In Vol. 2, of Hathaway's N. C. Historical & Genealogical Register, there is a long list of marriage bonds issued in BERTIE COUNTY, copied from the records of that County. These are published in different parts of the volume and in different issues. In order to aid the research worker in finding certain names, the writer has indexed the names of the bride and groom, the witnesses and the bondsmen, giving the sur-names only, in order to conserve space, and this index appears herein. During the period covered, which is nearly a hundred years, most of the THOMAS FAMILY of North Carolina, lived in BERTIE COUNTY. This list and index will be found of great value, and while the list appears short in the index, when properly checked, the results are surprising. For instance, the Thomas notation in the index is as follows:

THOMAS 320, 364-366, 368, 372
373, 374, 377, 590-593.

The hyphen between two numbers means that the name THOMAS occurs on all pages in the numbers given, and also the pages in between those numbers. In this way the information is conveyed, and space is saved. Thus, it is an accurate and dependable system, when carefully followed. By checking all THOMAS items included in the numbers thus given, we have found the following:

320. SARAH THOMAS m. BENJAMIN EDWARDS, Feb. 5, 1787. JOHN EDWARDS, Sec.
JOSIAH THOMAS, security on bond of JAMES THOMPSON m. ANNIE BAZEMORE, December 20, 1787.
364. JOHN THOMAS, security on marriage bond of JAMES OVERTON to MARY MITCHELL, Feb. 26, 1788.
365. JAMES THOMAS m. MARY STANDLEY, Sept. 6, 1790, WHITMELL WHITEACRE, Sec.
366. LEODICEA THOMAS m. BENJAMIN SHOLAR, Jan. 25, 1791. EZEKIEL THOMAS, Sec.
368. ZADOCK THOMAS m. DICEA BAZEMORE Jan. 12, 1783. JAMES WILFORD, Sec.
372. JAMES THOMAS security on marriage bond of MALACHI OLIVER to POLLY EDWARDS, April 29, 1798.
J. (JAMES) THOMAS, surety on marriage bond of PHILLIP STALLINGS to ELIZABETH BAZEMORE, August 15, 1798.
373. EZEKIEL THOMAS m. ELIZABETH WESTON, March 2, 1799. JONATHAN SPIVEY, Sec.
374. SARAH THOMAS m. JOHN BRAYBOY, November 26, 1800. JOHN THOMAS Security.
JOHN THOMAS m. SARAH BRITT, November 26, 1800. JOSEPH BURCH, Sec.
377. ELISHA THOMAS m. POLLY BURNS, October 15, 1805. HENRY BATE, Security.
590. JUDITH THOMAS m. JOHN FIFE, March 23, 1827. WILLIAM W. CHERRY, Security.
NANCY THOMAS m. ISAAC MYLES, March 10, 1827. WILLIAM W. ASBELL, Security.
591. JOSEPH THOMAS security on marriage bond of PEYTON BAZEMORE to PENELOPE JOHNSTON, February 20, 1828.
MARTHA THOMAS m. WILLIS GRIFFIN, March 1, 1828. W. C. BIRD, Security.
592. JOHN THOMAS m. SARAH RAYNER, March 13, 1829. JOHN THOMAS, Surety.
HANNAH THOMAS m. REDDIN BAZEMORE, April 11, 1831. M. THOMAS, Security.
MICHAEL THOMAS m. BETSY JOHNSTON, August 4, 1831. REDDIN BAZEMORE, Sec.
593. G. E. THOMAS m. DICEA RAYNER, October 30, 1832. JONATHAN S. TAYLOE, Sec.
ELIZABETH THOMAS m. CHARLES BUTTERTON, Jan. 1, 1833. WILLIS GRIFFIN, Sec.

The second item on the above notes, which appears on page 320, of Vol. II, of Hathaway's Register, shows that one JOSIAH THOMAS was security on the marriage bond of JAMES THOMPSON and ANNIE BAZEMORE, in Bertie County, on December 20, 1787. The marriage bond of this JOSIAH THOMAS, himself, does not appear among those listed by Mr. Hathaway, but eight pages farther over (Vol. 2 p. 328) is found an abstract of the will of one JOHN BAZEMORE, SR., which shows that he had a daughter SARAH BAZEMORE, who was the wife of JOSIAH THOMAS. It reads:

BAZEMORE, JOHN SR. July 10, 1789. May Term, 1790. Sons, John, Thomas, James and William, daughters Tamer Sowell (wife of Francis), SARAH THOMAS (wife of JOSIAH), grandchildren, MICHAEL, JORDAN, JOSIAH, ELIZABETH and SARAH THOMAS; daughter Elizabeth White (wife of William), Jesse and William Bazemore, and Francis Pugh, Exrs. Test. Francis Pugh, Josiah Collins and JOHN DAUGHTRY.

On the Chart of "203. Joseph Thomas and His Family", the JOSIAH THOMAS who was the son in law of John Bazemore, as shown above, is listed as 411. JOSIAH THOMAS m. SARAH BAZEMORE, and the grandson JOSIAH THOMAS, in the above will is "562. JOSIAH THOMAS m. TABITHA". The names of the children of 562 JOSIAH THOMAS come to us from family sources, which fortunately have been preserved, but bare of any mention of the maiden name of JOSIAH'S wife, TABITHA, leaving us to speculate frantically on that point.

As will be ascertained from the Chart, 411 JOSIAH THOMAS, who married SARAH BAZEMORE, was the son of 330 JOSEPH THOMAS, who married ANN, and grandson of 203. JOSEPH THOMAS whose name is at the head of the Chart. 203. JOSEPH THOMAS was the son of 100 JOHN THOMAS and either his first or second wife, SUSANNAH PORTIS or MARY LAWRENCE, and JOHN'S parents were RICHARD THOMAS and his wife ELIZABETH MARSHALL, daughter of HUMPHREY MARSHALL of Isle of Wight.

611. JAMES SHERROD THOMAS

(See Chart)

611. JAMES SHERROD THOMAS was the son of 562. JOSIAH THOMAS and his wife TABITHA, and he married HENRIETTA ELIZABETH COPPAGE, a member of the COPPAGE FAMILY of FRANKLIN COUNTY, North Carolina. The names of WILLIAM COPPAGE, CHARLES COPPAGE and JESSE COPPAGE appear on the census of 1800 in Franklin County, North Carolina, likewise the name of JAMES DEW is on the same list (See p. 207 of this work). HENRIETTA ELIZABETH COPPAGE was born in 1802, according to the family record, and she may have been a daughter of one or the other of these COPPAGES. THOMAS SHERROD and DURHAM HALL were members of the House of Commons from FRANKLIN COUNTY, N. C. in 1784 and 1785, while HENRY HILL was the member of the Senate. (Wheeler, p. 149). Fortunately we have been furnished with the entries in the old JOSIAH THOMAS BIBLE, now in the possession of a MRS. ADDIE McKELVEY, of MEDINA, TENNESSEE, which shows:

JOSIAH THOMAS was born 24 September, 1770.
TABITHA THOMAS was born 19 April, 1777.

BETSY THOMAS, daughter of JOSIAH and TABITHA THOMAS born 9 March, 1799.
JAMES THOMAS son of JOSIAH and TABITHA THOMAS born 4 March, 1801.
NANCY THOMAS, daughter of JOSIAH and TABITHA THOMAS born 28 April, 1803.
MARTHA THOMAS, daughter of JOSIAH and TABITHA, hi wife, born Sept. 29, 1805.
MARY THOMAS, daughter of JOSIAH and TABITHA, his wife, born May 20, 1808.
JOSEPH JOHN THOMAS was born August 30, 1810.
MATILDA W. THOMAS was born April 10, 1813.

JOSIAH THOMAS departed this life 5 April in his 59th year, 1830.
ELIZABETH THOMAS was born January 1, 1730, died Sept. 10, 1814.

There is a persistent tradition in this THOMAS FAMILY that the mother of JOSIAH THOMAS was ELIZABETH (last name unknown) and not SARAH (BAZEMORE), as shown on the 203. JOSEPH THOMAS CHART, and in the will of JOHN BAZEMORE, and the last Bible entry above strengthens the tradition. Who was this ELIZABETH THOMAS (b. 1730, d. 1814) at the age of 84 years? Certainly the mother of the children of 411 JOSIAH THOMAS was Sarah Bazemore, who was living in 1789, as the will of JOHN BAZEMORE SR. (2 Hathaway, p.328) shows. But SARAH (BAZEMORE) THOMAS may have died, and the first JOSIAH THOMAS may have married ELIZABETH as his second wife, and she could have been the subject of the last entry. Or, this ELIZABETH THOMAS, could have been 414 ELIZABETH THOMAS, sister of 411 JOSIAH and the spinster AUNT of 562 JOSIAH THOMAS who married TABITHA, living with her nephew's family in 1814 at the time of her death. After canvassing all angles of the problem, the compiler believes the actual records presented are correct, and that the explanation of ELIZABETH on the Bible is one or the other of the two suppositions above stated.

701. MARTHA JANE THOMAS

married, probably in SUMNER COUNTY, TENNESSEE, where both THOMAS and BARRETT families had removed from North Carolina, MARCUS LAFAYETTE BARRETT. After his death, the widow married second, WILLIAM CHAPMAN. The BARRETTS settled in West Tennessee, near or at the town of TRENTON, with many of their kinsmen on both sides of the house. Children of M. L. BARRETT and MARTHA JANE THOMAS were:

        800. WILLIAM FRANKLIN BARRETT (1846-1875)
        801. ISABEL BARRETT   (Died Young).
        802. LAVERA BARRETT
        803. LOVELLA BARRETT   (Twins - both died young.)
        804. MARCUS LAFAYETTE BARRETT II (b. 1855) (d. 194..)

804. MARCUS LAFAYETTE BARRETT II, married SARAH AMELIA BURNS, and moved from TRENTON, TENNESSEE, to BONHAM, TEXAS, where he settled, and raised an interesting family, several, or almost all of whom became prominent in the public life of the State. Among his children were the HON. A. P. BARRETT, who in 1906 missed going to the U. S. Congress from the Bonham District, by a fraction of a convention vote, based on the election returns, and who was again defeated by a close margin in the San Antonio district, whence he had removed. Later he settled in FORT WORTH, TEXAS, where he was the first President of the great Continental Air Line System. His brother ANDREW, also of Fort Worth is connected with a transportation concern, and HON. GRADY BARRETT, of San Antonio, is one of the leading members of the bar of that City, while another brother THURMAN BARRETT ranks high among the real estate owners and builders in the Alamo City. There were other children of this family, and only those have been mentioned with whom this writer has enjoyed an intimate business and professional acquaintance. MRS. DAISY BARRETT TANNER, one of the sisters, and an authority on the fine arts, recently of Boston, but back in Texas to live, has aided the compiler in his efforts to set down something of the history of this branch of the Thomas family.

      With reference to the marriage bonds copied from HATHAWAY, it will be noted that there are a number of intermarriages shown between the THOMAS and BAZEMORE families. Every Thomas shown in this list of marriages has not been placed, either in the Charts or the notes herewith presented. This is work that is left for other research workers who are interested in the THOMAS and allied families. Every entry shown has its significance in the THOMAS HISTORY.

333. JAMES THOMAS m. SARAH BARNES

JAMES THOMAS who married SARAH BARNES was a brother of 330 JOSEPH THOMAS whose wife was ANN. SARAH BARNES was the daughter of HENRY BARNES. Her sister MARY BARNES married a DUNNING and she had a brother HENRY BARNES. HENRY, MARY and SARAH BARNES were first cousins of JOHN, CADER and SOLOMON BARNES. An abstract of the will of 333 JAMES THOMAS appears on pp. 357-8 of Vol. 2, of Hathaway's N. C. Hist. & Gen. Register, and is as follows:

THOMAS, JAMES, October 22, 1780. November Term, 1780. Wife, SARAH; sons EZEKIEL, LUKE and JAMES, daughters SELAH DEMENT (wife of CHARLES), LUNDILL, SARAH and LYDIA. DAVID OUTLAW and son EZEKI-EL, Exrs. Test. ABNER EASON, JOHN EASON, MARY PRITCHARD.

The third son named in this will married MARY STANDLEY, Sept. 6, 1790, with WHITMELL WHITEACRE as security on the marriage bond. (Page 365, Vol. 2, Hathaway). This marriage is shown on the list of marriage bonds copied herewith. They had the following children and grandchildren:

Children:

1. CULLEN	2. TEMPERANCE	3. PERRY, SR.	4. STARKIE	5. MARY	6. JAMES	7. STANDLE
:	:	: Grnd-Ch:	:	:	:	:
ALFRED THOMAS	CLARISA THOMAS	ALBERT THOMAS	WILLIAM B.	married	EDWARD C.	ROBT. B.
PEYTON THOMAS		ALPHA THOMAS	STANDLEY	and had	CARRELL	HENRY C.
MARY THOMAS		ALLISON THOMAS	ADELINE	12 child-	INFANT	SARAH.
JAMES THOMAS		WILLIAM THOMAS	JAMES J.	ren.	CLARK	
EMELINE THOMAS		RUFUS K. THOMAS	ALFRED		POLLY	
JOHN C. THOMAS		FRANKLIN THOMAS	PEACHIE		AMANDA	
WILLIAM C. THOMAS		JAMES H. THOMAS	FRANCIS			
		PERRY THOMAS	BLUFORD			
		ELIZA THOMAS	PERRY C.		Children and Grand-	
THIS CHART SHOWS A TOTAL		CHILTON THOMAS	STARKIE A.		children of JAMES THOMAS	
OF FIFTY FOUR (54)		STARKIE THOMAS	MARY		and MARY STANDLEY.	
GRANDCHILDREN		JOSEPHINE T.				
		ETHA THOMAS				
		W. SCOTT THOMAS				

One of the sons of 1. CULLEN THOMAS of the above chart had a son named CHARLES CRAWFORD THOMAS (Called CRAFFORD on the old records), who married ELIZABETH COWAN, in TENNESSEE, and they were the parents of HON. CULLEN F. THOMAS, celebrated as an orator and lawyer, who died a few years ago in DALLAS, TEXAS, and whose wife was OLGA SHEPPARD, sister of HON. MORRIS SHEPPARD, the author of the Eighteenth Amendment to the Constitution, who for more than half his lifetime was the beloved United States Senator from Texas. Thus, the grandfather of HON. CULLEN F. THOMAS was one of the grandsons of JAMES THOMAS and MARY STANDLEY.

PERRY THOMAS, SR., one of the sons of 417 JAMES THOMAS and his wife MARY STANDLEY, and who was a second cousin of 562. JOSIAH THOMAS who married TABITHA, was 89 years old in 1885, and at that advanced age, wrote the following account of his father's family:

PERRY THOMAS SKETCH

A short biographical sketch of the paternal and maternal ancestry of Perry Thomas, Sr., which was written by his own hand August 18, 1885, and in the 89th year of his age, going back as far as his information enables him, as obtained from his father many years ago.

PATERNAL - JAMES THOMAS, his grandfather, was a native of ENGLAND. He emigrated to America and located in Bertie County, N. C., sometime between 1725 and 1740. He married a MISS SARAH BARNES, daughter of HENRY BARNES, sister of old HENRY BARNES and MARY DUNNING, by whom he had three sons and four daughters. Eldest son, Luke, Ezekiel and James, my father. Luke died in the Western part of North Carolina, leaving a son named William and a daughter named SALLIE. Ezekiel married a Miss Holland, by whom he had three sons and one daughter. Eldest son, Luke, Ezekiel and Eli, who died when a boy; the first two died in Tennessee. The daughter Sally married ROBERT HENRY; she died in NORTH CAROLINA. JAMES, my father, married MOLLIE STANDLEY, a daughter of Edmund Standley, by whom he had five sons and two daughters, towit: CULLEN, PERRY, STARKIE, JAMES, STANDLEY, TEMPERANCE and POLLY. They all married, lived and died in KENTUCKY. The names of the sisters of my father are as follows: SALLY, who married MR. EDWARDS, afterwards JAMES FOREMAN, then old MR. GREER. She died in TENNESSEE. UREDICA married BENJAMIN SHOLAR. She had two sons and one daughter, towit: ALLEN, BENJAMIN and SALLY. She died in Kentucky. SELY married CHARLES DEMENT; she lived and died in TENNESSEE. LYDIA married JAMES LAWRENCE. She had two sons and five daughters. She died in KENTUCKY.

Obviously, MR. THOMAS was a little mixed in his family history, but the statement has great value, just the same.

331. MICHAEL THOMAS

331. MICHAEL THOMAS was a brother of 330 JOSEPH THOMAS and 333. JAMES THOMAS, who married SARAH BARNES, and whose descendants went to Tennessee and Kentucky. This MICHAEL THOMAS was the son of JOSEPH THOMAS and his wife ALICE who went to BERTIE COUNTY, N. C., where most, if not all of his children followed, or had preceded him. But MICHAEL migrated in a different direction and about 1745-1748 patented 600 acres of land on Hog Creek and Rockfish river, in ALBEMARLE COUNTY, VIRGINIA, about the time that county was carved out of GOOCHLAND and the lands began to be parcelled out to the early comers. This MICHAEL THOMAS lived until 1802 and must have been of a ripe old age at the time of his death, since his father JOSEPH died in BERTIE COUNTY, North Carolina in 1735. In the 1780s MICHAEL THOMAS served ALBEMARLE COUNTY as a magistrate and also as Sheriff, and EDWARD MOORE and MENAN MILLS were two of his deputies. The name of his first wife is unknown (granting that he was only twice married) and he married ELIZABETH STATON as his second wife in 1792. The account (Wood's Albemarle County, p. 327) says that his son RALPH THOMAS, and his grown grandson JOHN CARROLL went across the mountains after the license. Of course there were probably no children by his last marriage. By his previous marriage 331. MICHAEL THOMAS had the following children:

    450. MICHAEL THOMAS (d. 1826).
    451. JOSEPH THOMAS (d. 1797)
    452. JESSE THOMAS
    453. RALPH THOMAS
    454. EDWARD THOMAS
    455. JAMES THOMAS
    456. ..... THOMAS (Dau.) m. CARROLL.

580. JOHN THOMAS

580. JOHN THOMAS was evidently a grandson of 331. MICHAEL THOMAS, of ALBEMARLE COUNTY, and a son of one of the sons listed above - which one, being a problem to which we are unable to find the answer. He lived in that part of old ALBEMARLE COUNTY, VIRGINIA, which became AMHERST COUNTY, and married FRANCES HENDERSON as his first wife. FRANCES HENDERSON was the daughter of JOHN HENDERSON, SR., a brother of SAMUEL HENDERSON, of GRANVILLE COUNTY, NORTH CAROLINA. JOHN THOMAS' wife was therefore a first cousin of JUDGE RICHARD HENDERSON, of GRANVILLE COUNTY. See pages 223-224 of this volume, for a previous account. JOHN HENDERSON sr. married the daughter of BENNETT GOODE, and JOHN THOMAS' wife was the sister of BENNETT HENDERSON who married ELIZABETH LEWIS, daughter of CHARLES LEWIS, who married MARY RANDOLPH, daughter of ISHAM RANDOLPH, so that BENNETT HENDERSON's wife was sister of ISHAM LEWIS (named for ISHAM RANDOLPH - down in HENRICO COUNTY), and JOHN THOMAS' children were first cousins of ISHAM HENDERSON, son of BENNETT HENDERSON. HOWELL LEWIS, ELIZABETH'S uncle in GRANVILLE COUNTY, N. C., had daughter MILDRED LEWIS who married JOHN COBBS - just another connection between the THOMAS and COBB families.

But from the marriage of this same 580 JOHN THOMAS, a second time to FRANCES LEWIS, sister of ISHAM LEWIS, came forth an ISHAM THOMAS, born in KENTUCKY in 1807, who married ADA...and moved to DALLAS, TEXAS, where in 1860 his son, W. H. THOMAS was the first Civil officer - County surveyor. This W. H. THOMAS was the father of HON. MIKE THOMAS, millionaire cotton dealer and a member for many years of the New York Stock Exchange. Another son of ISHAM THOMAS and his wife ADA was JAMES PINCKNEY THOMAS (born in Kentucky in 1840). Please note that 565 LUKE THOMAS on the 203 JOSEPH THOMAS CHART had a son 620 PINCKNEY THOMAS, whose mother ELIZABETH BARRADELL was from Kentucky, where the family probably lived. In Wood's account of the Albemarle County THOMAS FAMILY (p. 327) he says that 331. MICHAEL THOMAS came from down on the JAMES RIVER in Eastern Virginia, which means NANSEMOND or ISLE OF WIGHT COUNTY.

527. BENJAMIN I. THOMAS

This name will be found on the chart of 324 JOHN THOMAS AND HIS FAMILY, and he was one of the 22 children of REV. JOHN THOMAS JR., who after spending many years of his life in the ministry moved to HANCOCK COUNTY, GEORGIA, and settled between Sparta and Greensboro on SHOULDERBONE CREEK, and died about 1807.

527. BENJAMIN I. THOMAS settled in ALABAMA, coming there from GEORGIA as soon as the lands were opened up for settlement. Before 1820 he had settled in Texas. He had two sons:

    640. BENJAMIN THOMAS
    641. THEOPHILUS THOMAS

640. BENJAMIN THOMAS married MARTHA ENGLEDOW at NACOGDOCHES, TEXAS, Jan. 17, 1839. He served in the Texas revolution in Captain Kimbrough's Company. He died at San Antonio in 1891.

641. THEOPHILUS THOMAS was a Methodist Minister who served all but about five years of his life in Texas. He died in 1892 in his seventy-sixth year.

The wife of 641. THEOPHILUS THOMAS was SUSAN WINN, daughter of PETER WINN who probably lived in South Carolina, before emigrating to Texas, which he did. They had nine children.

410. MICHAEL THOMAS

410. MICHAEL THOMAS, the son of 330 JOSEPH THOMAS and his wife ANN, of BERTIE COUNTY, joined the POPES, McKINNIES and some of the BOONS, and removed to GEORGIA. The records, what few there are, in regard to his family and descendants, will be found in the two volumes of the "EARLY RECORDS of GEORGIA - WILKES COUNTY" compiled in recent years by MRS. WILLIAM LEE DAVIDSON. It may be that only his children went to GEORGIA, and that MICHAEL, himself, died in North Carolina, somewhere, but the inference is that he died in WILKES COUNTY, for on April 10, 1793, there is a record of MICHAEL and WILLIAM THOMAS, sons of MICHAEL THOMAS, deceased. The wills of PHILLIP THOMAS and MICHAEL THOMAS were recorded in the lost Will Book "D"D" for the years 1779-1792. From all of the items that appear on these records it is thought reasonable to assume that 410 MICHAEL THOMAS had:

530. MICHAEL THOMAS
531. PHILLIP THOMAS (d. 1786)
532. SAMUEL THOMAS

with a possibility that there were quite a number of other sons and some daughters. The above, however, are found on the Wilkes County records, with somewhat of their activities in GEORGIA. No trace except that there was one, has been found of the will of 530. MICHAEL THOMAS, and that he had at least two sons, MICHAEL and WILLIAM (vol. 1 p. 186 Davidson).

531. PHILLIP THOMAS died in Wilkes County, Georgia, will dated January 3, 1786 (Vol. 1, p. 50, Davidson), in which he mentions:

1. Wife MARY.
2. Son, JOHN THOMAS
3. Son, AUGUSTAIN THOMAS
4. Daughter, MARY THOMAS m. (1) NEWTON (2) MICHAEL WHATLEY.
5. Daughter, RACHEL THOMAS m. JOHN COOPER
6. Daughter, ANN THOMAS m. JONES.
7. Daughter, ELIZABETH THOMAS m. HOLMES.
8. Daughter, MARGARET THOMAS
9. Daughter, HANNAH THOMAS m. JOHN HOLMES
10. Son, BENJAMIN THOMAS (d. 1798, John Holmes, Admr.)
11. Son, EDWARD THOMAS (Minor, to be educated).

Exrs, WIFE MARY, and son BENJAMIN THOMAS
Witnesses, THOMAS BROWN and wife ANN BROWN.

532. SAMUEL THOMAS was member of the jury of WILKES COUNTY at the May term of the Court in 1790. Beyond that, no further record has been found of him

---

325. MICHAEL THOMAS

This MICHAEL THOMAS, who appears on the chart of 100 JOHN THOMAS and HIS FAMILY, was a son of 202 WILLIAM THOMAS and his wife MARTHA ROBINSON. He died in BERTIE COUNTY, NORTH CAROLINA, December 19, 1766. The following abstract of his will appears on page 357, Volume 2, of Hathaway's N. C. Hist. & Gen. Register:

THOMAS, MICHAEL, December 19, 1766. THOMAS PUGH, HARDY HAYNE and ANN THOMAS, Exrs. Son JOSEPH, daughter JUDY, wife, sister ELIZABETH THOMAS and brothers LEWIS and WILLIAM THOMAS. Wits, ROBERT CAKE, GEO. WINSLOW, ABAM RABY.

No further items regarding the family of this MICHAEL have been found and identified on the records.

THE STANDLEYS

EDMUND STANDLEY, my grandfather, married perhaps a MISS PERRY, by whom he had four sons and five daughters, WILLIAM, EDMUND, PERRY and JONATHAN. The daughters were JERUSHA, MOLLY, my mother, SALLY, MARGARET and ABRILLY. JERUSHA married JOHN BARNES. MOLLIE married JAMES THOMAS, my father. SALLY married JAMES BARADELL. MARGARET married JAMES MITCHELL, and ABRILLY married DUNNING BRUSE. The husbands of Sally and Margaret were soldiers in the war of 1812, and died in CANADA. WILLIAM, EDMUND, PERRY and JONATHAN all lived and died in NORTH CAROLINA. MOLLIE, SALLY and ABRILLY all lived and died in KENTUCKY. ABRILLA'S husband died in HOPKINS COUNTY, Kentucky; there she lived and died. JERUSHA and MARGARET MITCHELL died in OBION COUNTY, TENNESSEE. JERUSHA'S husband, JOHN BARNES, died in NORTH CAROLINA. OLD MARY DUNNING and old HENRY BARNES were my father's aunt and uncle. Old SOLOMON BARNES, CADER BARNES and JOHN BARNES were my father's cousins.

-- From the account written by PERRY THOMAS SR., son of 417 JAMES THOMAS, son of 333 JAMES THOMAS and his wife SARAH BARNES, in 1885.

THE ANCESTRY OF WILL ROGERS
OF THE LOST TRIBES OF OLD ALBEMARLE

The great AMERICAN STATESMAN, who never held a public office; the GREAT ENTERTAINER who never assumed a character other than himself, and the great writer and commentator who never wrote a single book, and who had as many warm personal friends in the forty-eight States of his native country as there were names on the latest UNITED STATES CENSUS, could have truthfully boasted that his forbears were among the children of OLD ALBEMARLE and that he was a descendant of the earliest settlers of the OLD NORTH STATE.

WILL ROGERS, whose towering personality, opened the doors of royal palaces throughout all Europe, won recognition and hearty welcome in the draperied drawing rooms of the orient, brought joy and laughter to the dingy hovels of the poor, and hurled stinging darts into the consciences of those who prayed on the misfortunes of their fellow men, throughout the civilized World, was at home even in the so-called cultural circles of the haughty, and the humble backwoods homes of mountains and plains. In haughty Boston he held the Mayflower Descendants that his own ancestors met theirs at the landing Beach, and his every utterance to the time of his demise, sent ripples of roaring laughter, and waves of spontaneous applause, flashing around the little old Earth, from pole to pole. His wit, his humor, his philosophy and his native wise-cracks, staved off endangering physical and economic ills, kept listening millions in a good humor during his brief life-time, and no sooner was his seething voice stilled by the ruthless scythe of Father Time, than, (as he might have said, himself) "hell broke loose in Georgia", and World War No. 2 arrived.

It is probably literally true that among the aborigines who met the Mayflower, and who came "down out of the woods" to meet the first vessel that arrived at Jamestown, were ancestors of WILL ROGERS. He was related to the CHEROKEE INDIANS through different branches and angles of his family, but this relationship came always through his maternal connections.

Instead of meeting the MAYFLOWER passengers at the "beach-head", the real ROGERS ancestor of the great commentator, one EDWARD ROGERS arrived in America and landed at JAMESTOWN on a vessel called the "ANNE" in 1623. On February 3, 1626, three years later, CAPT. WILLIAM EPPES patented 450 acres of land in ACCOMAC, which he claimed was due him for the transportation of nine persons, among whom were WILLIAM JONES, WILLIAM GALLAWAY, JOHN BARKER, EDWARD ROGERS and THOMAS WARDEN, "who all arrived in the "Anne" in 1623". (Nugent, p. 7).

At this point the reader's attention is called to two things: First, that one of the persons named above, with EDWARD ROGERS was WILLIAM GALLAWAY; second that the notes which follow will show that both the Grandfather and the Great Grandfather of the subject, WILL ROGERS, were named ROBERT ROGERS.

The last will and testament of a ROBERT ROGERS, of CHOWAN COUNTY, N. C., in the original, may be seen in the North Carolina State Department of Archives and History, in North Carolina Wills, 1663-1789, Volume 27, ROD-SCH p. 12, in which he mentions:
Daughter ELIZABETH, the now wife of SIMON DANIEL (She may have been married before or he may have been married before).
Two grandsons, ROBERT DANIEL and WILLIAM ROGERS (to have all my tract of land containing 630 acres, lying in BERTIE PRECINCT.
The children of my son ROBERT ROGERS and the children of my daughter ELIZABETH DANIEL.
Legacy to MARY GALLOWAY and one to THOMAS GALLOWAY..

Persons who came to VIRGINIA in the earlier years (1623 for instance) in the same vessel (the ANNE, for instance) as did EDWARD ROGERS and WILLIAM GALLAWAY, were possibly kinsmen in the first place. In the years and generations that followed they continued - usually - their original and previous intimate relations. This ROBERT ROGERS does not mention even the CHRISTIAN name of his wife. She may have been a GALLAWAY, and a descendant of WILLIAM, and these children may have been ROBERT ROGER'S step-children. Many such contingent relationships can be imagined, but it is safe to say they were at least relatives and certainly that they date back to the same WILLIAM GALLAWAY who came over in the "ANNE" with EDWARD ROGERS. These facts alone are sufficient to establish that the ROBERT ROGERS (will in 1736) was a descendant of EDWARD ROGERS of the ANNE. Other notes will strengthen these.

EDWARD ROGERS who came to VIRGINIA in the "ANNE" in 1623, settled at Capt. Christopher LAWNE'S plantation in Isle of Wight County, Virginia, where he had some distinguished and prominent neighbors who owned lands adjoining his own, in 1636. How long prior to that time he had owned lands there or been settled is problematical.

NICHOLAS REYNOLDS patented 1000 acres of land at LAWNE'S CREEK (Isle of Wight) S. S. E, up the same, N. N. E. upon the land of EDWARD ROGERS, North upon CAPT. WILLIAM PIERCE, down the Creek East and West into the woods. Dec. 23, 1636. (Nugent p. 53).

Here we have, beyond the slightest doubt, the ancestor of the ROGERS FAMILY of ISLE OF WIGHT and NANSEMOND COUNTY, Virginia. The ROBERT ROGERS, who left will in CHOWAN PRECINCT in 1736, was from either Nansemond or Isle of Wight. MICHAEL ROGERS, who left will in ISLE OF WIGHT in 1710

639

mentions four grandchildren named THOMAS, and appoints RICHARD THOMAS, a son in law, as the Executor of his will. Other members of the ROGERS family in ISLE OF WIGHT are shown by the following records:

In 1664 William Thompson bound himself to pay WILLIAM ROGERS 3500 pounds of tobacco and bound out his son THOMAS HARVEY to said WILLIAM ROGERS (Boddie p.544).

DEC. 10, 1677 WILLIAM ROGERS and his wife DOROTHY sold THOMAS PARKER 150 acres of land where ROGERS then lived. This was witnessed by JOHN PORTIS (See THOMAS CHART) Boddie. p. 578.

In 1693 JOHN PARKER, son of the above THOMAS refers to this same transaction - land his father bought of WILLIAM ROGERS in 1677, in an instrument witnessed by JACOB BARNES and DAN MILES. Boddie, p. 612.

CHRISTIE BODDIE, a daughter of OBEDIAH BOIDIE, son of JOHN BODDIE married a ROGERS, who was killed in the C. S. A. Beddie p. 383.

EDWARD ROGERS patented 300 acres in Isle of Wight in 1637 and also a tract in Nansemond the same year. Boddie p. 78. Another note says he patented 300 acres in May 1636 "adjoining THOMAS JORDAN". Boddie p. 658

NOV. 9, 1681 RICHARD BOOTH sold land to JOHN ROGERS on Beaverdam swamp in Isle of Wight, and says he "gives to his sister MARY ROGERS, wife of JOHN ROGERS, said land. Beddie p. 590.

JOHN ROGERS (JR.) was granted 200 acres in SURRY COUNTY by Gov. BERKELEY in 1682, and JOHN ROGERS SR. and his wife MARY is mentioned. Beddie, p. 593. RICHARD BOOTH again mentions JOHN ROGERS, April 20, 1680, along with THOMAS MANN and wife ELIZABETH. Boddie p. 608.

In 1672-73 JOHN FRIZZELL and his wife ANN sold land to LEWIS ROGERS he had bought from NICHOLAS COBB, in Isle of Wight. Boddie p. 569.

RICHARD ROGERS and GEORGE WILLIAMSON witnessed a deed to THOMAS MOORE on Lawne's Creek 1694. Beddie p. 616.

The foregoing notes show that in ISLE OF WIGHT COUNTY, before 1677, WILLIAM ROGERS had married DOROTHY; that JOHN ROGERS before 1681 had married MARY BOOTH, daughter of RICHARD BOOTH, and that they had a son JOHN ROGERS, JR. who patented land in 1682, so that he must have been born at least by 1660. That THOMAS MANN probably married his wife's sister, ELIZABETH BOOTH, and that LEWIS ROGERS was buying and selling lands in 1672; a RICHARD ROGERS witnessing deeds in 1694, and that MICHAEL ROGERS was an old man with grandchildren, when he died in Isle of Wight in 1710. Other records, not conveniently available, are several records of ROBERT ROGERS in the same section; and all of this gives a kind of bird's-eye view of the descendants of EDWARD ROGERS who lived in ISLE OF WIGHT and NANSEMOND before 1700.

THE ROGERS AND VANN CONNECTION

EDWARD VANN patented 250 acres on the Southern Branch of NANSEMOND RIVER, Isle of Wight County, Virginia, on APRIL 9, 1662, and a WILLIAM VANN and JOHN VANN appear on the records about the same time, one as a headright in ACCOMAC and the other in LOWER NORFOLK. (Nugent 393 and 553.). An EDWARD VANN in 1730 bought part of the lands patented by JOHN ALSTON in what is now GATES --then CHOWAN - in North Carolina. He died leaving a will in CHOWAN in 1752, with JOHN VANN and WILLIAM VANN as witnesses. (See page 172 of this volume). JOSEPH VANN left a will in CHOWAN also in 1753. (Ibid) In 1735 he witnessed a deed by ABRAHAM ODOM, and in 1739 he and JOHN THOMAS and WILLIAM LANGSTON witnessed a deed to lands. The witnesses to his own will were THOMAS and SARAH LANGSTON (Ibid). WILLIAM VANN left will in CHOTAN, naming children, in 1740 (Hathaway Vol. 1 p. 79. DORCAS LANGSTON married a VANN and died leaving a will in GATES COUNTY in 1793 (Hathaway Vol. 2, p. 77.) Then these items:

RICHARD ROGERS bought lands from JOHN ALSTON in 1733 (Hathaway Vol. 2, p. 610).
ROBERT ROGERS with JOHN LANGSTON, JR. in 1739 witnessed a deed to JOHN LANGSTON (Hathaway Vol. 3, p. 133; ROBERT ROGERS and MONTFORD LANGSTON, JR. were granted lands in 1733 together. (Hathaway Vol 1, p. 19).
ROBERT ROGERS was "of Nansemond County, Va." when he bought lands from JOHN WILLIAMS, and ROBERT ROGERS, SR. witnessed

the deed. ROBERT ROGERS SR., mentioned above, is the one who died in BERKELEY PRECINCT, North Carolina, in 1729 (Hathaway Vol. 3, p. 405), while the ROBERT ROGERS, JR. is the one who left will in CHOWAN COUNTY in 1736 (Vol. 1, Hathaway p. 69) naming the children of his son ROBERT ROGERS and his daughter ELIZABETH DANIEL, the "now wife" of SIMON DANIEL. (Page 143 of this volume).

WHEN JOSEPH VANN died leaving a will in CHOWAN COUNTY in 1753, he named two sons, GEORGE and JACOB VANN, and daughters JUDITH, ANN (who m. a LANGSTON), ELIZABETH, MARY and DORCAS VANN. The witnesses were THOMAS and SARAH LANGSTON and JACOB ODOM. (Hathaway Vol. 1, page 497). When EDWARD VANN died leaving a will in the same place in 1738, he named his son EDWARD VANN, his wife MARY, and daughters ANN, SARAH and ELIZABETH VANN. His will was witnessed by John Lewis and JOHN VANN and WILLIAM VANN.

These VANNS, ROGERS, and LANGSTONS, according to the old records lived near SARUM CHAPEL, an old landmark in what is now GATES COUNTY, which was at the head of SARUM CREEK about five or six miles Northwest of the present town of GATESVILLE in the BENNETT'S CREEK section. There were two INDIAN TOWNS not far from this same settlement. (Hathaway Vol. 1 p. 255) One of these was near the mouth of the Meherrin River which was occupied by the MEHERRIN INDIANS. In fact, Indians were all around them at that period and it was much later when the Indian lands were laid out lower down on the Moratuck or Roanoke, in the bounds of the present BERTIE COUNTY.

Among the neighbors of these three named families were the ROSS FAMILY, the ODOMS, the HARES and the BARNES, JONES and WILLIAMS, as well as the ALSTONS and DANIELS, with whom they were intimate, and with which families they probably intermarried then and later. (See Hathaway, Vol. 1, p. 450.) A hundred years later they were still intermarrying and keeping up this same intimate relationship. Attention is called to the fact that in all of the VANN FAMILY mentioned, the name of a DAVID VANN does not appear, but that there was a DAVID VANN in this family somewhere, is inescapable, as will later appear.

————

Among the ancestors of WILL ROGERS, as will appear later, was the CORDERY FAMILY. The following note from the record is of interest in that particular:

MRS. ANNA BERNARD patented 1000 acres in NORTHUMBERLAND COUNTY April 3, 1651. Upon South side of Potomac river, adjoining THOMAS PEAKES land. For the transportation of 20 persons, among whom were MR. RICHARD BERNARD, Mrs. Anna Bernard, MRS. ELLENER CORDEROY, ELIZA BARNETT, CORDEROY BARNETT, WILLIAM CORDERY, EDWARD CORDEREY and several persons named IRONMONGER. (Nugent, p. 211).

Another family that plays an important role in the history of the family of the inimitable WILL ROGERS, deceased, is the DOWNING FAMILY. Few names occur oftener among the yeomanry of OLD ALBEMARLE and its records than that of the DOWNINGS, and particularly WILLIAM DOWNING. Likewise the name is a familiar one on the Isle of Wight records.

ELIZABETH BARCROFT patented 1200 acres of land in ISLE OF WIGHT COUNTY, Virginia, June 17, 1647, near the head of Seward's Creek, adjoining Mr. Cooper (Justinian) and CAPT. BERNARD, for the transportation of 24 persons. Just a few of the names listed were: JOHN HARDY, ELIAS COLEWELL, EDMOND GREEN, OWEN MIDDLETON, JOHN GODWIN, JOHN LEWIS, MARTIN CRAFFORD, EDMUND GRAVES, and WILLIAM DOWNING. (These headrights were all living in ISLE OF WIGHT at the time the patent was taken out), and most of them continued there. (Nugent, p. 166)

In 1650, ROBERT BIRD patented 1400 acres on the North side of the Rappahanneck River, and named 28 persons he claimed to have transported to VIRGINIA, among them being RICHARD DOWNING. (Nugent, p. 192).

It is the writer's conviction that RICHARD DOWNING settled along the RAPPAHANNOCK river and became the ancestor of the numerous DOWNINGS of that section of Virginia, that married into the SAUNDERS FAMILY and whose descendants also married into the family of PETER PRESLEY and the REV. DAVID LINDSAY. (54 Va. Mag. p. 58). They were also intermarried with the THOMAS FAMILY, cousins of the Isle of Wight and Nansemond THOMAS FAMILY (See Charts). RICHARD DOWNING was the father of the WILLIAM DOWNING of that section, while WILLIAM DOWNING was perhaps the father of the DOWNINGS who remained in ISLE OF WIGHT for a time, but went early down into OLD ALBEMARLE, with members of the ROGERS, SAUNDERS, LAWRENCE and other families about whom we are writing herein.

Among the neighbors of the ROGERS, ODOMS, LANGSTONS, BARNES, HARES and others who resided together along the waters of BENNETT'S CREEK and in the neighborhood of the INDIAN TOWNS and SARUM CHAPEL were the JONES FAMILY, including WILLIAM JONES, WILLIAM HARDING JONES and COL. FREDERICK JONES, well known and preeminent in the History of OLD ALBEMARLE and CHOWAN PRECINCT. JOHN COTTEN, about whom much has been heretofore said in these notes, married as his second wife, MARTHA, a daughter of COL. FREDERICK JONES (His first wife was MARTHA GODWIN, from Isle of Wight County). This JONES FAMILY came from Isle of Wight and from NORTHUMBERLAND COUNTY. When CAPT. WILLIAM DOWNING died in Northumberland County in 1655, the witness to his will was WILLIAM JONES, and when his son by his first marriage died in 1683, the witnesses were JOSEPH TIPTON and WILLIAM HARDING, and out of this jumble of unknown but intimate relationship came forth WILLIAM HARDING JONES, the brother of COL. FREDERICK JONES, of CHOWAN COUNTY 50 or 60 years later. MARGARET, the widow of CAPT. WILLIAM DOWNING, of Northumberland County, married EDWARD TIPTON, and they were the ancestors of SAMUEL, JOHN and JONATHAN TIPTON, later of the Watauga Valley in TENNESSEE. All these folks were related to WILL ROGERS from away back, as will be shown below:

WILL ROGERS was a direct descendant of CAPT. WILLIAM DOWNING, of Northumberland County, Virginia, and his connection comes about in this way:

CAPT. WILLIAM DOWNING married MARGARET (who m. (2) EDWARD TIPTON) and had:
MAJ. JOHN DOWNING who married HANNAH FAWLING. (Major Downing is said to have been a Major in the British Army).
His wife HANNAH FAWLING was a full blood CHEROKEE INDIAN, of the Wolfe clan. They were the parents of the following children:

1. GEORGE DOWNING
2. JOHN DOWNING m. (1) JENNIE (2) NANNIE.
3. WILLIAM DOWNING
4. NANNIE DOWNING

4. NANNIE DOWNING m (1) PETTIT (2) CRITTENDEN (3) McSWAIN. By McSWAIN she was the mother of two children:

10. ELIZABETH McSWAIN m. DAVID WELCH
11. MARGARET McSWAIN m. AVERY VANN.

AVERY VANN and MARGARET McSWAIN were the parents of the following children:

100. JOSEPH VANN m. (1) CATHERINE ROWE (2) ELIZABETH ROWE.
101. DAVID VANN m. (1) JENNIE CHAMBERS (2) MARTHA McNAIR
102. MARGARET VANN m. DAVID WEBBER
103. ANDREW M. VANN m. (1) MARGARET LASLEY (2) SUSIE ALEXANDER.
104. NANNIE VANN m. JOHN CHAMBERS
105. CATHERINE VANN m. JOHN ROGERS (2) WILLIAM WILLIAMS
106. MARY VANN m. WILLIAM LASLEY
107. KESIAH VANN m. ROBERT WEBBER.
108. CHARLES VANN m. ELIZA WEST
109. CLEMENT VANN
110. SALLIE VANN m. (1) ROBERT ROGERS (2) WILLIAM ALEXANDER MUSGROVE.
111. ELIZABETH VANN (b. 1820) m. (1) GEORGE WEST (2) DAVID ROWE.
112. ELIZA VANN m. JOHN MARTIN
113. CLARA VANN.
114. JENNIE VANN

100. JOSEPH VANN, who bore the CHEROKEE name of TEAULTLE, was born on February 11, 1798. He was a member of the Constitutional Convention (Cherokee Nation) from the Hightower District, in 1827, and that of 1839. President of the Senate (Cherokee Nation), from 1841 to 1843. He died May 3, 1877.
100 DAVID VANN was born January 1, 1800. He was elected Treasurer of the Cherokee Nation 1839, 1843, 1847 and 1851. He was killed by the "PIN" Indians December 23, 1863.
103. ANDREW M. VANN was a resident of the TEXAS CHEROKEE NATION on July 30, 1833. He was elected Assistant Chief of the Cherokee Nation on June 28, 1840, in the place of his brother, JOSEPH VANN, who had resigned.

JOHN ROGERS who married (1) HETTIE MOSELEY and (2) CATHERINE VANN was a brother of ROBERT ROGERS who married SALLIE VANN.

ROBERT ROGERS who married SALLIE VANN, was the grandfather of WILL ROGERS, the subject of this sketch. He and his wife SALLIE VANN had only two children:

200. MARGARET LAVINIA ROGERS m. ALLISON WOODVILLE TIMBERLAKE
201. CLEMENT VANN ROGERS m. (1) MARY AMERICA SCRIMSHER (2) MARY BIBLE.

201. CLEMENT VANN ROGERS (Known in Oklahoma as "Uncle Clem") and his first wife MARY SCRIMSHER, were the parents of WILL ROGERS.

The full name of our WILL ROGERS, known to fame, was WILLIAM PENN ROGERS. COL. WILLIAM PENN, a revolutionary soldier, whose daughter, MARTHA, married a ROGERS, lived in GEORGIA. This MARTHA (PENN) ROGERS was living 50 years ago, one of the few REAL DAUGHTERS OF THE AMERICAN REVOLUTION.

THE ROGERS FAMILY OF WILKES COUNTY, GA.

Among the descendants of EDWARD ROGERS who came to VIRGINIA in 1623 with WILLIAM GALLAWAY, were MICHAEL ROGERS, who left will in Isle of WIGHT County, Virginia, in 1710, and whose daughter married a THOMAS; JOHN ROGERS who proved his headrights in North Carolina in 1701 (Hathaway, Vol. 1, p. 305) and who was Constable of BARTIE COUNTY between CASHEY RIVER and WICACON CREEK in 1744 (Ibid Vol. 2, p. 625); ROBERT ROGERS, of Isle of Wight, who died in BERKELEY PRECINCT, N. C. in 1729 (Ibid Vol. 3, p. 405; his son ROBERT ROGERS, who died in 1739, in the SARUM CHAPEL neighborhood along Bennett's Creek (whose will has been given heretofore in these notes); his son, ROBERT ROGERS, and his grandson WILLIAM ROGERS (mentioned in said will.) Also a JOSEPH ROGERS, who died leaving a will in NORTHAMPTON COUNTY, North Carolina, on February 18, 1752 (Grimes, p. 318) who mentioned the following children:

(1) JOSEPH ROGERS
(2) AARON ROGERS
(3) ISOM ROGERS
(4) REUBEN ROGERS
(5) JOHN ROGERS
(6) DRURY ROGERS
(7) MICHAEL ROGERS
(8) FAITH ROGERS
(9) SARAH ROGERS m. TARVER
(10) MARY ROGERS m. LOWREY.

The following records, all taken from MRS. WILLIAM LEE DAVIDSON'S two volumes of "Early Records of Wilkes County, Ga.", will be of interest:

OCTOBER 2, 1786. DOROTHY ASHFIELD, of Wilkes County sold to JAMES ALFORD, both of GREENE COUNTY, GA., 200 acres of land between BRIAR and REEDY Creeks. Witnessed by AARON ROGERS.

This was apparently (2) AARON ROGERS mentioned in the will of JOSEPH ROGERS above.

OCTOBER 15, 1773. DRURY ROGERS had arrived in GEORGIA, with a wife, 3 sons and 5 daughters, from 13 to 1 year old and applied to the LAND BOARD for 100 acres on OGEECHEE on a small creek above the lower Trading Path. Resigned November 8, 1773. This land was taken up on October 10th, a month later by MICHAEL WELCH, an Irishman. (DAVID WELCH m. BETTY McSWAIN, a sister of MARGARET McSWAIN, the Great grandmother of WILLIAM PENN ROGERS).

DAVID HOLMAN, of Wilkes County, died about 1779, and DRURY ROGERS was appointed administrator. Drury's brother, (4) REUBEN ROGERS, with JOHN HILL, appraised the estate. DRURY ROGERS died between 1779 and 1792 and his will was recorded on Will Book "D. D." which was destroyed by fire.

JUNE 9, 1785, IGNATIUS FEW sold JOHN ONEAL, JR. 200 acres on OGEECHEE river adjoining DRURY ROGERS and DAVID PHELPS. Rene Napier was a witness.

On the first Tax Digest of WILKES COUNTY (about 1790) it is shown that:
DRURY ROGERS owned 200 acres on the OGEECHEE river, and also 287 1/2 acres. 487 1/2 acres in Washington County.
BRITTAIN ROGERS, 575 and 287 1/2 acres in Washington County.
REUBEN ROGERS 350 acres in Wilkes County.
Each one of these owned one slave.

The wife of DRURY ROGERS (6) in will of his father JOSEPH ROGERS, of Northampton County, N. C., was TABITHA. She died in 1793, leaving a will in which she named their children:

1. BURWELL ROGERS
2. PHATA (?) ROGERS
3. POLLY ROGERS
4. MICHAEL ROGERS (a minor)
5. JOHN ROGERS
6. BRITTAIN ROGERS
7. TABITHA ROGERS m. SAMUEL STOKES
8. TABBY ROGERS m. KENDRICK
9. SALLY ROGERS m. WOMACK
10. CELIA ROGERS m. JOHN RINES.

This will was proved Feb. 11, 1794. JOHN RICE and ABRAHAM BELL, witnesses.

THE VANN'S CREEK BAPTIST CHURCH

Down in ELBERT COUNTY, GEORGIA, there is an old landmark known as "VANN'S CREEK BAPTIST CHURCH". Of course it is located on a stream that is called "Vann's Creek". In the official history of ELBERT COUNTY, by Col. John H. McIntosh and the members of the STEPHEN HEARD CHAPTER of the D. A. R., published in 1940, much is said about this community. In telling the story of this section, the book says (pp. 51 and 52) "Settlements sprang up almost over night, and with this mecurial activity horse racing, cock fighting, turkey shoots, gaming and fox hunting became the order of the day. Briefly, and very briefly indeed, did such state of affairs continue unchallenged, for in 1784, when GENERAL GEORGE MATTHEWS came to GEORGIA, he was accompanied by REV. DOZIER THORNTON. The item continues:

>Before the Act of the Georgia Legislature was passed creating the County of Elbert, DOZIER THORNTON was busily engaged in preaching throughout the entire area of WILKES COUNTY. For a time he and MIDDLETON MEEKS served as MISSIONARIES TO THE CHEROKEE INDIANS. Neither Thornton nor Meeks evidenced the least fear upon entering the most hostile Indian town, and never once were they molested.

>It was during this period that DAVID VANN, the famous CHIEF OF THE CHEROKEES, was converted by the preaching of Thornton, and they became fast friends.

>The first important act of DOZIER THORNTON in Georgia, was the establishment of VANN'S CREEK BAPTIST CHURCH, named in honor of his INDIAN FRIEND. This event took place early in 1785, and VANN'S CREEK became the sixth Church of the Baptist faith to be established in all Georgia.

The County of ELBERT was at this time a part of WILKES COUNTY and some of the records pertaining to ELBERT COUNTY at that early date apply to people who lived in ELBERT COUNTY as it is today. In this deductive study of the VANN and ROGERS family, we find the following notes to be considered: (Wilkes County) From Vol. 1, Davidson's Records.

>About 1783 one WILLIAM MOSELEY was deceased and JAMES VANN was appointed administrator.

>Before the WIGHTSBORO land board, December 7, 1773, one JAMES VANN, from South Carolina, himself and one child, applied for 100 acres on SAVANNAH RIVER adjoining ALEXANDER MACHAN. At the same time THOMAS WOOTEN, from North Carolina, with his wife, 7 sons and one daughter, from 18 to one year old, was awarded 200 acres on North side of Broad River opposite the mouth of LONG CREEK, and 300 acres on the South side of said river adjoining VANN'S OLD FIELD. (The first tract was in what is now ELBERT COUNY and the second tract in what is now WILKES COUNTY.)

>1780. Charles Williams, BENJ. MOSELEY, James Garnett, Charles Parks, Sr., JAMES VANN and JAMES YORK were appointed appraisers.

>August 16, 1786. GEORGE WALTON, late of the County of WILKES, to Thomas Wingfield of said County, 1150 acres adjoining the town of Washington, original grant in 1784 to said Walton. Witnesses: JAMES VANN, ARTHER CORDY (CORDERY), HENRY NAIL and JOHN CRUTHFIELD.

>WILLIAM BEAL, from South Carolina, a wife, two sons and three daughters from 20 to 11 years old, 200 acres on the North side of Broad River, adjoining the lower line of JOHN VANN. This item dated in December, 1773.

>September 27, 1773. WILLIAM GLASSCOCK, himself his wife and one daughter 16 years old, 1000 acres at the mouth of Buffalo Creek, where JOSEPH VANN, SR. lives.

>NOV. 16, 1773. JOSEPH VANN, from South Carolina, his wife, three sons and four daughters, from 16 to 7 years old, 500 acres on the NORTH FORK OF LONG CREEK. (This was in WILKES COUNTY).

>MARCH 8, 1787. JOHN CRUTCHFIELD, Indian trader and wife SUSANNAH, to WILLIAM GRAVES, 200 acres on Golden Grove Creek, original grant to said Crutchfield in 1787. Witnesses were BASIL LAMAR and QUILLA VANN.

And here is our old GATES COUNTY, NORTH CAROLINA, neighbor and relative of the VANN and ROGERS FAMILY, on the same WILKES COUNTY RECORDS:

>SEPT. 10, 1791. JOHN LEGETT, of Wilkes County, to NATHAN ACHESON, of ELBERT COUNTY, 200 acres on Fork Creek, ELBERT COUNTY, adjoining Robert Cowden and JOHN TALBOT; JACOB STEM and JACOB EVERHART, Witnesses. (Page 160 Georgia Chap' Hist Coll., Vol. 3.)

W I L L I A M   R O G E R S   O F   W I L K E S   C O U N T Y ,   G E O R G I A

WILLIAM ROGERS, the Great Great Grandfather of WILL ROGERS, the famous AMERICAN, was the "Grandson, WILLIAM ROGERS" mentioned in the last will and testament of ROBERT ROGERS, of CHOWAN COUNTY, N. C. in 1739. His father was ROBERT ROGERS, the "Son, ROBERT ROGERS", whose "children" are mentioned in the same will. Just who the other "children" (brothers and sisters of this William) were, is uncertain, since their names are not mentioned.

This writer has examined the records pertaining to this family as far as he has found them available. Though error is possible, he is convinced of this much: That the ROBERT ROGERS, who died in 1739, was the son of another ROBERT ROGERS, who died ten years previously, also in BERTIE COUNTY, and that the last mentioned ROBERT ROGERS was perhaps a brother of MICHAEL ROGERS who died in ISLE OF WIGHT COUNTY, Virginia, leaving a will in 1710, and of JOSEPH ROGERS, who died leaving will in NORTHAMPTON COUNTY, N. C. in 1752. Also that:

ROBERT ROGERS (Son of ROBERT) had children:

1. WILLIAM ROGERS m. MARY
2. ROBERT ROGERS (d. NASH COUNTY in 1791) m. ANN
3. THOMAS ROGERS (d. NASH COUNTY in 1782).

2. ROBERT ROGERS left will in NASH COUNTY, N. C., probated at the August Court in Nash County in 1791, in which he named his wife ANN, and three sons, JACOB, JESSE and ROBERT ROGERS, and daughters BETTY, NANCY, CHARITY, MOURNING and ZANA ROGERS. So far as the records reveal only one of these children went to GEORGIA, and that was CHARITY, the daughter, who died in WILKES COUNTY, Georgia, prior to May 11, 1792, and of her estate WILLIAM ROGERS was appointed administrator. I think this was her uncle 1. WILLIAM ROGERS.

3. THOMAS ROGERS. The records of the Broad River settlement in WILKES and ELBERT COUNTIES, in GEORGIA, show that practically ALL of the children mentioned in the will of this THOMAS ROGERS, settled there, though some of them have not been certainly identified. Out of the list of children mentioned in his will, we find that the son PELEG was in ELBERT COUNTY, and that OBEDIENCE ROGERS and her husband THOMAS BARRON was there; that UNITY, another daughter was there, and MOURNING and her husband WILLIAM or EDWARD MOORE was there, among the residents of the VANN'S CREEK BAPTIST CHURCH settlement. The oldest son, JOHN ROGERS married NANCY and died in ELBERT COUNTY about 1796, when Nancy applied for letters of administration on his estate. The daughter, MARY ROGERS, who married THEOPHILUS THOMAS, may not have come to GEORGIA, but at least one of her sons, MICAJAH THOMAS settled over in Hancock County, Georgia, near his uncle REV. JOHN THOMAS on Shoulderbone Creek. In Davidson's Wilkes County Records numerous deeds and instruments bear the names of JAMES and THOMAS ROGERS, possible sons of THOMAS, and nephews of 1. WILLIAM THOMAS.

In addition to the above we find that at least five of the six sons of WILLIAM THOMAS' uncle, JOSEPH ROGERS, who died in Northampton County, N. C. in 1752, appear on these same records.

In 1786 AARON ROGERS witnessed a deed in WILKES COUNTY.
In 1783 REUBEN was one of the appraisers of DAVID HOLMAN'S estate, while his brother DRURY ROGERS was the Executor. DRURY'S will with a list of all his children and his wife TABITHA, will be found in another place. January 3, 1787, the brother JOHN ROGERS and his wife AGNES sold lands to ROBERT CHAMBERS, and in 1787, MICHAEL ROGERS witnessed a deed of DOROTHY ASHFIELD, to lands in GREENE COUNTY, and this was the same DOROTHY ASHFIELD whose deed was witnessed by his brother AARON ROGERS in 1786 - the previous year.

1.   W I L L I A M   R O G E R S ,   E S Q .

1. WILLIAM ROGERS, the great, great grandfather of WILL ROGERS, was a lawyer and teacher. That he was a lawyer by profession see Georgia Historical Collections, D. A. R. Vol. II, page 311; that he was a teacher, see abstract of his inventory, given below, and the Estate of JESSE WALKER, in Wilkes County, Ga. (Davidson, Vol. 2, p. 308) where Baldwin Robinson paid WILLIAM ROGERS tuition for two of the minor children.

WILLIAM ROGERS settled in what was then BURKE COUNTY, in Georgia, while it was yet an almost unorganized province. He was probably in the vanguard of the Rogers family migration to that country. He practiced law for many years at AUGUSTA, GEORGIA, when that place was little more than a trading post. His business and professional associates were of the highest standing, and the names of some of them appear in the brief abstract accompanying the inventory of his estate, which appears on page 107 of Davidson's Early Records of Georgia and Wilkes County, Vol. No. 1. Numerous items relating to his business transactions, his associates and his clients are also to be found in Georgia Chapter Historical Collections, Vol. 2, of RICHMOND COUNTY.

The brief abstract or mention of the filing of the inventory of his estate, on August 9, 1794, reads as follows:

> WILLIAM ROGERS, deceased. Inventory August 9, 1794. A WONDERFUL LIBRARY OF CLASSICS. He seems to have been a teacher. His estate owned the notes and obligation against the following persons: WILLIAM MEAD, NATHANIEL COCKE, JOHN CRUTCHFIELD, PHILLIP CLAYTON, FIELDS PERDUE, JOHN GARRETT, GEORGE WALKER and NATHANIEL DURKEE. Appraisers of his Estate were SIDNOR COSBY, WILLIAM TRIPLETT and THOMAS LASLEY.

1. WILLIAM ROGERS numbered among his clients, the first named mentioned, WILLIAM MEADE, and had many business transactions with him. On April 28, 1788, WILLIAM MEAD gave a bill of sale to WILLIAM ROGERS of Augusta, for a slave. Doubtless in payment of legal services rendered. Witnessed by ZACHARIAH LAMAR, JR., and WILLIAM REILY. On May the 1st, following WILLIAM REILY also sold or transferred a slave to WILLIAM ROGERS.

NATHANIEL COCKE and his wife REBECCA in 1791 sold some lands in HALIFAX COUNTY, Virginia, to DANIEL ROBERTS. This was witnessed by JAMES BARNES and WILLIAM ROGERS.

JOHN CRUTCHFIELD was an Indian trader, from Spottsylvania County, Virginia, whose wife was SUSANNAH. This JOHN CRUTCHFIELD'S wife was a full blood CHEROKEE INDIAN, and their children were half-blood Cherokees. Many years after the death of WILLIAM ROGERS, JOHN CRUTCHFIELD, then living among the Indians in North Georgia, was killed by JAMES VANN, in a misunderstanding that had arisen between them. Vann was also part Cherokee. After Vann had slain Crutchfield, he adopted two of his sons JOSEPH and ROCK CRUTCHFIELD, raised and educated them, and left lands to them as legacies.

THOMAS LASLEY, also mentioned in this inventory, was the ancestor, no doubt of WILLIAM LASLEY who married MARY VANN, and MARGARET LASLEY, who married ANDREW M. VANN, who were brother and sister of SALLIE VANN, grandmother of our own WILL ROGERS.

These facts, which are real facts, backed up by the records, are links in the chain that tend to identify 1. WILLIAM ROGERS as the ancestor of WILL ROGERS.

The wife of 1. WILLIAM ROGERS was MARY. She was the administrator of his estate. By the time she made her returns for 1811, however, she had married again to a man named BRAGG, and made oath to the statement as MRS. MARY BRAGG, Administratrix. The fact that after fifteen years the administration of the estate of WILLIAM ROGERS was still pending in WILKES COUNTY, GEORGIA, shews that he left a considerable estate, besides "a wonderful library of classics", and doubtless a large family of children, most of whose names are lost. We can only guess at the identity of MARY ROGERS. This compiler has made three guesses, (1) that she was MARY PENN (2) or MARY VANN, or (3) possibly, MARY CORDERY. But these are pure guesses.

From the data presented above, and from a study of the ROGERS FAMILY and its allied connections, the following genealogical table of the descendants of 1. WILLIAM ROGERS and his wife MARY has been constructed:

---

1. WILLIAM ROGERS, married MARY.....
    and had:

(1) WILLIAM ROGERS married MARTHA PENN, daughter of COL. WILLIAM PENN.
(2) JOHN ROGERS married SARAH CORDERY, daughter of THOMAS CORDERY.
(3) ROBERT ROGERS married LUCY CORDERY, daughter of THOMAS CORDERY.

> (THOMAS CORDERY, a descendant of the CORDERYS of Northumberland County, married SUSANNAH. The Indian name of SUSANNAH CORDERY was "SONICOOIE" & she was a CHEROKEE, of the full blood.)

(3) ROBERT ROGERS and his half-Cherokee Indian wife, LUCY CORDERY, were the parents of:

(50) CATHERINE ROGERS married ALEXANDER McDANIEL.
(51) NANNIE ROGERS married (1) ALEXANDER JORDAN (2) JOHN ANDERSON
(52) ROBERT ROGERS married SALLIE VANN (Daughter of AVEY VANN and MARGARET McSWAIN).
(53) JOHN ROGERS married (1) HETTIE MOSELEY (2) CATHERINE VANN
(54) JAMES ROGERS.

When WILLIAM MOSELEY died in WILKES COUNTY, GEORGIA, in 1783, JAMES VANN was appointed Administrator of his estate. (Vol. 1, Early Recs. of Ga. p. 34).

HETTIE MOSELEY who married JOHN ROGERS, great uncle of WILL ROGERS was the daughter of SUSAN CORDERY (sister of Sarah and Lucy Cordery above) and JOHN MOSELEY, son of WILLIAM MOSELEY.

Through his grandfather, ROBERT ROGERS, WILL ROGERS was part Cherokee. This ROBERT ROGERS was one quarter Cherokee.

He married SALLIE VANN, daughter of AVERY VANN and his wife PEGGY (Margaret) McSWAIN. AVERY VANN was not an Indian, but his wife was a quarter blood, so that SALLIE VANN, grandmother of WILL ROGERS was one-eighth Cherokee. Thus, the Cherokee strain in WILL ROGERS from this part of his ancestry was almost drained by the time it reached him.

MISS MARY AMERICA SCHRIMSHER

MARY AMERICA SCHRIMSHER was the mother of WILLIAM PENN ROGERS. She was born October 9, 1839, and married CLEMENT VANN ROGERS, son of ROBERT ROGERS and his wife SALLIE VANN. Mary America Schrimsher was also part Cherokee.

JOHN GUNTER in 1814 was a powder maker, somewhere back
in the mountains of Tennessee and Georgia.
He married KATIE, a full blood Cherokee, of the
"Paint" clan. Both JOHN GUNTER and his wife KATIE
died in 1835. They had a daughter:

ELIZABETH HUNT GUNTER (b. 1804) m. MARTIN MATTHEW SCHRIMSHER, who was
born in 1806 in BLOUNT COUNTY, TENNESSEE.

Martin Matthew Schrimsher went with the "Gold Rush" to California in 1849, but did not remain long and returned and settled in the Cherokee Nation. His wife died in 1877 at their home at CLAIREMORE, OKLAHOMA, at the home of her son JOHN GUNTER SCHRIMSHER. JOHN GUNTER SCHRIMSHER was a Captain in the Confederacy during the war between the States. He was either the father or the uncle of Miss Mary America Schrimsher, who became the wife of Clement Vann Rogers. CLEMENT VANN ROGERS and MARY AMERICA SCHRIMSHER had children:

205. SALLIE CLEMENTINE ROGERS m. JOHN T. McSPADDEN
206. ROBERT MARTIN ROGERS died at the age of 17 years.
207. MAUD ETHEL ROGERS m. CAPT. LANE LANE.
208. MAY ROGERS m. JOHN MATTHEWS YOCAN (2) FRANK STINE.
209. WILLIAM PENN ROGERS m. BETTY BLAKE, of ROGERS, ARK.

Children of WILL ROGERS and his wife BETTY BLAKE

1. WILLIAM VANN ROGERS (b. 1911)
2. MARY AMELIA ROGERS (b. 1913)
3. JAMES BLAKE ROGERS (b. 1915)

1. WILLIAM VANN ROGERS served in the late World War No. 2, and made an excellent record, having been elected to Congress near the beginning of the conflict, he later resigned and resumed his military activities.

As all the World knows our WILL ROGERS was killed in an airplane accident when the ship crashed on the boggy tundras of Northern Alaska, a few years ago. Since then we have become resigned to his loss and have received much amusement from the hundreds of ambitious entertainers who have tried in vain to IMITATE HIM. He never had and never will have an equal in his sphere.

THE SCHRIMSHER FAMILY LIVED IN CHOWAN

Not only the ROGERS FAMILY and the VANN FAMILY were early residents of OLD ALBEMARLE, NORTH CAROLINA, and particularly CHOWAN PRECINCT and COUNTY, but the SCHRIMSHER FAMILY as well. On page 241, Volume 1, of Hathaway's N. C. Hist. & Gen. Register, containing the Marriage Bonds of Chowan County, will be found the following entry:

JOHN WYATT to ELIZABETH SCRIMPSHIRE, Feb. 17, 1768.

In the foregoing account of the family of WILL ROGERS, the compiler has been cramped for space, and has been compelled to "trim it down" to the point where much of the most interesting data he had gathered, must be left out. The real foundation of the account is to be found in the "HISTORY OF the CHEROKEES" by Emmett Starr.

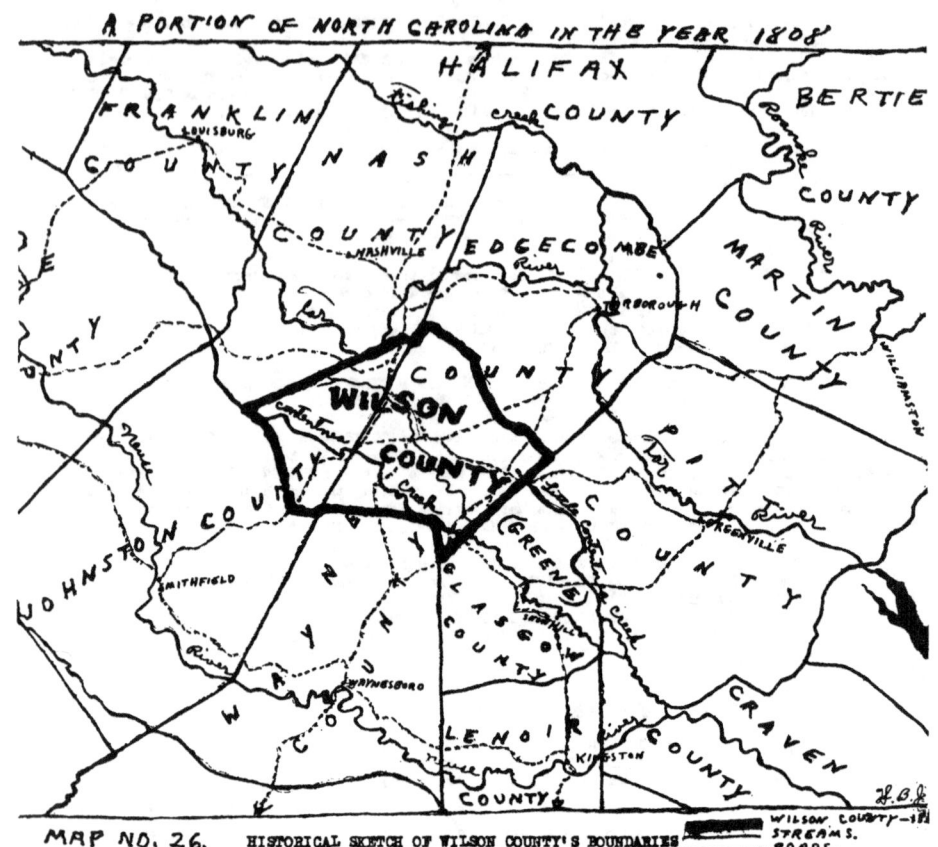

MAP NO. 26. HISTORICAL SKETCH OF WILSON COUNTY'S BOUNDARIES

By HUGH BUCKNER JOHNSTON

    Wilson County is so young that it is thought by many persons to have no history at all, and those who desire to look further are discouraged by the many complications arising from its fairly recent four-county origin or by the scanty published materials that feature such erroneous statements as the one that the territory was first penetrated by Scotch-Irish settlers about 1790. The fact is that the earliest citizens of what is now Wilson County were predominantly English and began arriving as early as 1740 from southeastern Virginia and the older settlements of northeastern North Carolina. The historian or genealogist is therefore confronted with a real problem in any attempt to trace the history of Wilson County and its people prior to its foundation in 1855, from parts of Edgecombe, Nash, Johnston and Wayne Counties.
    The settlement of Wilson County resulted ultimately from the gradual growth and focusing of the 1661 penetration North of Albemarle Sound, 1691 immigration to Pamlico River, and the 1704 movement up Neuse River. In 1712 the second was incorporated into Beaufort County and the third into Craven County (1) and in 1722 Bertie County was formed for the government of the inhabitants of the territory west of Chowan River and County. (2) The western boundary of Beaufort County was clarified by the subsequent formation of Edgecombe and Johnston Counties, and when Pitt County was formed in 1760 from the Western part of Beaufort County, the Edgecombe-Pitt boundary followed the original survey and is still retained in the present Wilson-Pitt County line.(3)
    The Governor and Council of North Carolina authorized Edgecombe Precinct on May 16, 1732 (4) to take care of the settlements south of Roanoke River from Bertie County, but the General Assembly did not give it formal sanction until November 12, 1734 (5) The western boundary was of no importance in that wilderness, but the eastern one was stated to begin near the present Hamilton (at the mouth of Conoconaro Creek on Roanoke River) and to run southwesterly in a straight line to Blount's Old Town on Tar River and to Neause River, passing thence to the northeastern branch of the Cape Fear River. Most of this territory was watered by the rivers originally incorporated into the Counties of Beaufort and Craven, but the majority of the affected inhabitants lived nearer to Bertie County and were governed by her until their own County government was established and Edgecombe became an independent County on April 7, 1741.
    The eastern boundary was now considered to begin at Jenkins Henry's house on Roanoke river and to proceed in a straight line to the mouth of Cheek's Mill Creek on Tar River, going from there in a straight line to the middle grounds between Tar and Neause Rivers, "and from thence up as high as may be, keeping the middle between the said two rivers, which shall be the dividing line between the Counties of Craven and Edgecombe, and Beaufort." (6) This was an improvement over the

first delineation of the boundary, but there was considerable confusion until 1748, when the line was drawn southwesterly in a straight line from Penny Hill at the mouth of Cheek's Mill (now Sugg's) Creek on Tar River to Contentnea Creek at the mouth of Toisnot Swamp, and thence northwesterly along the course of said Contentnea Creek towards its source (7). Part of this line is represented in the present Wilson-Greene County line.

The settlements in the upper part of Craven County had been growing all the while, and this newly peopled area was formed into Johnston County on June 29, 1746 (8). The course of Contentnea Creek formed its northern boundary and coincided with the southern boundary of Edgecombe County. In 1758 a straight line was drawn south-southwesterly from Boykin's Ford on Great Contentnea (a point about one and one-half miles west of the mouth of Bloomery Swamp) to the south of Mill Creek on Neuse River, and the territory east of this line became the new extinct Dobbs County. (9). The General Assembly that met on May 3, 1779, formed Wayne County from the Western part of Dobbs County by drawing a line due South from a point in Contentnea Creek about three quarters of a mile west of Ruffin's Bridge (Originally Samuel Peacock's Bridge). (10).

About this time the southern tip of the Edgecombe County line from Penny Hill to the mouth of Toisnot Swamp was pivoted westward about a half-mile to coincide with the northern tip of the Dobbs-Wayne County line, but with the formation of Wilson County in 1855 this line was restored to the survey of 1748. Dobbs County disappeared on December 5, 1791, the upper part becoming Glasgow County and the lower part becoming Lenoir County, with no effect on their outer boundaries (11). On November 18, 1799, without any alteration of the boundaries, the unpopular name of Glasgow County was changed to Greene County. (12). The General Assembly that met on April 8, 1777, had already formed Nash County from Edgecombe County by drawing a straight line from the Rocky Mount bridge at the Falls of Tar River to Widow Christian Rose's Ferry on Contentnea Creek (13) at the northern tip of the Johnston-Dobbs County line.

Wilson County was created by the General Assembly on February 13, 1855, (14) and a careful description of the new boundaries of Edgecombe, Nash, Johnston and Wayne Counties is necessary to show the territory that they lost to Wilson County:

> Beginning at a point in the Edgecombe-Pitt County line about a mile south of Turnage's Crossroads, go northwest five miles in a straight line to Pender's Hill, N. N. W. six and one-half miles in a straight line to Town Creek at the mouth of Col. David Williams' Mill Branch and up the branch to the mill, N. W. five and one-quarter miles in a straight line to the Edgecombe-Nash County line at Sharpsburg, S. S. W. two miles along the railroad, W. N. W. one and three-quarter miles in a straight line to a point about two miles S. E. of Tar River, S. W. twenty-one miles in a straight line across Turkey Creek Bridge near the old Pridgen Place to the Nash-Johnston County boundary at a pond and bridge across Moccasin (upper Contentnea) Creek, S. E. three miles along the run of Moccasin Creek to a point about one-half mile S. E. of the mouth of Turkey Creek, die South one and one-half miles, S. S. E. six and one-half miles in a straight line past Barnes' Store to the Red Hill (Henry Horn's Old Place) about a quarter-mile N. of Kenley, E. S. E. three and one-half miles in a straight line to a point in the Johnston-Wayne County line, N. N. E. one-half mile, E. thirteen and one-half miles to a point just S. of Contentnea Creek, due S. nearly a mile to the Wayne-Greene County line, N. E. nine miles in a straight line along the Greene County line (crossing Contentnea Creek about a half-mile below Samuel Ruffin's Bridge) to the Greene-Pitt County line on Little Contentnea Creek, and N. E. three miles in a straight line along the Pitt County line to the original point in the Pitt-Edgecombe County line.

1 William L. Saunders, The Colonial Records of North Carolina, Raleigh, 1886, III, p. 453; II, p. 172.
2 Op. cit., III, pp. 191 and 194.
   Walter Clark, The State Records of North Carolina, Goldsboro, 1904, XXIII, p. 100.
3 Second op. cit., pp. 531/4.
4 First op. cit., III, p. 417.
5 Ibid., p. 640.
6 Second op. cit., pp. 164/5.
7 Ibid., p. 287.
8 Ibid., pp. 248/9.
9 Ibid., pp. 469 and 495/6.
10 Walter Clark, The State Records of North Carolina, Goldsboro, 1905, XXIV, pp. 290/2.
11 Laws of North Carolina, 1791, Chapter XLVII.
12 Laws of North Carolina, 1799, Chapter XXXIX.
13 Third op. cit., pp. 139/141.
14 Public Laws of The State of North Carolina, Raleigh, 1855, pp. 30/34.

The compiler is indebted to MR. HUGH BUCKNER JOHNSTON, National Geographer of the NATIONAL GENEALOGICAL SOCIETY, and a native of WILSON COUNTY, N. C., for the execution of the MAP OF WILSON and surrounding Counties, shown above, and for the Historical Sketch accompanying the same. Considering the source and the authorities cited by Mr. Johnston, there can be no question as to its accuracy.

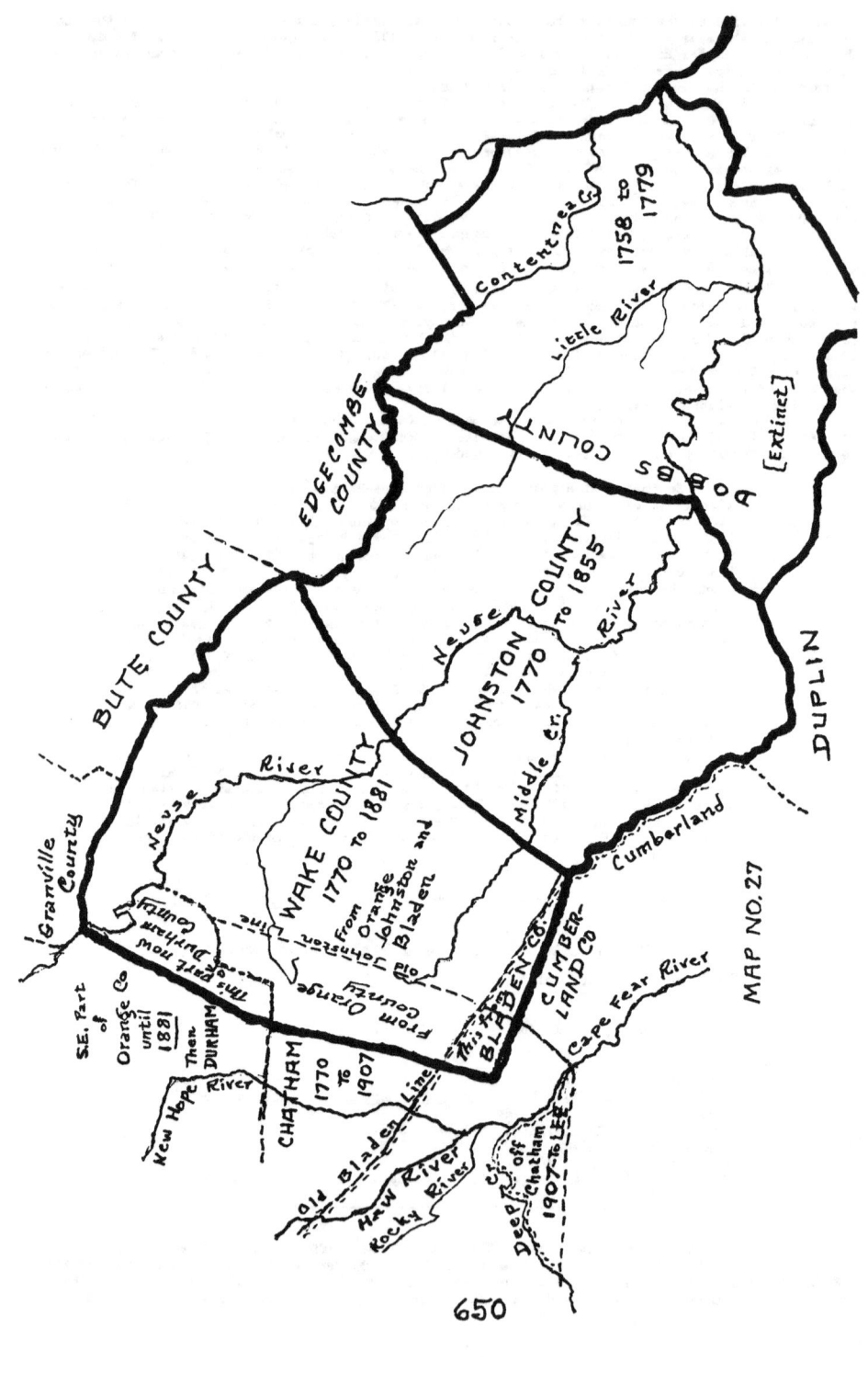

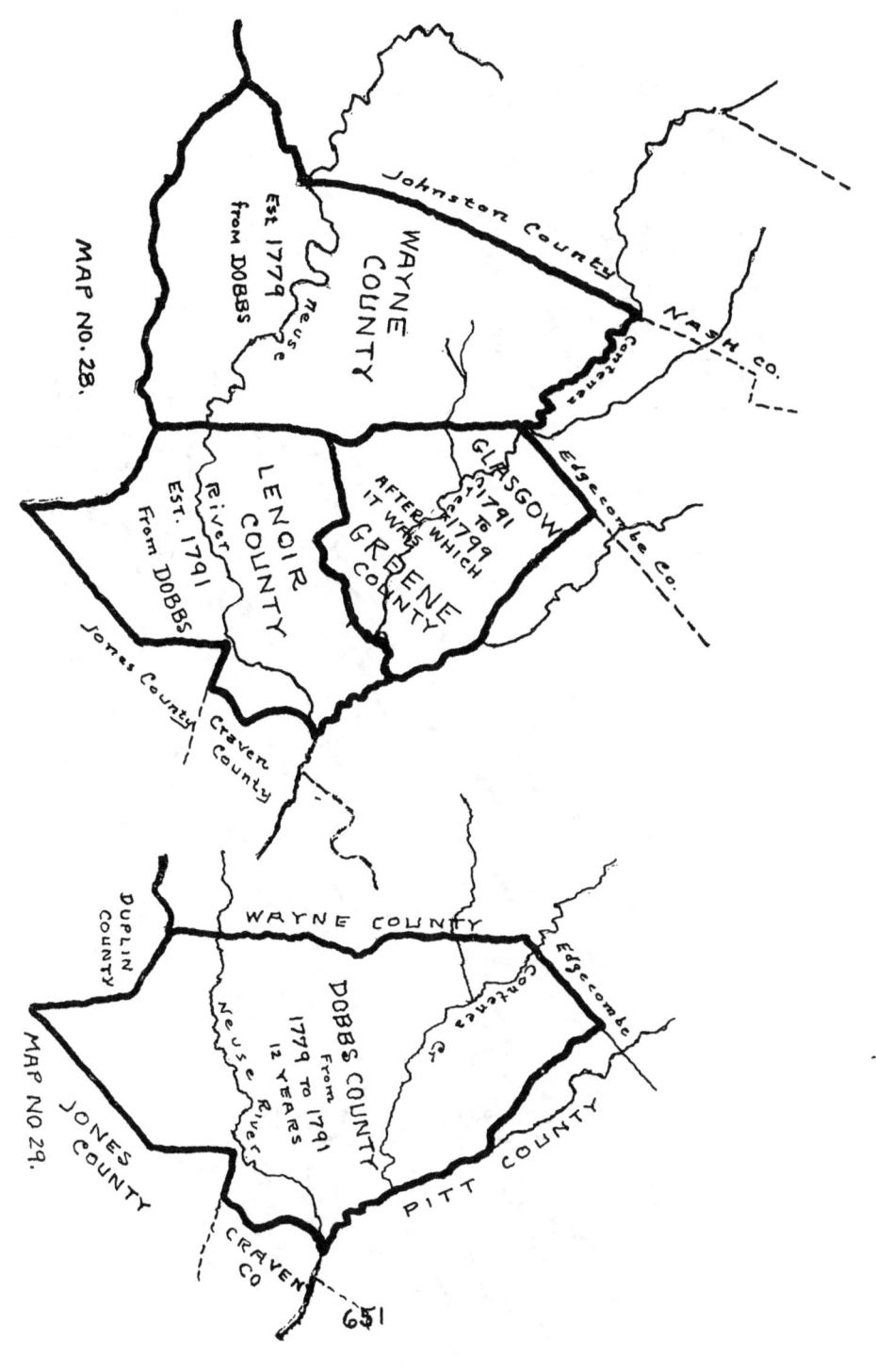

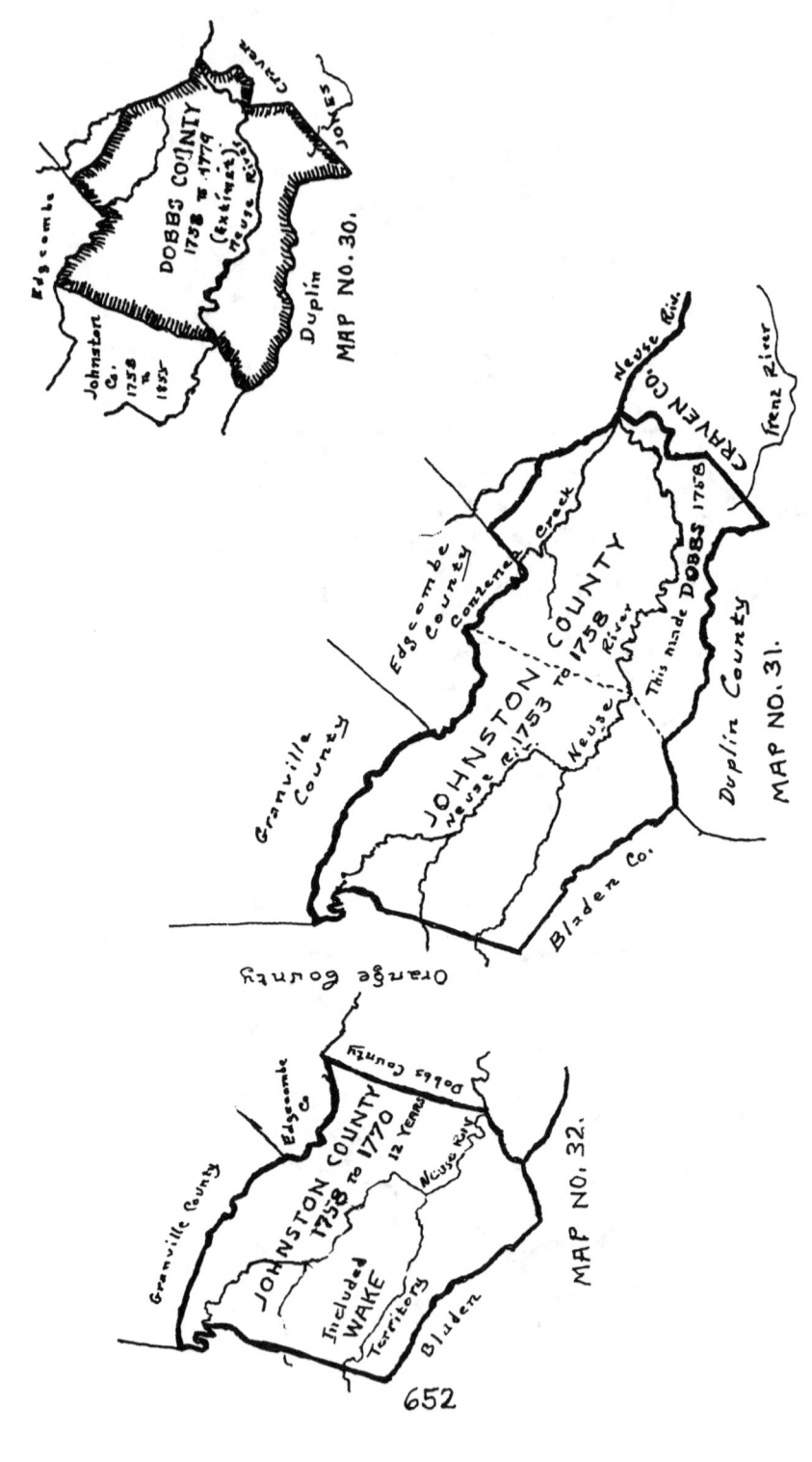

THE MARTINS OF OLD BATH TOWN

JOHN MARTIN of LOWER NORFOLK COUNTY appears to have been the ancestor of the MARTIN FAMILY that settled in OLD BATH TOWN on the banks of the PAMLICO RIVER in the early days of its establishment. The records disclose that he was living in Lower Norfolk County on October 1, 1646 when one Lancaster Levitt patented 300 acres "beginning at an island to the westward of JOHN MARTIN'S HOUSE, where Bennetts Creek (the one in that part of Virginia) divides itself into three branches in Lower Norfolk County, the island being between the south and west branch". (Nugent, p. 162.) Five years later, October 21, 1651, this JOHN MARTIN and his neighbor LANCASTER LOVETT patented 600 acres together in the same general neighborhood, same being in LYNHAVEN PARISH "at the mouth of the Eastern Branch, which is at the head of Bennett's Creek." (Nugent, p. 220.) He was related in some way to the WOODHOUSE FAMILY, as on July 16, 1655, he witnessed the will of HENRY WOODHOUSE, and on November1, the same year, that of THOMAS NEEDHAM, a relative of the BRYAN FAMILY, whose relationship has been heretofore mentioned (See notes on the Bryan family and the Hardys). On October 17, 1672, his old neighbor Lancaster Lovett died leaving a will in Lower Norfolk, in which he mentioned JOHN MARTIN "deceased". By inference we thus learn that JOHN MARTIN of this sketch had died not so very long before that time. He is also referred to, by inference, at least, in the will of ADAM KEELING, his son in law, who left a will in 1683. (See p. 231 of this book). It is obvious that the JOHN MARTIN of this sketch, who evidently died in LOWER NORFOLK, was a different JOHN MARTIN from the one who was related to ADAM DIXON, whose son HENRY MARTIN married a sister of WILLIAM BODDIE, heretofore mentioned. (Nugent p. 8).

The record as a whole discloses that this JOHN MARTIN, of LOWER NORFOLK and LYNHAVEN PARISH, had the following children:

1. JOEL MARTIN m. ELIZABETH
2. WILLIAM MARTIN
3. JONATHAN MARTIN
4. THOMAS MARTIN
5. ANN MARTIN m. ADAM KEELING.

1. JOEL MARTIN moved to OLD ALBEMARLE, as did the descendants of HENRY WOODHOUSE (See pp. 99 and 189 of this book). He patented lands in CURRITUCK PRECINCT on October 20, 1691. (Princess Anne County, Book I p. 13). This was perhaps in that part of CURRITUCK PRECINCT that lay South of ALBEMARLE SOUND at that time. Thereafter in 1702 he moved by water from Norfolk to the vicinity of PAMLICO RIVER. His wife was ELIZABETH (last name unknown) and their daughter, MARY MARTIN evidently married HENRY WOODWARD. After moving to OLD PAMTICOUGH PRECINCT, JOEL MARTIN patented several other large tracts of land in that vicinity and became prominent in the establishment of the settlements there. He made his will in BATH COUNTY, dated October 24, 1715, and named his children:

10. JOHN MARTIN, JR. m. REBECCA. (Probably LANGLEY).
11. WILLIAM MARTIN m. ELIZABETH
12. ANNE MARTIN
13. ELIZABETH MARTIN m. JOHN PENNY
14. FRANCES MARTIN m. JARVIS.
15. MARY WOODWARD wife of HENRY WOODWARD (In Va.)

11. WILLIAM MARTIN owned lands in PRINCESS ANNE COUNTY in 1704, some of which he sold in 1706. In 1715 he and Ledowick Martin (possibly another brother, or his own son) were on a list of freeholders in HYDE PRECINCT (Hathaway 3, p. 425). The will of a WILLIAM MARTIN of Princess Anne County - probably 5. WILLIAM MARTIN, son of JOHN - mentions the following children: HENRY, WILLIAM, ANN and REBECCA. But 11. WILLIAM MARTIN died in BEAUFORT COUNTY in St. THOMAS PARISH in 1745. (Grimes p. 240) He mentions his legatees as:

20. JOHN MARTIN
21. JOEL MARTIN
22. WILLIAM MARTIN
23. JOSEPH MARTIN
24. ANN MARTIN
25. ELIZABETH MARTIN
Other legatees: Cousin JOHN MARTIN
Wife MARY and HENRY SNOAD, Executors.

His wife was probably MARY SNOAD, sister of HENRY SNOAD.

22. WILLIAM MARTIN died in Beaufort County about 1769 leaving a will, in which he names his children as follows:

30. WILLIAM MARTIN
31. THOMAS MARTIN
32. JAMES MARTIN
33. HENRY MARTIN
34. EURANE MARTIN
35. MARY MARTIN
36. ANNE MARTIN

NOTE: Executors of this last will were MOSES HARE, HENRY BONNER and THOMAS JONES, which suggests that this last WILLIAM may have been of the ISLE OF WIGHT MARTINS. It is easy to get them mixed.

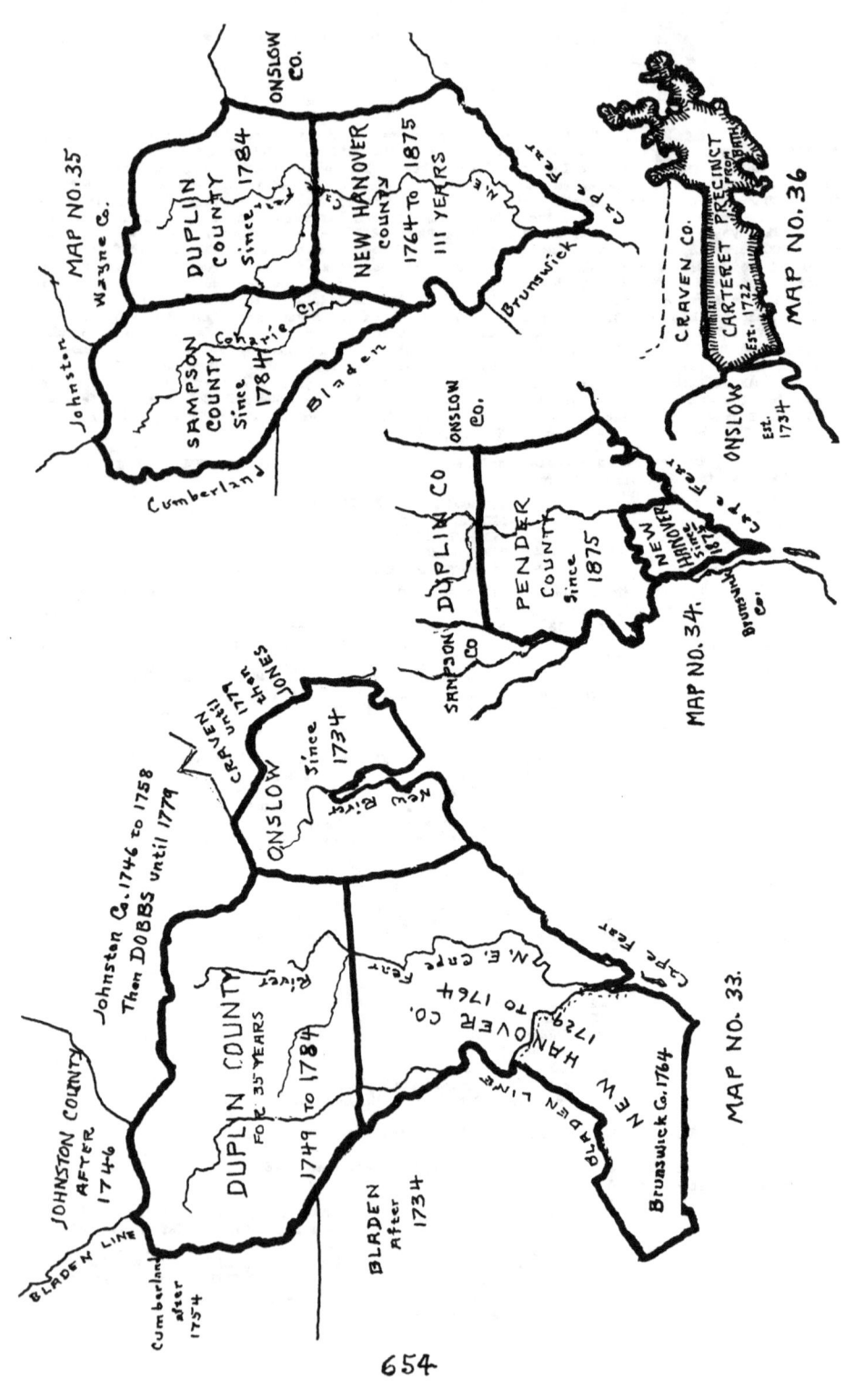

THE BRYAN FAMILY

Including the Ancestry of
HON. WILLIAM JENNINGS BRYAN

The ancient records of OLD ALBEMARLE and its descendant sub-divisions are filled with notes about the BRYAN FAMILY. Members of this family came down into NORTH CAROLINA early from ISLE OF WIGHT, SURRY and NANSEMOND COUNTIES.

The original emigrant ancestor of this family is not difficult to identify as the EDWARD BRYAN who came over from ENGLAND in the BONA NOVA in 1620. EDWARD WATTERS obtained his headright from THOMAS HAMOR, brother of CAPT. RALPH HAMOR, together with that of WILLIAM ARNALL who came over in the SEAFLOWER in 1621. Neither of them were brought to VIRGINIA by EDWARD WATTERS, but both of them were used by that worthy in 1624 when he patented 100 acres of land two miles below BLUNT POINT in ELIZABETH CITY COUNTY (Nugent p. 4).

EDWARD WATTERS who used the headright of EDWARD BRYAN in 1624 was one of two persons on the SEA ADVENTURE, all of whom were shipwrecked in the BERMUDAS, on their way over from ENGLAND in 1609, who liked the SOMERS ISLANDS so well that SIR THOMAS GATES was unable to persuade them to continue on their journey to VIRGINIA in the two small pinances that were built to bring them the rest of the way with GATES, SIR GEORGE SOMERS and others. But in 1618, on her way to VIRGINIA, the "DIANA" arrived at the BERMUDAS and among her passengers was GRACE O'NEILL, then 16 years old, who married EDWARD WATTERS and they came on the "Diana" to VIRGINIA, and settled on this 100 acres in ELIZABETH CITY COUNTY. Waters died before 1628 and his widow became the wife of OBEDIENCE ROBINS, but the son of EDWARD WATTERS settled in ACCOMAC and was the ancestor of the Waters family to which the old revolutionary "war horse" of South Carolina, COL. PHILEMON WATTERS was descended.

But back to EDWARD BRYAN. There is a blank period between 1624 and about 1665, when an EDWARD BRYAN (possibly a son, or maybe a grandson of the first EDWARD) married CHRISTIAN COUNCIL, the daughter of HODGES COUNCIL and LUCY HARDY. In the meantime, however, the first EDWARD BRYAN had found him a wife, in the person of a daughter of JOHN NEEDHAM, one of the "servants" of the famous GEORGE SANDYS, Treasurer of the Colony, whose headright he used in securing a patent to 400 acres of land in the precincts of ARCHER'S HOPE, and who came over with SANDYS in the "GEORGE". This patent was issued to SANDYS in 1624 at about the same time EDWARD WATTERS secured the 100 acre tract in ELIZABETH CITY COUNTY, close by. It takes no clairvoyant to sense that the EDWARD BRYAN who married CHRISTIAN COUNCIL was either a son or grandson of EDWARD the first and his wife MISS NEEDHAM, when one scans the long list of persons descending from this marriage who were saddled with the Christian name of NEEDHAM, beginning with the first NEEDHAM BRYAN. (Nugent, p. 4).

Nowhere on the VIRGINIA or NORTH CAROLINA records do we find a list, name by name, of the off-spring of CHRISTIAN COUNCIL and EDWARD BRYAN, but as the BRYAN-HARDY-COUNCIL parade passes along before us, emerging from the ancient archives of OLD ALBEMARLE and EASTERN VIRGINIA, it is comparatively easy to POINT THEM OUT. The BRYAN CHART runs something like this:

EDWARD BRYAN married CHRISTIAN COUNCIL, daughter of LUCY HARDY and HODGES COUNCIL; LUCY, the daughter of JOHN HARDY and his wife ALICE; JOHN the son of JOHN HARDY and his wife OLIVE COUNCIL who were married somewhere between 1620 and 1630. See "THE HARDY FAMILY". The children of EDWARD BRYAN and CHRISTIAN COUNCIL were:

1. NEEDHAM BRYAN
2. WILLIAM BRYAN
3. RICHARD BRYAN
4. JOHN BRYAN
5. LEWIS BRYAN
6. HARDY BRYAN

1. NEEDHAM BRYAN (No positive identified record. May have died young).
2. WILLIAM BRYAN had three sons, NEEDHAM, JOHN and WILLIAM. (Hathaway Vol. 1, 577)
3. RICHARD BRYAN (Settled in STAFFORD COUNTY, Va.) Ancestor of WILLIAM J. BRYAN.
4. JOHN BRYAN had EDWARD and WILLIAM BRYAN.
5. LEWIS BRYAN had Children, SIMON, EDWARD, ELIZABETH and ANN BRYAN.
6. HARDY BRYAN (Descendants unidentified).

SOME DESCENDANTS OF 2. WILLIAM BRYAN

10. NEEDHAM BRYAN (b. ca. 1790) m. ANNIE RAMBEAU Nov. 11, 1711. Settled at SNOWFIELD BERTIE COUNTY, N. C. and had:

50. RACHEL BRYAN m. WILLIAM WHITFIELD in 1741
51. WILLIAM BRYAN m. ELIZABETH SMITH
52. NEEDHAM BRYAN m. NANCY SMITH.

3. RICHARD BRYAN AND SOME OF HIS DESCENDANTS

3. RICHARD BRYAN, son of EDWARD BRYAN and CHRISTIAN COUNCIL settled in KING GEORGE COUNTY, whither many of those who flocked to the Northern Neck from the vicinity of ISLE OF WIGHT and SURRY COUNTY settled at about the same time. He bought land in KING GEORGE in 1694. This land descended to his son RICHARD BRYAN "late of King George" who left will dated JANUARY 18, 1747, leaving said lands to his son RICHARD BRYAN III. (W. & Mary Mag. Vol. 5, p. 277).

3. RICHARD BRYAN was the father of RICHARD BRYAN JR.
RICHARD BRYAN JR. was the father of:

55. RICHARD BRYAN III
56. JOSEPH BRYAN

In 1752/3 both RICHARD BRYAN III and his brother JOSEPH BRYAN were living in CULPEPPER COUNTY. 55. RICHARD BRYAN III married FRANCES BATTALY, daughter of MOSES BATTALY, of SPOTTSYLVANIA COUNTY, and had:

57. BATTALY BRYAN
58. ANNA BRYAN.
59. WILLIAM BRYAN.

The mother of the above children, according to the record, was ELIZABETH MATTHEWS, a daughter of CAPT. SAMUEL MATTHEWS, son of CAPT. JOHN MATTHEWS, son of LIEUT. COL. SAMUEL MATTHEWS, son of GOVERNOR SAMUEL MATTHEWS, whose WARWICK PLANTATION adjoined BLUNT POINT where EDWARD WATTERS secured 100 acres in 1624 with the headright of EDWARD BRYAN.

59. WILLIAM BRYAN
had sons:

60. JOSEPH BRYAN, who died leaving a will in CULPEPPER COUNTY in 1806, in which he gave the names of his children, as follows:

(1) JAMES BRYAN
(2) JOHN BRYAN m. NANCY LILLARD
(3) WILLIAM BRYAN
(4) AQUILLA BRYAN
(5) LUCY BRYAN m. DUNAWAY.
(6) ELIZABETH BRYAN.

NANCY LILLARD who married (2) JOHN BRYAN, was the daughter of JOHN LILLARD, a revolutionary soldier. Between 1810 and 1825 JOHN BRYAN sold out and went to Kentucky, then to Tennessee, and then to OHIO. He and his wife NANCY LILLARD were the parents of

61. SILAS LILLARD BRYAN.

In 1850 SILAS LILLARD BRYAN went to live with an older brother in MISSOURI. He married and had the following children:

62. FANNIE BRYAN m. BAIRD.
63. WILLIAM JENNINGS BRYAN m. BAIRD.
64. CHARLES BRYAN
65. ALLEN BRYAN (never married).
66. NANNIE BRYAN (never married).

---

4. JOHN BRYAN AND SOME OF HIS DESCENDANTS
had two sons:

100. EDWARD BRYAN (b. 1790)
101. WILLIAM BRYAN m. ANN DAWSON.

It was the descendants of 4. JOHN BRYAN who settled in CRAVEN COUNTY and in what is now JONES COUNTY, and intermarried with the HATCH and SIMMONS FAMILY, as well as the BUSH and HARRISONS and GREENS of that section.

101. WILLIAM BRYAN married ANN DAWSON, and they were the parents of a son:

200. JOHN BRYAN m. ELIZABETH OLIVER
and had:

300. WILLIAM BRYAN
301. OLIVE BRYAN m. CROOM.
302. JAMES BRYAN m. RACHEL HERITAGE
..................................:
Grand-daughter of 50. RACHEL BRYAN and WILLIAM WHITFIELD.

From this last marriage came JOHN HERITAGE BRYAN (m. MARY SHEPARD) and JAMES WEST BRYAN

100. EDWARD BRYAN (wife's name unknown)
(Son of 4. JOHN BRYAN) had:

201. HARDY BRYAN married MRS. SARAH (BONNER) MOSELEY, widow of JOHN MOSELEY, and the daughter of THOMAS BONNER. HARDY BRYAN was born ca. 1715-20. The BONNERS lived in BEAUFORT. Children:

    303. THOMAS BRYAN m. RACHEL LAVENDER (b. 1737). (She m. (2) A. B. SIMMONS).
    304. HARDY BRYAN m. SALLIE HATCH (Daughter of EDMUND HATCH) She m. (2) ROUNDTREE.
    305. WILLIAM BRYAN m. a sister of COL. JOSEPH GREEN.
    306. HON. NATHAN BRYAN, Mem. Cont. Cong. m. WINNIFRED BRYAN (Dau. of 52. NEEDHAM).
    307. LEWIS BRYAN (Sheriff of LENOIR CO.) m. ELIZABETH SASSER.
    308. MARY BRYAN m. EDMUND HATCH, son of LEMUEL HATCH.

303. THOMAS BRYAN and RACHEL LAVENDER were the parents of the following:

    400. SARAH BRYAN m. LEMUEL HATCH.
    401. NANCY BRYAN m. JOHN CROOM (2) WILLIAM HARDY.
    402. PENELOPE BRYAN m. (1) COL. JOHN HATCH (2) COL. THOMAS P. IVES.

    Children of 400 SARAH BRYAN and LEMUEL HATCH:

        (1) EDWARD HATCH
        (2) SAMUEL HATCH
        (3) BENJAMIN HATCH m. (1) MISS HOWARD (Dau of JOSIAH HOWARD)
            m. (2) SARAH WHITFIELD, daughter of
                NEEDHAM WHITFIELD and LUCY HATCH.

    Children of 402. PENELOPE BRYAN and COL. JOHN HATCH:

        (4) MARY HATCH m. JOHN T. BRYAN
        (5) ANTHONY HATCH m. MISS GARDNER
        (6) HASKELL HATCH (1) MISS FRANKS (2) MISS REYNOLDS.

304. HARDY BRYAN and wife SALLIE HATCH were the parents of the following:

    403. JAMES HARDY BRYAN m. his cousin, LUCY HATCH.
    404. WILLIAM HATCH BRYAN m. BETSY HERITAGE (Dau of JOHN HERITAGE and RACHEL
    405. ASHE BRYAN   WHITFIELD.
    406. EDMUND BRYAN
    407. THOMAS BRYAN

    RACHEL (LAVENDER) BRYAN widow of 303. THOMAS BRYAN m. in 1764 ABRAHAM BASSETT SIMMONS and had nine SIMMONS CHILDREN.

5. LEWIS BRYAN AND SOME OF HIS DESCENDANTS

102. LEWIS BRYAN married ELIZABETH HUNTER (From SURRY COUNTY VIRGINIA) and had:

    202. SIMON BRYAN m. ANN JACOCKS
    203. EDWARD BRYAN m. MARTHA WEST, (Daughter of THOMAS WEST)
    204. ELIZABETH BRYAN m. THOMAS WHITMELL.
    205. ANNE BRYAN m. JOHN GRAY.

203. EDWARD BRYAN m. MARTHA WEST (Daughter of THOMAS WEST and MARTHA BLOUNT, who was a daughter of JOHN BLOUNT and ELIZABETH DAVIS; JOHN BLOUNT was the son of JAMES BLOUNT and his wife ANNE, from ISLE OF WIGHT COUNTY, Va., to CHOWAN COUNTY, N.C. in 1669.) EDWARD BRYAN and MARTHA WEST had:

    310. THOMAS BRYAN
    311. EDWARD BRYAN
    312. MARY BRYAN m. LOCKHART.
    313. MARTHA BRYAN
    314. ELIZABETH BRYAN
    315. WINNIFRED BRYAN
    316. ANN BRYAN m. RYAN
    317. SARAH BRYAN m. a BAKER.
    318. JANET BRYAN m. (1) HARDY HILL (Son of MICHAEL HILL, son of NATHAN HILL and his
          wife ELIZABETH HARDY, daughter of JOHN HARDY and his wife REBECCA. JANET
          m. (2) THOMAS WHITMELL PUGH.

203. EDWARD BRYAN died in BERTIE COUNTY in 1762. His Executors were WILLIAM GRAY, EDWARD RAZOR and THOMAS WHITMELL JR.

    See further information about the BRYANS under sketch
        "THE WHITFIELD FAMILY".

THE WHITFIELD FAMILY

The prolific and prominent WHITFIELD FAMILY, whose representatives joined the tide of migrants from VIRGINIA and settled in OLD ALBEMARLE stem from WILLIAM and RICHARD WHITFIELD, who came with or shortly after SIR THOMAS DALE. RICHARD WHITFIELD, according to the records was a headright of one GREENLIEF, who used it in taking up lands in CHARLES CITY COUNTY in 1635. Nugent p. 34; while one JOHN CHANDLER claimed the headright of WILLIAM WHITFIELD in 1636 when he patented 1000 acres of land in ELIZABETH CITY COUNTY.

MATTHEW WHITFIELD who appears on the records of NANSEMOND COUNTY, VIRGINIA, in 1682, probably stems from one or the other of these two early emigrants to VIRGINIA. This Matthew Whitfield married PRISCILLA LAWRENCE, sister of MARY LAWRENCE, the second wife of 100. JOHN THOMAS, as shown on the Chart. MATTHEW WHITFIELD and his wife PRISCILLA had two known children:

(1) ELIZABETH WHITFIELD m. JOHN SMITH
(2) WILLIAM WHITFIELD m. ELIZABETH GOODMAN.

JOHN SMITH and ELIZABETH WHITFIELD had two daughters:
(3) ELIZABETH SMITH m. WILLIAM BRYAN
(4) NANCY SMITH m. NEEDHAM BRYAN.

(RACHEL BRYAN, sister of WILLIAM and NEEDHAM BRYAN married WILLIAM WHITFIELD, son of WILLIAM WHITFIELD and his wife ELIZABETH GOODMAN.)

(2) WILLIAM WHITFIELD and his wife ELIZABETH GOODMAN married in 1741, and had these children:

10. WILLIAM WHITFIELD married RACHEL BRYAN, daughter of NEEDHAM BRYAN and his wife ANNE RAMBEAU.
11. MATTHEW WHITFIELD married a MISS WARREN. (Wayne County, N. C. their home)
12. MARY WHITFIELD m. JOHN GRADY.
13. LUKE WHITFIELD married a MISS WARREN, sister of MATTHEW'S wife.
14. CONSTANTINE WHITFIELD m. BARBARA WILLIAMS
15. PATIENCE WHITFIELD m. EDWARD OUTLAW.
16. MARGARET WHITFIELD m. (1) BARFIELD (2) WINKFIELD or WINGFIELD.
17. ELIZABETH WHITFIELD m. JONATHAN TAYLOR.
18. SARAH WHITFIELD m. DANIEL HERRING.
19. CHARITY WHITFIELD m. FREDERICK O'DANIEL (2) DANIEL HERRING.

(4) NANCY SMITH and NEEDHAM BRYAN (Son of (2) WILLIAM BRYAN) had the following children:

210. NEEDHAM BRYAN JR. m. SALLY HINTON (Dau of Col. John Hinton).
211. LOVARD BRYAN m. ELIZABETH GREEN (Dau. of JOSEPH GREEN and wife SARAH).
212. BENJAMIN BRYAN m. MRS. MARY SASSER.
213. SALLY BRYAN m. JACK HINTON
214. KEDAR BRYAN m. (1) ELIZABETH SMITH (2) MARY WHITFIELD (3) BETSY JAMES (4) DICKSON.
215. WINNIFRED BRYAN m. COL. NATHANIEL BRYAN, member Continental Congress.
216. NANCY BRYAN m. BRYAN WHITFIELD
217. RACHEL BRYAN m. GIBSON SLOAN

COLONEL NATHAN BRYAN and his wife 215. WINNIFRED BRYAN had the following children:

320. MARY BRYAN married GEN. WILLIAM CROOM of LENOIR COUNTY, N. C.
321. JOHN THOMAS BRYAN m. (4) MARY HATCH.
322. NATHAN BRYAN m. RACHEL WHITFIELD
323. WINNIFRED BRYAN m. GEN. BRYAN WHITFIELD
324. NANCY BRYAN
325. FREDERICK BRYAN m. HOLLAND S. BUSH.
326. NEEDHAM BRYAN m. SUSAN BARFIELD

and had :

410. MARY BRYAN m. ANDREW HAMILTON
411. NATHAN BRYAN m. (1) ELIZABETH WHITEHEAD (2) MARY UNDERWOOD
and they settled at DEMOPOLIS, ALABAMA.
412. NEEDHAM BRYAN
413. SUSAN BRYAN m. COLLIER
414. WINNIFRED BRYAN m. HOGAN.
415. NANCY BRYAN m. JOHN THOMPSON.

For more information on the BRYAN FAMILY in this Volume see pages 16 and 17.
For further information on the WHITFIELDS in this Volume see page 183.
For information on the WHITMELL FAMILY see page 184 of this Volume.

Compilation From Old Newspaper Files

THE CHARLOTTE OBSERVER

SUNDAY, JUNE 30, 1929

Married:

Near Salisbury by Rev. Mr. Stafford, January 24, 1831, James B. Hampton to Mrs. Susan A. Locke.

In Charlotte by Rev. R. H. Morrison December 22, 1831, Pinckney C. Caldwell to Miss Sarah R., daughter of the late Joseph Wilson.

(Dr. Caldwell, leading Charlotte physician. Active in politics. Member constitutional convention of 1861. Brother of Green W. Caldwell who represented this district in Congress 1841-1843.)

Near Beattie's Ford by Rev. R. J. Miller May 8, 1833, Michael Hoke of Lincolnton to Miss Frances, daughter of Robert H. Burton.

(Michael Hoke, distinguished citizen of Lincoln county, democratic candidate for governor in 1844; father of Gen. Robt. F. Hoke and grandfather of Hoke Smith of Georgia.)

In Lincoln county, March 11, 1834, Simon Rhyne, 4 1-2 feet high, and weighing 230 pounds, to Susan Lay.

In Charlotte by John Sloan, Esq., June 26, 1834, Thomas J. Holton to Miss Rachel R. Jones.

(Mr. Holton was for more than 30 years publisher of Charlotte Journal and Charlotte Whig.)

By Rev. M. Adams, November 20, 1834, John Graham to Miss Bridget Little.

In Salisbury by Rev. P. J. Sparrow, Feb. 15, 1835, Peter M. Brown of Charlotte to Miss Martha Gay of Salisbury.

(Mr. Brown was father of the late Col. John L. Brown and grandfather of late Peter Marshall Brown, once mayor of Charlotte.)

In Pittsboro Dec. 21, 1835, Rev. Wm. M. Green, pastor of Episcopal church, Hillsboro, to Miss Charlotte I. Fleming.

(Late bishop of Mississippi diocese, Protestant Episcopal church.)

In Salisbury, Dec. 24, 1835, Dr. Lucco Mitchell to Miss Jane E. daughter of Archibald Henderson.

(Three years later Dr. Mitchell died and his widow married Hon. Nathaniel Boyden, and was mother of Col. Archibald Henderson Boyden of Salisbury, who died June 19, 1929.)

At Butterwood Dec. 22, 1835, James B. Hawkins of Warren to Miss Arilla, daughter of Willis Alston of Halifax.

March 31, 1836, A. B. Davidson of Charlotte, to Miss Mary L., daughter of John Springs of York, S. C.

(Mr. A. Brevard Davidson, a notable citizen of this county and father of Baxter Davidson of Charlotte.)

In Rowan, May 26, 1836, Allen Alexander of Lincolnton, to Miss Adelaide, daughter of Moses Graham of Rowan.

In New Bern, 8 June, 1836, Wm. A. Graham to Miss Susan, daughter of John Washington of New Bern.

(Wm. A. Graham, governor 1844-1848, United States senator, secretary of navy 1852, one of the great citizens of the state.)

In Burke, Sept. 15, 1836, Burton Craige, to Miss Eliza P. daughter of Col. James Erwin of Burke.

(Burton Craige, a distinguished citizen of Salisbury, member of congress, author of the North Carolina secession ordinance in 1861.)

On Jan. 12, 1837, Cadawaller Jones, Jr., of Hillsboro, to Miss Annie, daughter of Hon. James Iredell.

In Lincoln county, Sept. 6, 1838, by Rev. Adam Miller, James Abernethy to Miss Mary Rankin, John Abernethy to Miss Jane Rankin. All Whigs.

In Lincolnton, Jan. 10, 1833, by Rev. A. L. Watts, Mr. Caleb Phifer of Concord to Miss Adeline, daughter of David Ramsour, Esq., of Lincolnton.

In Philadelphia Nov. 8, 1838, Col. John H. Wheeler, supt. of Charlotte Mint, to Miss Ellen, daughter of Thos. Sully, the sculptor.

(Col. John H. Wheeler, the North Carolina historian, later lived at Beattie Ford and represented Lincoln county in the house of commons 1852.)

In Washington City by Rev. Henry Slicer, April 9, 1830, Hon. Henry W. Connor, member of congress from this district, to Mrs. Lucy Ann Coleman, daughter of the late Governor Hawkins.

(Henry W. Connor, 1793-1866, of Lincoln county. On staff of Gen. Joseph Graham with rank of major in war against Creek Indians of Alabama in 1814. Member of congress from this district 1821-1841. Senator from Lincoln county 1848.)

In Charlotte by Rev. John Watts. August 11, 1841, Rev. Colin Murchison of South Carolina conference, to Miss R. E. Pearson of Abingdon, Va.

At Beatties Ford by Rev. M. Forbes, Oct. 6, 1841, Eli Hoyle to Miss Elizabeth, daughter of Alfred M. Burton.

In Iredell county by Rev. Wm. M. Jordan, Oct. 13, 1841, Dr. Avery M. Powell of Caldwell to Miss Mary Caroline, daughter of Robert Allen of Iredell.

Near Charlotte by Rev. J. Williamson, Nov. 17, 1841, G. W. Logan of Rutherford to Miss Amelia D. Wilson of Mecklenburg.

(G. W. Logan was member of Confederate congress and judge superior court, 1868-1874.)

In Lincolnton by Rev. J. H. Crawford, Nov. 17, 1841, L. E. Thompson, attorney at law, to Miss Harriet, daughter of Jacob Ramsour.

In Cabarrus by Rev. Angus Johnson, Dec. 30, 1841, Gen. W. C. Means to Miss Jane C., daughter of Gen. Paul Barringer.

(They were the parents of the late Col. Paul Barringer Means and Wm. G. Means of Concord.)

Dec. 16, 1841, Rev. Paul F. Kistler of Lincolnton to Miss Mary Wingard of Lexington, S. C.

In Fayetteville by Rev. A. Gilchrist, Jan. 13, 1842, Alexander Bethune to Miss Catherine McGilvary of Fayetteville.

(Parents of the late Miss Sallie Bethune who taught for 40 years in the Charlotte city schools.)

In Charlotte by Rev. J. Williamson, April 1842, James W. Osborne to Mrs. Mary A. Moore, daughter of John Irwin, Esq.

(Judge James W. Osborne, a brilliant lawyer and eloquent orator and judge of superior court. Father of the late Judge Frank Irwin Osborne of this city.)

In Cabarrus by Rev. D. A. Penick May 31, 1842, Robert W. Allison to Miss Sarah Ann, daughter of John Phifer.

(Mr. Allison was a notable citizen of Concord and father of Mrs. J. M. Odell of that city.)

Near Knoxville, Tenn., June 11, 1842, Richmond M. Pearson, attorney of Rowan and member of house of commons, to Miss Margaret C., daughter of Col. John C. Williams of Knoxville.

(Richmond M. Pearson, afterwards superior court judge, 1836-1848, associate justice supreme court, 1848-1858, and chief justice supreme court, 1858-1877.)

In Davidson county by Rev. Thales McDonald, in Dec. 1842, William Overman to Miss Mary E., daughter of Fielding Slater.

(Parents of Senator Lee Slater Overman of Salisbury.)

In Lincolnton by Rev. E. M. Forbes, Jan. 3, 1843, Dr. John M. Happoldt of Charlotte to Miss Sarah A. daughter of Robert Williamson of Lincolnton.

(Dr. Happoldt volunteered for service in yellow fever epidemic in New Orleans in 1878, and died there and then of that disease.)

In Lincolnton by B. S. Johnson, Esq., Nov. 11, 1843, W. R. Edwards to Miss Sarah E. Detter.

In Catawba by Rev. R. H. Morrison, Nov. 1843, Hugh C. Hamilton, to Miss Susan L. Massey.

In Anson county, December 20, 1843, Col. Absalom Sherrill of Catawba to Miss Sarah McAlpine of Anson.

In Iredell county, Aug. 29, 1844, by Rev. Dr. Morrison, Robert I. McDowell to Miss Rebecca Brevard.

(Parents of F. Brevard McDowell of this city.)

By Rev. Cyrus Johnson, Feb. 27, 1845, R. M. Miller of Lancaster, S. C., to Miss Ann Cureton.

(Parents of the late R. M. Miller, Jr., of this city.)

In New Bern, March 12, 1845, Joseph M. Graham to Miss Mary A. daughter of John Washington.

In Lincoln county, by Rev. Mr. McDaniel, March 19, 1846, Amos Morris to Miss Mary, daughter of William Davenport.

In Cheraw, S. C., April 23, 1846, by Rev. James Stacy, Rev. Dr. Albert M. Shipp to Miss Mary Jane Gillespie.

(Dr. Shipp was member N. C. University faculty for 10 years, president of Greensboro Female college, Wofford college and professor in Vanderbilt University School of Religion.)

In Cabarrus, Dec. 9, 1846, by Rev. Mr. Pharr; Joseph H. Wilson to Miss Mary L. Phifer.

(Mr. Joseph Harvey Wilson was a prominent Charlotte lawyer and grandfather of Mr. George E. Wilson the present mayor of Charlotte.)

In York county, S. C., by Rev. Cyrus Johnston, Dec. 15, 1846, Wm. R. Myers, attorney of this place, to Miss Sophia, daughter of John Springs, Esq.

(Col. Wm. R. Myers, a prominent Charlotte citizen for many years. Grandfather of Rawlinson Myers Dr, Wm. Myers Hunter, and Hamilton C. and Wm. Myers Jones of Charlotte.)

In Charlotte by Rev. J. F. W. Freeman, April 24, 1847, Maj. Benjamin Morrow to Miss Mary Jane, daughter of the late Governor Hawkins.

In Lincoln by Rev. Dr. Morrison, Sept. 2, 1847, Dr. W. J. Hayes to Miss Isabella, daughter of Dr. M. W. Alexander.

In Charlotte, by Rev. Cyrus Johnson, Nov. 2, 1847, Dr. Henry M. Pritchard of Lincoln to Miss Sarah, daughter of Maj. Benj. Morrow.

At Greenwood, in Catawba county, the residence of Hon. Henry W. Connor, March 30, 1848, by Rev. Jacob Hill, Mr. John W. Morrow of Mecklenburg to Miss Mary Ann Nuttall of Granville county.

In Gaston county by Rev. Samuel Lander, May 24, 1848, Uriah Cloyd of Caldwell to Miss Rosanna Moore of Gaston.

In Iredell by Rev. C. H. Pritchard, Aug. 9, 1848, Dr. J. H. Ward to Miss Ann, daughter of James Lemley.

By Rev. Mr. Freeman, Oct. 27, 1848, Mr. M. L. Wallace of this county to Miss Elizabeth, youngest daughter of Robert Williamson deceased of Lincoln county.

By Rev. R. H. Morrison, Nov. 6, 1848, Major D. H. Hill, 4th regiment U. S. artillery, to Miss Isabella, daughter of Rev. Dr. Morrison of Lincoln county.

(Gen. D. H. Hill, lieutenant general Confederate army, father of Joseph M. Hill, once chief justice of Arkansas, and of the late Dr. D. H. Hill of Raleigh.)

By Rev. Cyrus Johnson, Dec. 22, 1847, Lewis H. Russell of Warren county, to Miss Matilda Martha, daughter of Major Benj. Morrow.

(Parents of Mr. J. A. Russell, assistant clerk superior court, Mecklenburg county.)

At Brackettown, Burke county, Rev. Mr. Parker, Oct. 30, 1850, Capt. John F. Hoke of Lincoln to Miss Catherine, daughter of Col. Wm. Julius Alexander.

(Col. John F. Hoke was a prominent Lincoln county lawyer and father of the late Wm. Alexander Hoke, for 35 years on the N. C. bench and in his latter years chief justice of N. C. supreme court.)

By Rev. R. H. Lafferty, Oct. 28, 1851, Dr. E. O. Elliott to Miss Martha McRae, all of this county.

(Grandparents of Esley A. Anderson and Fred Anderson of this city.)

At Blandwood near Greensboro by Rev. Dr. Chas. F. Deems, April 6, 1852, Rufus Lenoir Patterson to Miss Marie Louise, daughter of Governor Morehead.

(Parents of the late Lindsay Patterson of Winston-Salem.)

In Charlotte by Rev. Cyrus Johnson, May 13, 1852, John Sloan of Greensboro, to Miss Eliza P. daughter of John D. Graham of Lincoln county.

In Charlotte, May 18, 1852, Dr. E. Nye Hutchison to Miss Mary A., daughter of David Parks, Esq.

(Dr. E. Nye Hutchison, a prominent physician, was father of R. S. Frank and J. J. Hutchison. Father too of Misses Charles and Bessie Hutchison of the Charlotte city schools.)

In Morganton by Rev. Mr. Sheets, May 27, 1852, Victor C. Barringer of Charlotte to Miss Marie A. Massey.

(Judge Barringer was for many years one of the judges of the Egyptian International Court by appointment of President Grant.)

In Raleigh by Rev. B. H. Rice, Oct. 10, 1853, Thomas W. Dewey, cashier of the State bank, to Miss Bessie, daughter of Rev. Dr. Drury Lacy.

In Gaston county, by Rev. Mr. Little, Oct. 30, 1853, D. H. Byerly of Charlotte, to Miss J. H. C., daughter of Hugh Jenkins of Easton.

In this county by Rev. R. F. Taylor, Aug. 22, 1854, Robert C. Bell, a merchant of Charlotte, to Miss Mary J. daughter of Dr. W. A. Ardrey.

(Parents of Mr. James Ardrey Bell of the Charlotte bar.)

In Charlotte, by Rev. Mr. Smith, April 15, 1855, John L. Morehead of Greensboro to Miss Sarah Smith, daughter of Wm. F. Phifer.

(Son of Governor John M. Morehead and father of the late John M. Morehead of Charlotte.)

In Charlotte by Rev. J. R. Pickett, Sept. 25, 1856, C. W. Abernethy to Miss Mary A. daughter of D. Kistler of Charlotte.

At residence of bride's parents in Lincoln county by Rev. Dr. Drury Lacy, July 16, 1857, Major T. J. Jackson, professor in Lexington (Va.) Military Institute, to Miss Mary Ann, daughter of Rev. Dr. R. H. Morrison.

(Stonewall Jackson, one of the Immortals of the Southern Confederacy.)

Near Wadesboro by Rev. T. R. Walsh, Oct. 28, 1857, Rev. Hilliard C. Parsons of South Carolina conference, to Miss Cornelia F. daughter of Walter F. Leake of Anson county.

(Parents of Mr. Walter Leake Parsons of Rockingham and late W. P. Parsons of Wadesboro.)

In Charlotte, by Rev. Mr. Sinclair, Nov. 24, 1857, Wm. J. Yates, editor of The Western Democrat, to Miss Sarah, daughter of the late Alexander Springs.

(Wm. J. Yates, late of Charlotte, a notable citizen and an editor of wide influence.)

In this county by Rev. James Sinclair, Aug. 15, 1858, Rev. Alexander Sinclair, pastor Presbyterian church, to Miss Laura, daughter of A. B. Davidson.

In Christ's church, New Bern, by Rev. T. J. Haughton, Aug. 11, 1858, Hon. John W. Ellis of Salisbury to Miss Mary McKinley, daughter of the late John P. Devane.

(Governor Ellis of North Carolina was elected governor of North Carolina 1858, re-elected in 1860, died in office 1861.)

In Union, S. C., by Rev. E. W. Thompson, Aug. 10, 1858, Eli H. Flenwider of Shelby, to Mrs. Mary C. McConnell of Union, S. C.

In Charlotte by Rev. E. J. Maynardie, Sept. 15, 1858, Thomas H. Brem, a merchant of Charlotte, to Mrs. Harriet Jones, daughter of Dr. D. R. Dunlap.

(Col. Thomas H. Brem, a leading business man, father of the late Walter Brem of this city.)

In Lincolnton, by Rev. R. N. Davis, August 24, 1859, William Tiddy to Miss Pattie A. daughter of Dr. J. C. Rudisill.

(Mr. Tiddy for many years operated the Lincoln Paper Mills of Lincolnton, and supplied paper to a wide section of country.)

In Lincolnton, August 25, 1859, at residence of bride's parents, David Schenck, attorneys to Miss Sallie W. daughter of Jacob A. Ramsour.

(David Schenck, grandson of Michael Schenck, pioneer cotton factor in the south, brilliant lawyer member of constitutional convention, 1861, judge superior court 1874-1881. Father of Judge Michael Schenck of Hendersonville.)

In Morganton, April 27, 1860, Dr. R. C. Pearson to Miss Emma daughter of Col. B. S. Gaither.

(Col. Gaither was a leader of the Whig party and member of Confederate congress. Once superintendent Charlotte mint.)

In Dallas, Nov. 29, 1860, Dr. Wm. Sloan to Miss E. E., daughter of the late Larkin Stowe.

In Charlotte by Rev. A. Sinclair, April 30, 1861, Lewis S. Williams to Miss Della S. White.

May 15, 1861, Rev. R. Z. Johnston, to Miss Kittie, daughter of R. B. Caldwell.

(Rev. R. Z. Johnston was 40 years, 1871 to 1911, pastor of the Lincolnton Presbyterian church.

DIED.

Near Beatties Ford, April 26, 1832, James King, 87.

In Lincolnton, Oct. 9, 1832, George McCulloh, 70.

At Georgetown, D. C., Feb. 2, 1834, Lorenzo Dow, a well known itinerant preacher.

In Charlotte, Oct. 7, 1834, after a lingering illness, Mrs. Mary Wilson, relict of the late Joseph Wilson.

In Lincoln county, Feb. 1, 1835, William Price, 78, a soldier of the Revolution.

Alfred Graham, 82, (son of Gen.

Joseph (Graham), Nov. 16, 1835, at home of his brother, John D. Graham in Lincoln county.
In Washington, D. C., Dec. 2, 1835, Dr. James Otis Freeman noted teacher and preacher.
At residence of Henry T. Sloan in Iredell county, April 21, 1836, Governor Hutchins G. Burton, after a very short illness.
(Gov. Burton of Halifax county, journeying to Beatties Ford, to visit relatives there, was taken violently ill en route and died. His body is buried in Unity church graveyard near Beatties Ford.)
Joseph Graham, 40, son of Gen. Joseph Graham, in Memphis, Sept. 18, 1837.
At his plantation near Haynesville, Alabama, Jan. 1, 1838, Dr. Lueco Mitchell of Salisbury.
John Wilfong of Lincoln, 76, a soldier of the Revolution, June 16, 1838, on his way to the springs some 14 miles from his home was found dead in woods near the road. His horse was tied to a nearby tree. It is supposed he took suddenly sick and lay down to rest.
In Greensboro, Oct. 24, 1841, Miss Jane E. Johnston, 18, daughter of Dr. William Johnston of Lincoln.
Miss Johnston was a sister of the late Gov. Robt. D. Johnston and Gov. James Forney Johnston of Alabama.
At Beatties Ford, Lincoln county, April 26, 1842, Hon. Robert H. Burton, widely known as an able lawyer.
(One time judge superior court and later treasurer of the state).
In Lincolnton Nov. 2, 1843, Major Lawson Henderson, 70.
(An influential citizen, one time sheriff of Lincoln county and clerk superior court 1807-1835. Father of Gen. James Pinckney Henderson who figured notably in the early history of Texas.)
In Charlotte, Michael Hoke of Lincolnton, died of bilious fever, Sept. 9, 1844. He was a candidate for governor against William A. Graham in August, 1844.
(Hoke and Graham were both natives of Lincoln county. Graham, the whig candidate, defeated Hoke, democrat, by about 3000 vote.)
In Catawba county, Feb. 10, 1850, Mrs. Lucy Connor, wife of Hon. Henry W. Connor.
Near Lenoir, Jan. 23, 1852, Mrs. Susan Mott, 38, wife of Rev. T. W. S. Mott, an Episcopal clergyman.
(Rev. T. W. S. Mott was once rector of St. Peter's Episcopal church of Charlotte and was father of the late Dr. J. J. Mott of Statesville.)
In Lincoln county, June 8, 1852, Mrs. Adelaide M. Cansler, wife of Col. A. P. Cansler and daughter of the late George Conley of Caldwell county.
In Lincolnton, Feb. 15, 1857, Col. William Julius Alexander, a brilliant lawyer.
(Grandfather of the late William Alexander Hoke, chief justice of our supreme court.)
In Charlotte, Dec. 23, 1857, Mrs. Catherine W., wife of Capt. John F. Hoke of Lincolnton, and daughter of the late Col. Wm. Julius Alexander.
Senator J. P. Henderson of Texas in Washington, D. C., June 4, 1858, just three months after he entered the senate.
(Born in Lincolnton 1808, son of Major Yawson Henderson, secretary of state Texas republic under President Sam Houston, minister to France from Texas, first governor of Texas 1848, general in Mexican war, for gallantry congress voted him a sword.)
In Concord, June 27, 1858, Mrs. Eugenia Barringer, wife of Rufus Barringer, Esq., and daughter of Rev. Dr. R. H. Morrison of Lincoln county.
(Mother of Dr. Paul Brandon Barringer of Charlottesville, Va.)
In Lincolnton, Dec. 21, 1858, Robert Williamson, 45, clerk superior court of Lincoln county.
In Shelby, August 24, 1859, Rev. William I. Langdon, president of High Point seminary.
In this county near Beatties Ford, April 10, 1835, James Connor, a patriot of the Revolution at advanced age of 81. Native of Ireland, but for more than 60 years a citizen of this county and greater part of his life in this county.
(Great grandfather of the late F. Brevard McDowell of Charlotte, father of the late Henry Workman Connor, Charleston, S. C., banker and one time mayor of that city.
In Lincoln county, August, 1846, Robert Henry and William Sidney, infant sons of Dr. Sidney X. and Mrs. Harriet C. Johnston.
In Gaston county, Jan. 19, 1859, Hugh Jenkins, 71.
In this county, June 22, 1861, Dr. W. A. Ardrey, aged 63.
In Charlotte after a lingering illness caused by an accident on his way to Monroe when he was thrown from his buggy, Thomas J. Holton, publisher of The Charlotte Whig, died in January, 1861.

The MINERS AND FARMERS JOURNAL was an early publication in Mecklenberg County, North Carolina. It begat the CHARLOTTE JOURNAL, which, in turn begat the CHARLOTTE WHIG, published by THOMAS J. HOLTON, and there finally came forth from these worthy ancestors the present modern, stream-lined daily newspaper, THE CHARLOTTE OBSERVER, the great grandchild of the first publication named, from which the very interesting notes above, were taken. Even newspapers have ancestors that it is sometimes interesting to trace. Aside from the OBSERVER, who first gave space to these old notes, credit is due to REV. WILLIAM L. SHERRILL, who later gave to the World his "ANNALS OF LINCOLN COUNTY". It was to this revered author, who thumbed the musty pages of the yellow files of the old JOHNAL, the WHIG and the FARMERS JOHNAL, tribute should be paid for preserving these priceless records of the distant past. Every day History is being made and the newspapers are preserving its details for future generations.

The ancestors of THOUSANDS of people scattered over, not only the OLD NORTH STATE, but the entire OLD SOUTH are mentioned in the above items. We regret that a full reproduction requires the type to be so small, but even if a glass is needed to read it, it will be time well spent, and will yield up information that would otherwise have been lost in the ashes of the past.

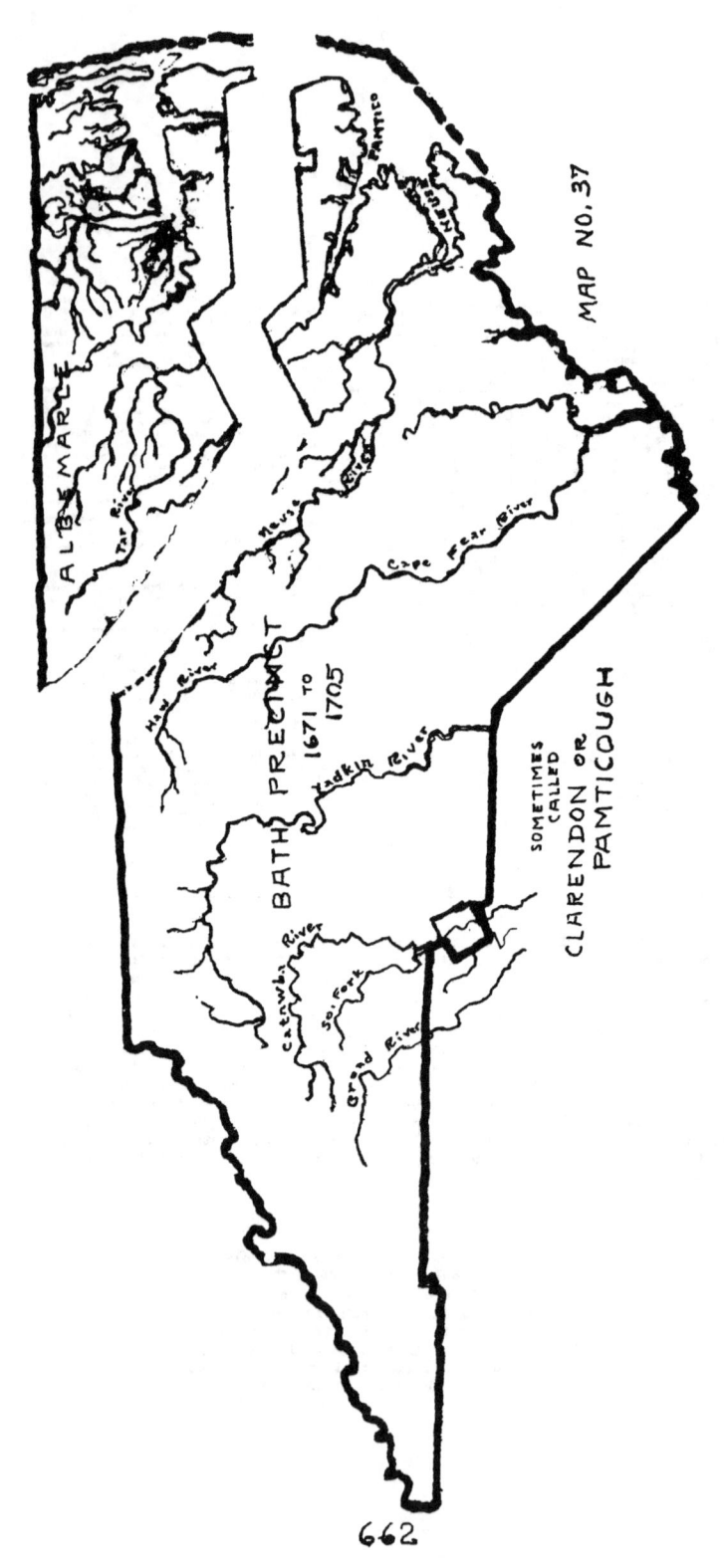

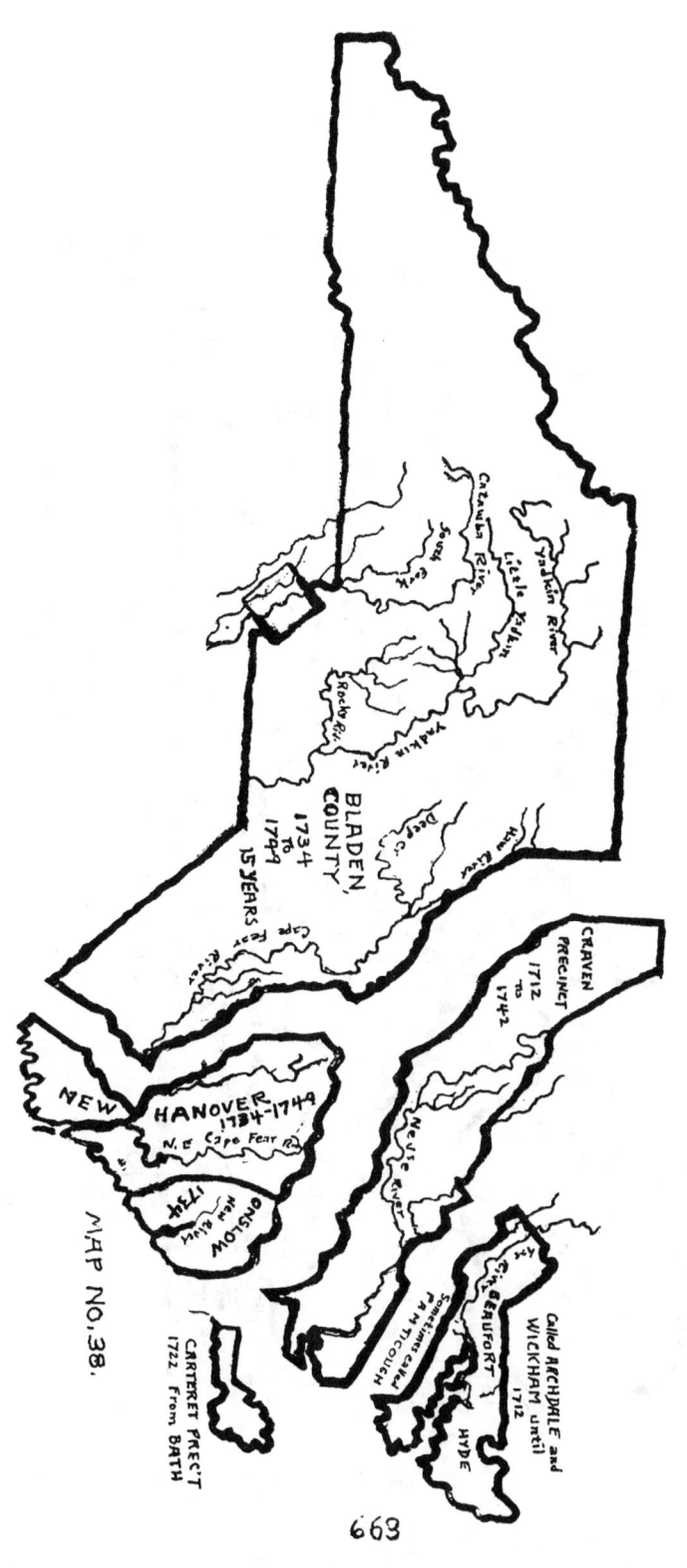

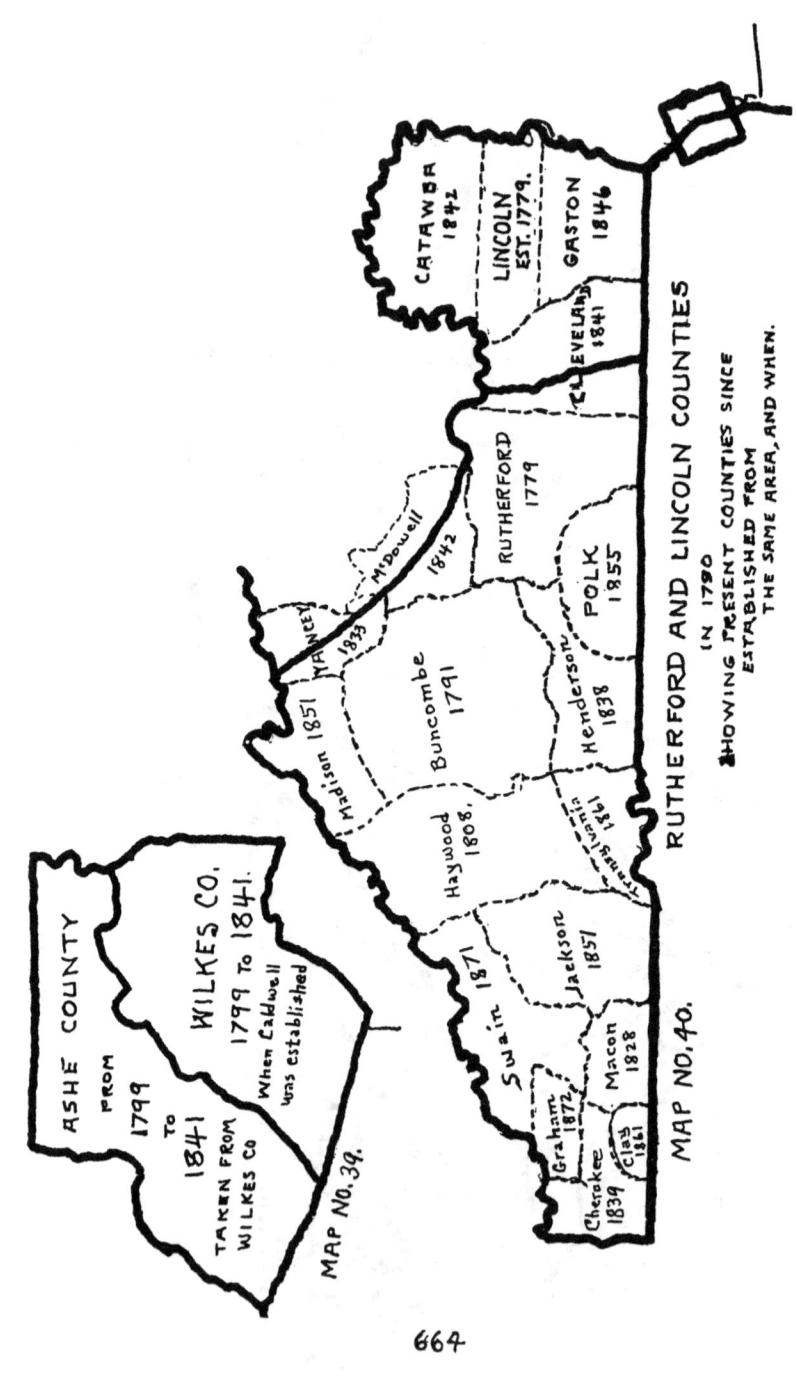

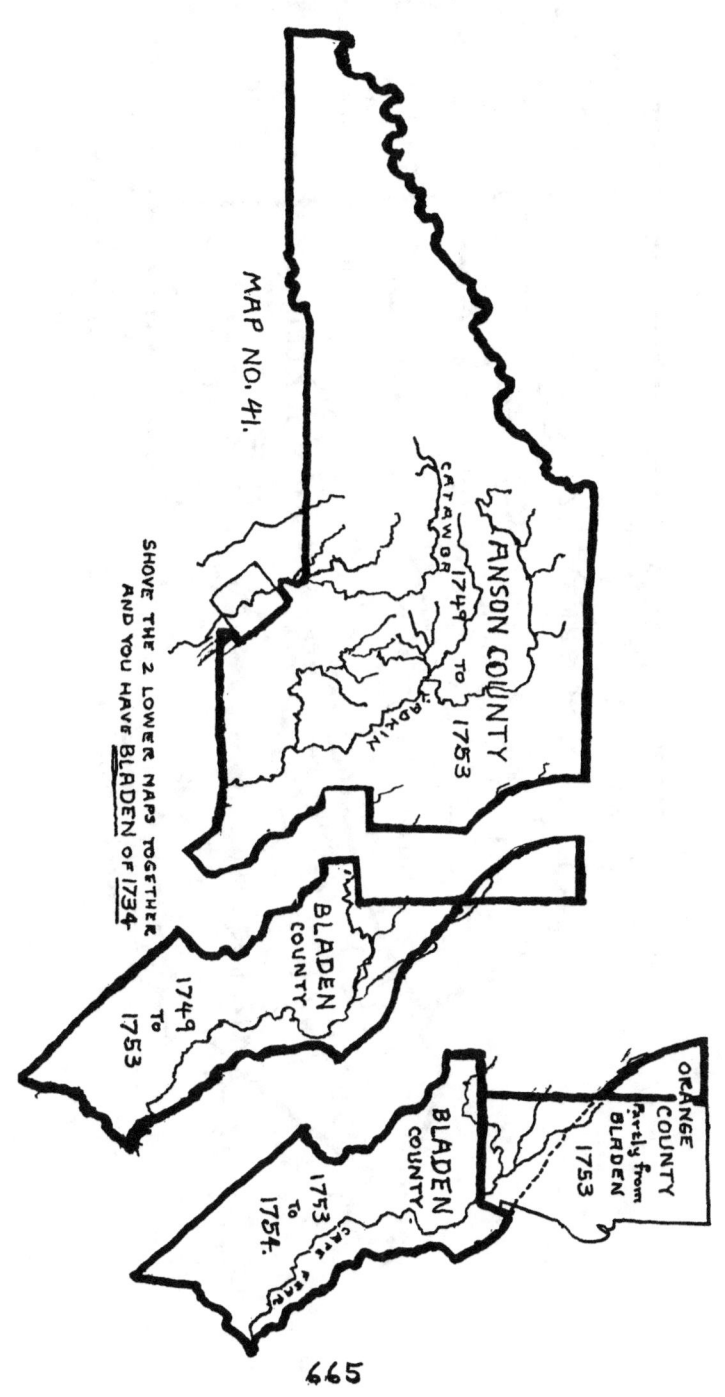

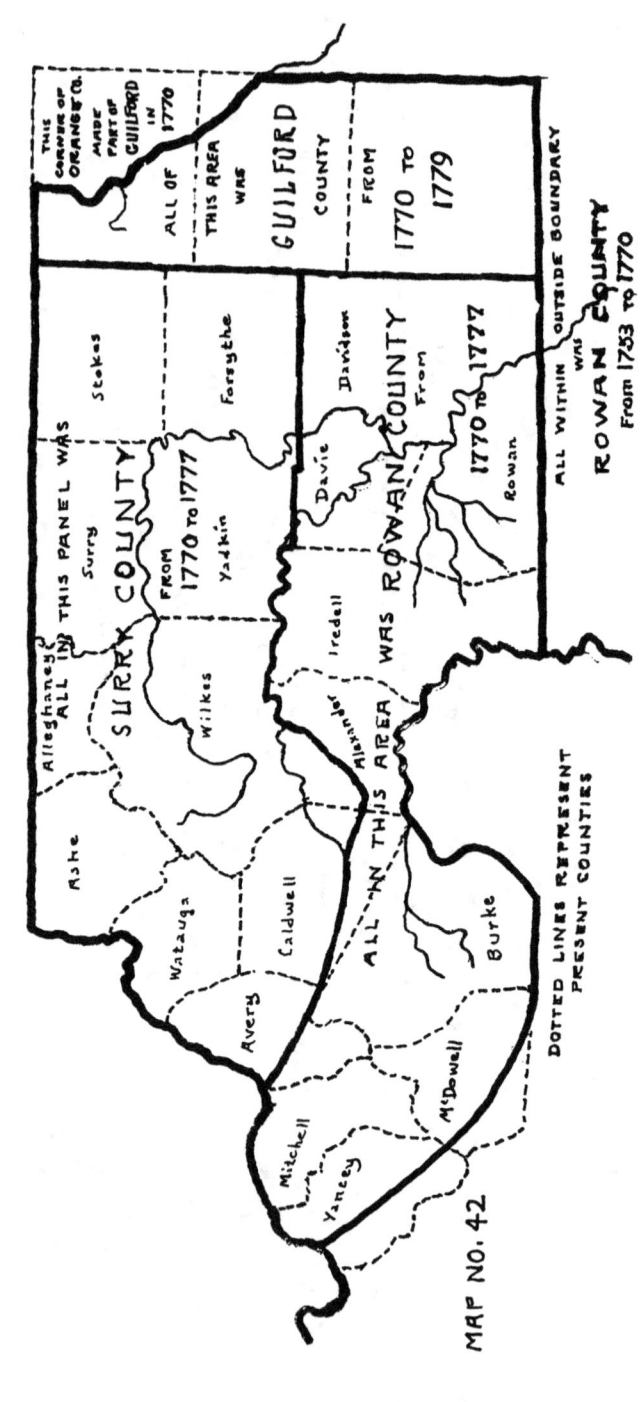

MAP NO. 42

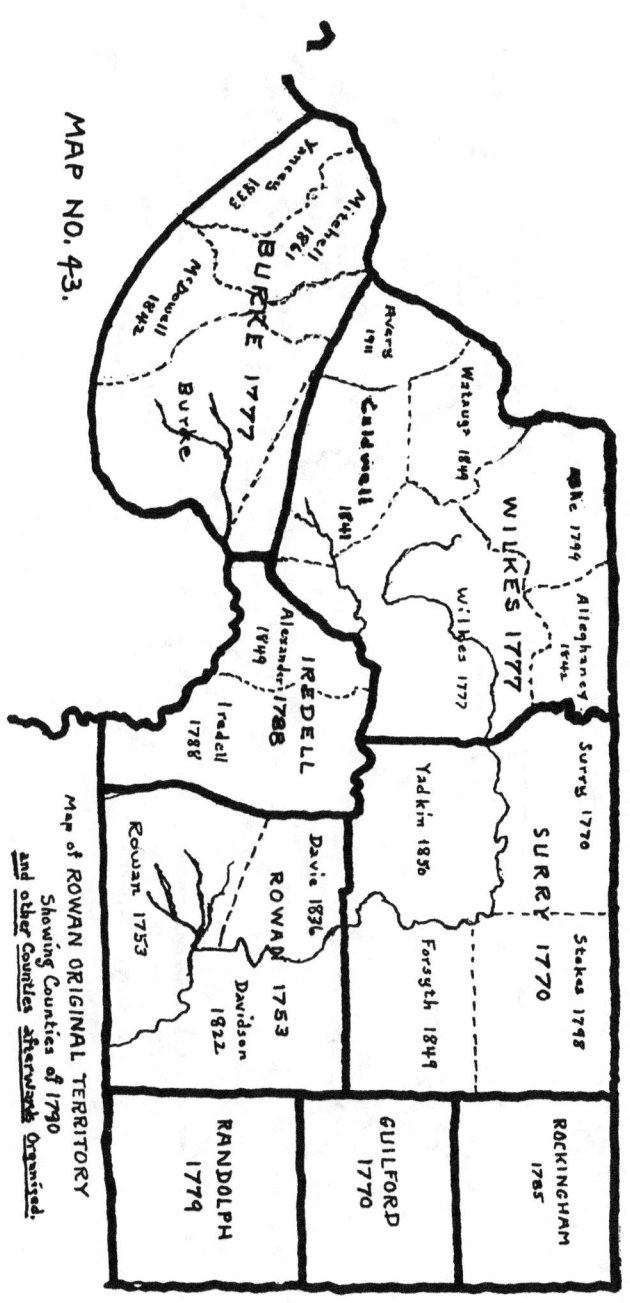

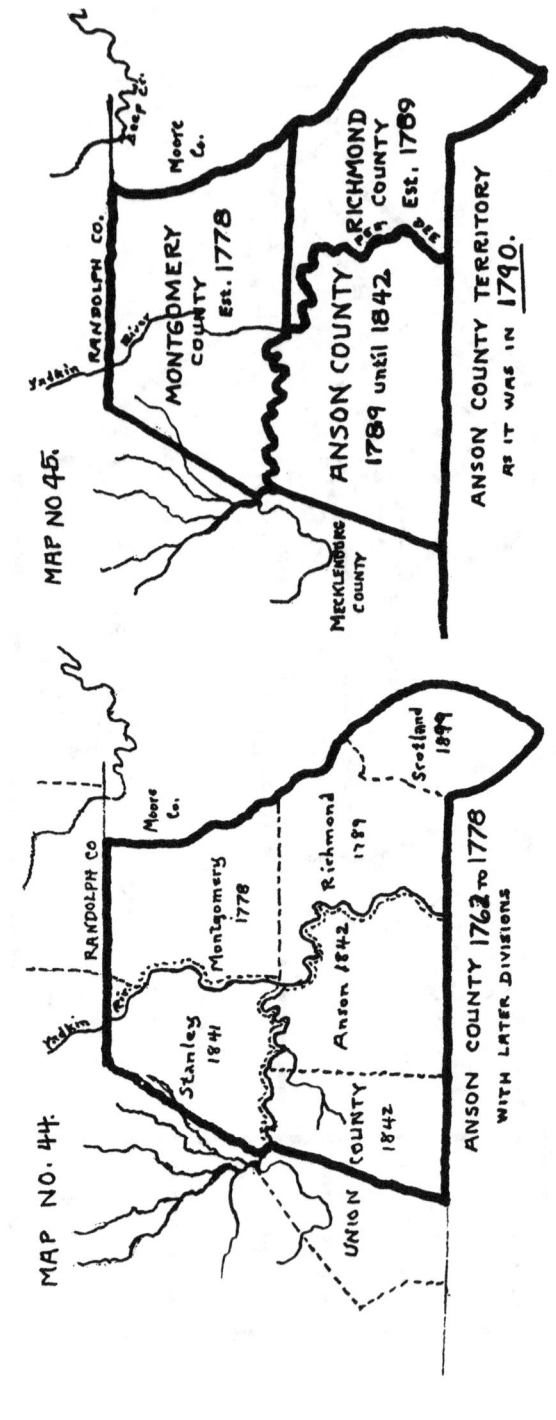

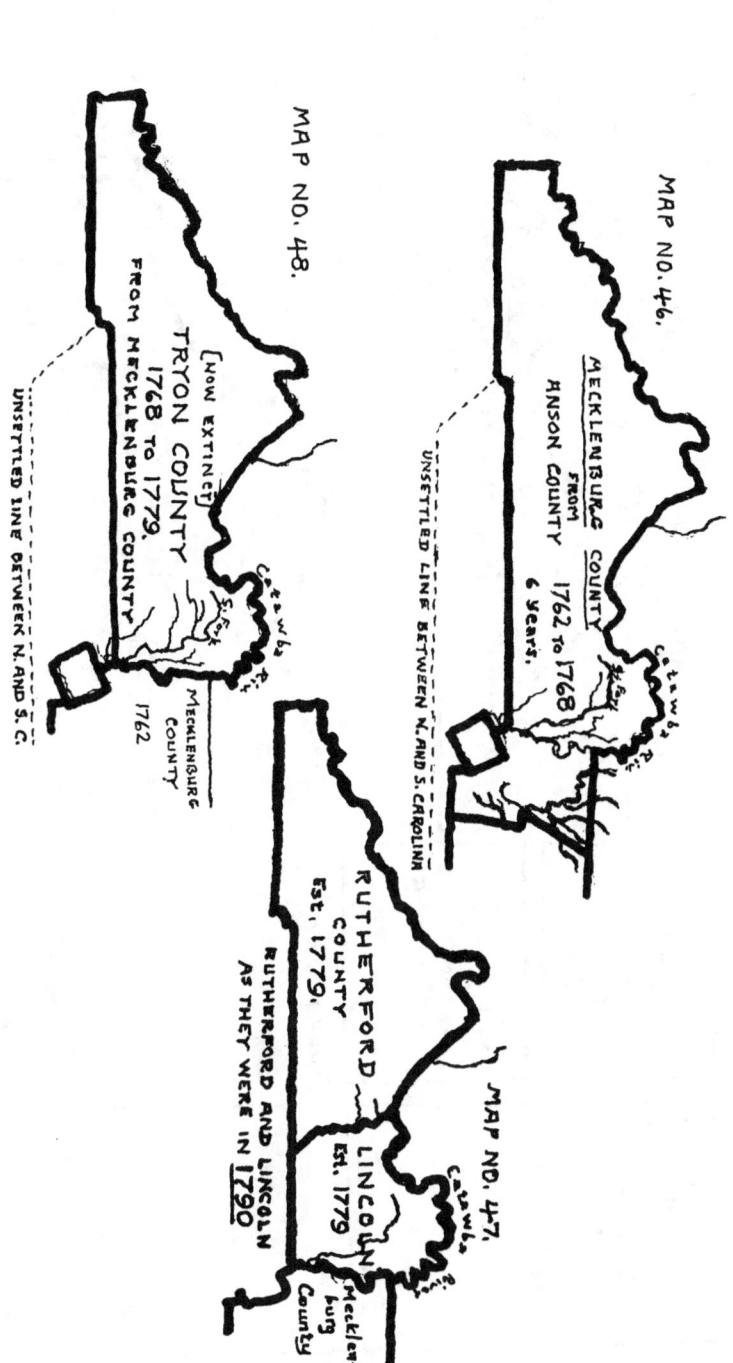

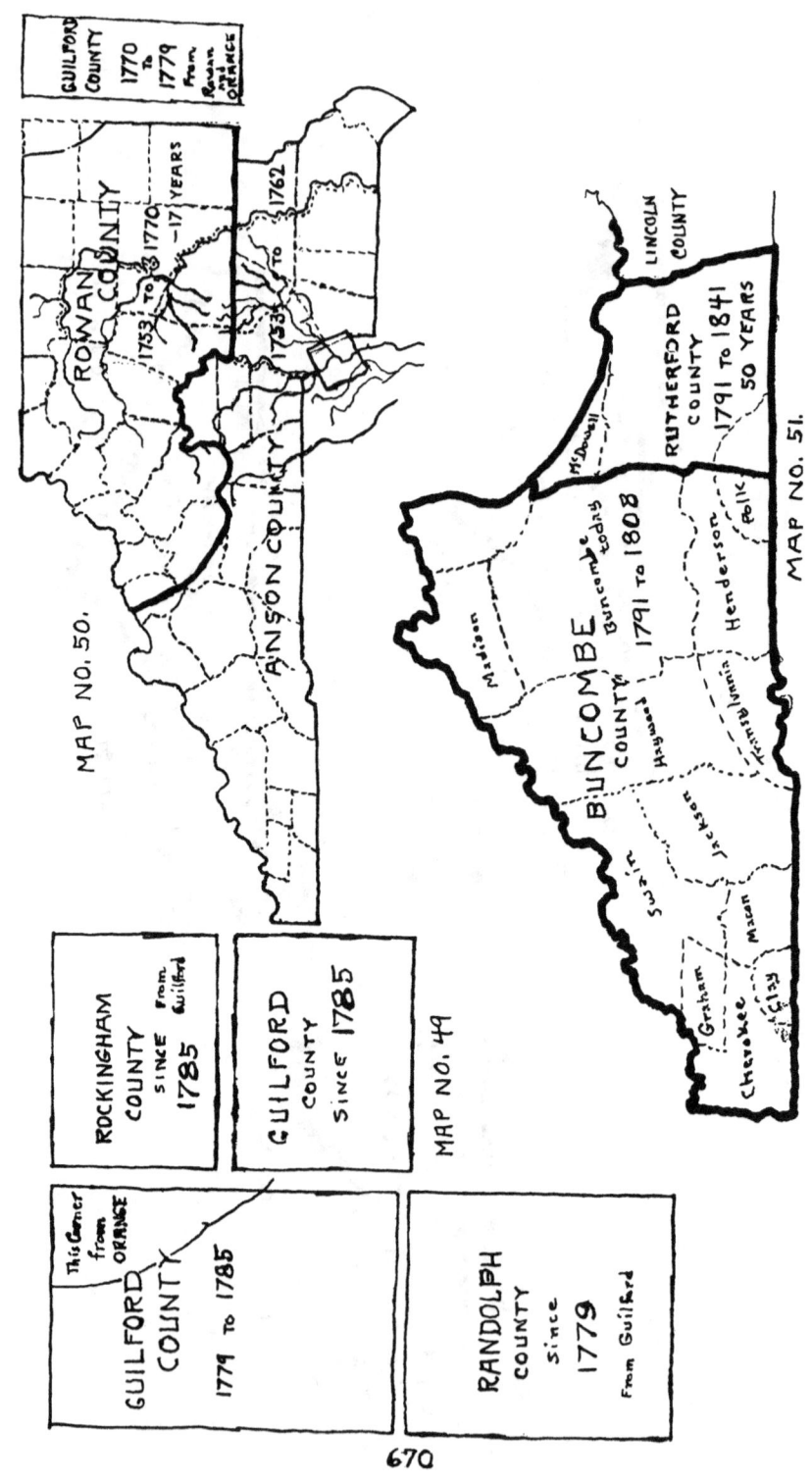

NORTH CAROLINA PRECINCTS
HISTORY

How often you hear even natives of the Old North State say: "Originally, North Carolina was divided into THREE PRECINCTS." Some will tell you there were FOUR precincts, and sometimes they say "four counties", etc. That of course samples only a popular conception - not the student's ideas. But even the student is to be excused, in view of the various statements to be found in books dealing with the State's history, which are confusingly out of harmony with the facts.

From first to last there were no less than TWENTY-TWO subdivisions of OLD ALBEMARLE, designated as "PRECINCTS", up to 1738, when the use of the name PRECINCT was abolished and the term COUNTY or COUNTIES adopted. This compiler may have made a miscount. If so, it has been an honest one. I am counting CARTERET PRECINCT twice, because there were two of them, one NORTH of ALBEMARLE SOUND, which was abolished in 1684, and one on Cape Fear, established in 1722. I am also counting OLD ALBEMARLE as a precinct, which it was often called, though many of the oldest records refer to it as ALBEMARLE COUNTY, before the name COUNTY came into official use in the Province. It is interesting to consider a brief history of these several early sub-divisions.

ALBEMARLE PRECINCT. You may call it a County, if you prefer, but it represented and embraced the entire habitable portion of what is now NORTH CAROLINA. Out of its wide domain came all of the other PRECINCTS and COUNTIES. It was the "grand-daddy" of the whole family, now consisting of one round hundred (100) counties, the youngest of which was named AVERY in 1911, after HON. WAIGHTSTILL AVERY, an early patriot, Judge and statesman, who was one of the signers of the MECKLENBURG DECLARATION. (See page 381 of this book). Much other material herein deals with the history of OLD ALBEMARLE, more in detail, to which the reader's attention is called.

BERKELEY PRECINCT. Named for SIR WILLIAM BERKELEY, or his brother, who were among the "Proprietors" of the Province of North Carolina. It was one of the three precincts established in 1671, at which time the first "division" of Old Albemarle was made. This precinct lay between the present CHOWAN and PASQUOTANK COUNTIES, and embraced all of the territory now known as PERQUIMANS COUNTY, plus a four or five mile strip off the East side of the present GATES COUNTY, which extended to the VIRGINIA LINE (which at that time was unknown and unsettled). It also embraced a large block of territory immediately South of the present PERQUIMANS COUNTY on the lower side of ALBEMARLE SOUND, then often referred to in the ancient records as "Carolina River". This strip of land extended from ALBEMARLE SOUND indefinitely Southward, and was for a long period of time undefined and unknown as to either its extent or character. BERKELEY PRECINCT lasted for approximately thirteen (13) years, when the name BERKELEY was dropped and it was called thereafter PERQUIMANS PRECINCT. This was about 1684.

CARTERET PRECINCT. This Precinct was established in 1671, and was named for another Proprietor. See "Old Albemarle and Its Absentee Landlords" herein. The territory of which it was comprised lay immediately East of BERKELEY PRECINCT and embraced all of the present Counties of PASQUOTANK, CAMDEN and CURRITUCK, which at that time was on the North side of ALBEMARLE SOUND. The territory of CARTERET presumably also took in all lands within an even area below the Sound, extending Southward indefinitely into unknown and unexplored regions. North of the Sound, and perhaps Southward as well, the country was infested with Indians and there are legends of pirates who made their homes along the rivers and arms of the sea that jutted inward. This Precinct also lasted for thirteen years, until 1684, when its name was changed by making it two precincts called PASQUOTANK and CURRITUCK PRECINCTS.

SHAFTSBURY PRECINCT. It embraced all of the present CHOWAN COUNTY, most of GATES, and presumably all territory West of the CHOWAN RIVER in the present North Carolina that was habitable or might thereafter become habitable. It was also named for one of the "Proprietors" or absentee landlords. Its territory also jumped the Sound and extended Southward for an indefinite distance. In 1684 the name of SHAFTSBURY was dropped and the name CHOWAN substituted. All three of these first precincts being changed in name, and the new names based on the then established names of the principal water ways North of the Albemarle Sound.

BATH PRECINCT. The exact date of the actual birth of BATH PRECINCT is shrouded in mystery. Presumably it came into existence ON PAPER ONLY about the time of the establishment of the three other precincts mentioned above - in 1671 - but as it was designed to embrace lands lying South of the Albemarle Sound, which were at that time perhaps inhabited by wild tribes of Indians, its actual coming into physical existence, may have been somewhat later. At the home of old man JOHN HECKLEFIELD in 1705, in PASQUOTANK PRECINCT, the Council of Assembly granted a charter for the incorporation of BATH TOWNE, away below the Sound in what for several years had been called on the records PAMTICOUGH. Thereafter many of the inhabitants of EDENTON (or what afterwards became EDENTON) settled at this place, and thereafter you will find them referred to for several years as "of Bath" and sometimes "Bath Town". Thus the name of Bath came into general use. BATH PRECINCT was sometimes referred to as CLARENDON, also. This writer believes they were the same, contemporaneously and perhaps embraced ON PAPER the same territory.

CLARENDON PRECINCT. As heretofore stated, this name was applied to what was commonly called "BATH" Precinct on the records. It is likely that CLARENDON was the official name for it, adopted from another one of the "Proprietors", the intention having been to name a precinct for each of them, though it appears they never got around to all of them. The incorporation of the Old Town of BATH in 1705 appears to have pre-empted the title, because of the popular conception that anybody who settled in the vicinity of the town, was from BATH. What is said about the later disposition of the territory of BATH, therefore, applies to CLARENDON.

CHOWAN PRECINCT. This was originally called SHAFTSBURY, and the name was changed to CHOWAN in 1684, the new title, like other substitutions, being adopted from the name of the principal stream or river penetrating the territory. In theory CHOWAN PRECINCT, like SHAFTSBURY, extended indefinitely Westward, presumably even over the mountains into what is now TENNESSEE, and on to the MISSISSIPPI, or the "Western Waters" about which little was known. Otherwise, until the erection of BERTIE PRECINCT in 1722, it comprised the original territory of SHAFTSBURY. It took in most of GATES COUNTY, HERTFORD, NORTHAMPTON and on West, unless it may be said that at the time BATH came into existence, CHOWAN stopped at the line of PERSON and CASWELL COUNTIES as they are today. Consult the accompanying maps for details.

PERQUIMANS PRECINCT. Originally called BERKELEY. It embraced, so far as the record appears, the same identical territory included in BERKELEY until TYRRELL PRECINCT was established below ALBEMARLE SOUND in 1729, which took away from it the last of its territory below the Sound. In 1705, however, the lower part of its Southern territory had been absorbed by BATH or CLARENDON, and as early as 1696 the almost legendary PAMPTICOUGH PRECINCT. Its territory North of Albemarle Sound remained intact until GATES COUNTY was established in 1779 and absorbed the narrow strip of land that connected it with the Virginia line, now comprising a part of the Eastern boundary of GATES COUNTY, which Mr. Hathaway, from an examination of the ancient deed records, conceived to be about three or four miles in width on that side.

PASQUOTANK PRECINCT was established in 1684, out of the Western part of the older CARTERET PRECINCT, which went out of existence in that year. Until CAMDEN COUNTY was formed in 1777, Pasquotank's Eastern boundary was CURRITUCK, but nearly all of the new sub-division - CAMDEN - was taken from PASQUOTANK, leaving CURRITUCK as it had been previously, with all of its territory SOUTH OF ALBEMARLE SOUND, intact, as originally, except that part of it which had been first, in PAMPTICOUGH, second in BATH, and finally in WICKHAM and HYDE. This territory was finally taken away from CURRITUCK when DARE COUNTY was set up in 1870. Of course, in 1738, like all the other Precincts, PASQUOTANK became a COUNTY.

CURRITUCK PRECINCT, as stated above, was until 1684, a part of the first CARTERET PRECINCT, when that Precinct was divided into PASQUOTANK and CURRITUCK. Included in this Precinct, as well as today, when it is a County, its jurisdiction included the lands and territory embraced in the peninsular formations East of CURRITUCK SOUND, on down to and including ROANOKE ISLAND, "NAG'S HEAD", etc. In the early exploratory era these bays and inlets furnished piratical harbors and havens for such characters as "Blackbeard", Stede Bonnett, and others of that ilk, who raided not only the surrounding waters of the Gulf and bays, but harrassed would-be industrious settlers for half a century. Even today there is an "OLD BRICK HOUSE" standing on the banks of the PASQUOTANK RIVER, perhaps in what is now CAMDEN COUNTY, which is pointed out as one of the traditional haunts of "Blackbeard" the pirate.

BERTIE PRECINCT. This Precinct was established by the General Assembly of North Carolina, in 1722. It took away from CHOWAN PRECINCT all of its territory lying West of Chowan River, and extending South to the lower bends of the ROANOKE, following the high water shed between the Tar and Neuse to the line of Virginia (still unsettled) at a point now comprising the boundary between PERSON and CASWELL COUNTIES. It remained thus for a period of nineteen (19) years, or until 1741, when from BERTIE was taken NORTHAMPTON and EDGECOMBE COUNTIES. Neither EDGECOMBE (which embraced large areas) or NORTHAMPTON COUNTY were ever known as PRECINCTS, since they were established after the Act of the General Assembly of 1738, which abolished the use of the term PRECINCT. See sketches of the Counties and the accompanying maps.

TYRRELL PRECINCT was erected out of most of the territory left of the original ALBEMARLE and its subsequent sub-divisions, lying South of ALBEMARLE SOUND, with the execption of the larger part of what is now DARE COUNTY, which at that period (1729) was still a part of CURRITUCK PRECINCT. In 1729 when TYRRELL PRECINCT was established it extended East ACROSS ALLIGATOR RIVER, as is shown by deeds to lands on the East side of ALLIGATOR, stated to have been in TYRRELL PRECINCT. On the West TYRRELL PRECINCT when first established, included all of the present MARTIN COUNTY, except a block off the WEST END, between the ROANOKE and the present line of EDGECOMBE COUNTY, which was taken from HALIFAX COUNTY in 1774 to make MARTIN. The Southern boundary of TYRRELL PRECINCT was the BATH - CLARENDON - PAMPTICOUGH line, though at that time the Northern lines of BEAUFORT and HYDE PRECINCTS. MARTIN COUNTY, in 1774, WASHINGTON COUNTY, in 1799, and DARE COUNTY in 1870, taken from what was formerly TYRRELL PRECINCT (long after it became a COUNTY) has trimmed TYRRELL COUNTY down considerably. Today WASHINGTON COUNTY embraces the site of most of the important early settlements there.

PAMPTICOUGH PRECINCT. This is the name applied to that certain area lying immediately South of the present Counties of MARTIN, WASHINGTON, TYRRELL and DARE COUNTIES from 1696 to the year 1705, including both sides of the PAMLICO RIVER and the present CRAVEN COUNTY. It appears in certain deeds to lands and other items relating to people living at that period in that section. It may have been another name for BATH, or regarded as a different Precinct, carved out of BATH and CLARENDON. No record of this name has been found after 1705, when the name of ARCHDALE and WICKHAM PRECINCTS came into existence, the first applying to the BEAUFORT TERRITORY and the second to the area known after 1712 as HYDE PRECINCT. Of course the name came from the PAMPTICOUGH RIVER, since designated as the PAMLICO on modern records.

ARCHDALE PRECINCT. So called, perhaps, for GOVERNOR ARCHDALE. It comprised the territory now embraced in BEAUFORT & PITT COUNTIES. It lasted for seven (7) years and went out of existence as a Precinct of that name in 1712. Here was the scene of the Indian uprisings of 1711 around old BATH TOWN, then regarded as the capital of that section, which for a time almost emptied the community of its residents.

WICKHAM PRECINCT. This was the name of the Precinct, which embraced the territory now comprising HYDE COUNTY, from its establishment in 1705 and its ending in 1712, when WICKHAM PRECINCT went out of existence and was superceded by HYDE PRECINCT.

BEAUFORT PRECINCT. Came into existence in the place of ARCHDALE and comprised the same territory. It was established as a precinct in 1712. The present PITT COUNTY and BEAUFORT COUNTY includes all of the old original territory of BEAUFORT PRECINCT. The town of WASHINGTON at the conjunction of PAMLICO and the TAR RIVER is now the capital. This town was laid off by one of the BONNER FAMILY, and was the birthplace of a notable, modern day, diplomat and newspaper man, JONATHAN DANIELS. BEAUFORT PRECINCT automatically became BEAUFORT COUNTY by Act of the Assembly in 1738.

HYDE PRECINCT was the successor, so far as the same territory is concerned, of WICKHAM PRECINCT, mentioned above. It went out of existence, after a period of twenty-six years, when it became one of the original THIRTEEN COUNTIES of North Carolina, after the name of PRECINCT was abolished. It is now HYDE COUNTY.

CRAVEN PRECINCT. In 1712, at the same time that BEAUFORT and HYDE PRECINCTS to the immediate North of PAMLICO RIVER, came into existence on the map, CRAVEN PRECINCT was established. Two years prior to that time, in 1710, CHRISTOPHER de GRAAFFENREIDT and his so-called Palatines, from Switzerland, had acquired a large tract of land on the Neuse River and settled in this territory, naming their headquarters NEW BERN. New Bern is still the official county seat of the present CRAVEN COUNTY. Craven Precinct was made up of territory considered as belonging to BATH or CLARENDON PRECINCTS, and Col. Fred Olds, whose views have been adopted by this compiler in regard to CRAVEN'S origin, so states. CRAVEN PRECINCT remained intact as a sub-division of OLD ALBEMARLE, until its name as a Precinct was dropped by the General Assembly in 1738, after which it was called CRAVEN COUNTY. It was one of the Original Thirteen Counties of NORTH CAROLINA. See map.

CARTERET PRECINCT. Established in 1722. It was the same in area then as it is today, under the name of CARTERET COUNTY. The fact that among the three original first divisions of OLD ALBEMARLE, the territory now comprising PASQUOTANK and CURRITUCK COUNTIES was set apart as a CARTERET PRECINCT has confused even the historians, but one has only to study the documentary declarations that occur in Wills and Deeds of the two periods to understand and differentiate between them. The illustrious JOHN H. WHEELER in his HISTORY OF NORTH CAROLINA who forgot more than this writer will ever knew about North Carolina History, became confused about this matter and inadvertently referred to this latter sub-division as "One of the Original Precincts of the Lords Proprietors" - thinking of the first and writing of the second CARTERET. (See his Vol. 2 p. 72.) No other sub-divisions were ever taken from this area, and it became one of the ORIGINAL THIRTEEN COUNTIES of NORTH CAROLINA in 1738. It came out of BATH PRECINCT.

NEW HANOVER PRECINCT. JUDGE WHEELER says this sub-division was formed in 1728 and called in honor of the House of Hanover, in England, but wholly fails to designate the name of the territory from which it was taken. COL. FRED OLDS declares it was established in 1729- and that it came - like CRAVEN - from BATH COUNTY, and adds that "it was the last came out of that" territory. In other words, when NEW HANOVER PRECINCT was established in 1728-29, it embraced all of the remaining and unappropriated territory originally or that ever belonged to BATH or CLARENDON PRECINCT, and the latter sub-division became extinct. We have endeavored to show on the accompanying maps the full extent of NEW HANOVER PRECINCT, which extended Westward indefinitely to the "Western Waters" whatever that may have implied at that time.

BLADEN PRECINCT, which was erected out of the vast area of the territory allotted to NEW HANOVER mostly to the West of Cape Fear River (see map) came into existence in 1734. It remained a "PRECINCT" for only four years, and then came in under the wire as one of the ORIGINAL THIRTEEN COUNTIES of NORTH CAROLINA. Its numerous sub-divisions will be shown later.

ONSLOW PRECINCT was cut out of the Southeast corner of NEW HANOVER in 1734 at the same time that CRAVEN was established. Thereafter it remained intact until the present day, having four years later automatically progressed into ONSLOW COUNTY. Thus ONSLOW COUNTY became also, one of the Original Thirteen North Carolina Counties, to be mentioned later in these notes.

THUMB-NAIL HISTORIES OF
THE ONE HUNDRED NORTH CAROLINA COUNTIES

ALAMANCE COUNTY. The territory comprising ALAMANCE COUNTY was a part of ORANGE COUNTY for almost 100 years, from 1753 to 1849. The outburst of the "Regulators" and the "Battle of the ALAMANCE" occurred on ALAMANCE CREEK in what is now a part of this County. The leaders of the "regulator movement" in ORANGE COUNTY were HERMAN HUSBANDS, one R. HOWELL and one MADDOCKS at whose mill in what is now ALAMANCE the Regulators held their first general meeting. GRAHAM, the county seat of ALAMANCE is 59 miles from RALEIGH, the present capitol. BURLINGTON is the largest town in the county. It is an up to date town, with good hotels, factories, etc, and near many points of historic interest. This was the home of many Quakers in the early days. MEBANE is another town, which bears the name of an ancient family of this section, of which one ALEXANDER MEBANE was the head. He served in the House of Commons and the Senate from Orange in the early days, was a kinsman of the ARMSTRONG family, and the MEBANE descendants are scattered throughout Tennessee, Kentucky, North and South Carolina, Alabama and Texas. The Ruffin family also lived in this county. The Haw River runs through a part of the county, and rises in the county.

ALEXANDER COUNTY. This County was established in 1847. TAYLORSVILLE is the County seat, and is a town of about 1000 population. There is at least one mill there. The County was named for NATHANIEL ALEXANDER, of Mecklenburg County, Governor of the State. The territory comprising ALEXANDER COUNTY had been settled about 100 years before the County was established, and at one time it was all a part of ROWAN COUNTY. See maps. BARRETT'S MOUNTAIN is located a little West of the town of TAYLORSVILLE. The first state-wide prohibitionist in North Carolina lived on the banks of the Catawba River not far away. He was an Indian Chief. There is a so-called emerald mine in the county, and the records show that a gem weighing nine ounces was found there once upon a time.

ALLEGHANEY COUNTY was established in 1859 from ASHE COUNTY. Its northern boundary is the State of VIRGINIA. New River runs through the Northwestern corner of the County. SPARTA is the name of the county seat. Originally (1753) this territory was a part of ROWAN COUNTY, taken out of ANSON. This is the home county and the birth place of BOB DOUGHTON, the famous North Carolina "Mule Doughton". The county is also somewhat noted as being the home at one time of the so-called "SIAMEZE TWINS" made famous by P. T. BARNUM. The story prevails locally that they were married in the old DOUGHTON HOME.

ANSON COUNTY. This is one of the older counties of the Old North State, which has been in existence since 1749. In genealogical terms ANSON COUNTY was the grandson of NEW HANOVER, one of North Carolina's Original Thirteen Counties, its parent being BLADEN COUNTY, established from New Hanover in 1734. Anson County at the time of its establishment (1749) comprehended almost the entire western part of North Carolina to the Tennessee line. A large slice of it was allocated to ROWAN COUNTY in 1753, and nine years later to MECKLENBURG and TRYON COUNTIES went the most of the remainder. Today it is a small county on the banks of the Pee Dee River, some fifty miles East of Charlotte, with WADESBORO as the County seat. Many of the old original records of this county are still preserved in the little county courthouse at Wadesboro, and some abstracts of these records will be found published in this book on pages 195 and 196. Also see maps.

ASHE COUNTY. It was taken out of WILKES COUNTY in 1799. It was named for GOVERNOR SAMUEL ASHE. Its northern boundary is the Virginia line next to GRAYSON COUNTY, Virginia. Here was the home of the CALLAWAY, CLEVELAND, MILLER, HARDEN and McMILLAN families, members of which served the county in the General Assembly at different times. BENJAMIN HOWARD, of Maryland settled here before the revolution, and his descendants and the descendants of other families mentioned peopled Tennessee and the West long afterwards. A splendid source of information in regard to these early settlers of ASHE COUNTY is Arthur's History of Western North Carolina. BENJAMIN CLEVELAND, the revolutionary leader, lived in what is now Ashe County, in the Yadkin Valley.

AVERY COUNTY is the youngest child of OLD ALBEMARLE, named for a signer of the Mecklenburg Declaration, when it was born in 1911, Hon. WAIGHTSTILL AVERY. For 112 years the territory comprising AVERY COUNTY was a part of ASHE COUNTY, though at the time it was established none of its territory came directly from ASHE, but from other counties surrounding that had been taken from ASHE previously. Its Western boundary is the line of TENNESSEE, and the town of NEWLAND is the county seat. Good highways run through the county and over the mountains into Tennessee valleys.

BEAUFORT COUNTY. Its territory came out of BATH PRECINCT originally. It was BEAUFORT PRECINCT (formerly ARCHDALE PRECINCT) from 1712 until it became known as BEAUFORT COUNTY in 1738. Thus it was one of the Original Thirteen Counties of North Carolina. For a long period the old town of BATH was the capital of this territory, and later the town of WASHINGTON was established at the confluence of the TAR and PAMLICO rivers, which has since been the county seat. Many of the old landmarks of the town of BATH are yet intact, including the old St' Thomas Church (See illustration), built in 1734, though the Church was organized in 1701. The first public library in North Carolina was started here by Rev. Thomas Bray in 1700. This was the scene of the Tuscarora massacre. BATH is said to be the oldest town in NORTH CAROLINA and it is claimed was at one time the Capital of the Province. It was the home of Governor Eden at one time. The county seat of the county was moved from BATH to the town of Washington in 1785. Bath and Back Creeks coming in from Pamlico river furnish water fronts for BATH and there is now a bridge across the river at Washington. The BONNERS, BLOUNTS, EDENS, BLACKLEDGES, LANIERS, STANLEYS and WILLIAMSES were prominent families in BEAUFORT COUNTY in its earlier days.

BERTIE COUNTY was one of the Thirteen Original North Carolina Counties, by reason of the fact that BERTIE PRECINCT (established in 1722) was in existence in 1738, when the names of these precincts were changed to COUNTIES. WINDSOR, located on the CASHIE RIVER is the County seat. They call it the "Valley of the Cashie River" and there are hills that overlook the town. One JOHN GRAY donated land for the town site in 1722, the year BERTIE PRECINCT was established out of CHOWAN COUNTY. Three miles from the town is the site of the home of DAVID STONE, Governor of North Carolina in 1808. Eleven miles East of Windsor is the location of the old estates of the Dukenfields, and it was in the forks of the Cashie and the Roanoke river, according to tradition, that the grant of land was made to REV. ROGER GREEN in 1653, by Governor Berkeley, with the understanding that he and a hundred followers would locate along the Roanoke. It is claimed that the settlement was never made, though there is plenty of evidence that there were white settlers in the vicinity by this time. The Tuscarora Indian reservation granted them in 1717 are located about five miles West of the highway between Windsor and WILLIAMSTON (South of the Roanoke) in BERTIE COUNTY. It is called the Indian Woods. So many notable persons lived in BERTIE COUNTY and others are descendants of people who lived there that it would be folly to undertake to list even a few of them. See the genealogical section of this work for references to many of them.

BLADEN COUNTY. The territory for BLADEN came out of NEW HANOVER in 1734, at which time it was called BLADEN PRECINCT. Four years later (in 1738) it became BLADEN COUNTY, and by virtue of this fact it became one of the THIRTEEN ORIGINAL COUNTIES of NORTH CAROLINA. (See Map). Eleven years later BLADEN lost the greater part of its territory when ANSON COUNTY was organized in 1749, which territory covered most of the Western part of North Carolina. Mr. Wheeler in his history of BLADEN COUNTY says that in 1840 a certain WILLIAM PRIGDEN lived in this County, who was the eldest man on the U. S. census for that decade, and that he was 112 years old at that time, and lived until he was 122 years old. ELIZABETHTOWN, on the Cape Fear River is the county seat, and it was at this place that a battle took place between the opposing forces during the American revolution. Among the prominent families represented on the records of BLADEN COUNTY during and after the revolution were the following: WHITE, OWEN, STEWART, JOSIAH LEWIS, COWAN, SELLERS, BEATTY, McMILLAN, HOLMES, CROMARTIE, ASHFORD, RICHARDSON, (AMOS), GILLASPIE, LYON and JONES.

BRUNSWICK COUNTY. This County, lying West of the Lower Cape Fear River, was cut off from NEW HANOVER COUNTY in 1764. It fronts on the coast to the South. (See maps). Although Brunswick County was not created from New Hanover until 1764, there was an early settlement on the Cape Fear River much sooner. In 1725 COL. MAURICE MOORE laid off the town of BRUNSWICK and named both town and county for the Prince of Brunswick. In 1731 Dr. Brickell in his "Natural History" wrote: "BRUNSWICK TOWN is most delightfully seated, on the South side of that noble River Cape Fear; and no doubt it will be very considerable in a short time, by its great trade, the number of merchants and rich planters that are settled upon its banks." Its exact location is not known to the writer, but one authority places it on the Southwest side of Cape Fear River, which, it seems to me, locates it in what is now BRUNSWICK COUNTY. It is claimed that no less than three colonial Governors of North Carolina lived at one time at OLD BRUNSWICK, i. e., GABRIEL JOHNSTON, ARTHUR DOBBS and GOVERNOR TRYON. It was to these parts that JOSIAH MARTIN fled to escape the wrath of the aroused populace, when the revolution got hot, and boarded His Majesty's vessel to make good his escape out of the country. But old BRUNSWICK gave way to WILMINGTON, which later became the Capital of the State, and the once thriving settlement practically vanished. It is now a "ghost town". Wilmington and Old Brunswick were ports of entry, and it was through vessels landing in this area that Flora McDonald's hordes of Scotch setlers arrived. Likewise from the vicinity of OLD ALBEMARLE, after the Tuscarora War was over, came a long list of migrants to this same settlement. Among the families in that catagory were: SWANN, PORTER, HARNETT, MOORE, McREE, RICE, GRAINGER, HOLT, WALKER and others.

BUNCOMBE COUNTY. This county was established in 1791 and the territory comprising it, which was extensive, was taken partly from BURKE COUNTY, but mostly from RUTHERFORD COUNTY. The portion contributed by BURKE was small compared to the other part. (See maps). Afterwards practically all of the counties in the extreme southwestern portion of North Carolina were taken from the territory Rutherford had contributed to Buncombe. On pages 193 and 194 of this volume will be found published abstracts of some of the very early records of BUNCOMBE COUNTY, showing the names of some of the earliest settlers and families. Haywood County was the first county established out of Buncombe in the year 1808 and most of the other counties then came out of Haywood.

BURKE COUNTY was established in 1777, from territory taken out of ROWAN COUNTY. MORGANTON is the County seat. This was the home of JUDGE WAIGHTSTILL AVERY and his descendants are still living there. Here it was that GOV. JOHN SEVIER, of Tennessee, was rescued by some of his followers when he had been arrested and brought back to North Carolina in his political mix-ups. All records of Burke County were burned during the War, 1861-5.

CABARRUS COUNTY. This County came into existence in 1792. Its territory was for a long time part of MECKLENBURG COUNTY, which was taken from ANSON in 1762, thirty years prior to that time. It was named for STEPHEN CABARRUS, one of three brothers, AUGUSTUS, BARTHOLOMEW and STEPHEN CABARRUS. Stephen Cabarrus was from CHOWAN COUNTY, and died at Pembroke, in Chowan County, in 1807. (See page 21 of this book). The county seat of Cabarrus County is CONCORD, historic old town of North Carolina, which had its representatives in the Mecklenburg Convention in 1775. See pages 369, 380 and 381 in this book. The Cabarrus family was from France. The first gold discovered in North Carolina was on Meadow Creek in Cabarrus County in 1799, on the farm of one George Reed, and this excitement preceded other discoveries made later (notably in Rutherford County) and the eventual location of a branch of the U. S. mint at Charlotte, in Mecklenburg County. Among the prominent families of CABARRUS COUNTY were the HARRIS, BARRINGER, PHIFER, McLEAN and ALEXANDER clan. Also the WHITE FAMILY, members of which participated with "Blackface Billy" Alexander in the so-called "gun powder plot" about the time the army marched through towards Hillsboro to quell the "Regulators".

CALDWELL COUNTY. This county was taken from BURKE and WILKES COUNTY, both of which, however, consisting of territory that came out of ROWAN COUNTY. It was named for DR. JOSEPH CALDWELL, noted educator and first President of the University of North Carolina. It was one of later counties, established in 1841. The town of LENOIR is the County seat. Here was the home of the famous Western North Carolina revolutionary patriot, WILLIAM LENOIR, for whom LENOIR COUNTY back over in Eastern North Carolina, was named, as well as the County seat of Caldwell. The Lenoir family scattered over the entire Southland, to South Carolina, Georgia, Alabama, Tennessee and even Texas. Todd Robinson Caldwell represented Caldwell County in the General Assembly in 1850, and was Governor of North Carolina in 1873 and 1874.

CAMDEN COUNTY. This County was composed of territory taken away from one of the Original Thirteen (13) Counties of North Carolina - PASQUOTANK, and was organized in 1777. Its northern line is the line between Virginia and North Carolina, established by William Byrd and his party of surveyors, who served on the commission appointed for that purpose. Part of the Dismal swamp is in the Northern part of this county and extends over into Virginia. Among the prominent historical characters who resided in CAMDEN COUNTY after its organization were ISAAC GREGORY, WILLIAM AND THOMAS BURGESS, CALEB PERKINS, ARTHUR OLD, DEMPSEY SAWYER, BENJAMIN JONES, NATHANIEL SNOWDEN and others, nearly, if not all, of whom were revolutionary soldiers.

CARTERET COUNTY. This was one of the Thirteen (13) Original North Carolina counties, which was established as a Precinct in 1722. Its boundaries have never changed materially since it was organized. See sketch under "North Carolina Precincts". Early public characters in this County after the revolution were OTWAY BURNS, for whom BURNSVILLE, NORTH CAROLINA, was named, David W. and William H. Borden, John and Samuel EASTON, Jacob Henry and John Robards.

CASWELL COUNTY. Territory for this County was taken from ORANGE COUNTY in 1777. This particular part of ORANGE COUNTY came out of BLADEN COUNTY and had been prior thereto a part of NEW HANOVER PRECINCT. (See maps). The County seat is named YANCEYVILLE, doubtless for the noted BARTLETT YANCEY and his family, famous in the political history of that section of North Carolina. The County, of course, is named for RICHARD CASWELL, the first Governor of North Carolina, after the adoption of a Constitution, following the revolution, or during same, who lived in LENOIR COUNTY. The northern boundary line is the line between North Carolina and Virginia. It is a great tobacco country and as you drive along its well paved highways there are tobacco barns on all sides. After the war between the States there were many members of the Ku Klux Clan in this section. It was the breeding place of the LEA FAMILY (The LUKE LEA, of Tennessee), of the WILLIAMS FAMILY, one of whom served in Congress from the District (Hon. Marmaduke Williams) and then moved to Alabama, where he was a Judge at Tuscaloosa, and was narrowly defeated for Governor of that State by one of the BIBBS. The famous JOHN SHARP WILLIAMS, of Mississippi, was of this family also. Other notable families in this County were the GRAVES, MOORES, WALKERS, DIXONS and RAYS.

CATAWBA COUNTY. This county was formed in the bend of the Catawba River on the North, out of LINCOLN COUNTY, which came from TRYON, out of ANSON, that came from BLADEN. The County was established in 1842. It is claimed that it was named for the INDIANS and not for the RIVER that almost surrounds it. NEWTON is the County seat. HENRY W. CONNOR, whose name is often mentioned in this book, a member of the U. S. Congress, resided in CATAWBA COUNTY. Its history is closely linked with LINCOLN and MECKLENBURG COUNTIES.

CHATHAM COUNTY was formed in 1770 from the territory given to ORANGE out of BLADEN COUNTY in 1753. It is a very interesting old County and PITTSBORO is the County seat. On pages 199 to 201 in this volume will be found numerous abstracts from the early records of this county, and which will give a fair idea of who lived there in the early days. Pittsboro is only 34 miles from Raleigh, the Capital of the State, southwestward. It was the home of the MARSH, STEDMAN, STEWART, RAMSEY, MEBANE, ALSTON and McQUEEN families, and many others who might be mentioned.

CHEROKEE COUNTY   This County was established in 1839 from Macon County, both of which came out of territory formerly belonging to BUNCOMBE COUNTY. It was named, presumably for the Cherokee Indian tribes. It is in the extreme southwestern corner of the Old North State.

CHOWAN COUNTY. This was one of the Thirteen (13) Original Counties of North Carolina and had been CHOWAN PRECINCT from 1684 until the name "Precinct" went out of use in 1738. It's first title as a sub-division of OLD ALBEMARLE had been SHAFTSBURY PRECINCT, which was altered to CHOWAN in 1684. This sub-division once included all of the territory extending westward that was considered habitable, until the territory assigned to BATH (or CLARENDON) was defined to include territory South of the line of Virginia immediately West of the later Granville County. (Consult maps herein). Since QUEEN ANNE'S TOWN was established (the original name for the present EDENTON) that place has been the County seat at all times, and is today. These notes have much material about the people of this sub-division of the Old North State, which need only be pointed out here. Such notables as Governor EDEN, SAMUEL JOHNSTON, HUGH WILLIAMSON, JUDGE JAMES IREDELL, of the Supreme Court of the United States, JOSEPH HEWES, signer of the Declaration of Independence, STEPHEN CABARRUS , and the BLOUNTS, HOSKINS, SKINNERS, BROWNRIGGS, BULLOCKS and STALLINGS were all of CHOWAN COUNTY and are closely linked with its earliest history. The reader is referred to other material on this County.

CLAY COUNTY, is a small bit of territory taken from CHEROKEE COUNTY, in the extreme southwestern part of North Carolina, named for the famous statesman, HENRY CLAY, of Kentucky. At one time it was a part of RUTHERFORD and later of BUNCOMBE COUNTY, when only the Indians (Cherokees) held sway there and made it their home. It was the home of the PENLAND family of North Carolina. MICAJAH THOMAS, JR. mentioned on the genealogy of the "THOMAS FAMILY" herein, who was very wealthy, owned lands in this county, or in the territory that now comprises the county. (This was perhaps a descendant of the MICAJAH THOMAS of that compilation, though it is said he had no male descendants, and he, himself could hardly have been the one who built a hotel at BUCK FOREST on little river just prior to the Civil War). Hayesville is the County seat. Some of the ALEXANDERS and MARTINS from Wilkes County settled in this county. From this county came REV. GEORGE W. TRUETT, the late beloved Baptist Minister of Dallas, Texas, also. He was related to the Penlands and the KIMSEYS, of "KIMSEY MOUNTAIN" over the line in Tennessee.

CLEVELAND COUNTY was established in 1841, from parts of both LINCOLN and RUTHERFORD COUNTIES, and the territory of which those two sub-divisions were comprised came from the short-lived and now extinct county of TRYON, taken from ANSON COUNTY in 1762. A few abstracts of the early records of CLEVELAND COUNTY will be found on page 202 of this volume. The County was named for the old Revolutionary soldier, BENJAMIN CLEVELAND, who came from WILKES ASHE and WATAUGA COUNTIES on the Yadkin. The spelling was afterwards changed. SHELBY is the County seat, named for ISAAC SHELBY another well known and famous patriot. Many of the men who fought at King's Mountain, located close by, came from this county.

COLUMBUS COUNTY was established in 1808, from territory taken from the counties of BLADEN and BRUNSWICK COUNTY. The county seat is WHITEVILLE, named for a family of that section who settled there in the early days when it was all in NEW HANOVER PRECINCT. The names of JAMES B. WHITE, LUKE R. SIMMONS (afterwards in ALABAMA), CALEB STEPHENS, JAMES GUYTON, MARMADUKE POWELL and RICHARD WOOTEN occur often on the early records of COLUMBUS COUNTY. (See map).

CRAVEN COUNTY. Established as CRAVEN PRECINCT in 1712, from territory belonging to BATH (or CLARENDON). One writer has said that it came out of territory belonging to ARCHDALE, although that territory went out of existence with the name ARCHDALE attached to it in the same year, and our impression is that ARCHDALE'S lines only included what is now known as BEAUFORT and PITT COUNTIES. NEW BERN, perhaps first established by the Swiss "empresario" CHRISTOPHER de GRAFFENREIDT and his colony in 1710, is the county seat. This was the home of many ancestors of people who are now scattered throughout the Southland. Among the notable residents of the early CRAVEN COUNTY were WILLIAM BLOUNT, later Indian Agent and Governor of Tennessee, ABNER NASH (born in Prince Edward County, VIRGINIA, and a relative of the HEADS and HILLS), RICHARD DOBBS SPEIGHT, named for GOV. ARTHUR DOBBS, who also lived in CRAVEN when Governor, JOHN and EDWARD STANLEY, who came there from EDGECOMBE and BERTIE COUNTIES, WILLIAM GASTON, THE BRYANS, HARRISONS, BADGERS, DONNELLS, SHEPARDS, SITGREAVES, ALLENS, COORS, NEALES and others. CRAVEN was one of the THIRTEEN ORIGINAL COUNTIES of NORTH CAROLINA, that were changed from the designation of Precincts to Counties by th General Assembly in 1738. The largest part of its territory on the Northwest went to form JOHNSTON COUNTY in 1746. See maps.

CUMBERLAND COUNTY. Fayetteville was the County seat of the County. It was one of the early Counties formed in 1754 from what remained of BLADEN COUNTY, after it had given up most of its territory to ANSON. When formed its northern line joined what is now WAKE, JOHNSTON and CHATHAM COUNTIES. See maps. Fayetteville was first called CAMPBELLTOWN and later Cross Creek. It was at Cross Creek, now FAYETTEVILLE that Allan and Flora McDonald, from Scotland settled shortly prior to the revolution and it was here also that the battle occurred during the revolution between the forces under McDonald for the King and under JAMES MOORE for the colonies clashed, resulting in a great victory for Moore and his troops and the capture of McDonald, who was thrown into jail at HALIFAX, North Carolina. The Scotch highlanders who fought under the McDoanlds for the King, many of them, remained in this section, and became good loyal Americans, notably some of the CAMPBELLS. They are now scattered over the entire South. Among these might be mentioned the McKAYS, McNEILLS and others.   The ROWANS, WINSLOWS, TAYLORS, COCHRANS, ARMSTRONGS, McALLISTERS, TAYLORS, MATTHEWS, ECCLES, STRANGE, ROWANS and GOODWINS also lived in CUMBERLAND during the latter part of the eighteenth century. The MURCHISONS, BETHUNES, DOBBINS and SHAWS are also found on the records after 1800.

CURRITUCK COUNTY. This was another one of the Original Thirteen Counties of North Carolina, that previous to 1738 had been called PRECINCTS. One writer says that it was formed in 1670, but is in error,for the reason that from 1670 to 1684 the territory of which it is comprised was a part of CARTERET PRECINCT. But in 1684, this CARTERET PRECINCT (named for one of the "Proprietors" of the Province of North Carolina) was abolished and the territory divided into TWO PRECINCTS called PASQUOTANK and CURRITUCK. There was a tribe of Indians called CURRITUCKS, from which the name perhaps was obtained. This County is located in the extreme Northeastern part of the State, and until 1870 its domain extended across ALBEMARLE SOUND on the South and took in the territory assigned that year to the present DARE COUNTY. Many of the names that appear on the records for CURRITUCK PRECINCT and COUNTY in the early days were names of people who lived South of Albemarle Sound along the ROANOKE SOUND and ALLIGATOR RIVER. The name of the County seat is CURRITUCK, a small town or Village on the Western shore of CURRITUCK BAY, some fifteen or twenty miles from ELIZABETH CITY. Some call it CURRITUCK SOUND. CURRITUCK COUNTY takes in ROANOKE ISLAND, the site of the first English landing in North America. Among the early and prominent residents of CURRITUCK, a list of whom will be found in other parts of these notes, were the SANDERSONS, LINDSAYS, WHITES, WILLIAMS, HUMPHRIES, FEREBEES, GARRETTS, BELLS, BALLS, BARNARDS and HARRISONS. See maps and other notes.

DARE COUNTY. This county, which is bounded on the East by ROANOKE SOUND (or Bay) has been in existence as a separate county only since 1870. When it was formed, most of its area was taken from CURRITUCK COUNTY, now confined to the islands on the East and the territory lying North of ALBEMARLE SOUND, with a small area from HYDE COUNTY and narrow strip on the East bank of the ALLIGATOR RIVER, from TYRRELL COUNTY. It was named for VIRGINIA DARE, the almost legendary "first child born of English parents in America", whose parents were among the passengers that came over in Sir Walter Raleigh's adventure in 1685 to Roanoke Island, all of whom are supposed to have perished afterwards before aid could be brought to them. The county has several small towns among them being Buffalo City not far from the banks of the ALLIGATOR RIVER.

DAVIDSON COUNTY. The territory from which this county was formed in 1822 was taken from ROWAN COUNTY. It lies immediately East of the present ROWAN COUNTY and is cut off from it by the YADKIN RIVER. The name of the County seat of Davidson is LEXINGTON. The County was named for General William Lee Davidson, who was killed during the revolution at COWAN'S FORD in Mecklenburg County. The HARGROVE, HOGAN, HAMPTON, WISEMAN, SPURGEON, THOMAS and LEACH FAMILIES were numerous in the early days of its formation and took an active part in its political affairs. The town of LEXINGTON is a prosperous and thriving little City, about midway between SALISBURY in Rowan, and High Point, in Guilford County.

DAVIE COUNTY. This County was established from territory taken from ROWAN COUNTY in 1836. The old town of MOCKSVILLE is the County seat and the lower Yadkin is the line between it and the present ROWAN COUNTY. This territory was the home of HON. RICHMOND MONTFORT PEARSON, distinguished North Carolina Judge, and the Pearson family to which he belonged. The KERR, MILLER, LILLINGTON and DOUTHIT families were among those who resided in DAVIE COUNTY along about the time it was established. Some of the WILLIAMS family also lived there much earlier. The County was named after HON. WILLIAM RICHARDSON DAVIE, distinguished statesman and revolutionary patriot, who is buried at the old WAXHAW CHURCH in Lancaster County, South Carolina, but who adopted North Carolina as his home for the greater part of his active life and where his political career had its beginning and ending. He married a daughter of the noted GEN. ALLEN JONES, of Halifax County.

DUPLIN COUNTY. This County came into existence in the year 1749 and was composed of the northern part of NEW HANOVER COUNTY. Its northern line joined WAYNE and JOHNSTON COUNTIES, and in 1784, the County of SAMPSON was established out of the Western half of its original territory. Mr. Wheeler in his fine "HISTORY" says that its early settlers were IRISH, and while this is probably true, it drew to it representatives of many families who had previously resided in the older sub-divisions to the North and East of it. Among these were the COOPERS, Kennans , CANNONS, DICKSONS and others. Among the families who settled in DUPLIN were the GRIMES families, from which came HON. JESSE GRIMES who emigrated,first, to ALABAMA, and finally to Texas, where he served in the Congress of the Republic in the days of Sam Houston. The RHODES, CLINTON, GILLASPIE, WATKINS, WRIGHT, GLISSON, HUSSEY and HILL families were prominent in the political life of DUPLIN COUNTY. There were also members of the THOMAS FAMILY, from EDGECOMBE and BERTIE COUNTIES, who lived there. On pages 203, 204, 205 and 206, of this work will be found many abstracts of early records of DUPLIN COUNTY pertaining to the families who settled there. In these will be found the names of CARROLL, LANIER, HILL. THOMAS, GREEN, HERRING, SLOAN, O'DANIEL, PEARSALL, OUTLAW and others. Its records are a veritable mine of valuable genealogical material.

DURHAM COUNTY. This is one of the younger counties of North Carolina, and has been in existence only since 1881. Its territory was appropriated from ORANGE COUNTY, principally, with a small slice off of Wake County. The City of Durham is the county seat, and Durham (the City) is also the home of the famous DUKE UNIVERSITY, established by the philanthropy of a member of the old North Carolina family of that name. The name DURHAM was adopted in honor of DR. BARTHOLOMEW DURHAM and applied to both the County and the City that bears it. The City of Durham is only a short drive in these modern days from RALEIGH, the Capital of the State, and likewise from CHAPEL HILL, the seat of the Great University of the State of North Carolina. In addition to this DURHAM is a tobacco manufacturing town, the products from which are sold around the World. It is a thriving, throbbing North Carolina metropolis, the seat of factories, banks and commercial institutions, as well as a veritable hub in the wheel of EDUCATION.

EDGECOMBE COUNTY. This county was established in 1741, the same year that NORTHAMPTON COUNTY came into existence, both being comprised of territory that had been a part first, of BERTIE PRECINCT, and after 1738, of BERTIE COUNTY. BERTIE COUNTY was one of the Thirteen (13) Original Counties of North Carolina. The original territory of Edgecombe consisted of all of the territory now comprising GRANVILLE, part of PERSON, VANCE, WARREN, FRANKLIN, NASH, HALIFAX and a proportionate part of WILSON COUNTY. GRANVILLE COUNTY, when established out of EDGECOMBE in 1746, absorbed all of WARREN, FRANKLIN, VANCE, most of PERSON and the present GRANVILLE. (See maps). In 1758 another large slice of EDGECOMBE was given to create HALIFAX COUNTY; NASH COUNTY was carved out in 1777, and WILSON long later in 1855, leaving EDGECOMBE COUNTY trimmed down to its present proportions. The county seat is TARBORO. Early and active residents of EDGECOMBE were THOMAS BLOUNT, ETHELRED PHILLIPS, RICHARD HARRISON, JOHN LEIGH, JEREMIAH HILLIARD, JOHN COTTON, LOUIS D. WILSON, JUDGE JOSEPH J. DANIEL, BENJAMIN SHARPE, JOHN HORN, MOSES BAKER, NATHAN MAYO, HARDY FLOWERS, WILLIAM GRAY and JOSHUA BARNES.

FORSYTH COUNTY. This County was established in 1849 from STOKES COUNTY, whose territory came out of SURRY COUNTY, which came out of ROWAN COUNTY. The up to date metropolis of FORSYTH COUNTY is WINSTON-SALEM, reputedly one of the richest towns in all North Carolina. Its wealth comes from tobacco. The town of SALEM (Now Winston-Salem) was first established by the MORAVIANS, and it is an old, old settlement, whose history is absorbingly interesting. Winston-Salem is the county seat. JOSEPH WINSTON, from whom the WINSTON part of the name came, was a native of the parent county, STOKES. When the county of STOKES was first established JOSEPH WINSTON was its first Senator. Forsyth County was named for COL. BENJAMIN FORSYTH a soldier in the War of 1812.

FRANKLIN COUNTY was established in 1779, from the lower portion of old BUTE COUNTY, which went out of existence at the same time. BUTE was abolished because one half of it went to WARREN COUNTY and the other half to FRANKLIN COUNTY. Bute came into existence in 1764 (out of territory taken from the original Granville County) and lasted for fifteen years. Franklin County was named for BENJAMIN FRANKLIN. The town of LOUISBURG on the TAR RIVER is the county seat. Notes and abstracts of the records of FRANKLIN COUNTY will be found on pages 207 and 208 of this book. Also see maps herein. Among the early families who settled and lived in FRANKLIN COUNTY were the following: HILL, CHRISTMAS, HARRIS, DAVIS, BRICKELL, HALL, GREEN, FOSTER, SHERROD, ALSTON, LEWIS, WILLIAMS, STONE, HAWKINS, HOUSE, COLLINS, BRANCH, LANIER, BATTLE, HOWERTON, HARRISON and JEFFREYS. The famous WAKE FOREST COLLEGE is located just over the line from FRANKLIN COUNTY, in the extreme upper portion of WAKE COUNTY.

GASTON COUNTY. This County was established in 1846 from the lower part of LINCOLN COUNTY, and was named in honor of JUDGE WILLIAM GASTON, who, however, never lived in the County. GASTONIA is the county seat. WILLIAM GASTON lived in CRAVEN COUNTY and his name has been mentioned under the sketch of CRAVEN COUNTY. He was a Judge of the Supreme Court of North Carolina. The early history of LINCOLN COUNTY necessarily includes the early annals of GASTON, which sprang from LINCOLN. GASTON COUNTY territory (when it was, of course, known as LINCOLN) was the home of REV. HUMPHREY HUNTER, one time pastor of STEELE CREEK CHURCH in Mecklenburg County; of MAJ. WILLIAM CHRONICLE, who lead his Catawba Fork Boys at the battle of King's Mountain; of the ARMSTRONGS, the RANKINS, the MOORES, ADAIRS, ALEXANDERS, CALDWELLS, and of JAMES HENDERSON, grandfather of JAMES PINCKNEY HENDERSON, the first Governor of the great STATE OF TEXAS. James Picney Henderson was born at Lincolnton, in the present LINCOLN COUNTY, but his grandfather rests on a high bluff on the East side of of the South Fork of the Catawba River in the present GASTON COUNTY.

GATES COUNTY. This County joins the line of Virginia and is in the heart of the old original ALBEMARLE PRECINCT or COUNTY, though this sub-division was not laid off and made into a County until 1779. Territory to comprise the area was taken at that time from three different counties, viz, HERTFORD (as originally established in 1759), CHOWAN, to whom all of the territory taken had belonged until 1759, except the strip of about three or four miles in width that was appropriated from PERQUIMANS for the benefit of the new GATES COUNTY. (See maps). This GATES COUNTY has remained unchanged, so far as the records seem to show, from the time it was established up to the present. It embraces an interesting area, and one that perhaps was the first selected by migrants of ISLE OF WIGHT, NANSEMOND and other VIRGINIA COUNTIES, across the then wholly imaginative line between OLD ALBEMARLE and VIRGINIA. Among these were JOHN ALSTON, ROBERT and JOHN LAWRENCE, ROBERT, THOMAS and MICHAEL ROGERS (ancestors of the famous WILL ROGERS), and innumerable others, whose names will be found in connection with the accounts of the earliest settlers in the Old North State, in this volume. Also consult the maps of the region shown herein. BENNETT'S CREEK, probably deriving its name from WILLIAM BENNETT, was a navigable slough or stream rising, perhaps in Nansemond County, Virginia, and flowing Southward to ALBEMARLE SOUND via the CHOWAN RIVER, was the principal stream. Vessels plied its waters and Indians (who had their villages round about), and migrants from the outside, found the fishing profitable - and do yet, for that matter. Contacts are constant between the Indians and the whites, and there were even intermarriages between them, to which were born children of the half and quarter-blood, who bore the names of their English fathers. Out of this jumble of social relations grew strange and interesting complications in family histories, and out of it also, came forth many of the great "white Chiefs" among the different tribes, who wielded great influence and furnished leadership when the tribes were finally driven to the reservations in the far West. Out of this strange admixture of the races came forth such rare personages as the late lamented and beloved WILL ROGERS. (See other notes.)

GRAHAM COUNTY. This is another one of the late counties, established in 1872 from CHEROKEE COUNTY, away down in the Southwestern corner of the State next to the Tennessee line. The county was named in honor of WILLIAM A. GRAHAM, who was Governor, United States Senator and also Confederate States Senator and Secretary of the Navy. The name of the County seat of GRAHAM COUNTY is ROBBINSVILLE, where Junaluska, the Cherokee Chief, sleeps in a marked grave. Lafayette GHORMLEY, an early settler lived near the mouth of Mountain Creek, DAVE ORR between Bear and Slick Rock creeks, and Rev. Joseph A. Wiggins, distinguished Methodist minister was born in Graham County. A family named STEWART came there from GEORGIA, and another by the name of STRATTON came from Monroe County, over the line in Tennessee. A noted character from POLK COUNTY, TENNESSEE, named JOHN DENTON, settled in Graham County, who was six feet, three inches high and whose mother JANE MERONEY, is said to have been a first cousin of JEFFERSON DAVIS. (See Arthur's Western N. C. p. 212.)

GRANVILLE COUNTY. This county was erected in 1746 from EDGECOMBE COUNTY, and is one of the older, though not one of the thirteen original counties of the State. When first established GRANVILLE COUNTY included practically all of the present PERSON COUNTY, that which is now GRANVILLE, all of VANCE, WARREN and FRANKLIN. (See maps). Also pages 264-265 herein. See also notes and records from page 209 to 304 inclusive, of this volume, all of which material has been separately bound and published under the title "COLONIAL GRANVILLE COUNTY AND ITS PEOPLE". OXFORD is the county seat of GRANVILLE COUNTY.

GREENE COUNTY. This county was established in 1791 and named for General Nathaniel Greene, of the American Revolution. The history of the territory of which its is composed is about as follows: Originally it was part of CRAVEN PRECINCT, cut out of BATH in 1712. In 1746 it was part of JOHNSTON COUNTY, which was established that year, out of CRAVEN, which had been known as a COUNTY since 1738. Then in 1758 a county called DOBBS was formed out of the lower end of JOHNSTON COUNTY. In 1779 half of the County of Dobbs on the West was made into Wayne County and the other half became LENOIR and GLASGOW counties. Then in 1791, the name GLASGOW was dropped and the territory comprising it was called GREENE COUNTY. For a better understanding of this geographical muddle see the maps of this area herein. The county seat of GREENE COUNTY is SNOW HILL. The HOOKERS, SPEIGHTS and MOYES, the WILLIAMS, HARPERS and TAYLORS were prominent in GREENE COUNTY.

GUILFORD COUNTY came into existence in 1770. Judge Wheeler tells us it was created out of ROWAN and ORANGE COUNTY. As a matter of fact only a small part of it came from ORANGE COUNTY, that being now a part of ROCKINGHAM COUNTY. No part of the present day GUILFORD COUNTY was ever in ORANGE COUNTY. (See maps herein). When first established GUILFORD COUNTY consisted of all of the territory now included in ROCKINGHAM, GUILFORD and RANDOLPH COUNTIES. In the year 1779 RANDOLPH COUNTY was cut off of the southern end of GUILFORD, and in 1785 ROCKINGHAM was established out of the Northern end of Guilford. The county seat of GUILFORD COUNTY is GREENSBORO, though the great battle fought during the revolution was at what is called GUILFORD COURTHOUSE, located in the same general vicinity. Among the historical characters who lived in GUILFORD COUNTY were REV. DAVID CALDWELL, noted teacher and minister; ALEXANDER MARTIN, who served in the Senate, RALPH GORRELL, DANIEL GILLESPIE, SAMUEL LINDSAY, JONATHAN PARKER, ROBERT HANNAH, WILLIAM ARMFIELD, HANCE McCAIN, JOHN RANKIN, DAVID WORTH, JOHN M. MOREHEAD, JAMES McNAIRY and numerous others, not forgetting to make it of record that GUILFORD COUNTY was the native home of one WILLIAM SYDNEY PORTER, better known all over the world as "O. HENRY", which will explain the presence in the present GREENSBORO of a handsome modern hotel bearing the name.

HALIFAX COUNTY. This is one of the historic old counties of NORTH CAROLINA, which came into existence in 1758, out of territory taken from the original EDGECOMBE COUNTY, lying between the ROANOKE RIVER on the North and Fishing Creek on the South. (See maps). The town of HALIFAX was made the county seat, which had been previously (for Edgecombe) located at ENFIELD, a small village, which is still in existence. HALIFAX was the home of GENS. ALLEN and WILEY JONES, COL. NICHOLAS LONG, WILLIAM RICHARDSON DAVIE (from South Carolina, who married SARAH, a daughter of GEN. ALLEN JONES), COL. NICHOLAS LONG, JUDGE JOSEPH J. DANIEL, GOV. HUTCHINS GORDON BURTON (who married SARAH, the daughter of COL. WILEY JONES), and many other distinguished characters. Here lived also representatives of the LONGS, MONTFORTS, QUARLES, ALSTONS, BRANCHES, WHITAKERS, MATTHEWS, JOYNERS and others. The ancestors of thousands scattered over the Southern States trace back to some of these old families in HALIFAX COUNTY.

HARNETT COUNTY. In 1855, less than a hundred years ago the upper portion of CUMBERLAND COUNTY was erected into HARNETT COUNTY, and named for CORNELIUS HARNETT, a celebrated revolutionary patriot, said to have lived at WILMINGTON. 101 years prior to that time (in 1754) the County of Cumberland had been established out of BLADEN COUNTY, formerly BLADEN PRECINCT, from 1734 to 1738. Many people, therefore, who are listed as having lived in Cumberland County prior to 1855, lived just over the line from WAKE and JOHNSTON COUNTIES, which form the northern boundary of HARNETT. The town of LILLINGTON is the county seat of HARNETT COUNTY. Consult the maps of this area.

HAYWOOD COUNTY. This county was established out of BUNCOMBE COUNTY in Western North Carolina, in 1808, and named for JOHN HAYWOOD, who was State Treasurer of North Carolina for a long period of years. See notes on page 193 of this volume. Many of the earliest settlers of HAYWOOD COUNTY came from over in Lincoln and Mecklenburg County, including the HOWELL FAMILY, mentioned at some length in ALLEN'S "Annals of Haywood County". The county seat of HAYWOOD COUNTY is WAYNESVILLE.

HENDERSON COUNTY This county is now a little over a hundred years old. It was established in 1838 and the territory of which it is comprised was taken from BUNCOMBE COUNTY. We are told that it was named in honor of JUDGE LEONARD HENDERSON, of Granville County, North Carolina, who had a distinguished career on the bench of the Old North State, and who was a son of JUDGE RICHARD HENDERSON, of Transylvania fame. The county seat of HENDERSON COUNTY is called HENDERSONVILLE. The line between North and South Carolina constitutes its southern boundary.

HERTFORD COUNTY. On some of the old maps this is called HARTFORD COUNTY, but the name HERTFORD is now the accepted name, as shown by the modern records. The county was formed in the year 1759, and in order to secure sufficient territory for the county, all of CHOWAN on the northern side of CHOWAN RIVER and West of Bennett's Creek was taken from that county, and strip was cut off the east side of NORTHAMPTON COUNTY, and the balance of the territory used had comprised the upper part of what was then left of BERTIE COUNTY. Thus BERTIE COUNTY received its final cut, and was left as it is today. The town of WINTON, located South of the Meherrin River and West of Chowan River, is the county seat. HARDY MURFREE or MURPHY lived in what is now Hertford County, from whom the town of MURFREESBORO in Hertford, and in TENNESSEE derives their names. It was also in this county that HON. JOHN H. WHEELER, the great North Carolina Historian, was born, the son of a certain JOHN WHEELER, who was once postmaster of the little town of MURFREESBORO, N. C., mentioned above. The WHEELERS of this family came from ELIZABETHTOWN, NEW JERSEY, where REV. JAMES CALDWELL, of the Charlotte County (Va.) CALDWELLS was killed during the revolution. JOHN HILL WHEELER, the Historian, was born August 2, 1806, at MURFREESBORO, HERTFORD COUNTY, North Carolina. HERTFORD COUNTY was also the home of the SUMNERS, the WYNNS, the BOONS, CARTERS, HILLS (HENRY HILL), PERRYS, MONTGOMERYS, BRICKELLS, MANNEYS, BAKERS, JORDANS and the SHARPES.

HOKE COUNTY. This county and AVERY COUNTY must have been twins, since they were both established and came into existence the same year - 1911. It has been said by one historian that AVERY COUNTY was the last county established in North Carolina. Not having found the exact dates for either, the compiler is unable to say which is the younger of the two and must accept the claims of AVERY, as has been asserted. HOKE'S territory was taken from CUMBERLAND and ROBESON COUNTIES about half and half. (See the maps pertaining to these counties for more detailed information.). The town of RAEFORD is the county seat.

HYDE COUNTY. This county was formerly known as WICKHAM PRECINCT, which had been a part of PAMPTICOUGH PRECINCT, which came from BATH PRECINCT, all now extinct. HYDE PRECINCT was the name of the territory until 1738, when it became HYDE COUNTY. This was one of the THIRTEEN ORIGINAL North Carolina Counties. Swan Quarter is the name of the county seat. In 1870 a small corner of this county fronting east on ROANOKE SOUND was taken from HYDE COUNTY to help provide territory for the establishment of DARE COUNTY. The County and precinct is said to have been named for EDWARD HYDE, Colonial Governor in 1712, when the name of WICKHAM PRECINCT was changed to HYDE PRECINCT. The RUSSELLS, JONES, SELBYS, SANDERSONS, JASPERS, PUGHS, CARTERS, JORDANS, GIBBS, FARROWS and SINGLETONS have lived in HYDE COUNTY since days before the American revolution.

IREDELL COUNTY. The name of the county seat is STATESVILLE, which before the days of actual towns was known as FOURTH CREEK. The County of IREDELL was formed in 1788 from territory taken from ROWAN COUNTY, which came out of ANSON COUNTY in 1753. It was named for JUDGE JAMES IREDELL, a member of the Supreme Court of the United States. This county was the home of the WHITE FAMILY, represented by MOSES WHITE, father of JAMES WHITE, of Knoxville, Tennessee fame, and grandfather of JUDGE HUGH LAWSON WHITE. Since the line between MECKLENBURG and IREDELL COUNTY long remained in doubt, there is some doubt as to whether the WHITES belonged to one county or the other. It is known that HUGH LAWSON, whose daughter married JAMES WHITE is buried in MECKLENBURG COUNTY at the Baker's Graveyard, but it may be that some of the WHITES are buried in the "upper Baker's Graveyard", which is in what is now IREDELL COUNTY. (See page 425 of this volume). The original families in what is now IREDELL COUNTY were the OSBORNES, CALDWELLS, NESBITS, DAVIDSONS, MATTHEWS, HARTS, HUGGINS, TORRENCE, CONNORS, ALLISONS, YOUNGS and HILLS.

JACKSON COUNTY. This county is over in Western North Carolina, and was formed in 1751, from territory taken from HAYWOOD and MACON COUNTIES, all of which came from BUNCOMBE, originally. See maps. The county was named for ANDREW JACKSON, President of the United States. The present county seat is SYLVIA, but when the county was first laid off the name of the county seat was WEBSTER, which name was adopted because the famous DANIEL WEBSTER had just died. Among the notable characters of that early day, who were then living were THADEUS D. BRYSON, of Scott's Creek, COL. W. H. THOMAS, J. W. TERRELL, ABRAHAM BATTLE, and ABRAHAM ENLOE, said to have given a home to an orphan girl, NANCY HANKS, who became the mother of ABRAHAM LINCOLN, long before. REV. WILLIAM HICKS lived in Webster after the war between the States, having come there from SULLIVAN COUNTY, TENNESSEE.

JOHNSTON COUNTY. This county was established away back in 1746, and extended all the way from the eastern and southern boundary of LENOIR COUNTY of today, to the line between Virginia and North Carolina on the northwest corner of the present ROCKINGHAM COUNTY (approximately). See maps. The town of SMITHFIELD is now the county seat of JOHNSTON COUNTY. A large part of this county's original territory was taken to establish ORANGE COUNTY in 1752-3. Then another big batch was set aside for WAKE COUNTY in 1770. In 1758 DOBBS took all the lower end of the county, which was later split up into Wayne and Lenoir and Greene counties. So the county was gradually trimmed down to its present proportions. See maps. The name of BRYAN, WILLIAMS, SMITH, TOMLINSON, RICHARDSON, SAUNDERS, BOONE, INGRAM, WILDER, WHITLEY, ADAMS, BRIDGES, GRAY, RAIFORD and THOMPSON are all common to this county on the ancient records.

JONES COUNTY. This county was established in 1778, from CRAVEN COUNTY, and derived its name from the old States Rights Wiley Jones, of HALIFAX, North Carolina. (The town of Washington, Tennessee, is said to have been named for his brother, ALLEN JONES). TRENTON, is the name of the county seat of JONES COUNTY. This was the home of a number of notable personages who played important roles in the early history of North Carolina, including NATHAN BRYAN, who served in the Congress of the United States, and whose antecedents are shown in an account of the BRYAN FAMILY to be found elsewhere in this volume. Many of these same Bryans lived farther up in JOHNSTON COUNTY, but still on the waters of the Neuse river. Others were ABNER NASH, JOHN ISLER, JOHN, EDMUND and DURANT HATCH (See Bryan Family for mention of these also), WILLIAM BUSH, BENJAMIN FORDHAM, AMOS SIMMONS, BENJAMIN SIMMONS, LEWIS and NATHAN FOSCUE, JAMES SHINE; WILLIAM DANIEL, JAMES HARRISON, JOSIAH and JAMES W. HOWARD.

LEE COUNTY. This county must be next to the youngest county in North Carolina, as it was established in 1907. A part of it was taken from CHATHAM COUNTY and a part from MOORE COUNTY. The county was named in honor of GEN. ROBERT E. LEE. It is watered on the Northern boundary by DEEP CREEK, and is split by the upper Cape Fear or HAW RIVER, which is augmented at the Lee boundary by the waters of Rocky River coming down from the Northwest. As it is a very young county its ancient history is linked with that of CHATHAM and MOORE COUNTIES.

LENOIR COUNTY. This county was named in honor of another revolutionary patriot, GEN. WILLIAM LENOIR, of Western North Carolina. The county seat is KINGSTON. The county was established in 1791, and the United States Census of 1790 - the first taken - shows the names of the then residents of LENOIR COUNTY as living in DOBBS, which a year later was split in two parts, the old county abolished, and LENOIR and GLASGOW substituted. Nine years later the county of GLASGOW was wiped out of existence by the General Assembly, and the county of GREENE established in its place and territory. The Indian tribes who formerly lived in this section of North Carolina made up a large part of the contingent who massacred the settlers along the Pamlico River at the old town of BATH in 1711. The space available here will not permit a discussion of the reasons actuating the Assembly in abolishing the county of GLASGOW. That is a Chapter of unwritten history which is seldom discussed anywhere. Quite a number of notable families, who afterwards scattered over "Dixie Land" and made their impression on its history, resided in what is now LENOIR COUNTY. Among these might be mentioned the CROOMS, who went to MISSISSIPPI; the WHITES, GOODMANS, SIMON BRUTON, NATHAN B. WHITFIELD, WILLIAM D. MOSELEY, EDWIN G. SPEIGHT, the BRIGHTS, WOOTENS, KILPATRICKS, LOFTINS, BYRDS, PIERCES and DAVISES. The NEUSE RIVER runs through LENOIR COUNTY.

LINCOLN COUNTY. This county occupies space on the map that back in 1749 was allotted to ANSON COUNTY. ANSON transferred it to MECKLENBURG and then it became TRYON COUNTY, which in 1779 was split in two and made into RUTHERFORD and LINCOLN COUNTY. Originally in 1779, Lincoln County included all of the present GASTON, CATAWBA and an undefined part of the present CLEVELAND COUNTY. Much of the history of the early settlers of LINCOLN will be found in that section of this volume dealing mainly with MECKLENBURG COUNTY (Pages 313 to 558.) including the indexes thereto). Some more of it is pointed out as appearing in the article headed "COMPILATION FROM OLD NEWSPAPER FILES" to which the attention of the student and the reader is directed. Also see maps of this section.

MACON COUNTY. This county will be found on the map of North Carolina away down in the extreme southwestern portion of the State. It was formed and organized in 1828 from a part of Haywood County, which came out of BUNCOMBE. The name was given it in compliment to NATHANIEL MACON, a distinguished WARREN COUNTY statesman who was once Speaker of the House of Representatives in the United States Congress. Macon County was the home of JACOB SILER, head of a well known North Carolina tribe, which is still numerous. It was also the home of Gen. THOMAS LOVE; of the PATTONS, BARNARDS, GUINNS, DOBSONS, HOWARDS, McDOWELLS, COLEMANS and DICKEYS. Arthur's Western North Carolina appears to give the most accurate and complete account of these early settlers in MACON COUNTY. The town of FRANKLIN is the county seat of MACON COUNTY.

MADISON COUNTY was erected from BUNCOMBE and YANCEY COUNTIES in 1851. It is directly on the line of East Tennessee and North Carolina. It was named for JAMES MADISON, President of the United States, and the town of MARSHALL is the county seat. It is said that the TOWN of MARSHALL was named for Chief Justice JOHN MARSHALL. In 1858 MARSHALL (the town) was called LAPLAND. This writer finds some very interesting names among the early residents of MADISON COUNTY. Some of these are the ASKEWS, LUSKS, GARRETTS, MOODYS, DUCKETTS, WOODYS, MARTINS, ALEXANDERS, GUDGERS, PENLANDS, HAWKINS, LOWRIE, SWAIN and JONES. I have found that the county records will still give up information to those who are looking for history pertaining to these families, and others.

MARTIN COUNTY. The territory from which Martin County was formed came out of TYRELL, mostly, with a considerable square of territory taken off the southeastern end of HALIFAX in 1774, which reduced the size of Halifax somewhat from its original area. It is stated that this county was named for JOSIAH MARTIN, the last royal Governor of the Province, who left the country on board ship out of Wilmington in a kind of hurry, when he found how the sentiment of the people ran. The county seat of this county is WILLIAMSTON on the South side of the Roanoke river. This county, Wheeler says, was the home of WHITMELL HILL, who married WINNIFRED BLOUNT, of Chowan County. It is interesting to note that a WHITMELL HILL lived in Mecklemberg County (see page 341 herein). Other interesting families in MARTIN COUNTY were the WILLIAMS, SMITHWICKS, MAYOS, SLADES, McKENZIES, BAKERS, HYMANS, COOPERS, SHEPPARDS, JOYNERS and CHERRYS.

McDOWELL COUNTY. This is another Western North Carolina County, established in 1842, from parts of two other counties, RUTHERFORD and BURKE. The lower part was taken from RUTHERFORD and the upper portion from BURKE. The town of MARION is the county seat, it being named for GENERAL FRANCIS MARION, while the county was named for COL. JOSEPH McDOWELL, the old war horse of the Indian days, and Indian boundary commissioner. Although the territory of McDOWELL came partly from BURKE and partly from RUTHERFORD, and BURKE COUNTY came out of the original ROWAN COUNTY area, while RUTHERFORD came out of the TRYON COUNTY area, yet, when you trace back the genealogy of McDOWELL COUNTY you will find that its ancestrial county was ANSON and before that BLADEN, then NEW HANOVER and BATH. BLADEN gave the territory to ANSON, and ANSON gave territory to ROWAN in 1753, and to TRYON (later Rutherford) in 1768. Thus McDOWELL COUNTY came out of ANSON entirely, when you go back to the early part of the territory's history.

MECKLENBURG COUNTY. This county was created in 1762 from ANSON COUNTY, and the county seat is CHARLOTTE, now the largest and most populous City in North Carolina. In 1768, all of the territory of Mecklenburg County West of the CATAWBA RIVER (now the line between Mecklenburg and Lincoln) was given to what was called TRYON COUNTY. After that time Mecklenburg's area covered the county as it is today and all that territory now embraced in CABARRUS COUNTY, and about all of the West half of the present UNION COUNTY. In 1791 Cabarrus County was established, which took away that territory, and in 1842 Union County was established and absorbed the lower end of the county, thus trimming MECKLENBURG COUNTY down to what it is at the present day. Mecklenburg County, of course, was the home of the "Mecklenburg Signers". (See pages 313 to 558 herein).

MITCHELL COUNTY. This county was established in 1861 from parts of five different Western North Carolina counties, viz, BURKE, CALDWELL, McDOWELL, WATAUGA and YANCEY, an undefined area, short of the original field notes, being taken from each county. The county seat is BAKERSVILLE. In 1866 a part of the land on which the town of Bakersville was built was deeded to the county commissioners by ROBERT N. PENLAND. Bakersville became the county seat after the war between the States, but prior to that time court was held at a place called CALHOUN, not far from Spruce Pine. Among the names of residents of MITCHELL COUNTY were JOHN B. PALMER, TILMAN BLALOCK, LYSANDER CHILDS and MOSES YOUNG. The county of Mitchell was named for DR. ELISHA MITCHELL, of the University of North Carolina, in whose honor MT. MITCHELL was also named.

MONTGOMERY COUNTY was established out of territory taken from ANSON COUNTY in 1779. TROY was and is the county seat. It is named for General Richard Montgomery of the American revolution, I believe. The county is situated immediately South of RANDOLPH COUNTY. It originally comprised all of its present territory with all of the present county of Stanley, which now lies to the immediate west of it. Among the notable names attached to the history of this county we find CHARLES ROBERTSON (who went to Tennessee); THOMAS CHILDS, EDMUND DEBERRY, THOMAS BLEWETT (went to Mississippi and GEORGIA and some of them to Kentucky), WEST HARRIS, GEORGE W. GRAHAM, JAMES LEGRANDE, GEORGE W. DAVIDSON, ANDREW WADE, CLEMENT LANIER, CLAIBORNE HARRIS, SILAS BILLINGSLEY, and the DARGANS, DUNNS, ALLENS, RANDLES and others.

MOORE COUNTY. This county was established from Cumberland County in 1784, and named for JUDGE ALFRED MOORE, of North Carolina. The county seat is CARTHAGE. HON. BENJAMIN WILLIAMS, who was Governor of North Carolina in 1809 lived in this county at one time and died in MOORE COUNTY. Interesting residents of MOORE COUNTY, taken at random from the old records, are PHILLIP ALSTON, THOMAS OVERTON, MALCOLM GILCHRIST, WILLIAM MARTIN, CORNELIUS DOWD, ALEXANDER McNEILL, JOHN MURCHISON, JAMES SEAWELL, WILLIAM BARRETT, GIDEON SEAWELL, JOHN CARROLL, BENJAMIN PERSON, DUNCAN MURCHISON and FRANCIS BULLOCK.

NASH COUNTY. This county was established out of EDGECOMBE COUNTY in 1777. It was named for General Francis Nash, of ORANGE COUNTY, revolutionary soldier. the town of NASHVILLE is the county seat. The genealogical material in this volume frequently mentions NASH COUNTY and some of the people who lived there. See the THOMAS FAMILY, particularly. Among the persons and families whose names appear on the ancient records of NASH COUNTY are HARDY GRIFFIN, JOSEPH ARRINGTON, JOHN BOND, MICAJAH THOMAS, WILSON VICK (Of the Vicks of Vicksburg, Miss.) JAMES BATTLE, MICHAEL COLLINS, GEORGE BODDIE, EDWARD NICHOLSON, WILLIAM W. BODDIE, JOSEPH TERRELL, JOHN H. DRAKE, W. D. HARRISON, R. C. HILLIARD and DAVID RICKS.

NEW HANOVER COUNTY. As this sub-division was established out of BATH PRECINCT as late as 1729, it was first called NEW HANOVER PRECINCT. Then in 1738, it automatically became a COUNTY, and it was one of the Thirteen (13) ORIGINAL Counties of North Carolina. While it was still a precinct, however, most of the vast territory that it comprised when first established in 1729, was taken away from it, by the establishment of two other PRECINCTS, both in 1734. They were BLADEN PRECINCT and ONSLOW PRECINCT, both of which in 1738 became COUNTIES in name and were of the thirteen ORIGINAL Counties of North Carolina. (Consult the maps herein for a visual explanation of the details). When New Hanover was first established we are told that the first two representatives sent to the ASSEMBLY were JOHN SWANN and JOHN PORTER, who had come to that lower country from OLD ALBEMARLE above the Sound. The old town of BRUNSWICK "on the southwest side of Cape Fear River" appears to have been, for a time, the seat of Government in New Hanover. It was even briefly the Capital of the State, and the home of at least three Governors and as many "Acting Governors" of the Province. The town of WILMINGTON, however, had advantages, and Old Brunswick soon passed away. CORNELIUS HARNETT maintained a public ferry across the Cape Fear River, and his son CORNELIUS HARNETT was a noted Inn Keeper' JOSHUA GRAINGER, one of the founders of WILMINGTON, was the son of CALEB GRAINGER. JOHN SWANN, FREDERICK JONES, SAMUEL ASHE, EDWARD MOSELEY and JOHN PUGH WILLIAMS lived in WILMINGTON. THOMAS CLARK, SR. was Sheriff of NEW HANOVER in 1741.

NORTHAMPTON COUNTY. The County was created out of a portion of BERTIE PRECINCT in 1735, and it was apparently NORTHAMPTON PRECINCT for the first four years. The boundaries of NORTHAMPTON COUNTY were never changed but one time after it was established and that was when HERTFORD COUNTY was established in 1759, when it lost the territory North of the MEHERRIN RIVER BETWEEN the Meherrin and Chowan, where they enter North Carolina from Virginia, and a narrow triangle of land off its Eastern boundary between the Meherrin and the Roanoke. Thereafter HERTFORD lost a part of its eastern territory to GATES in 1779, but NORTHAMPTON was in no way affected. (See maps). The county seat of NORTHAMPTON is Jackson, which Mr. Wheeler tells us "preserves the name of Andrew Jackson", but fails to give the name of the county seat of Northampton County in the first instance, since the county was in existence for some thirty years before Andrew Jackson was BORN. ALLEN JONES, brother of WILEY JONES, of Halifax, lived in Northampton County. Early names on the records of NORTHAMPTON County include JAMES VAUGHAN, ALLEN JONES, JOHN M. BINFORD, ROBERT PEOPLES, WILLIAM AMIS, NICHOLAS EDMUNDS, SAMUEL TARVER, BENJAMIN WILLIAMSON, RICHARD FREEAR, COLLIN W. BARNES, HENRY BOONE, CHARLES HARRISON, DAVID BARNES, JOHN B. ODOM, PETER WOODLIEF, GREEN TURNER, JOS. M. S. ROGERS, J. H. PATTERSON, ANDREW JONES, FRANCIS A. BYNUM and CORNELIUS MOORE.

ONSLOW COUNTY. Established as ONSLOW PRECINCT out of NEW HANOVER PRECINCT in 1734. The name of its county seat is JACKSONVILLE. It was one of the Thirteen (13) ORIGINAL COUNTIES in North Carolina. Some of the early names found on its old records are CHRISTOPHER DUDLEY, EDWARD WARD, JOHN MITCHELL, JOHN FULWOOD, EDWARD STARKEY, JAMES HOWARD, REUBEN GRANT, ZACHARIAH BARROW and HENRY RHODES.

ORANGE COUNTY. This county was established in 1753 from GRANVILLE, JOHNSTON and BLADEN COUNTIES. The part that came out of GRANVILLE COUNTY consisted of a block of territory in its extreme northwestern end, which afterwards comprised a triangle half of the present PERSON COUNTY. The part taken from BLADEN COUNTY was that part of the present CHATHAM COUNTY lying South and West of the HAW RIVER. All the rest of the newly established ORANGE COUNTY came out of JOHNSTON COUNTY. The territory as a whole, included in ORANGE consisted of all the territory now embraced in CHATHAM, CASWELL, PERSON, ALAMANCE, DURHAM and the present day ORANGE, together with that part of LEE COUNTY, taken from Chatham in 1907, which lies South of Deep River. See maps herein. HILLSBORO, the county seat of ORANGE was laid out in 1759 and was at first called CHILDSBURG, but pretty soon changed to HILLSBORO, which name it has retained ever since. It is generally stated that ORANGE COUNTY was the seat of the Regulator trouble that arose near the outbreak of the revolution. There were many Quakers in this section of North Carolina and several meeting places where they worshiped along the waters of the HAW RIVER in Orange County, and many of the regulators appear to have been affiliated with the Quakers or Friends, as they were called. The following historic personages lived in ORANGE COUNTY: THOMAS BURKE, who was Governor of the State and a member of the U. S. Congress; one THOMAS HART (ancestor of Thomas Hart Benton); ALEXANDER MEBANE (mentioned under ALAMANCE COUNTY); FRANCIS NASH; ARCHIBALD D. MURPHY, famous Lawyer and Historian; PLEASANT HENDERSON-brother of JUDGE RICHARD HENDERSON; Hon. WILLIAM A. GRAHAM, Governor and Secretary of the Navy; WILEY PERSON MANGUM, a United States Senator from North Carolina; DAVID L. SWAIN and WILLIAM H. BATTLE. Names mentioned in the old records: William Courtney, Thomas Tullech; JOHN TAYLOR, WILLIAM NASH, DAVID RAY, JOHN SCOTT and many others.

PAMLICO COUNTY. This county was established in 1872 from CRAVEN and BEAUFORT COUNTIES. It is a small county bordering on the PAMLICO SOUND and on the South side of the mouth of PAMLICO river. The county seat is BAYBORO. Being a comparatively new county its history is included in the story of the other sub-divisions around it. See map.

PASQUOTANK COUNTY. This is one of the original thirteen counties of North Carolina, which was known as PASQUOTANK PRECINCT from 1684 until 1738, when it became automatically a COUNTY instead of a Precinct. Lists of many of its early settlers and their land grants and activities are included in other notes in this volume, to which, with the maps pertaining to this County and its surroundings, attention of the reader is called. ELIZABETH CITY county seat.

PENDER COUNTY. This County was cut out of the upper part of NEW HANOVER COUNTY, as then constituted, in 1875, and named in Honor of GEN. WILLIAM DORSEY PENDER a North Carolina general in the Confederate States Army. Burgaw is the county seat of PENDER. Even the pre-civil war history of Pender County belongs to NEW HANOVER COUNTY, and the U. S. Census from 1790 up to and including 1870 contains the residents of this county under the name of NEW HANOVER. It is probable that among the PENDER pioneers were the HOWARDS, MOORES, JONES; DANIEL HENDERSON, JOHN HENDERSON, NATHAN HILL and others.

PERQUIMANS COUNTY. Known as PERQUIMANS PRECINCT until 1738, when it became officially known as PERQUIMANS COUNTY and was one of the thirteen original counties of North Carolina. Its territory consisted of the present area known as PERQUIMANS COUNTY, and most of the territory on the South side of ALBEMARLE SOUND now composing TYRRELL CO!TY. The town of HERTFORD is the county seat. Elsewhere in these notes will be found lists of the earliest settlers of Perquimans Precinct and county, to which the attention of the reader is called. Prior

PERSON COUNTY. This county was established in the year 1791, out of territory taken from CASWELL COUNTY. Originally this territory was partly in EDGECOMBE and GRANVILLE and partly in JOHNSTON COUNTY. Its evolution is made more understandable by a study of the maps herein shewing its geographical development. The town of ROXBORO is given as the county seat. Early PERSON COUNTY records contain many references to the ATKINSON, VANHOOK, WILLIAMS, EDWARDS, HESTER, WILLIAMSON and CUNNINGHAM families.

PITT COUNTY. PITT COUNTY was established in 1760 out of the upper or Eastern f BEAUFORT COUNTY, (Formerly PRECINCT). The town of GREENVILLE is the county e of PITT County, while SNOW HILL is the county seat of GREENE COUNTY, which joins PITT on the West. So far as the writer can tell PITT COUNTY as originally established has remained intact since the day of its establishment. The lower end of the TAR RIVER runs all the way through PITT COUNTY from the northwest to the southeast, and makes its confluence with the PAMPLICO RIVER near the southern line of the county, close to WASHINGTON, the capital of BEAUFORT COUNTY. Among the early residents of what is now PITT COUNTY were the SALTERS, MOYES, WILLIAMS, BRYANS, MAYS, JOYNERS, DANIELS, SMITHS, SHEPPARDS, EVANS and ALBRITTONS.

POLK COUNTY. This is another county in Western North Carolina, which was established in 1855, out of territory taken from the counties of RUTHERFORD and HENDERSON, situated on the line of South Carolina, and of which COLUMBUS is the county seat. Historians say it was named for COL. WILLIAM POLK, of Mecklenburg County, revolutionary soldier.

RANDOLPH COUNTY. This is one of the very interesting old counties of North Carolina, which was established in 1779 from the territory set aside for GUILFORD COUNTY from ROWAN in the year 1770 - nine years previously. The county seat of RANDOLPH County is ASHEBORO, in between LEXINGTON and PITTSBORO, and a place of much interest, because so many ancestors of so many people once lived there. Some of the outstanding leaders of the "regulators" lived along Sandy Creek in this county, including HERMAN HUSBANDS, whose two sons, settled on DEEP RIVER, near what was called in the old days BUFFALO FORD. It was on SANDY CREEK in this or the adjoining county of CHATHAM that the "Sandy Creek Baptist Church" was established about 1756 on the lands belonging to SEYMOUR YORK, by REV. SHUBAL STEARNS and others, and to which congregation OBEDIAH HOWARD belonged. Hon. JOHN LONG resided in RANDOLPH COUNTY and became a member of the United States Congress in 1821. ASHEBORO was also the home of JONATHAN WORTH, Governor of the Old North State from 1866 to 1868. His home is still standing in ASHEBORO, with an appropriate marker. His family furnished this writer a good Christian name. Other notable families of RANDOLPH COUNTY whose names occur often on the ancient records were the COLLIERS, SHARPES, WADDELLS, GRAYS, HARVEYS, WOODS, BAILEYS, ARNOLDS, WADES, BRANSONS, LYNDONS, ARMISTEADS, STALEYS, LANES, HOOVERS (ancestors of the President), CRAVENS, WALKERS, CUNNINGHAMS, ELLIOTTS, RUSH, HAWKINS, LANES and MARSHES.

RICHMOND COUNTY. This county was established in 1779 from ANSON COUNTY, just thirty years after the latter county had been taken out of BLADEN and set apart with a vast territory of its own. (See maps). The town of ROCKINGHAM is now the county seat of RICHMOND COUNTY. A man named CHARLES MEDLOCK had much to do with the affairs of this county when it was first organized and represented it many years in the State Senate. The WEBBS, WALLS, McFARLANDS (Duncan), ALEXANDER McMILLAN, STEWARTS, STEELES, McLEODS, WEBBS, WALLS, SPEEDS, THOMASES, POWELLS, COLES, ARCHIBALD McNAIR, ERASMUS LOVE, GEORGE THOMAS, and ALFRED DOCKERY, were all prominent. This was the home of THOMAS BLEWETT, who ran a ferry on PEE DEE RIVER, and whose descendant, THOMAS GARTEN BLEWETT (THOMAS BLEWETT married a GARTEN) owned a vast plantation near COLUMBUS, MISSISSIPPI, before the war between the States. It seems that ALEXANDER MARTIN also lived in this county.

ROBESON COUNTY. This county was formed in 1787 from a part of BLADEN COUNTY. (See map). It was named for a COL. THOMAS ROBESON, a soldier of the revolution. The county seat is LUMBERTON. There is a tribe of strange people in this county that is linked by tradition with the ill fated expedition that landed in 1685 at Roanoke Island, who appear to be of a mixed blood with some strange race, the explanation that it was with the Croaten Indians and white settlers of the expedition, being sometimes accepted. The earliest representative of ROBESON COUNTY in the State Senate of North Carolina was a JOHN WILLIS, and his successor was an ELIAS BARNES, probably a descendant of the BARNES FAMILY of Eastern Virginia, who had penetrated by 1800 to this part of the Old North State. This was also the home of BENJAMIN LEE, ALFRED ROWLAND, JOHN GILCHRIST, SHADRACH HOWELL, KENNETH BLACK, a ZACHARIAH JORDAN (one went to Texas, and I knew him), HUGH BROWN, DUNCAN McALPIN, JOHN REAGAN, JAMES McQUEEN, JOHN PURCELL, ALEXANDER WATSON and others. Here, too, in ROBESON COUNTY is buried a DR. JAMES ADAIR or ROBERT ADAIR, said to have been the ADAIR who was the father of all the CHEROKEE INDIANS bearing the name, and also reputed to be the "ROBIN ADAIR" famed in song and story. (See "KINFOLKS" by William C. Harlee).

ROCKINGHAM COUNTY. This county was established out of GUILFORD COUNTY in 1785 and the name was adopted from a certain Duke of Buckingham. The little village of WENTWORTH is the home of the county courthouse and the county seat. This was the home of the famous JUDGE THOMAS SETTLE, a pioneer jurist of the Old North State. It is in the midst of a great tobacco raising country. Familiar names on its ancient records are the GALLOWAYS, WILLIAMS, PHILLIPS, SCALES, HILLS, TAYLORS, LEAKS, BETHELS, DOUGLASS, BLACKWELLS, GENTHYS, LANIERS, MOREHEADS and MARTINS. Also DAVID S. REID of REIDSVILLE.

ROWAN COUNTY. Established out of ANSON COUNTY in 1753, and containing at that time a large part of the territory North of the Catawba River bend on westward to the line of Tennessee, across the mountains. As a matter of fact, it is supposed to have taken in all that part of Tennessee, west of the Alleghaneys in the "Watauga Settlements" including Sullivan County and the Jonesboro country, later ceded to Tennessee by North Carolina. Space, here, of course, is wholly inadequate to portray the long and interesting history of Rowan County. By consulting maps in this work, the evolution of this vast territory can be better grasped and understood by the reader. Much material in regard to its people will be found recorded on other pages of this volume, to which the reader is referred.

RUTHERFORD COUNTY. This county was established in 1779 from the territory of TRYON COUNTY, and TRYON COUNTY had been established in 1768 out of the Western part of MECKLENBURG COUNTY. (See page 379 herein). TRYON COUNTY was divided into two counties in 1779, one being RUTHERFORD and the other LINCOLN. The territory comprising RUTHERFORD extended westard to the extent of the habitable country, and in theory to the MISSISSIPPI RIVER, taking in a good part of what is now TENNESSEE. The county of RUTHERFORD was named for Gen. Griffith Rutherford, patriot of the revolution and Indian fighter. The town of RUTHERFORDTON is the county seat. In an early day there was a "gold rush" to Rutherford County, when gold was discovered in that region, after some of the same metal had been found in what is now CABARRUS COUNTY, mentioned elsewhere in these notes. The ancient records of RUTHERFORD COUNTY will still yield up valuable data to those who visit RUTHERFORDTON and examine them. This was the home of ANDREW HAMPTON, whose ancestry has long been a knotty problem for research workers. The U. S. Census for the year 1790 includes the heads of families who at that time lived not only in the present RUTHERFORD COUNTY but in all of the other counties to the West of it, clear to the TENNESSEE line, and this fact has confused many people. The maps of that region shown herein will make clear to the reader just what territory was then included in Rutherford County. Among the early families of RUTHERFORD were the PORTERS, WALKERS, HOLLANDS, MILLERS, WHITESIDES, SINGLETONS, HAMPTONS, GREENES, HYDERS, WALTONS, SHUFORDS, CARSONS, GRAHAMS, MOORES, DAVIDSONS, McINTYRES, MORROWS, TERRELLS and VAN ZANDTS.

SAMPSON COUNTY. This county was established in 1784 from DUPLIN COUNTY, which territory had been appropriated from NEW HANOVER COUNTY in 1749 to make DUPLIN. SAMPSON comprised all of the western side of the original DUPLIN COUNTY and it was bounded on the North by the counties of JOHNSTON and WAYNE, and this will explain why so many of the same names one finds of families in DUPLIN are to be found also in JOHNSTON and WAYNE COUNTIES. There was only the county line between them, and many families lived on both sides of the line. SAMPSON COUNTY was also the home of HON. WILLIAM R. KING, who became Vice President of the UNITED STATES, after he moved over into ALABAMA. SAMPSON was also the home of the CLINTONS, (DeWitt's relatives), HOLMES (Gabriel), KENNANS, GAVINS, BLACKMANS, MATTHEWS, BRYANS, SELLERS, INGRAMS, MOBLEYS, THOMPSONS, KINGS, BOYKINS and UNDERWOODS. The town of CLINTON is the county seat of SAMPSON COUNTY.

SCOTLAND COUNTY. Established in 1899, from a part of RICHMOND COUNTY. The name SCOTLAND is said to have been chosen because of the fact that its residents were so many of them descended from the early Scotch emigrants, many of whom came over with Allan and Flora McDonald before the revolution. LAURENBURG is the name of the county seat. What has heretofore been written about RICHMOND COUNTY and its early residents, of course, applies to SCOTLAND'S history.

STANLEY COUNTY. This county was formed out of the territory lying west of the YADKIN RIVER in its passage through MONTGOMERY COUNTY. Its western border is the eastern line of the present CABARRUS COUNTY, formerly a part of the original MECKLENBURG COUNTY. STANLEY was created in 1841, and has therefore been in existence for a period of 105 years at this writing. The county is said to have been named for JOHN STANLEY, of NEW BERN, who was several times elected speaker of the House of Commons of North Carolina, and whose forbears lived in BERTIE and EDGECOMBE COUNTIES. (See Genealogy of the Thomas Family in this volume). RUFUS BARRINGER, of CABARRUS or MECKLENBURG COUNTY represented STANLEY County in the General Assembly and Senate, shortly after it was organized. The county seat of STANLEY COUNTY is named ALBEMARLE, which seems to be the only vestage of official recognition of the original ancestor of all North Carolina - OLD ALBEMARLE.

STOKES COUNTY. This County was organized in 1789 from a part of SURRY COUNTY, and was named, it is said, for COL. JOHN STOKES, a gallant officer of the American Revolution. DANBURY is the county seat of STOKES COUNTY. It was in the territory now included in STOKES COUNTY, where a colony of MORAVIANS settled, the first contingent of which arrived in November, 1753 from the country farther North by way of WINCHESTER, VIRGINIA, and other points. The tract of some seventy thousand acres of land conveyed to their agent JAMES HUTTON in 1782 was located near where the present town of Winston-Salem is situated in FORSYTHE COUNTY, which was taken from the lower half of STOKES COUNTY in 1849. Besides the Moravian leaders who made the very finest citizens, many notables of history resided in STOKES COUNTY, among them being JOSEPH WINSTON, COL. JOHN MARTIN, HON. JOHN HILL, AUGUSTUS H. SHEPPERD, MATTHEW BROOKS, PETER HAIRSTON, HENRY DOBSON, EMMANUEL SHOBER, ANDREW BOWMAN, ISSAC NELSON, JOSEPH ALLEN and ISAAC DALTON. The town of DANBURY is the county seat.

SURRY COUNTY. Surry County was established in 1770 from ROWAN COUNTY, the same year that GUILFORD was carved out of the same territory. It has been claimed that the county was named after SURRY, ENGLAND. DOBSON is the county seat. At the time this county was organized in the year 1770 it embraced all of the Northern half of North Carolina west of the original GUILFORD COUNTY, clear to the TENNESSEE line. See map of the original SURRY COUNTY of 1770 which will be found herein. SURRY COUNTY was the home of MAJ. JOSEPH WILLIAMS, whose distinguished sons moved over into TENNESSEE, and whose grand-daughter became the wife of JUDGE RICHMOND PEARSON. HON. JESSE FRANKLIN, a kinsman of BENJAMIN CLEVELAND, was a resident of STOKES COUNTY, and became Governor of the STATE. The SHEPPARDS, ARMSTRONGS, WINSTONS, EDWARDS, FRANKLINS, WRIGHTS, GRAVES, HORNS, POINDEXTERS, WAUGHS and DOBSONS were all from STOKES COUNTY and prominent in its early history.

SWAIN COUNTY was established in 1871 from JACKSON and MACON COUNTIES and will be found on the map away over in the Southwestern corner of North Carolina, with BRYSON CITY as the county seat. It was named for DAVID L. SWAIN, Governor and University President.

TRANSYLVANIA COUNTY. This county was established in 1861 from parts of HENDERSON and JACKSON COUNTIES, off-shoots of BUNCOMBE and RUTHERFORD territory, as shown by their respective histories herein. The county seat is called BREVARD, after an old IREDELL, ROWAN and MECKLENBURG COUNTY family of that name. See maps herein.

TYRRELL COUNTY. This was orginally a PRECINCT established away back in 1729 from territory taken from CHOWAN, PERQUIMANS and PASQUOTANK PRECINCTS, lying south of ALBEMARLE SOUND. In 1738, nine years after its establishment as TYRRELL PRECINCT it became TYRRELL COUNTY, and thus one of the original thirteen counties composing the Province of North Carolina. COLUMBIA is the County seat of TYRRELL COUNTY. It was, long before it became a separate precinct or county, the home of the SPRUILLS, BLOUNTS and a lot of other families from the vicinity of EDENTON, North of the Sound, who had removed to that section. JOHN WARRINGTON, RICHARD DAVIS, JOHN B. BEASLEY, EPHRAIM MANN, THOMAS PENDER, ELIJAH WARRINGTON, JEREMIAH WYNNE, SOLOMON AND ENOCH HASSELL, THOMAS LEIGH, DANIEL N. BATEMAN, GEORGE ALEXANDER, THOMAS HOSKINS and SILAS and FREDERICK DAVENPORT were among the prominent residents of this territory from 1777 up to 1850.

UNION COUNTY. About half of this county, which was established in 1842, was taken from MECKLENBURG COUNTY while the other half on the East came out of ANSON COUNTY. The town of MONROE is the county seat. Many of the early residents of the present UNION COUNTY are mentioned in that section of this volume dealing with the early history of MECKLENBURG County, extending from pages 313 to 558, to which reference is here made.

VANCE COUNTY was, until 1881 a part of GRANVILLE COUNTY, and was the last part of that county to be appropriated to the establishment of other counties or sub-divisions so far as this writer is informed. It has a most interesting history and background and has been referred to as "Historic Vance County" in an interesting volume published by JOHN BULLOCK WATKINS, a native of the county, and of HENDERSON, the county seat. Mention of nearly all of its earliest residents has been made in that section of this volume dealing with "Colinial Granville County and Its People" embraced in pages 209 to 312, to which reference is here made. It was the home of the WILLIAMS, HENDERSON, DANIEL, SEARCY, YANCEY, BULLOCK, HARRIS and other interesting families.

WAKE COUNTY. Raleigh, the county seat, is the present Capital of the State of North Carolina. The County was taken from territory formerly embraced in ORANGE, JOHNSTON and CUMBERLAND COUNTIES, but the amount of territory that was taken from ORANGE and CUMBERLAND was negligible, as the great bulk of the territory came out of JOHNSTON COUNTY. There is a map appearing herein which is designed to make plain the details of the geographical construction of the county, with the changes made in it from time to time, so that it can be understood. WAKE COUNTY was established in 1770. Space will not permit in this brief sketch an adequate showing of its earliest citizenship and history. The stalwarts of the early days of Wake County and of RALEIGH, the capital, include such men as MICHAEL RODGERS, JOEL LANE, JAMES HINTON, TIGNAL JONES, JOHN HINTON, SAMUEL WHITTAKER, HENRY SEAWELL, NATHANIEL JONES, WILLIAM H. HAYWOOD, WILLIAM POLK, HARDY SAUNDERS and many others.

WARREN COUNTY. This county was created in 1779 from OLD BUTE COUNTY (established in 1764 and abolished in 1779) out of its northern half. Originally it had been a part of EDGECOMBE and later GRANVILLE COUNTY. On pages 302, 303 and 304 of this volume will be found a number of interesting abstracts gathered by this writer from the ancient records of WARREN COUNTY which will add materially to the history of the people of the county, and substitute for a more extended sketch here.

WASHINGTON COUNTY. This county, named, presumable for the "father of his country" was created from territory taken from TYRRELL COUNTY in 1799. PLYMOUTH is the name of the county seat. On the west it is joined by Martin County and immediately east is the remnant of TYRRELL COUNTY, which at one time embraced not only the present WASHINGTON but most of what is now MARTIN COUNTY. The early history of TYRRELL COUNTY includes the early story of WASHINGTON as well. Consult maps herein for an understanding of its geographical history.

WATAUGA COUNTY. This county lies in the extreme Western part of North Carolina, and was established in 1849 from ASHE, CALDWELL, WILKES and YANCEY COUNTIES. It takes its name from the WATAUGA RIVER which winds around its mountain peaks through the county. The town of BOONE is the county seat. Early politicains in this county were MARK HOLTSCLAW, THOMAS GREEN and WILLIAM HORTON. The first court was held on the farm of JOSEPH HARDIN, one mile East of the town of BOONE. E. C. BARTLETT was the Clerk. MICHAEL COOK, JOHN HORTON, W. M. CALLAWAY and D. C. REAGAN were among the first Sheriffs of the county. W. L. BRYAN ran a hotel in BOONE as did T. J. COFFEY and his brother. The CABLES, FARTHINGS, MASTS, BROWNS and COUNCILS were all early residents of the county.

WAYNE COUNTY was established in 1779 from DOBBS COUNTY. It was named for Anthony Wayne. GOLDSBORO is the county seat. The McKINNIES and MOORINGS, the CROOMS, SMITHS and RHODES, and the SHERARDS, EXUMS, BROGDENS and BARNES families took a prominent part in the affiars of WAYNE COUNTY. The COBBS and BOONES also lived in Wayne. DOBBS county went out of existence when LENOIR and GLASGOW were established out its territory. See maps.

WILKES COUNTY. This county was created out of SURRY COUNTY in 1777. WILKESBORO is the name of the county seat. Montfort Stokes, afterwards Governor, was a resident of WILKES COUNTY. He was a revolutionary soldier and died in the far west whither he had gone to attend to matters as Indian Agent in his old age. He was buried in OKLAHOMA. See data on maps.

WILSON COUNTY. This county was created in 1855 from four counties surrounding it, viz. EDGECOMBE, NASH, JOHNSTON and WAYNE. It was named for the HON. LOUIS D. WILSON, a prominent citizen who resided in the county and served as a Colonel of troops in the War with Mexico. In a special article written by MR. HUGH BUCKNER JOHNSTON, a native of WILSON COUNTY and an outstanding writer, historian and genealogist, a complete account of the geography and history of WILSON COUNTY is set forth on other pages in this volume, to which reference is here made. The County seat of WILSON COUNTY is the town of WILSON.

YADKIN COUNTY was established in 1850 from SURRY COUNTY. YADKINVILLE is the county seat. The YADKIN RIVER furnishes its northern and eastern border.

YANCEY COUNTY. This county was established in 1833 from parts of both BURKE and BUNCOMBE COUNTIES. BURNSVILLE is the name of the county seat of YANCEY COUNTY. It is the home of the RAY and BAILEY FAMILIES, and when this compiler happens along through the town he stops at the Ray hotel, gets gas at a Bailey filling station, visits a RAY County Clerk at the courthouse and calls for his mail from a Bailey postmaster. It is an attractive little town, watered by the Cane River subsidiaries with its courts, schools, churches, stores, hotels, filling stations, restaurants and hamburger stands all conducted by the Baileys and the Rays, and the records at the courthouse with most of the instruments of record being under either the Rs or the Bs. When city life gets too strenuous in Burnsville, one can go over to Spruce Pine and have a grand time, only a few miles up the road, and I was told that some of my kinfolks had been as far away as Ashville, which is quite a "fur piece" for home-loving tar heels. The long time Judge of the local courts, JUDGE BIS RAY has been deceased now for several years, but left a numerous progeny.

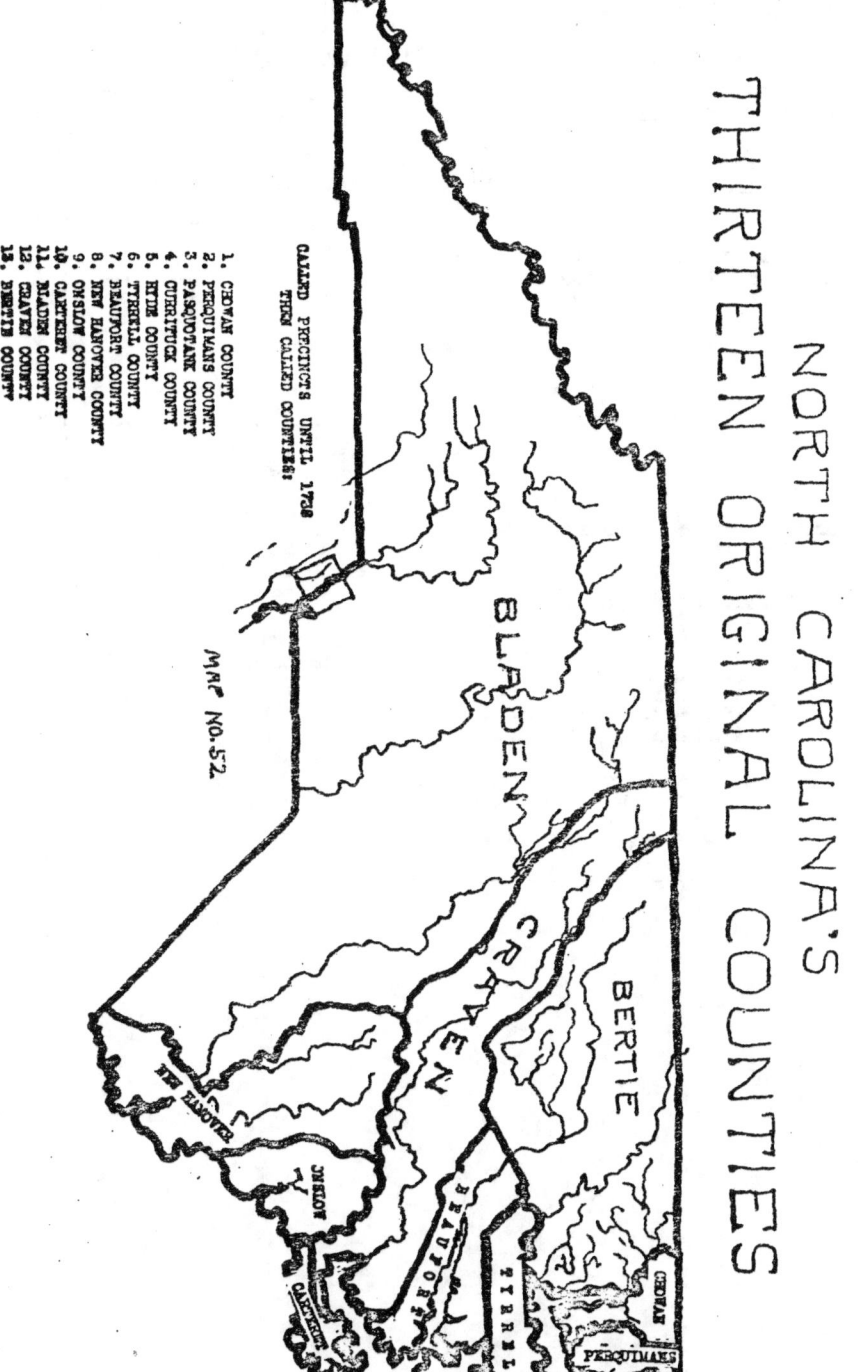

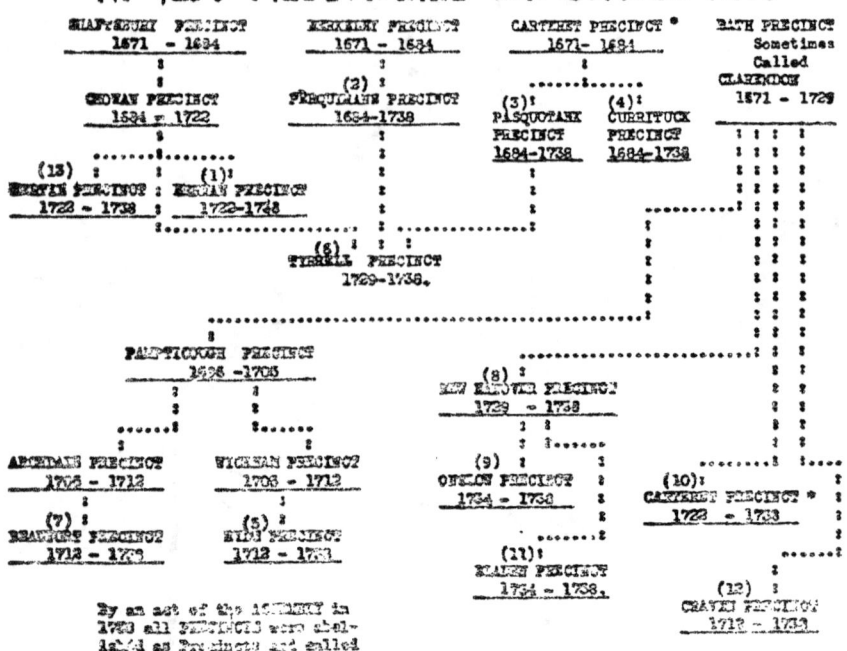

OLD ST. THOMAS CHURCH
BATH

OLD ST. PAUL'S CHURCH
EDENTON

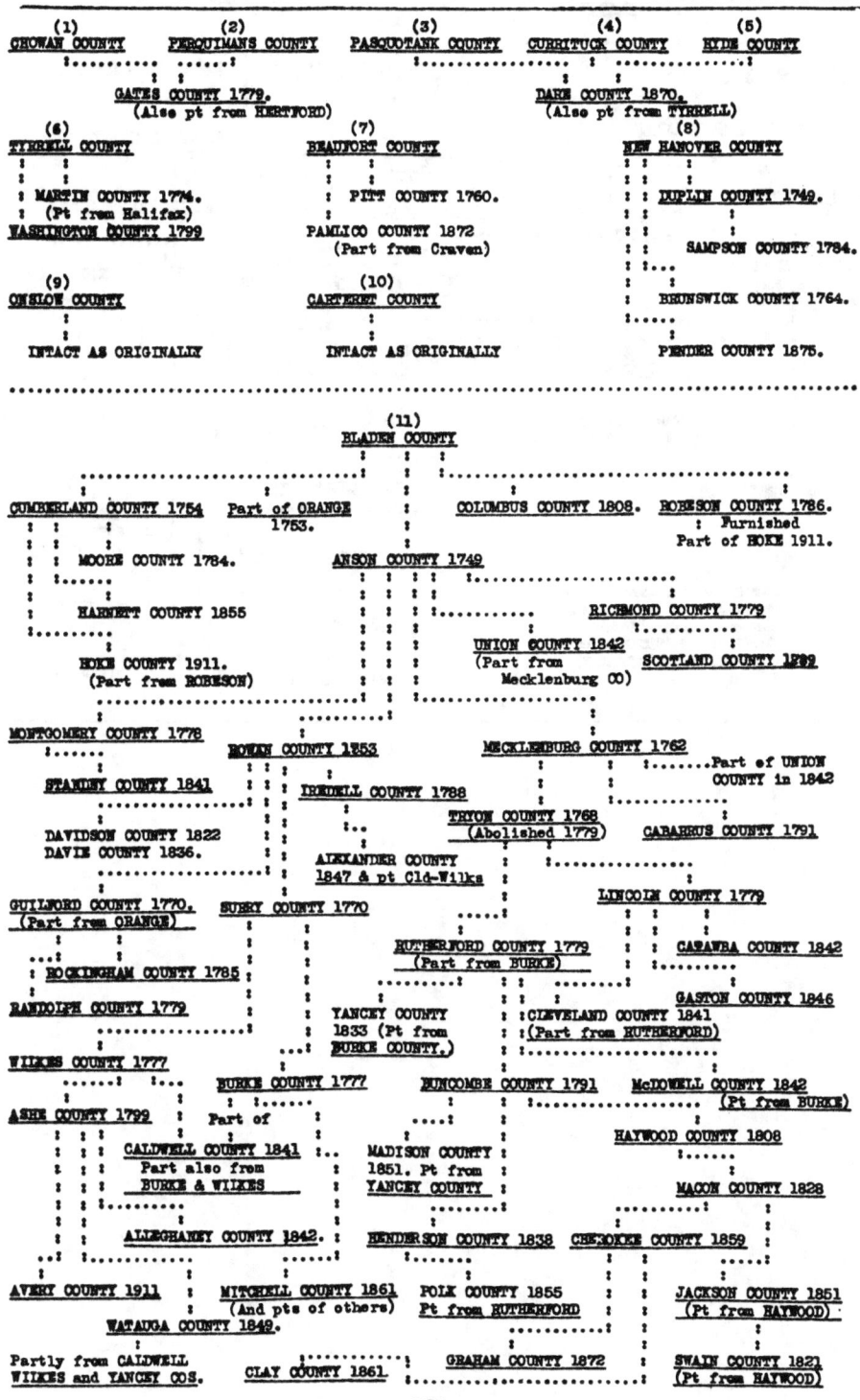

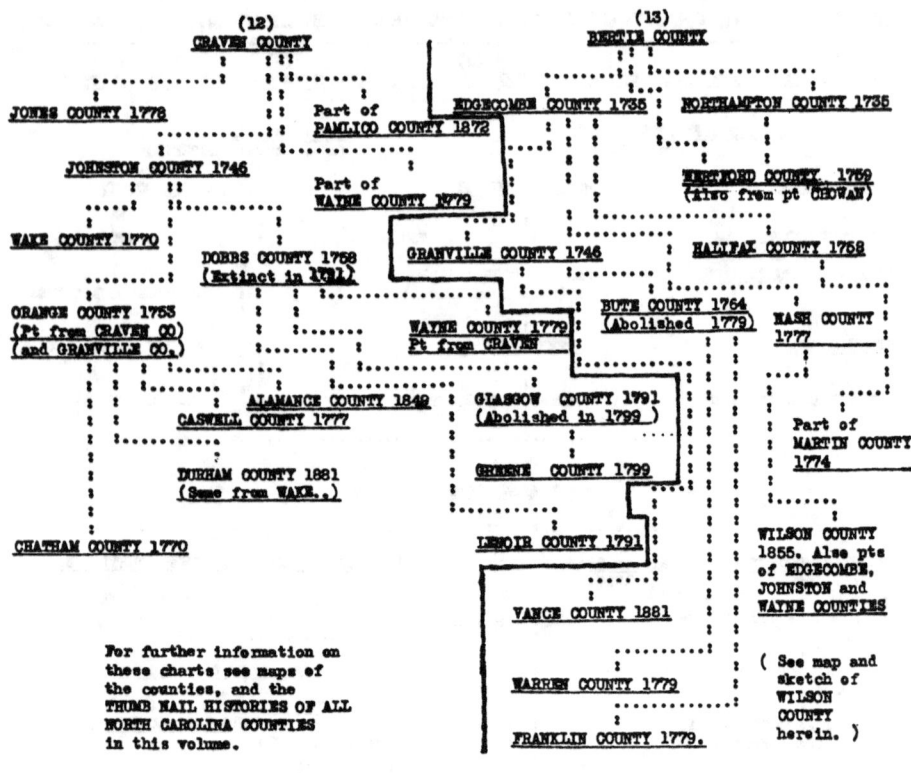

HISTORIC VANCE COUNTY

NOTE: What follows is material from "HISTORIC VANCE COUNTY" by JOHN BULLOCK WATKINS, of Henderson, N. C. in 1941, which is used by his permission in this volume.

SAMUEL HENDERSON OF ASHELAND

Thomas Henderson came from Dumfries Scotland to Jamestown, Virginia in 1607, living at Blue or Yellow Springs and having several children. He was a Burgess in 1619. A son, Richard Henderson moved to Hanover County, Virginia, marrying "Polly" Washer, a daughter of Ensign Washer. Samuel Henderson, 1700-1783, married, in 1732, Elizabeth Williams, who was eighteen years old and an aunt of Judge John Williams of Montpelier. They moved to Granville County North Carolina about 1740. (*)

Samuel Henderson was the first Sheriff of Granville County in 1746, and had a "Red Tavern" in Williamsboro, which was modeled after an English Coffee House. Also, before 1750, he started a mill just beyond Flemingtown, and the old dam there can be seen today. It is just above where the road crosses Henderson Mill creek.

He had seven sons and four daughters. The oldest son, Judge Richard Henderson, 1735-1785, married, in 1763, Elizabeth Keeling, an eighteen year old daughter of George Keeling of Nine Oaks. He was a partner with his first cousin, Judge John Williams of Montpelier in "Williams & Henderson", Judges and Attorneys.

was a Judge. Another son, Chief Justice Leonard Henderson is written up in our "City of Henderson" section, as the man for whom the City was named.

Asheland was built by Samuel Henderson probably when he came over from Hanover County, Virginia, and, as far as I know, it is the oldest house in Vance County. It has a small hall, with a side stairway, and a large room back of this, all on one side, with two rooms about the same size on the other side. The same arrangement was upstairs. There were two large chimneys at the back, all facing the south. There probably was a porch in the front.

After Judge Richard Henderson's death, Asheland was sold to his son, Archibald Henderson of Salisbury, who probably sold it to Richard Bullock, who is said was the richest man in Granville County around 1820. He was the only son of Len Henley Bullock. In 1820, Archibald Henderson, a son of Chief Justice Leonard Henderson, married the only daughter of Richard Bullock, "Annie Bullock" and this Richard Bullock gave Asheland to them, so that his daughter could live near him.

EAST VIEW OF ASHLAND, our oldest house; the lower part built about 1740 by Samuel Henderson.

Of the many children of Judge Richard Henderson, "Archibald" moved to Salisbury, being an attorney and Mayor, and there is a monument to him there.

The youngest son, John Lawson was Clerk of the Supreme Court, member of Congress, and very brilliant. Another son, William was a hero and killed at the battle of Eutaw Springs. Pleasant Henderson

Archibald Henderson took off the front porch and added a hall and a large "ball room", in which he put a glass pendant chandelier. He was seven years doing this, and this turned the house to face the east, instead of the south. After the death of the widow of Archibald Henderson, Asheland was sold, and the late Thomas F. Wiggins lived there. Later it was sold to the late Eugene White, whose widow and children live there now.

(*) This is the traditional account, but much of it is obviously erroneous. See pages 221 et seq.

PATRICK HAMILTON OF BURNSIDE

In 1750, Joseph Davenport bought several tracts of land from Lord Granville around this location, and it looks like he lived at this place and built the present house. This is as near as I can answer the question I am often asked, "Who built Burnside"?

BURNSIDE, two miles northwest from Williamsboro.

In 1768, he sold this tract, 611 acres, to Charles Kinnon, and from there the records are clear.

In 1786, son John Kinnon sold this 611 acres to Vinckler Jones, who lived across the creek. Later, Vinckler Jones gave this to a son, John Jones. In 1820, John Jones of Maury County Tennessee, sold this as then 1589 acres, to Dr. Thomas Hunt, a son of Menucan Hunt, who was the first State Treasurer of North Carolina. Dr. Hunt repaired the house, adding the frescoing. In 1824. Dr. Hunt sold this place as 2000 acres to Patrick Hamilton. There is a book called "Patrick Hamilton of Burnside", which tells much about him. He was State Senator, and filled other positions.

After Patrick Hamilton's death in 1850, the place became the property of his son, Robert Hamilton. Since that time it has changed owners about ten times, and now is the property of R. B. Crowder, of Raleigh.

HENDERSON GRAVE

The grave of Judge Richard Henderson (1735-1785), father of Chief Justice Leonard Henderson is about one mile beyond Ashland.

The stone was put up by Archibald Henderson of Chapel Hill. It reads as follows:

Richard Henderson (1735-1785) Jurist, Pioneer, Colonizer, Founder of Boonesboro, Ky. and Nashville, Tenn., President Colony of Transylvania, Author Cumberland Compact.

693

Richard Bullock Built the "Dick" Henderson House

Around 1900, Rev. Lewellyn Bullock of Rugby, England wrote "Bullock Genealogies", in which he traced this family back to "Oswald", who, around the Eleventh Century, took the surname of Bullock.

They have long been established in Wales, from which place, Captain Hugh Bullock came to York County, Virginia, about 1630. After his death, his son, William Bullock, returned to London, and wrote on the beauties of Virginia, the "Virginia Impartially Examined". But he is not our ancestor.

Another William Bullock, son of John Bullock of Darley, England, came to Virginia, on the ship "Planter", about 1650. Tradition is that he was an elderly man and that he brought a part of his family at that time and that these raised tobacco and caught herrings to pay the fare of the rest of the family. That because of the congestion on the northern side of the James River, he settled "Over the River", possibly in Surry county, as there are many old Bullock records there.

In 1704, we find Richard and Edward Bullock on the "King's Rent Roll" in New Kent County, Virginia. Edward Bullock, Jr., in 1722, bought land in Hanover County, which county had been cut from New Kent, and I think that he is the Edward Bullock that, in 1752, moved to just north of Oxford, North Carolina, and that he is the grandfather of Captain Micajah Bullock of the Revolution, who lived near Creedmoor, North Carolina. The Bullocks of Oxford and Creedmoor are descendants of the above Captain Micajah Bullock.

Now to my family. Richard Bullock, Jr., in 1728, bought land in Hanover County, Virginia, and around 1732, he was granted five tracts of four hundred acres each in that seection, and he was a merchant.

In 1753, owing to the French and Indian War, he sold all his property, and moved to Granville County North Carolina. He settled between Drewry and Nutbush Creek, place now called "Bullocksville". He built the old house that is now falling down. Richard Bullock's ten children, some married, settled around him.

The home place was left to a son, Len Henley Bullock, who was a Captain in the Colonial Army, and Sheriff of Granville County. This Len Henley Bullock left the home place to his only son, Richard Bullock. He also had five daughters.

The above Richard Bullock left the place to his grandson namesake, Richard Bullock Henderson, who was called "Dick Henderson", and it is b, that name the place is known today.

It is today the property of a sister of Robert Taylor of Townsville, North Carolina.

Will of Richard Bullock, died 1764

In the name of God Amen I Richard Bullock of the County of Granville and Provence of North Carolina being very sick though of a perfect sense and memory thanks to Almighty God and calling to mind the uncertainties of this life and that all flesh only yields unto Death whensoever it shall please God to call there for I appoint this my last will and Testament in manner and form following faith and principally I give my Soul unto God that gave me and my Body to be the Earth to be Buryied in such manner as my Executors hereinafter shall think fit in Sure and Certain hopes of Eternal Life through the merits of Jesus Christ my Mediator and Redeemer and for my Temporal Estate wherewith it has pleased God to bless me with I give and bequeath as followith after my Just debts are paid

Item I give and bequeath to my Daughter Sarah Sims one shilling.

Item I give and bequeath My Vandyk one shilling sterling

Item I give and bequeath my Daughter Agnes Williams one shilling sterling

Item I give and bequeath my son Zachariah one shilling sterling

Item I give and bequeath my son William Bullock one shilling sterling

Item I give and bequeath my son John Bullock one shilling sterling

Item I give and bequeath my daughter Susannah Sims one shilling sterling

Item I give and bequeath to my granddaughter Ann Vandyck one feather bed and furniture to the value of Eight pounds Virginia money

Item I give and bequeath to my grandson Zachariah Nucholls one feather bed and furniture to value of eight pounds Va money

Item I give and bequeath to my granddaughter Agatha Nucholls one shilling sterling

My will and desire is that my lands on Elerbees Creek in Orange County be sold to pay part of my debts and I leave the Land and planation whereon I now live to my wife during her Natural Life likewise the remainder of my Estate

After my Just Debts is paid Item I give and bequeath to my son Nathaniel Bullock after my wife decease the land and planation whereon I now live and after my wifes Decease I give and bequeath to my Two youngest sons Leonard Henley Bullock and Nathaniel Bullock all my Estate that is not otherwise divided between them and my Desire is that my Estate be not appraised I likewise appoint my said wife and son Leonard Henly Bullock my Executrix & Executor of this my last Will and Testament in witness whereof I have herewith set my hand and affixed my seal this 27th day of October 1764.

Richd Bullock

Signed and sealed and declared to be his last will and Testament in presence of
William H Shaw (his mark)
Philemon Hawkins
Julius Howard
Will proven in Granville Court Nov. 1766

The above will is a continuous writing with no commas, rearranged by me   John B. Watkins, Jr

JOHN TAYLOR OF MACPELAH

"Trailerer" came with William the Conqueror to England, and is the founder of the Taylor family.

James Taylor, 1615-1680, a descendant of the Earl of Hare, came to Virginia in 1635. James Taylor, Jr., 1635-1689, was in the Royal Army, and had 10,000 acres in Orange County, Virginia. He married, first Frances Walker, and a son by this marriage, James Taylor III, is ancestor of President James Madison, President Zachary Taylor, Mrs. Jefferson Davis, and others too numerous to try to mention. James Taylor, Jr., married, second, in 1862, Mary Gregory. A son by this marriage, John Taylor, married Catherine Pendleton, of a family very prominent in Virginia history. About 1860, they moved to "Macpelah", south of Townesville, North Carolina. They had eleven children, most of whom settled around their parents. Together, they owned around 20,000 acres of land, also they owned Taylor's Ferry on the Roanoke River. A daughter, Catherine Taylor married Moses Penn, who was the parents of John Penn, a Signer of the Declaration of Independence. Another daughter, Elizabeth, married, first, Colonel James B. Lewis, second, 1766, Colonel William Bullock, and is the writer's ancestor by both marriages. The youngest son, Joseph Taylor was a Colonel in the Revolution, and inherited Macpelah. His daughter Elizabeth married Col. William Hunt, a son of Menucan Hunt, the first State Treasurer of North Carolina, and inherited Macpelah.

A daughter of Col. William Hunt married Captain Joseph Townes of the Confederate army, they living at Macpelah. Captain Townes built a race track across the road, which was used for drilling soldiers for the Civil War.

Macpelah was later sold to Edward O. Taylor of a different family of Taylors, and his son, Robert Taylor now owns the place.

The house burned around 1880, and E. O. Taylor rebuilt it. The only antique is the old office in the yard. Many of the John Taylor family are buried here, and I have a chart of the graves.

"John Taylor of Macpelah" is an ancestor of the writer of this history.

BUENA VISTA, old Burwell place one mile north of Williamsboro.

NOTE: For "The Bullocks of Granville" see page 238. The versions differ.

GEORGE KEELING OF NINE OAKS

There is a tradition that Lord Keeling was a member of Parliament, and because of his outspoken Protestant sympathies, he had to flee to Virginia. A descendant, George Keeling married Agnes Bullock, a daughter of Richard Bullock, in Hanover County, Va., and he doubtless came to Granville County in 1753 with the Bullock family.

He settled at "Nine Oaks", two miles west of Williamsboro. The last of the nine oaks died a few years ago.

He died soon after settling at this place, leaving three daughters and a son, John, who never married. His widow married in 1757, Judge John Williams of Montpelier. In 1770, a daughter, Frances Keeling married Bromfield Ridley, who built the present house as a present to his bride. The location may not be the same as George Keeling lived though. Bromfield Ridley was very rich, had much land, and gave "Ridley Park" to Oxford.

A daughter married James Hamilton, a brother of Patrick Hamilton of Burnside, they living here. Nine Oaks later became the property of Smith Cooper. It now belongs to his great-granddaughter, Miss Ethel Crowder, of Henderson, North Carolina.

OLD CHURCHES IN VANCE

The following is a list of the churches in Vance county, with the date of organization. I also have the names of the first pastors, and other items about them.

Baptist: Middleburg 1861, Island Creek 1820, Rock Spring 1885, Dexter 1906, Poplar Creek 1836, Kittrell 1908, Oak Ridge 1873, New Bethel 1872, New Sandy Creek 1895, Carey 1888.

Methodist: Middleburg 1854, Drewery 1922, Tabernacle 1842 (but there was a meeting house there in 1784), Hargrove 1911, Marrows Chapel 1825, Herman 1858, Kittrell 1880, Cokesbury 1784.

Protestant (now Methodist) Spring Valley 1905, Harris Chapel 1857, Union Chapel 1829, Rehobeth 1828, Antioch 1869, Gillburg 1894.

Presbyterian: Young's Memorial 1894, Nutbush 1757, St. Andrews 1912, Brookston 1900.

Congregational - Christian: Fullers Chapel 1900, Antioch 1895, Liberty 1858.

Episcopal: St. John 1754, Trinity 1914.

I want histories of Tar River, Shocco, Spring Valley, Silver Springs, Middleburg Episcopal, Flat Rock, Rock Spring Methodist, Catholic, and any others I have not mentioned.

NINE OAKS, two miles west of Williamsboro, built in 1770 by Bromfield Ridley as a present to his bride. Now owned by Miss Ethel Crowder.

COLONEL JOHN HARGROVE OF HIBERNIA

This place is three miles northeast of Townsville, North Carolina. The Hargrove family came over from Virginia before the Revolution, and settled around this section. They married with the Woodworths, which caused that name to a village north of Townsville. Colonel John Hargrove said that all he knew about when the present house was built was that he was born in it in 1815. However, the smokehouse there is "Colonial", and a lady with whom I visited this place a few years ago, took a picture of that for the Congressional Library. But the boxwood and flower gardens are worth a trip to the place.

Hibernia, today, is owned by a grandson, Hargrove Bellamy of Wilmington, North Carolina, who "summers" there. Many Hargroves are buried in the graveyard at the place.

MARROW'S CHAPEL Methodist

GRAVE OF ANNIE LEE.

About twelve miles southeast of our city in Warren county is the grave of Annie Bell Lee. She died while on a visit to friends at Jones Springs near here, during the Civil War.

Her father, General Robert E. Lee, was unable to attend the funeral, but visited the grave later. Recently, the Warren County Daughters of Confederacy had a memorial service at the grave and a State Historical Commission marker is on the Warrenton-Louisburg highway for it.

Judge R. Hunt Parker is a descendant of John Taylor and Catherine Pendleton of Macpelah. By his decisions, Judge Parker is making Vance county and this section of the State "a better place to live in." He lived in our city a few years ago for a short time.

HIBERNIA, the Hargrove place, three miles northeast from Townsville.

For notes on KEELINGS turn back to pages 221 to 232.

WILLIAM HENRY BOYD OF BELVIDERE

Lord Robert Boyd, died 1469, was a "most courteous, wise and kind knight, peer of Parliament and Governor of the realm, who negotiated a marriage between King James III, and a daughter of King Christian of Norway, and who, himself married King James' sister, Lady Mary."

This writer further states there are 228 Boyd Revolutionary Veterans, and many other things about this family.

Alexander Boyd, 1743-1801, known as "Alexander the Great" in the family, was one of four brothers who came from Kilmarnock, Ayreshire, Scotland to Virginia. He married Ann Dandridge Swepson (The Dandridge family is an illustrious Colonial family, Martha Dandridge being the widow Martha Custis, who married George Washington, President of the United States).

Alexander Boyd settled at Boydton, Virginia, and is considered the founder of that city. He had ten children. The third son, Richard Boyd married Panthea Burwell, they lived near Boydton, and having ten children.

The youngest of these, William Henry Boyd, 1819-1892, married in 1848, Susan Davis, who died soon, leaving no children. At that time, William H. Boyd bought and moved to Belviere, building the present house. This place is twelve miles northeast of Henderson, on the Drewry-Townsville road.

Around 1763, David Mitchell bought three tracts of land, all together 640 acres, which' being a part of this, he sold to Benjamin Belvidere. In 1810, he sold this as 680 acres to John Rust Eaton of Bloomsbury, an adjoining plantation. In 1848, a son, James W. Eaton, sold "Belvadier", as the deed spells it, to William H. Boyd. This place was mostly between Big and Little Nutbush Creeks, but later William H. Boyd added several hundred acres on the north, across Little Nutbush Creek.

William H. Boyd married, second, 1856, Sallie Virginia Daniel of Tranquility, which place is eight miles northwest of Oxford, North Carolina. At that time there was a lane about a half of a mile long, in front of Belvidere, and my mother said that when the "bride", who was her Aunt, rode into the place. there were sixteen white calves grazing in this lane. Also there was a row of sycamore trees on each side of the lane. Of these, there is one left, it being near the well.

Here they raised thirteen children, and there are many descendants in this section today.

Belvidere is now owned by a granddaughter of William H. Boyd, Mrs. Lucy Boyd Harris, of our City, and her mother and sisters live there.

Kittrell, when the railroad was run about 1838, George Kittrell gave the land for the station. He refused the honor, so they named it for his young son, George, who was father of our Joe and Bob Kittrell.

DREWRY MARROW OF GROVE HILL

There were many Marrows around the Revolutionary period in the "Marrows Chapel" section of our county, which church the family started in 1825.

From about 1850 to 1900, Drewry Marrow lived at Grove Hill, being the father of the late Joseph T. Marrow, of Henderson. J. P. Zollicoffer got that large boxwood bush at his home from this place. Lately, this farm of around 2000 acres was sold to Thomas Morgan. Mr. Morgan started life as a poor boy on a farm near here, joined the Navy, was assigned to help a Mr. Sperry, and is now President of the Sperry Gyroscope Co., of New York. A brother lives at Grove Hill, another has a new brick house nearby, and Mr. Morgan has built a bungalow for himself. Also an airplane landing field.

GROVE HILL, the Drewry Marrow home, now owned by Thomas A. Morgan, New York industrialist and native of this section.

THE MORROW (Marrow) FAMILY. DRURY MORROW was the son of DANIEL MORROW and his wife ELIZABETH. DANIEL MORROW died in 1817 and his widow, ELIZABETH in 1836, both leaving wills recorded in GRANVILLE COUNTY, and in which they named their children, including DRURY MORROW, mentioned above.

For abstracts of both these wills copied from the records at OXFORD, turn back to page 212.

SPOTTSWOOD BURWELL OF SPRING GROVE

The late Mr. Walter Burwell of our City had a book that tells much of this family. The name, as Boralle, Borel, Burrell and Burwell appears in England about the time of Richard III, and there are many old references to them.

For our Burwells, Edward Burwell of Bedfordshire, England, married Dorothy Bedel, and was granted land in Virginia from James Ist., in 1607. His son, Major Lewis Burwell, 1625-1658, settled about 1645, on Carter's Creek, Gloucester County Virginia, marrying Lucy Higginson, whose father was a Captain in the Colonial Army. Major Burwell was a Sergeant Major. One son went to Lake Erie, and has descendants in Canada.

Another son, Major Lewis Burwell, Jr., who died 1710, married first Abigal Smith, a niece of Nathaniel Bacon, Sr., who was uncle to Nathaniel Bacon of "Bacon's Rebellion", Abigal inheriting much land from this uncle.

A son. Lewis Burwell III, 1684-1744, married a Miss Armistead. Their son, Armistead Burwell, 1718-1754, started "Stoneland", in Mecklenburg County Virginia. He married Christian Blair, a daughter of Honorable John Blair, who was President of the Council and Acting Governor of Virginia.

A son of Armistead Burwell, Lewis Burwell, 1745-1800, was a Colonel in the Revolutionary Army. He married, first, 1768, Ann Spottswood, a daughter of Governor Spottswood. Colonel Lewis Burwell married, second, Elizabeth Harrison, a cousin of President Harrison. A son by this second marriage, Henry Harrison Burwell and his wife died from burns they received from the burning of "Stoneland" in 1815.

Colonel Lewis Burwell and his first wife, Ann Spottswood, had twelve children. Of these, "Ann Spottswood" was the second wife of Bishop Ravenscroft. "Panthea" married Richard Boyd, they being the parents of "William H. Boyd of Belvidere."

Another child, Spottswood Burwell, 1785-1855, married Mary Green Marshall, they living at "Spring Grove", on the Townesville-Hargrove Road. The house burned some years ago, so, lately, a tenant house has been built at the location. They had nine children, and many descendants, some of whom are listed on charts I have of this family.

NEW DISCOVERIES, CORRECTIONS AND AFTER-THOUGHTS

It has taken the compiler TWO YEARS to write this book, which contains 700 pages. The research necessary has taken a still larger toll in time and effort, before a line could be written. Being unusually compact the material produced would have made three large volumes in the ordinary type used in most books. Naturally, where so much material has been handled, it has been wholly impossible to prevent many errors creeping into the manuscript. Also, while the work was being transcribed, the research campaign continued ahead, resulting in new discoveries, after it was too late to insert them in the text. Likewise new ideas were born of the intense concentration centered on the subjects treated. It is impossible to detail all of the errors, correct all the mistakes, or insert an adequate recital of the new discoveries, at this point. But following herewith, are a few random notes pertaining to these matters, to which the attention of the student and reader is here called, as a matter of fairness to both the reader and the author:

Page 83. There is a line at the bottom of this page attempting to correct the sketch of COL. FREDERICK JONES, in which it is stated that JOHN COTTEN married MARTHA GODWIN instead of MARTHA JONES. The truth is that there are deeds extant and shewn in Hathaway's Register that prove beyond question that JOHN COTTEN did marry MARTHA JONES, daughter of FREDERICK JONES, and in Isle of Wight County there is an early marriage record shewing also that JOHN COTTEN married MARTHA GODWIN. John Cotten was twice married, first to MARTHA GODWIN and second to MARTHA JONES.

Pages 98-99. Since writing the notes on the LANE, LANIER and LINDSAY families on the two pages the writer has made many new discoveries on all of them and the sketches should be rewritten to include them.

Page 114. Many new discoveries and a wealth of new material on the MOORE FAMILY has come to hand, and much can be added to the MULKEY sketch also.

Page 146. Much new material has been found on the ROBERTSON (ROBINSON) family, which is referred to in the last half of this volume. It dove-tails however with the facts set out in this sketch so far as it goes, but expands it very widely. We hope to rewrite this family history later. JOHN, the father of GEN. JAMES ROBERTSON of Nashville, Tennessee, and the WATAUGA settlement, undoubtedly spelled the name ROBINSON, or permitted it to be so spelled on the records. This discovery leads to the identification of much new material about the family, which it is too late to remedy in this volume.

Page 213. The sketch of the "Daniel Families of Granville County" appearing on this page is erroneous in several respects. In a footnote on page 242 an ineffectual attempt is made to correct this error. It will take a new account in full to clear up this error, at some future time.

Page 224. In connection with the (5) WILLIAM HENDERSON family dealt with at the bottom of this page, the reader is directed to turn to page 486 for additional data on this particular branch of the HENDERSON FAMILY, on that and pages 487, 488 and 489, all of which dove-tails with the first account.

Page 251. Much new material has been discovered and gathered by the writer since the material about the HARRISON FAMILY on this and several succeeding pages were written and particularly that on pages 258, 259, 260 and 261 were written, which should all be revamped to conform to these new findings, so far as the earliest families mentioned are concerned. The later tables are correct, but the earlier ancestrial lines will vary considerably in any later accounts.

Page 274. Much new material has been found on the MEMUCAN HUNT family, which is intensely interesting. No room to detail it here.

Page 277. "1. ROBERT LANIER" on this page, it has been found, married a daughter of REV. HENRY PATILLO, from which marriage sprang many descendants, something the writer did not find until too late to make the corrections and additions. I think from this marriage came the LANIERS of West Point, Georgia.

Page 280. Richard Bullock, shown near the bottom of this page was not "daughter" of course, but a "son" of Edward Bullock.

Page 270. Peter Bennett lived on TAR RIVER and not HAW RIVER as here inadvertently stated.

Page 260. Jemimah Jenkins was a daughter and not a son of Thomas Jenkins.

Page 278. The account of "The Bullocks of Granville" starting on this page, while in the main correct as far as it goes, should be rewritten now to include more about the descendants of a DAVID BULLOCK, revolutionary soldier, who settled in North Carolina, in EDGECOMBE COUNTY, as early as 1768, where he left a will in 1782, naming twelve children. Mr. Hugh Buckner Johnston, my Edgecombe County authority is convinced that he came from Hanover County and should have been included in the Granville group of BULLOCKS. Mr. Johnston has gathered a great deal of material pertaining to the Bullocks of this branch from the Tarborough and other records, which is most valuable and enlightening. In addition the writer has found a number of other Bullock data in Isle of Wight and the lower Eastern Virginia Counties that perhaps belongs to the Granville families lines, and the whole Bullock set-up should be re-written and re-arranged to include all of these.

Page 289. "The Harris Family of Granville County" which begins on this page should all be rewritten; first, because of a wealth of new material that has been found, and second, because the early ancestry here given may be erroneous in many particulars, though not wholly so. The BUCKNER HARRIS (No. 50) in the Harris Chart on page 290, we have since discovered, married NANCY EARLY of the famous Early family of Virginia, and had four sons, EARLY HARRIS who married MARY HARRISON (see page 255), WILEY P. HARRIS, CHARLES WALTON HARRIS, WILLIAM CRAWFORD HARRIS, and EARLY HARRIS and MARY HARRISON were the parents of JUDGE WILEY P. HARRIS, of Mississippi, a member of the Constitutional convention of Mississippi in 1751, and a distinguished jurist of his State, who died at Jackson, Mississippi, Dec. 3, 1891. Other material could be added, so that a revamping of the Harris chronology would make it most interesting.

Page 305. "Index to Names" for pages 193 to 304 inclusive is defective in this, that the name JONES, which appears throughout the entire text of the pages given, is inadvertently omitted altogether from the Index, which is to be regretted.

Page 379. The map on this page, after a thorough going over the history of the section shewn, turns out to be erroneous, so far as the boundary lines of BLADEN COUNTY is concerned. The balance of the map is in accordance with the facts. For a correct map of BLADEN COUNTY see Map No. 24, page 633.

Page 471. Attention is called to the list of the children of 17 JAMES CUNNINGHAM, in which the son DAVID is listed with the statement that he was the David who died in York County, Virginia, in 1719/20. This is wrong, both in the list and in the last note on the page, which erroneously restates the same thing. The DAVID who died in York in 1720, was a brother of 17 James Cunningham and not his son. Since writing this account of the CUNNINGHAM FAMILY, beginning on page 464, many new angles have been discovered, which will necessitate a re-writing of these accounts at some future time, and in order to include DANIEL and JAMES CUNNINGHAM, possible brothers of the WILLIAM CUNNINGHAM named as the emigrant ancestor of this family in the account presented.

Page 477. On this page starts an account of the "BARRY AND MOORE FAMILIES". New discoveries changing the whole set-up of these MOORES have been found since the article was written, so far as the MOORE FAMILY is concerned. In the main, the family units do not need changing except as to the children of CHARLES MOORE and MARGARET BARRY. Some of the children given to this couple belong to EPHRAIM MOORE on page 492, and it will be necessary to re-write the entire account at some future time, in order to get the arrangement of the family properly allocated, and in doing this a new phase of the MacLEAN family has been discovered with numerous ramifications that spread out over the country, with many surprising connections hitherto never brought out in any genealogical account of these families.

Page 505. A correspondent has dug up material and sent us in relation to a JONATHAN POLK of North Carolina that he believes belongs to the Polk family here presented. Any change in our account of the Polk family, still seems unnecessary notwithstanding that material, which we are not convinced belongs to the Polks of Mecklenburg. No effort was made by us to attempt a widely inclusive account of the Polks, so that mention was not made of a number of its distinguished members, who are well identified in the history of the country. Space in a book of this character must be conserved in order to give the volume a wider variety of interesting families, and long lists of descendants shortened as much as possible.

Page 532. One of the most common errors which it is difficult to avoid and carrying genealogical dates is the use of figures designating the centuries. In several instances the writer has inadvertently used 1700 for 1600. Scarcely a genealogical book of any kind has been able to avoid this class of errors. On page 532 in the last line of the second paragraph David Merryws will is stated to have been proven in Lower Norfolk about 1789, when the intention was to say 1689.

Page 536. This is an error of similar import to the one immediately preceding, in which the last will and testament of STEPHEN HORSEY is said to have been in 1772, when the facts are that he died and it was probated in 1672 just 100 years earlier. It was the intention to so state in the text, but the inadvertance happened, as it so often does in such recordings.

Page 545. In the "Index to pages 313 to 536" there is another omission of a family name, without which no history of the "Signers" of the Mecklenburg Declaration, or of Mecklenburg County could be written. The name omitted from the index is MORRISON. One of the signers was Neill Morrison, and the name Morrison appears innumerable times throughout this section of the volume. How it was omitted the writer is unable to understand, but it certainly does not appear.

Other parts of this book not reviewed in the foregoing notes may likewise contain some such erroneous inadvertances, but efforts will be made to hold them to a minimum.

INDEX TO NORTH CAROLINA MAPS

ALAMANCE COUNTY from 1849 to 1947. Map 19,p 600
ALBEMARLE PRECINCT-COUNTY before
   settlement about 1650............Map 37.. 662
   The original precinct............Map 1...560
   Divided into 3 precincts 1671-84.Map 2...569
   Four precincts after 1684........Map 3...571
ALEXANDER COUNTY 1847 to date........Map 42...666
                                   Map 43...667
ALLEGHANEY COUNTY 1859 to date......Map 43...667
ANSON COUNTY when established 1849..Map 41...665
   Same from 1753 to 1762............Map 50...670
   Same from 1762 to 1778............Map 44...668
   Same from 1778 to 1789............Map 45...668
   Same from 1789 to 1842............Map 45...668
   Same from 1842 to 1947............Map 44...668
ARCHDALE PRECINCT 1705 to 1712......Map 6...587
ASHE COUNTY 1799 to 1841............Map 39...664
   Same as at present -1947........Map 42...666
AVERY COUNTY 1911 to 1947..........Map 42...666

BATH PRECINCT from ca 1671 to 1705 Map 37...662
BEAUFORT PRECINCT from 1712-1738...Map 21...601
BEAUFORT COUNTY from 1738 to 1760..Map 23...632
                                   Map 52...689
BEAUFORT COUNTY 1760 to 1947........Map 23...632
BERKLEY PRECINCT 1671 to 1684......Map 2...569
BERTIE PRECINCT 1722-1735..........Map 8...591
   Same less EDGECOMBE 1725-1741....Map 13...598
BERTIE COUNTY 1735-1741............Map 13...598
   Same from 1741 to 1759............Map 10...592
   Same from 1759 to 1947............Map 8...591
   As an Original County in 1738....Map 52...689
BLADEN PRECINCT from 1734 to 1738..Map 38...663
BLADEN COUNTY from 1738 to 1749....Map 39...663
   Same from 1749 to 1753............Map 41...665
   Same from 1753 to 1754............Map 41...665
   Same from 1754 to 1786............Map 26...633
   Same from 1808 to 1947............Map 23...632
   Same - part given to ORANGE Co...Map 41...665
   Same - part given to WAKE Co.....Map 27...650
   Same as an Original County 1738..Map 52...689
BRUNSWICK COUNTY as established 1764 Map 33...654
BUNCOMBE COUNTY 1791 to 1808.......Map 51...670
   Same - as in 1792................Map 40...664
BURKE COUNTY as (1st census)1790..Map 43...667
   Same as in 1947..................Map 42...665
BUTE COUNTY (Extinct) 1764-1779...Map 15...599
CABARRUS COUNTY 1792-See Mecklen-
   burg, page.....................................369
CALDWELL as in 1841..............Map 42...666
CAROLA (See Albemarle)..........Map 3...571
CARTERET PRECINCT 1671-1684.......Map 2...569
CARTERET PRECINCT (No. 2) in 1722.Map 36...654
   Same............................Map 38...663
   Same............................Map 23...632
CARTERET COUNTY from 1722-1947....Map 52...689
CASWELL COUNTY 1777-1791..........Map 19...600
   Same from 1791 to 1947...........Map 19...600
CATAWBA COUNTY Est 1842 to 1947...Map 40...664
CHATHAM COUNTY 1770 to 1907.......Map 19...600
CHEROKEE COUNTY as Est. in 1839...Map 40...664
CHOWAN PRECINCT 1684 to 1722......Map 7...588
   Same............................Map 5...580
   Same............................Map 3...571
CHOWAN COUNTY as an Original
           County in 1738........Map 52...689
CLAY COUNTY from 1861 to 1947.....Map 40...664
CLEAVELAND COUNTY 1841-1947.......Map 40...664
COLUMBUS COUNTY 1808 to 1947......Map 25...633
CRAVEN PRECINCT 1712 to 1738.....Map 38...663
CRAVEN COUNTY as an Original County..Map 52...689
   CRAVEN COUNTY 1738 to 1742......Map 38...663
   Same from 1742 to 1746..........Map 21...601
   Same 1746 to 1872...............Map 21...601
   Same 1872 to 1947...............Map 23...632

CUMBERLAND COUNTY 1754 to 1784....Map 24...633
   Same from 1784 to 1855..........Map 25...633
CURRITUCK PRECINCT 1684 to 1738..Map 3...571
CURRITUCK COUNTY as original
           County..................Map 52...689

DARE COUNTY 1870 to 1947..........Map 23...632
DOBBS COUNTY (Now Extinct) from
   1758 to 1779....................Map 27...650
   Same and for same dates.........Map 30...652
   Same County 1779-1791...........Map 29...651
DUPLIN COUNTY 1749-1784...........Map 33...654
   Same county 1784 to 1947........Map 35...654
DURHAM COUNTY from 1881 to 1947...Map 20...600

EDGECOMBE COUNTY 1735 to 1746.....Map 13...598
   Same county 1746 to 1758........Map 14...598
   Same county 1758 to 1777........Map 16...599
   Same County 1777 to 1855........Map 16...599
   Same County 1855 to 1947........Map 13...598
   Same............................Map 26...648
   Same as Original County 1738...Map 52...689

FORSYTH COUNTY 1849 to 1947......Map 43...667
FRANKLIN COUNTY 1779 and 1808....Map 26...648
FRANKLIN COUNTY 1808 to 1947.....Map 17...599

GASTON COUNTY 1848-1947..........Map 40...664
GATES COUNTY 1779-1947...........Map 12...593
GLASGOW COUNTY (Now Extinct)
   1791-1799.......................Map 28...651
GRAHAM COUNTY 1872 to 1947.......Map 40...654
GRANVILLE COUNTY 1745-1753.......Map 22...602
GRANVILLE COUNTY 1764-1881.......Map 15...599
   Same county 1881 to 1947........Map 19...599
GREENE COUNTY 1799 to 1947.......Map 22...601
   Same in 1808...................Map 23...633
GUILFORD COUNTY 1770-1779........Map 42...666
   Same in 1st census 1790........Map 43...667
   Same from 1779 to 1785..........Map 49...670
   Same 1785 to 1947...............Map 49...670
   Part taken from Orange in 1770.Map 42...666

HALIFAX COUNTY 1758-1774.........Map 14...598
   Same after 1774.................Map 15...599
   Same............................Map 26...648
HARNETT COUNTY since 1855........Map 25...633
HAYWOOD COUNTY as Est. in 1808...Map 40...664
HERTFORD COUNTY 1759 to 1779.....Map 11...592
HENDERSON COUNTY 1836............Map 40...664
HYDE COUNTY 1911 to 1947.........Map 23...633
HYDE PRECINCT 1712 to 1738.......Map 23...632
   Same............................Map 21...601
HYDE COUNTY as an original
           County in 1738.........Map 52...689
   Same from 1738 to 1870..........Map 23...632

IREDELL COUNTY at 1st census 1790.Map 43...667

JACKSON COUNTY in 1851............Map 40...664
JOHNSTON COUNTY 1746 to 1753......Map 22...602
   Same County 1753-1758...........Map 31...652
   Same County 1758-1770...........Map 32...652
   Same County 1770-1855...........Map 27...650
   Same County in 1855.............Map 26...648
JONES COUNTY 1779-1947...........Map 23...632

LEE COUNTY 1907-1947.............Map 19...600
   Same-parts from Chatham and
       Cumberland shown..........Map 25...633
LENOIR COUNTY in 1791 until now..Map 28...651
LINCOLN COUNTY in 1779...........Map 47...659
   Same in the year 1790...........Map 40...664
MACON COUNTY in 1828.............Map 40...664

MADISON COUNTY of 1851.....................Map 40...664	ROWAN COUNTY 1753-1770................Map 42...666
MARTIN COUNTY 1774 to 1947..............Map 23...632	Same County 1770-1777.............Map 42...666
McDOWELL COUNTY of 1842....................Map 40...664	Same County 1753-1770.............Map 50...670
MECKLENBURG COUNTY 1762-1768........Map 46...669	Same County in 1790...............Map 43...667
MECKLENBURG COUNTY 1768 - 1791......Map ___...380	RUTHERFORD COUNTY 1779.................Map 47...669
Same.........1791-1842........................380	Same County in year 1790.........Map 40...664
Same 1842-1947...............................380	Same County in 1791-1841........Map 51...670
MONTGOMERY COUNTY in 1790..............Map 45...668	Same County 1841-1947............Map 40...664
MOORE COUNTY 1784 to date................Map 25...633	
	SAMPSON COUNTY 1784....................Map 35...654
NASH COUNTY 1777-1855.......................Map 16...599	SCOTLAND COUNTY 1899...................Map 44...668
NASH COUNTY 1855-1947.......................Map 26...648	STANLEY COUNTY 1841....................Map 44...668
NEW HANOVER PRECINCT 1729-1734.....Map 38...663	SHAFTSBURY PRECINCT 1671-1684.....Map 5...580
Precinct 1734 to 1738...............Map 33...654	Same Precinct...................Map 2...569
NEW HANOVER COUNTY 1738-1749........Map 33...654	Same Precinct...................Map 7...588
Same 1749-1764...............................Map 33...654	SURRY COUNTY 1770-1777.................Map 42...666
Same 1764-1875...............................Map 35...654	Same County in 1790.............Map 43...667
Same 1875-1947...............................Map 34...654	Same County in 1947.............Map 43...667
NORTHAMPTON COUNTY 1741-1759.......Map 10...592	SWAIN COUNTY 1871......................Map 40...664
Same County 1759-1947.............Map 11...592	STOKES COUNTY 1789-1947...............Map 40...664
ONSLOW PRECINCT 1734-1738................Map 33...654	TRANSYLVANIA COUNTY 1861..............Map 40...664
ONSLOW COUNTY 1738-1947..................Map 33...654	TRYON COUNTY (Extinct) 1768-1779..Map 48...669
Same as an Original County 1738 Map 33...654	TYRRELL PRECINCT 1729-1738...........Map 9...591
ORANGE COUNTY 1753-1770..................Map 19...590	TYRRELL COUNTY 1738-1774.............Map 9...591
Same county 1770-1777................Map 20...600	Same County since 1870..........Map 23...632
Same County 1777-1849................Map 19...600	
Same County 1849-1947................Map 19...600	UNION COUNTY 1842-1947................Map 44...668
Same- part given to Wake............Map 27...650	VANCE COUNTY 1881-1947................Map 18...599
PANTICOUGH PRECINCT 1696-1705.........Map 3...571	WAKE COUNTY 1770-1881.................Map 27...650
PAMLICO COUNTY 1872-1947..................Map 23...632	Same County showing parts taken
PASQUOTANK PRECINCT 1684-1729........Map 3...571	Orange and Bladen Map 27...650
Same as Original County 1738....Map 52...689	Same County part given DURHAM Map 27...650
PENDER COUNTY 1875-1947..................Map 34...654	WARREN COUNTY 1779-1947..............Map 17...599
PERQUIMANS PRECINCT 1684-1729.......Map 3...571	WASHINGTON COUNTY since 1799.......Map 23...632
PERQUIMANS COUNTY (As Orig) 1738..Map 52...689	WATAUGA COUNTY 1849-1947............Map 43...667
PERSON COUNTY 1791-1947..................Map 19...600	WAYNE COUNTY 1779......................Map 28...651
PITT COUNTY 1760-1947.....................Map 23...632	WICKHAM PRECINCT 1705-1712.........Map 6...587
Same as in 1790.........................Map 26...648	WILKES COUNTY 1777.....................Map 43...667
POLK COUNTY since 1855....................Map 40...664	Same County 1799-1841...........Map 39...664
	Same County in 1790.............Map 43...667
RANDOLPH COUNTY 1779-1790.............Map 43...667	Same County 1947................Map 43...667
RICHMOND COUNTY in 1790.................Map 45...668	WILSON COUNTY 1855-1947..............Map 26...648
ROBESON COUNTY 1786........................Map 25...663	
Same - part given to Hoke 1911..Map 25...663	YADKIN COUNTY 1850-1947..............Map 43...667
ROCKINGHAM COUNTY 1785..................Map 43...667	Yancey County 1833.....(to date)...Map 42...666
Same in the year 1790.............Map 49...670	

SOURCES AND RESOURCES

PAGES 559 TO 700

S O U R C E S :

ALLEN'S ANNALS OF HAYWOOD COUNTY, N. C....680
ARTHUR'S HISTORY OF WESTERN N. C....674...680
BELL'S "OLD FREE STATE"....................620
BODDIE'S 17TH CENTURY ISLE OF WIGHT
    COUNTY, VIRGINIA........ 566, 567
    608, 614, 616, 618, 625, 629, 631..640
CHAPMAN'S ABSTRACTS OF THE RECORDS OF
    ISLE OF WIGHT COUNTY, VIRGINIA 616.631
"CHARLOTTE WHIG" FILES OF.........659....661
"CHARLOTTE JOURNAL", FILES OF.............659
"CHARLOTTE OBSERVER" from FILES OF........661
CHOWAN COUNTY (N.C.) MARRIAGE INDEX.......586
DODD'S "THE OLD SOUTH".........563........589
FLEET'S COLONIAL ABSTRACTS OF VA....608...623
FOTHERGILL'S WESTMORELAND WILLS...........612
GEORGIA RECORDS (D. A. R. COLLECTIONS)
    VOL. 1, 645, 646; VOL. 2, 645,VOL 3.644
GEORGIA RECORDS by MRS. DAVIDSON, 638,
    643, 644.............................655
HATHAWAY'S N. C. HIST. & GEN. REGISTER
    562, 563, 564, 567, 568, 570, 573
    574, 575, 576, 581, 586, 589, 590
    596, 603, 631, 634, 635, 638, 640
    641, 643, 647........................655

HARLEE'S "KINFOLKS"....................... 685
HENNINGS' VIRGINIA STATUTES............... 629
ISLE OF WIGHT COUNTY RECORDS......613.... 631
MARTIN'S HISTORY OF NORTH CAROLINA........ 572
MASON'S GLOUCESTER COUNTY (VA) RECORDS... 608
NORTH CAROLINA COLONIAL RECORDS....570.... 627
NUGENT'S "CAVALIERS AND PIONEERS" OF
    VIRGINIA...........................564,
    565, 567, 568, 608-614, 616 -622,
    639, 641, 653, 655.................. 658
PASCHALL'S HISTORY OF THE NORTH CAROLINA
    BAPTISTS............................ 628
STARR, EMMETT'S HISTORY OF THE CHEROKEES... 647
SAUNDER'S VA. EARLY SETTLERS OF ALABAMA... 618
VIRGINIA COUNTY RECORDS................... 564
VALENTINE PAPERS.......................... 617
WESTERN DEMOCRAT, OF CHARLOTTE, N. C.
    ITEMS FROM OLD FILES................ 660
WILKES COUNTY, GEORGIA RECORDS, COMPILED
    BY MRS. DAVIDSON...........638...... 643
WILLIAM & MARY QUARTERLY, VOL. 7.......... 620
WILLIAM & MARY QUARTERLY, VOL. 6.......... 656
WOOD'S HISTORY OF ALBEMARLE COUNTY,
    VIRGINIA............................ 637

NOTE: The above are just a few references cited in the text on the pages indicated. To publish here a BIBLIOGRAPHY of the contents of this entire volume would simply require a catalogue of the compiler's private library and documents of several thousand items, which would be tiresome reading - a condition better to be avoided in a book of this kind.

RESOURCES - COLLABORATORS

This volume is not the work of just one person.

The contents represents the combined efforts of many persons. The compiler is responsible for the errors and mistakes and takes the blame for them, while most of the credit for the good parts of the book should be given to the small army of COLLABORATORS mentioned below, who by correspondence and otherwise placed in the hands of the writer the material that goes to make up the valuable features of what is printed here. Not all of those who rendered assistance are included in this list, but the author is proud of them all and especially of those mentioned.

MAJ. GEN. JAMES BREAINER ALLISON, Retired, of WASHINGTON, D. C. and YORK, South Carolina, author of "THE ALLISON FAMILY" 1941, and "JAMES MEEK and SUSANNAH BYERS",1942. GEN. ALLISON is the grandson of ROBERT TURNER ALLISON and MARTHA BURNETT CLINTON, and the Great Grandson of HUGH ALLISON (will in 1799). The writer is indebted to General Allison for copies of his rare volumes and other data.

MISS ZELLA ARMSTRONG, Chattanooga, Tennessee, the beloved and outstanding Tennessee genealogist, whose sparkling letters and volumes "NOTABLE SOUTHERN FAMILIES" have been drawn upon freely by the compiler, at her gracious invitation. She is the possessor of an inexhaustable store of rich material and has been an inspiration to the author of this book.

MR. H. E. C. (Red Buck) BRYANT, of MATTHEWS, N. C. whose articles in the Charlotte Observer has added to the writer's "resources" most materially. Mr. Bryant is a member of the famous Gridiron Club, of Washington, D. C. and a famous writer.

MRS. BLANCHE ADAMS-CHAPMAN, of Smithfield, Virginia, author of the "WILLS AND ADMINISTRATIONS" of Elizabeth City County, Virginia, and "Abstracts of Isle of Wight County", from whose work many valuable genealogical facts have been gleaned and used herein.

HON. WILL H. DANIEL, attorney, of Huntington, West Virginia, one of the moving spirits and leaders in the Historical and Genealogical circles of his State. His letters and generous contributions have greatly enriched this volume. May he live long and prosper.

DR. JOSEPH D. EGGLESTON, of Hampden-Sydney and Farmville (Prince Edward County) Virginia. We have a priceless collection of letters and genealogical material gathered by Dr. Eggleston, during the years, and which he has sent us from time to time. We are proud to number him among our collaborators, and it is from such "resources" as this on which many statements relating to that section of Virginia are based. They can be depended upon.

MRS. JEROME A. ESKER, Washington, D. C. one of the balance wheels of the Daughters of the American Revolution, officer in the National Genealogical Society and a regular contributor to the Virginia Magazine of History and Biography. She is a busy individual, who, however, has found time to write a few letters and furnish some valuable material to this work, or which has been drawn upon by the author.

HON. BEVERLY FLEET, of the old, old town of RICHMOND, VIRGINIA, ancient records expert and profound student of early Virginiana, whose Virginia Colonial Abstracts have centered the bright lights into the dark vaults of forgotten corners and brought forth things that were all but lost in the mists of antiquity. He lives and breathes the atmosphere of the "ancient planters" as if he had known them personally. The footprints of his ancestor, HENRY FLEETE, have been followed across Virginia and Maryland and his "Abstracts" constitute an oasis in the desert of research. Here is one of our real "resources" in the time of dire need. Hail to this collaborator!

MRS. NATHANIEL GIST GEE, of GREENWOOD, S. C. A tireless worker, a civic genius, and a true daughter of the "Old South". Many a member of the "Lost Tribes" have been restored to the family fold through her efforts. In our files are her abstracts of the old records of LAURENS DISTRICT and COUNTY, which, if published, would prove a treasure trove to research workers. They are the key that unlocks many a closed door to the average researcher, and are among our most treasured "resources". She has never failed to answer a call.

MISS CLARA C. HARRIS, of CONCORD, N. C. She is a descendant of the ancient HARRIS FAMILY, of early Mecklenburg and Cabarrus County, which has no less than two "Signers" of the Mecklenburg Declaration to its credit. She has given unstinted devotion to her study of this interesting tribe - and its allies. Much that is said in this volume is founded upon the documentary evidence that came from her letter files.

HON. FRANCIS BURTON HARRISON, of Charlottesville, Virginia; one time Governor General of the Philipines, under Woodrow Wilson; descendant of the "Skimeno Harrisons" and co-editor, with his brother, HON. FAIRFAX HARRISON, of that volume; author of that most valuable series of articles on the early Harrisons of Virginia, recently published in the Virginia Magazine of History & Biography; world traveler and industrialist; diplomat and statesman. Our BURTON HARRISON FILE is a rich storehouse of "resource" and his collaborating aid has been a source of pride and joy to the writer.

DR. THOMAS PERRIN HARRISON, SR., educator and scholar, now retired and resting on his honors at ASHVILLE? NORTH CAROLINA. To the writer he has been a link between the present and the past, and his letters have always teemed with rare items that needed to be preserved, and will be. He is a descendant of James Harrison and Elizabeth Hampton, with a blend of the ancient family of EARLES, of South Carolina, whose progeny now resides in many of the States of the "Old South". To him we make our bow.

MR. W. S. HENDERSON, Davidson, N. C. Mr. Henderson's contribution to the pages of this book have added no little to the story of Mecklenburg and Lincoln Counties. Sketches of BETHEL and GILIEAD CHURCHES were much enhanced in value through Mr. Henderson's generosity and enterprise. He has made no pretense of being a historian, but his contributions have great value.

MRS. HALE HOUTS, of Kansas City, Missouri, a leader in the Daughters of the American Revolution, and an earnest seeker after facts about early families in the South, has been a source of great value to the writer of these lines. Her file in our correspondence corner is fat with rich and wealthy material. Thanks.

MRS. CASTRA DANDRIDGE HENLEY HOWARD, daughter of the Henleys and Dandridges, great grand-daughter of ALEXANDER SPOTTSWOOD MOORE and the wife of an old school mate of the compiler, who now lives in BLOUNT COUNTY, TENNESSEE, at Marysville. Her mother "Aunt Kittie" Henley was a nationally known genealogical authority and author, and she, herself, has been so busy working as a leader in the Daughters of the American Revolution she has had little time for correspondence, but she says much in a few words, and her collection of letters are priceless on genealogical and historical matters.

HUGH BUCKNER JOHNSTON, native of WILSON, N. C. and historian for that county in the Old North State; is Geographer for the National Genealogical Society, and at the present writing absent temporarily at or near Santiago de Chile on an educational mission. A young man with a keen eye and mind for genealogical subjects, and a long life before him, his is a bright and shining future. His sketch of WILSON COUNTY herein is by-lined for recognition. His absolute accuracy dominates his writing. In this work it may be truthfully said he has been our "Chief of Staff". Here is hoping for his early return to the States and a resumption of his genealogical activities.

MRS. J. M. JONES, of EDENTON, N. C. Mrs. Jones is the grand-daughter of the late J. R. B. HATHAWAY, founder and publisher of the North Carolina Historical & Genealogical Register, upon which, it may be stated, a large part of this volume is founded. Like her grandsire Mrs. Jones takes an intense interest in the field of research and has been of much encouragement to the writer.

MRS. EDITH (ZEBULON) JUDD, of AUBURN, Alabama. Descended from the HIGH and HOYSTER families of GRANVILLE and WAKE COUNTIES, in North Carolina, Mrs. Judd has been one of our most active lieutenants in that particular field of research. She is active in Alabama in all civic affairs and leader in the D. A. R. Only the excessive demands upon her time from various sources have curtailed her labors in behalf of this work.

MISS MIRAM LANDRUM, of Austin, Texas, a descendant of the Earles and Landrums of upper S. C. Her constant and untiring efforts in behalf of the completion of this work has been an inspiration.

MISS LAURA LUTTRELL, Knoxville, Tennessee, an active member of the East Tennessee Historical Society. Miss Luttrell has been an unfailing source of information, and through the East Tennessee Publications and the State Historical Magazine has contributed much information suitable for use and reference in this volume.

MRS. JOHN TROTWOOD MOORE, of Nashville, Tennessee the beloved archivist and librarian, has been often called upon and has never failed to respond when help or information was wanted or needed by the writer. Her always dependable assistance has been most valuable to this effort.

MRS. STELLA (W. M.) REEDER, of Elizabethton, Tennessee, has for several years been an active "field worker" for the writer, in locating old graves, cemeteries and tombstone inscriptions throughout ALABAMA, TENNESSEE and the CAROLINAS. Without her co-operation and aid the merits of this work would undoubtedly have suffered. Mr. Marvin Reeder, her husband and their sprightly daughter, Miss Jane Reeder, commandeered by our representative, have responded when called upon; have torn their clothes, muddied their shoes, burned up their gasoline and worn out their automobile tires, helping their mother in her determined quest for information gathered and printed in this volume. They are certainly entitled to mention as aides in this work. All of them deserve the equivolent of a Congressional medal from the genealogical fans who have already reported finding the records that admitted them to membership in the patriotic organizations they have since joined on the data found by our "collaborating Reeders". Many, many thanks!

DR. THADEUS BROCKETT RICE, of GREENSBORO, GA. The assistance rendered this compiler by DR. T. B. RICE extends back for so many years and covers such a wide range of investigation and research that it is hard to say definitely when it all began. The Rice home in GREENSBORO, GEORGIA, has been used as a kind of "way station" by Mrs. Ray and myself for at least a part of two decades. This collaborator is beyond question the greatest living Georgia Historian. He is a grandson of ROBERT McALPIN WILLIAMSON, called the "Patrick Henry of Texas" in his day, and his good wife, MAMIE (BOWEN) RICE is a real daughter of the Republic of Texas. It is likely that the RICE PAPERS in the writer's files will eventually be preserved in the Archives of Texas.

PETER BRYCE SEARCY, of Austin, Texas, and a native of TUSCALOOSA, ALABAMA, is an outstanding artist. On pages 264 and 265 of this volume is a reproduction of the Peter Bryce Searcy Map of Colonial Granville County. The idea set the pace for the inclusion of many other maps of North Carolina areas to be found herein. P. B. Searcy is the Great Grt. Grandson of REUBEN SEARCY, one of the first Sheriffs of GRANVILLE COUNTY, N. C.

MRS. ESTELLE SEAWELL, of Kershaw, South Carolina has been furnishing the writer material for many long years. It was Mrs. Seawell, who preserved the issue of the CHARLOTTE OBSERVER containing so much valuable genealogical matter about the people of that section, which has been reproduced in this volume. Other material from her stack of preserved letters in our files have been a souce of information of much value.

REV. E. M. SHARP, of New Albany, Mississippi, is pastor of the Methodist Church at that place. Being a minister, and subject to being "shuffled" by his Bishop and the Conference, Dr. Sharp has lived in various sections of the State; has a wide acquaintance, and is a student not only of theology, but of genealogy and history. Light on many old Southern and pre-revolutionary families has been collected by Dr. Sharp, who has generously furnished much of this to the writer, fully documented. For a minister he is a live wire.

CHARLES E. SPARKS, Route 2, UNION, S. C. This man lives on the very ground where many of the persons mentioned in this volume once resided. What is more, he knows a lot about them and their histories. His map of the area is treasured by the writer, and his letters are most informative and useful as reference.

MRS. MARION HARRISON (MRS. HENRY) SCHIFFERS, of San Antonio, Texas. Mrs. Schiffers is a real genealogist, interested in a number of families having their origin in Virginia. Her file fairly sparkles with valuable data she has discovered.

MRS. JULIAN S. STARR, SR., Lancaster, S. C. is a most well versed person on the early families of her section, particularly on the WAXHAW CHURCH SETTLEMENT. Her correspondence is prized most highly.

MRS. HELEN MONTAGUE TURNER, of NEWPORT NEWS, Virginia, has a wide range of genealogical information on early Virginia families, which she gives away to her friends and to this writer. Hers is a most interesting letter file to us.

HON. JOHN BULLOCK WATKINS, of HENDERSON, N. C. Mr. Watkins is the author of a little volume "HISTORIC VANCE COUNTY", which, by his generosity, has furnished several pages for this volume. His permission to use this is greatly appreciated.

ALMA DANIEL (MRS. T. I.) WESTON, of COLUMBIA, S. C. has been a "feeder" of information to the compiler for many years. She is a sister of the late DR. DANIEL of S. C.

SAMUEL WHEELER WORTHINGTON, of WILSON, N. C. But for the enthusiasm of this collaborator this book might never have appeared.

ANCIENT "CEDAR GROVE" CEMETERY, NEAR NEW BERN

NAME INDEX

PAGES 559 TO 700

ABERNATHY 659, 660
ABEY 597
ACHESON 644
ADAIR 679, 685
ADAMS 567, 587, 657, 681
ADDISON 597
AKEHURST 574
ALBERTSON 575
ALEXANDER 597, 642, 659, 660, 674, 676, 677, 679, 682, 687.
ALFORD 643
ALLEN 639, 586, 611, 659, 677, 683, 686
ALLINGNOW 596
ALLISON 659, 681
ALSTON 593, 618, 625, 640, 641, 659, 676, 679, 680, 683
AMBROSE 593, 594
ANDERSON 568, 660
APPLEWHITE 616, 622
AP THOMAS 609
ARCHDALE 563
ARCHDEACON 596
ARDRY 660, 661
ARMFIELD 680
ARMISTEAD 685, 696
ARMSTRONG 567, 674, 677, 679, 686
ARNALL 655
ARNOLD 575, 685
ARRINGTON 683
ARTHUR 595
ASBELL 634
ASHE 674, 683
ASHFIELD 643, 645
ASHFORD 675
ASHLEY 586, 597
ASKEW 616, 624, 629, 682
ATKINS 590
ATKINSON 684
ATTAWAY 568
AVERY 671, 675

BACHELOR 587
BACON 622, 696
BADGER 677
BAIHAM 593
BAILEY 568, 574, 596, 627, 685, 688 (See BAYLEY)
BAIRD 656
BAKER 565, 573, 657, 679, 681, 682
BALL 597, 678
BALLARD 594
BANKS 567, 587
BARBER 594, 597
BARCKHURST 608
BARCLIFT 568, 575
BARCOCK 574
BARCROFT 641
BARD 564
BARDEN 596
BARFIELD 658
BARKER 566, 639
BARNARD 678, 682
BARNES 573, 593, 620, 622, 626, 636, 638, 640-642, 646, 649, 679, 683, 685
BARNUM 674
BARNWELL 566
BARRADELL 626, 637, 638
BARRETT 567, 607, 609, 622, 623, 625, 635, 683

BARRINGER 659, 660, 661, 676, 686
BARRON 573, 645
BARROW 568, 575, 684
BARRY 698
BARTLETT 610, 687
BASSE 634
BASTNET 573
BATE 634
BATEMAN 568, 573, 687
BATMASON 610
BATTALY 656
BATTLE 565, 679, 681, 683, 684
BATTS 570, 609
BAXTON 567
BAYARD 575
BAYLEY 565, 572
BAZEMORE 626, 634, 635
BEALL 644
BEASLEY 575, 595, 687
BEATTY 675
BEDEL 696
BELL 573, 587, 597, 618, 643, 660, 678
BELLAMY 695
BELMAN 574
BELSON 566
BENBURY 590
BENFORD 684
BENNETT 573, 593, 594, 612, 616, 617, 620, 623, 625, 697
BENTON 593, 617, 684
BERKELEY 559, 562, 563, 570, 575, 616, 640, 671, 675
BERNARD 613, 641
BERRYMAN 593
BERWICK 589
BEST 608
BETHEL 685
BETHUNE 659, 677
BIBB 676
BIBLE 642
BIGGS 563
BIRD 567, 634, 641
BILLETT 573
BILLINGSLEY 683
BLACK 626, 685
BLACKLEDGE 675
BLACKMAN 686
BLAIR 696
BLAKE 573, 647
BLALOCK 683
BLANCHARD 595
BLAND 612
BLEWETT 683, 685
BLOUNT 567, 589, 590, 594, 597, 616, 621, 629, 657, 675, 677, 679, 682
BODDIE 607, 610, 611, 614-618, 620-622, 624, 625, 627, 629, 630, 640, 653, 683
BODITH 587
BOGUE 575
BOND 568, 586, 621, 683
BONNER 573, 587, 589, 590, 593, 594, 595, 596, 653, 657, 675
BOONE 596, 619, 638, 681, 687
BORDEN 676
BOOTH 589, 640
BOSWELL 575
BOUCHER 611
BOULKON 574
BOWMAN 686
BOYCE 586, 593

BOYD 696
BOYDEN 659
BOTKIN 622, 686
BRAGG 620, 646
BRANCH 589, 594, 679, 680
BRANSON 685
BRASWELL 596, 622
BRAY 593, 594, 574, 674
BRAYBOY 634
BREAD 574
BREM 660
BRESSIE 623
BRETT 622
BREVARD 660
BREWER 567, 620
BRICKELL 679, 680
BRIDGERS 607, 617, 619
BRIDGES 565, 681
BRIGHT 687, 682
BRINKLEY 593
BRITT 587, 634
BROACH 608
BROMFIELD 620
BROOKS 686
BROWN 567, 593, 596, 638, 659, 685, 687
BROWNE 615, 616, 618, 622, 629
BROWNRIGG 677
BRUCE 620, 638
BRUTON 682
BRYAN 589, 594, 607, 614, 620, 653, 655-658, 660, 677, 681, 682, 685, 686, 687.
BRYANT 622
BULLARD 567
BULLER 567
BULLOCK 565, 567, 573, 677, 683, 687, 693, 694, 695, 697
BUNDY 574
BURCH 634
BURGESS 676
BURKE 684
BURNETT 620
BURNS 626, 634, 635, 676
BURNSBY 574
BURRINGTON 563
BURT 597
BURTON 564, 610, 611, 659, 661, 680
BURTONSHALL 573, 597
BURWELL 694, 696
BUSH 658, 682
BUTTERTON 634
BYRUM 684
BYRD 562, 597, 676, 682
BYSHOP 574

CARABEUS 676
CARLES 687
CARE 638
CALDWELL 659, 660, 676, 679, 680, 691, 687
CALLOWAY 575, 674, 687
CANADY 575, 596
CANNINGS 597
CANNON 574, 594, 676
CAUSLER 661
CAPP 566
CAREW 566
CARLINGTON 593
CARR 651
CARROLL 596, 637, 676, 683.

CARNEY 596
CARTER 681
CARTRENT 559, 563, 568
CARTWRIGHT 574
CARY 563, 567, 587
CASWELL 573
CASEY 618
CASNEY 596
CASWELL 573, 676, 684
CATCHMAID 564, 565, 570
CATTON 622
CHAMBERS 642
CHAMPION 586, 594
CHANCEY 568
CHANDLER 656
CHAPMAN 566, 635
CHARLES 594
CHARLTON 589, 593, 594, 595
CHERRY 634, 682
CHESSON 575
CHERVIN 593
CHILDS 683
CHRISTMAS 596, 679
CHRONICLE 679
CHURCH 573
CROOM 656
CLAIBORNE 616
CLARK 611
CLARK 683
CLAY 677
CLAYTON 595, 646
CLEAVER 575, 611
CLEAVES 587
CLEVELAND 677, 686
CLINTON 678, 686
CLOYD 660
COACH 610
COALS 574
COATES 597
COBB 615, 621, 640
COBBS 611, 657
COCHRAN 677
COCKRANE 677
COCKE 646
COCKRELL 590
COFFEY 687
COLE 574, 575, 685
COLEMAN 632, 682
COLLETON 570, 589
COLEWELL 641
COLLIER 638, 685
COLLINS 574, 593, 594, 654,679
COLSON 596
COMMANDER 574, 575
COMBS 597
COMINFORT 573
COMBES 617
CONE 588
CONLEY 661
CONNOR 597, 659, 660, 661, 676
CONROLL 573
COOK 597, 687
COOKE 575
COPELAND 586, 590
COPPAGE 624, 635
CRYPTS 596
COOPER 559, 573, 589, 615, 678
    682
COOR 677
CORBIN 617
CORBERY 641, 644, 646
CORNELIUS 565
COREY 573
COSBY 646
COSBY 574
COTTON 607, 617, 619, 621, 622
    635, 637, 650, 642, 679,
    687
COUNCIL 611, 614, 615, 620
    655, 656, 687.

COURTNEY 684
COWAN 636, 675
COWDEN 644
CRADDOCK 597
CRAFFORD (See CRAWFORD) 565, 625,
    630, 641
CRAIG 574
CRAIGH 659
CRAVEN 685
CRAWFORD (See CRAFFORD) 568, 659
CRISP 589
CRITTENDEN 642
CROMARTIE 575
CROMEY 597
CROMWELL 589
CROOM 656, 657, 685, 682
CROPLEY 589, 590
CROSBY 596
CROSSAN 606, 611, 617
CROWDER 693, 695
CRUDUP 607, 616, 686, 635, 637
CRUMPLER 615
CRUTCHFIELD 644, 646
CRUTCHINGSON 575
CULLEN 568
CULPEPPER 562, 563, 568, 572
CULVER 596
CUNNINGHAM 684, 685, 686
CURETON 680
CURTIS 696

DAIN 638
DALTON 596
DANIEL 565, 666, 596, 615, 622
    639, 641, 673, 679, 680,
    683, 684, 685, 687, 696.
DARDEN 596, 622
DARE 678
DARGAN 683
DAUGHTRY 593, 622, 680, 684
DAVENPORT 597, 660, 687, 693
DAVIDSON 636, 643, 649, 680, 681,
    685, 686
DAVIS 678
DAVIES 563, 564, 566, 567, 569,
    574, 575, 587, 595, 609,
    622, 637, 660, 679, 680,
    682, 687, 694, 696
DAVS 587, 589
DAWSON 607, 614, 616, 618, 619,
    621, 624, 625, 651, 656
DEAL 575
DEAR 589, 590
DEBERRY 683
DEENS 660
DE GRAFFENREIDT 677
DELAMARE 574
DEMPSEY 636, 686
DENNIS 566, 567
DENTON 597
DENTON 596, 680
DEPTER 680
DEW 596, 607, 617, 619, 630, 635
DEWEY 660
DICKEY 682
DICKSON 688, 676
DIXON 607, 616, 621, 637, 663,
    676
DOBBINS 677
DOBBS 675, 677
DOBSON 682, 686
DOCKERY 685
DOMRANTER 567
DONNELL 677
DOUGHTON 674
DOUGLASS 685
DOUTHIT 678
DOW 660
DOWD 683
DOWNING 641, 642

DRAKE 596, 683
DRAPER 573
DRIVER 620
DRUMMOND 562, 563, 570
DUCKETT 682
DUDLEY 684
DUCKENFIELD 568, 594, 595, 597.
DUNAWAY 656
DUNLAP 660
DUNN 685
DUNNING 636, 658
DURANT 561, 568, 578, 589
DUKE 594
DUNHAM 678, 684
DURHAM 646
DYE 568

EARLY 589, 698
EASON 636
EASTON 676
EASTCHURCH 565, 568
EATON 696
EBORN 587
ECCLES 677
EDEN 562, 563, 675, 677
EDGERTON 593, 595
EDMONDS 564, 597, 684
EDWARDS 587, 597, 607, 609,
    610, 611, 614, 620, 654,
    656, 680, 684, 686
EICHORN 593
ELLIOTT 596, 640, 685
ELLIS 660
ELLWOOD 619
EIMES 566
ELY 615
ENGLEDOW 637
ENGLISH 565
ENLOE 681
EPPES 639
ERVIN 659
EVANS 565, 574, 575, 590, 685
EVERARD 563
EVERHART 644
EXUM 615-615, 617, 619, 620.

FAISON 622
FALCONER 595
FANDALL 575
FARLOW 589, 590, 593, 594, 681
FARTHING 687
FAWLING 642
FELTON 585
FERRIBEE 678
FEW 643
FENNIX 597
FIBUSH 596
FIKE 634
FISHER 595, 597
FLAKE 585
FLEMING 639
FLETCHER 575
FLEMMILIN 584
FLINN 587
FLOWERS 679
FLOYD 596
FOLK 564, 596
FORBES 639, 640
FORCE 574
FORD 584, 596
FORDHAM 682
FORDYCE 589, 590
FORMAN 587
FORSYTH 579, 686
FORTSON 566, 567
FOSCUE 682
FOSTER 566, 572, 588, 595, 679
FOWLER 622
FOX 575, 587
FRANKS 687.

FRANKLIN 679, 686
FREEAR 684
FREEMAN 660, 661
FRISSELL 566, 618, 640
FROST 594
FRYER 597
FULLINWIDER 660
FULLER 573
FULWOOD 684
FURRH 574

GAID 574
GAINEY 596
GAITHER 660
GALE 594, 624, 631
GALLOWAY 639, 643, 695
GARD 573
GARDNER 596, 597, 657
GARLAND 597
GARNETT 574, 644, 646
GARRETT 589, 593, 594, 595, 678, 682
GARTEN 685
GASKINS 568
GASTON 677, 679
GATES 607, 655
GAVIN 686
GAY 613, 614, 659
GAYLORD 597
GENTRY 685
GERVAISE 577
GESPER 573
GHORMLEY 680
GIBBS 681
GIBSON 564
GILBERT 590, 593, 594
GILCHRIST 659, 683, 685
GILES 566
GILLESPIE 660, 675, 678, 680
GILLIAM 589, 590, 593
GLASSCOCK 644
GLISSON 678
GLOVER 563, 564
GODFREY 568, 575
GODWIN 613, 616, 617, 621, 622, 630, 641, 697
GONSOLVO 575
GOODE 637
GOODIN 587
GOODMAN 564, 658, 682
GOODWIN 677
GORHAM 589
GORRELL 680
GOSBY 575
GOWER 621
GRAHAM 574, 628, 659, 660, 661, 680, 683, 684, 686
GRAINGER 675, 683
GRANDY 573
GRANT 660, 684
GRAVES 617, 641, 644, 676, 686
GRAY 575, 619, 657, 675, 679, 681, 685
GREEN 559, 561, 562, 564, 565, 586, 587, 589, 622, 641, 656, 657, 658, 659, 675, 678, 679
GREENE 566, 567, 680, 686
GREENLIEF 658
GREER 636
GREGORY 574, 676, 694
GRIFFIN 562, 574, 597, 610, 611, 615, 616, 620, 634, 683
GRIGSBY 628
GRIMES 678
GUDGER 682
GUINN 682
GUN 568
GUNFALLIS 568
GUNTER 647

GUTTON 677

HACKLEY 593
HAIRE 624, 631
HAIRSTON 686
HALFORD 568
HALL 575, 587, 593, 631, 679
HALLUM 566
HALSEY 590, 595
HALSTED 593
HAMBLIN 612
HAMILTON 658, 660, 693, 695
HAMOR 655
HAMLIN 587
HAMMOND 566, 620
HAMPTON 566, 609, 619, 659, 678, 686
HANCOCK 565, 567
HANKS 681
HANNAH 680
HAPPOLDT 660
HARDIN 674, 687
HARDING 589, 642
HARDY 597, 607, 619, 620, 641, 655, 657
HARE 565, 641, 642, 653
HARGROVE 678, 695
HARLOWE 593
HARMAN 566
HARNETT 675, 680, 683
HARPER 567, 680
HARRIS 566, 573, 574, 593, 617, 676, 679, 683, 687, 696, 698
HARRISON 564, 609, 617, 619, 623, 624, 631, 656, 677, 678, 679, 682, 683, 696, 697
HART 628, 681, 684
HARTLEY 568
HARVEY 561, 563, 564, 566, 567, 575, 587, 594, 595, 640, 685
HARUDI 568
HASSELL 597, 626, 687
HASWELL 568
HATCH 656, 657, 659, 682
HATHAWAY 576
HAUGHTON 593, 594, 660
HAVITT 595
HAWKINS 568, 573, 574, 597, 625, 659, 660, 679, 682, 685, 694
HAWLEY 565, 567
HAYES 562, 596, 620
HAYNES 660
HAYWOOD 624, 631, 680, 681, 687
HAZLEWOOD 566
HEALE 589
HEARIN 597
HECKLEFIELD 561, 563, 575, 671
HEK 597
HENDERSON 597, 637, 659, 661, 679, 681, 684, 687, 693, 694, 697
HENDRICKS 566, 574
HENRY 626, 629, 648, 676
HERITAGE 656, 657
HERON 590
HERRING 658, 678
HERTFORD 561, 672
HESTER 684
HEWES 596, 677
HIBBINS 595
HIBUINOS 575
HICKS 590, 593, 594, 681
HIGGINSON 696
HIGH 365
HILL 565, 568, 587, 609, 611, 612, 623, 628, 629, 635, 643, 657, 660, 677, 678, 679, 681, 682, 684, 685, 686
HILLIARD 566, 628, 679, 683
HINDS 596

HINES 597
HINTON 656, 687
HOBBY 596
HODGKIN 564
HOGAN 658, 678
HOKE 659, 660, 661
HOLBROOK 597
HOLDER 566
HOLLAND 617, 626, 635, 686
HOLLOM 566
HOLLOWAY 575
HOLLOWELL 562, 586
HOLMAN 643, 645
HOLMES 565, 587, 638, 675, 685
HOLT 622, 675
HOLTON 659, 661
HOOKER 680
HOOPER 594
HOOVER 685
HOPKINS 575, 589, 595, 597
HORN 627, 679, 686
HORNE 587, 596
HORNSBY 574
HORSEY 696
HORTON 590, 595, 687
HOSKINS 568, 589, 594, 677, 687
HOUGH 610
HOUSE 679
HOUSTON 661
HOWARD 587, 657, 674, 682, 684, 685, 694
HOWCOTT 594
HOWELL 586, 611, 674, 680, 685
HOWERTON 679
HOYLE 659
HUDNALL 618
HUDSON 586
HUGGINS 681
HUGHES 593
HUMPHRIES 678
HUNT 574, 575, 596, 607, 610, 611, 615, 616, 620, 693, 694, 697
HUNTER 574, 593, 594, 657, 660, 679
HURDLE 586
HURSING 587
HURST 615
HUSBANDS 674, 685
HUSSEY 678
HUTCHINSON 596, 660
HUTTON 565, 686
HYNE 563, 659, 681
HYDER 686
HYMAN 682

INGE 626
INGRAM 681, 686
IREDELL 659, 677, 681
IRWIN 659
IRONMONGER 641
ISLER 682
IVES 657

JACKSON 568, 574, 587, 594, 596, 610, 618, 620, 660, 681
JACOB 587, 608
JACOCKS 657
JAIKES 593
JAMES 574, 656
JANSEN 567
JARNIGAN 596
JARVIS 563, 564, 575, 589, 653
JASPER 681
JEFFREY 566
JEFFREYS 566, 620, 635, 679
JELPS 573
JENKINS 563, 567, 568, 660, 661, 697

JENNINGS 566, 567, 574
JEREMY 608
JOHNSEY 566
JOHNSON 573, 574, 575, 597, 660
  659
JOHNSTON 562, 634, 645, 649,
  661, 675, 677, 684, 688,
  697
JONES 566, 573, 574, 589, 590
  593, 594, 595, 613, 617,
  625, 629, 638, 639, 641,
  642, 653, 659, 660, 675,
  676, 678, 680, 681, 682,
  683, 684, 687, 693, 697,
  698
JORDAN 586, 594, 597, 607, 608
  613, 617, 629, 640, 646,
  659, 681, 685
JOYNER 596, 616, 680, 682, 685

KASWELL 573
KEARNEY 625, 630
KEELE 565, 566, 567
KEELING 653, 693, 695
KEELY 565
KEETON 574
KELLEY 565, 566, 567, 575
KENDRICK 643
KENNON 678, 686
KERR 678
KIMBERLY 568
KIMBROUGH 637
KILPATRICK 682
KINCHEN 625
KING 568, 589, 593, 597, 660,
  686
KINNON 693
KISTLER 659, 660
KITCHING 573
KITTRELL 593, 696
KNOX 565

LACY 660
LAFFERTY 660
LAKER 575
LAMAR 646
LANDER 660
LANGDON 561
LANE 615, 622, 647, 685, 687,
  697
LANGLEY 627
LANGSTON 593, 596, 640, 641,
  642
LANIER 675, 678, 680, 683, 685
  697
LANSTON 593
LASLEY 642, 646
LASSITER 590, 593, 594
LATEN 624
LAVENDER 657
LAW 626
LAWLER 593
LAWLEY 593
LAWNE 639
LAWRENCE 565, 607, 613, 614,
  615, 624, 626, 627, 629,
  630, 631, 634, 636, 641,
  658, 679
LAWREY 566
LAWSON 597, 681
LAY 659
LAMAR 644, 646
LEA 676
LEACH 678
LEAKE 660, 685
LEARY 575
LEE 682, 685, 695
LEGETT 644
LE GRANDE 683

LEIGH 679, 687
LEMLEY 660
LENOIR 682
LEONARD 565
LEWELTON 568, 589, 592, 594
LEWIN 573
LEWIS 587, 590, 593, 594, 637,
  641, 675, 679, 682, 694
LILES 594
LILLARD 656
LILLINGTON 575, 678
LINDSAY 573, 641, 678, 680, 697
LINGFIELD 587
LITTLE 573, 618, 659, 660
LOADMAN 575
LOCKE 659
LOCKHART 657
LOFTON 589, 595, 682
LOGAN 659
LONG 597, 610, 615, 680, 682, 685
LOVE 685
LOVELL 609
LOVETT 653
LOVICK 595
LOWD 573
LOWREY 566, 574, 643, 682
LUDWELL 563
LUMBROZIER 574
LUSK 682
LUTON 589, 590, 594, 595
LYNDON 685
LYON 675

MACHAN 644
MACKERAHE 596
MACKIE 574
MACON 623, 681, 682
MADREN 574
MADISON 682, 694
MAN (See MANN) 565, 568, 640, 697
MANNEY 681
MANWARING 575
MARKHAM 574
MARION 683
MARR 566
MARROW 696
MARKS 590, 594
MARSH 676, 685
MARSHALL 566, 567, 587, 607-610,
  612, 616, 618, 621, 623, 624,
  627, 629, 630, 631, 634, 682,
  696
MARTIN 587, 593, 607, 616, 618,
  621, 642, 657, 675, 680,
  682, 683, 685, 686
MASON 567, 574, 587
MASSAGHEY 574
MASSEY 660
MASTS 687
MATKIN 568
MATTHEWS 567, 575, 610, 612, 616,
  617, 644, 656, 677, 680, 681,
  686
MAULE 597
MAYER 596
MAYHARDIE 660
MAYO 574, 620, 679, 682
MAYS 685
McALPINE 660, 685
McALLISTER 677
McCAIN 680
McCLENDON 593, 595
McCLENNY 586
McLEOD 685
McCONNELL 660
McCULLOCH 660
McDANIEL 575, 590, 595, 660, 646
McDONALD 596, 677
McDOWELL 586, 660, 661, 682, 683

McFARLAND 685
McGILVARY 659
McGUE 575, 594
McINTOSH 644
McINTYRE 686
McKAY 677
McKELVEY 635
McKENZIE 682
McKEYENTE 610
McKIEL 574
McKINNIE 607, 610, 611, 614, 615
  616, 620, 621, 638
McLEAN 676
McMILLAN 674, 675, 685
McNAIR 642
McNAIRY 680
McNEILL 677, 683
McQUEEN 676, 685
McQUINNIE (See McKINNEY) 610
McREA 675
McSPADDEN 647
McSWAIN 642, 643, 646, 647
MEAD 573, 574, 646
MEANS 659
MEBANE 674, 676, 684
MEDLOCK 685
MEEKS 644
MELTON 627
MENIFEE 609
MERCER 618
MEREDITH 586
MERONEY 680
MERRICK 565
MIDDLETON 641
MILES 640
MILLER 562, 563, 572, 574, 659,
  660, 659, 674, 678, 685
MILLS 637
MINGE 611
MINTY 568
MITCHELL 634, 638, 659, 661,
  683, 696
MOBLEY 696
MOHLIN 575
MOLINES 568
MOLSON 596
MONCK (MONK) 559, 596
MOODY 682
MOORE 566, 593, 615, 628, 637
  640, 645, 659, 660, 685,
  676, 677, 679, 683, 684,
  686, 697, 698
MOREHEAD 660, 680, 685
MONTAGUE 575, 587, 607, 608,
  613,
MONTFORT 680
MONTGOMERY 680, 683
MOREY 590
MORGAN 565, 567, 575, 696
MORFELL 575
MOREY 565
MORRIS 587, 660
MORRISON 660, 659, 696
MORROW 660, 686, 696, 698
MOSELEY 590, 593, 594, 642, 644,
  646, 657, 682, 683
MOSES 566, 567
MOTT 661
MOWBRAY 574
MOYE 680, 685
MULKEY 697
MULLINS 573
MUNDAY 564, 574
MUNDS 594
MURCHISON 659, 677, 683
MURDAH 565
MURFREE 681
MURPHY 614, 615, 627, 681, 684
MYERS 660.   MYLES 610, 634.

708

NAIL 644
NAIRN 597
NAPIER 643
NASH 586, 682, 683, 684, 688
NEAL 677
NEEDHAM 653, 655, 657
NELSON 596, 686
NESBITT 681
NEWBY 575
NEWLAND 590
NEWSOM 622, 628
NEWTON 566, 622, 638
NUCKOLS 694
NICHOLSON 575, 683
NIXON 575
NOAKES 565, 567, 568
NOEL 568, 575
NORMAN 597
NORSWORTHY 631
NORTHCUTT 575
NORTON 587
NOWELL 568, 573, 575
NUGENT 623
NUTALL 660

O'DANIEL 658, 678
ODELL 659
ODOM 589, 593, 640, 641, 642
  644, 684
OGLETHORPE 623, 624, 629
OLD 675, 676
OLIVER 634, 656
O'NEAL 574, 643, 645
ORR 680
OSBORNE 659, 681
OUTLAND 614
OUTLAW 568, 636, 658, 678
OVERMAN 660
OVERTON 634, 683
OWEN 675

PADGETT 590, 593, 594
PAGE 596, 614
PALIN 564, 566, 574
PALL 573
PARHAM 566, 567
PARISH 568
PARIS 567
PALMER 574, 617, 620
PARKER 573, 586, 590, 593,
  607, 608, 640, 660, 680
  695
PARKS 644, 660
PARNELL 566, 616, 619, 630,
  631
PARSONS 573, 609, 660
PARROTT 589
PATCHETT 589
PATE 597
PATILLO 697
PATMAN 565
PATTERSON 596, 660, 684
PATTON 682
PAULS 567
PEAKE 641
PEARSALL 678
PEARSON 659, 678, 686
PECKRIM 597
PELL 573
PENDER 684, 687
PENDLETON 574, 694, 695
PENLAND 677, 682, 683
PENN 642, 646, 694
PENNY 653
PENRICE 568
PEOPLES 684
PERDUE 646
PERKINS 676
PERRY 596, 609, 638, 681
PERSON 683, 684

PETERSON 513, 593
PETTIVER 594
PEYTON 573, 622
PHELPS 575, 597, 643
PHINER 659, 660, 676
PHILLIPS 587, 679, 685
PHILPOTT 564
PICKETT 660
PIERCE 575, 590, 639, 682
PIERCY 574
PIERSON 565
PITT 619, 620
PLOWMAN 589, 597
POINDEXTER 686
POLK 685, 687, 698
POLLOCK 563, 589, 594, 595, 629
POND 622
POOLE 566
POONE 565
POPE 574, 615, 622, 637
PORTER 574, 589, 590, 593, 594,
  595, 675, 680, 683, 686
PORTIS 607, 616, 618, 619, 620,
  622, 634, 629, 634
POU 586
POWELL 608, 659, 677, 685
PRESTON 565, 566
PLATTO 568
PRICE 587, 597, 660
PRIDGEON 627, 675
PRIME 618
PRITCHARD 574, 636, 660
PRIVETT 586, 590
PROCTOR 587, 596
PROSSER 609, 617
PRYOR 587
PUGH 593, 634, 657, 681
PURCELL 586, 614, 685

QUARLES 680

RABY 638
RAINFORD 681
RAMBEAU 655, 658
RAMON 574
RAMSEUR 659, 660
RAMSEY 676
RANDLE 683
RANDOLPH 567, 637
RANKIN 659, 679, 680
RATLIFF 597
RAWLYNSON 574
RAY 593, 610, 676, 684, 688
RAYNOR 634
RAZOR 657
READ 564, 567, 677
REAGAN 685, 687
REDITT 597
REED 563, 596, 676
REGNAUD 573
REID 685
REILY 646
RELLE 562, 566
REEVES 615, 621
REYNOLDS 615, 639, 657
RHODES 678, 684
RHYNE 659
RICE 643, 660, 675
RICH 567
RICHARDS 573
RICHARDSON 675, 681
RICHMOND 565
RICKS 596, 615, 683
RIDLEY 695
RINES 643
RISROD 568
ROBARDS 676
ROBERDS 597
ROBERTS 567, 575, 594, 620, 628
  646

ROBESON 685
ROBERTSON 621, 683, 687
ROBINS 655
ROBINSON 566, 567, 573, 589, 594,
  595, 607, 609, 621, 624,
  625, 629, 630, 631, 638,
  645, 687
ROGERS 564, 566, 593, 596, 607,
  610, 621, 625, 628, 630,
  639, 640, 641, 642, 643,
  644, 645, 646, 647, 679,
  684, 687
ROOKES 568, 575
ROPER 566, 567
ROSE 597, 649
ROSS 566, 573, 641
ROUNDTREE 593, 594, 657
ROUSE 566
ROWAN 677
ROWDEN 574
ROWN 642
ROWLAND 685
RUDISILL 660
RUFFIN 649, 674
RUMMELS 586
RUSH 685
RUSSELL 660, 681
RUTTER 660, 681
RUTHERFORD 686
RUTTMAN 687

SADLER 594
SAIFER 685
SANDERS (See SAUNDERS) 566, 614,
  620, 625, 630, 641
SANDERSON 573, 678, 681
SANDY'S 655
SARGEN 590, 597
SASSER 658
SAUNDERS (See SANDERS) 587, 614,
  623, 624, 629, 641, 681, 687.
SAWYER 575, 676
SCALES 685
SCARBOROUGH 573, 575
SCHENCK 660
SCONE (SCOWAN) 610
SCOWEN 607, 608, 610, 612
SCOTT 568, 572, 575, 610, 612,
  615, 617, 684
SCRIMSHER 642, 647
SEARCY 687
SEAWELL 683, 687
SELBY 681
SELLERS 675, 686
SESSIONS 589
SETTLE 685
SEVIER 575
SEWARD 566
SHANDS 566
SHARPE 564, 565, 607, 611, 623,
  679, 681, 685
SHARPMAN 568
SHAW 677, 684
SHEARARD 619
SHEARER 607, 618, 619, 624, 630
  631
SHELBY 677
SHEPARD 612, 656, 677
SHEPPARD 636, 683, 685, 686
SHERRILL 660
SHERROD 575, 586, 607, 638, 678
SHERWOOD 564, 575, 607, 638.
SHINE 682
SHIPP 660
SHOLAR 654, 636
SHORES 686
SHREWSBURY 568
SHUFORD 686
SILER 682
SILVER 596

SILVERTHORNE 587
SIMS 631
SIMONS 568, 590, 595, 595
SIMMONS 575, 589, 621, 656, 657, 677, 682
SIMPSON 525
SINCLAIR 660
SINGLETON 597, 681, 686
SITGRAVES 677
SYMONDS 621
SKINNER 561, 590, 593, 621, 677
SKITTLETHORPE 597
SLADE 573, 587, 682
SLATER 660
SLIGER 659
SLOCUM 568, 589, 594
SLOAN 658, 660, 661, 678
SROWIN 568
SMITH 564, 566, 567, 573, 575, 586, 587, 595, 596, 609, 612, 616, 623, 624, 627, 629, 655, 658, 659, 660, 681, 685, 696
SMITHWICK 568, 589, 593, 594, 682
SNEED 608
SNELL 575
SNOAD 653
SNOWDEN 595, 676
SOJOURNER 622
SOMERS 607, 655
SOTHEL 561, 563
SOUTH 564
SOWELL 593, 594, 634
SPARROW 659
SPEARS 617
SPEED 685
SPEIGHT 575, 589, 593, 677, 680, 682
SPERRY 696
SPILLMAN 575
SPIVEY 593, 631, 634
SPOTTSWOOD 696
SPRINGS 587, 659, 660
SPROSS 574
SPRUILL 597
SPURGEON 678
SQUIRES 587
STACEY 589, 593, 594, 660
STAFFORD 659
STALEY 685, 686
STALLINGS 634, 677
STAMPE 565, 567, 574, 575, 613, 617
STANDING 593
STANLEY (STANLEY) 597, 607, 626, 634, 636, 638, 675, 677
STANTON 575
STAPLES 567
STANKEY 684
STATON 637
STRANGES 685
STEDMAN 676
STEELE 573, 685
STEPHENS 563, 565, 677
STEVENS 559, 562, 585, 568, 570, 594, 620
STEVENSON 567
STEWART 575, 597, 675, 680, 685
STINE 647
STOKELEY 616
STOKES 642, 687
STONE 566, 617, 675, 679
STONEHOUSE 596
STOWE 660
STRANGE 677
STRATTON 680

STRICKLAND 627
STROUD 565
STUART 559
STUBBS 587
SULLIVANT 587
SULLY 659
SUMMER 681
SUTTON 567, 568, 575, 594, 597, 681
SWAIN 595, 682, 684, 686
SWANN 675, 683
SWEPSON 696

TALBOT 644
TALIAFERRO 609, 623
TANNER 589, 635
TARKINGTON 597
TARVER 643, 684
TAYLOE 634
TAYLOR 568, 573, 574, 575, 590, 594, 595, 596, 614, 621, 658, 660, 677, 680, 684, 685, 694
TEMPLE 574
TERRELL 681, 683, 686
THIGPEN 576
THOMAS 574, 607-610, 612, 614-631, 634-638, 640, 641, 677, 678, 681, 683, 685
THOMPSON 634, 640, 658, 681, 686
THORNTON 590, 644
TIDDY 660
TIMBERLAKE 642
TINES 622
TIPTON 642
TITTMAN 589
TYCE 587
TOCINSON 573
TOMES 575
TOMLIN 568, 574, 575
TOMLINSON 681
TOMS 572
TORRENCE 621, 681
TRAVIS 622
TRIPLETT 646
TRUEBLOOD 574
TRUEIT 677
TRYON 675
TULLE 573, 587
TULLOCH 684
TURNER 565, 596, 597, 575, 684
TWEEDY 575
TYLER 564

UNDERWOOD 658, 686
UPTON 574

VAIL 590, 593
VANN 593, 640, 641, 642, 644, 646, 647
VARNHAM 564, 570, 589, 590, 595
VANDERMERLIN 573
VAN DYKE 694
VAN HOOK 684
VANTUSIN 597
VAUGHAN 684
VICK 683
VINCE 573
VINSON 596
VOSS 568

WADE 683, 685
WADDELL 685
WAHL 626
WALKER 563, 567, 589, 595, 597, 645, 646, 675, 676, 685, 686, 694
WALL 685
WALLACE 574

WALLER 575
WALSH 660
WALSTON 589, 590, 595, 597
WALTON 644, 686
WARBURTON 589, 594
WARD 567, 593, 595, 639, 660, 684
WARDEN 639
WARNER 567
WARREN 564, 573, 594, 658, 682
WARRINGTON 687
WASHER 693
WASHINGTON 562, 659, 660, 686
WATERS 655, 656
WATKINS 608, 620, 675, 687, 693, 694
WATSON 587, 685
WATTS 609, 659
VAUGH 686
WAYNE 587
WEBB 615, 638, 685
WEBBER 642
WEBSTER 681
WELCH 574, 585, 642, 643
WELLS 565, 566, 589, 593
WEST 566, 574, 594, 595, 597, 607, 622, 642, 657
WESTER 634
WHEATLEY 658
WHEATLEY 589
WHEELER 568
WHEELER 617, 659, 673, 680, 681, 682
WHERRY 593
WHITBY 575
WHITE 564, 565, 567, 568, 574, 575, 586, 590, 593, 594, 597, 634, 660, 676, 677, 678, 681, 682, 693
WHITACRE 634, 636
WHITAKER 680, 687
WHITFIELD 607, 614, 656, 657, 658, 682
WHITEHEAD 614, 658
WHITESIDES 686
WHITLEY 681
WHITMELL 619, 657
WHITTY 685
WICKER 590
WIGGINS 680, 693
WILDER 681
WILFONG 661
WILFORD 634
WILKINSON 563, 572, 587, 589, 594, 595, 597
WILLIS 685
WILLS 564, 565, 617, 625
WILLIAMS 566-568, 575, 589, 590, 593, 594, 597, 619, 630, 640-642, 644, 649, 658, 660, 675, 676, 678, 679-683, 685-687, 693, 695
WILLIAMSON 566, 597, 617, 639, 640, 659, 660, 661, 677, 684
WILLOUGHBY 559, 568, 575
WILSON 575, 590, 593, 594, 659, 660, 679, 688
WIMBERLY 627
WINBORNE 594, 624, 631
WINDLEY 587, 594
WINGARD 659
WINGATE 574, 597
WINKFIELD 658
WINGFIELD 658
WINN 637
WINSLOW 638, 677, 679
WINSTON 686

710

WISEMAN 678
WINN 557, 631, 637
WYATT 566, 647
WOODARD 556
WOODHOUSE 576, 655
WOODLEY 590, 593, 594
WOODLIEF 634
WOOD 565, 594, 685
WOODWARD 566, 567, 568, 578,
   586, 593, 594, 595, 653.

WOODWORTH 695
WOODY 682
WOOLARD 575, 593
WOOTEN 620, 644, 677, 682
WOLFE 557
WOMACK 645
WOMBWELL 566
WORSLEY 609
WORTH 679, 680
WRIGHT 621, 678

YANCEY 687
YATES 590, 607, 680
YIELDING 565
YEO 615
YOGAN 647
YORK 644, 685
YOUNG 575, 681, 685

ZOLLICOFFER 694.

PLACES
PAGES 559 TO 700

ABBINGDON, VA. 659
ACCOMAC COUNTY, VA. 616, 640
ALABAMA 687
ALAMANCE COUNTY 674, 684
ALAMANCE CREEK 674
ALBEMARLE, N. C. 686
ALBEMARLE CO. VA. 637
ALBEMARLE PRECINCT 671, 674
ALBEMARLE SOUND 559, 561½, 575
   679, 684
ALEXANDER COUNTY N. C. 674
ALLEGHANEY COUNTY N. C. 674
ALLIGATOR RIVER 573, 672, 678
AMELIA COUNTY? VA. 631
AMHERST COUNTY, VA. 637
ANSON COUNTY, N. C. 560, 674,
   675, 676, 677, 681, 682,
   683, 685, 687
APPOMATTOX RIVER VA 567
ARCHDALE PRECINCT 587, 673, 677
ARCHER'S HOPE, VA 609, 655
ARRENGUSH CREEK 566, 574
ASHE COUNTY? N. C. 674, 677, 687
ASHBORO, N. C. 685
ASHLAND N S. 693
ASHEVILLE, N. C. 688
AUGUSTA, GA. 645, 644
AVERY COUNTY, N. C. 674, 681

BACK RIVER, VA. 610
BACON'S REBELLION 565, 684
BAKERS GRAVEYARD 681
BAKERSVILLE, N. C. 683
BARNEY'S MOUNTAIN 674
BATH PRECINCT 573, 587, 671,
   677, 680, 681, 683
BATH TOWN, N. C. 671, 674
BATT'S GRAVE 562
BATTLE OF ALAMANCE 674
BAYBORO, N. C. 684
BEAR SWAMP 590
BEATTIE'S FORD 659, 661
BEAUFORT COUNTY, N. C. 622,
   648, 657, 674, 677, 684,
   685
BEAUFORT PRECINCT 587, 673
BEAVER DAM SWAMP 590
BEDFORDSHIRE, ENGLAND 694
BELVEDERE PLACE 694
BENNETT'S CREEK 562, 590, 595
   594, 641, 642, 655, 679,
   681
BERKELEY PRECINCT 570, 571,
   572, 589, 619, 641, 671.
BERMUDA ISLANDS 607, 655, 623
BERTIE COUNTY? N. C. 605, 617,
   618, 622, 626, 629, 630,
   631, 634, 636, 637, 638,
   641, 645, 648, 655, 657,
   675, 677, 678, 681,
   686.

BERTIE PRECINCT 587, 605, 672,
   675, 679, 684
BLADEN COUNTY, N. C. 674, 675,
   676, 677, 680, 683, 685,
   697
BLADEN PRECINCT 680, 676, 680.
BLOUNT COUNTY, TENN. 647
BLOUNT'S OLD TOWN 648
BLUNT POINT 655, 656
BLUE SPRINGS, VA. 693
"BONA NOVA" (Ship) 655
BOONSBORO, KY. 695
BONHAM, TEXAS 635
BRACKSTOWN, N. C. 680
BREVARD, N. C. 687
BRIAR CREEK (Ga.) 643
BROAD RIVER (Ga.) 644
BRUNSWICK COUNTY, Va. 631, 677
BRUNSWICK COUNTY, N. C. 675, 683
BRYSON CITY, N. C. 685
BUCK FOREST, N. C. 677
BUCKLAND 609
BURKE COUNTY, GA. 645
BURKE COUNTY, N. C. 659, 675,
   676, 683, 686
BUTE COUNTY, N. C. 679, 687
BUENA VISTA, N. C. 684
BUFFALO CITY, N. C. 676
BUFFALO FORD 685
BUFFALO CREEK, GA. 644
BUNCOMBE COUNTY, N. C. 675, 676,
   677, 680, 681, 682, 686
BURGAW, N. C. 684
BULLINGTON, N. C. 674
BURNSIDE N. C. 683, 685
BURNSVILLE, N. C. 676, 686

CABARRUS COUNTY, N. C. 659, 676,
   677, 683, 684
CALDWELL COUNTY, N. C. 660, 661,
   676, 683
CALHOUN, N. C. 685
CALIFORNIA 647
CAMDEN COUNTY, N. C. 575, 676
CAMPBELLTOWN, N. C. 677
CANE RIVER 686
CAPE FEAR 572, 671
CAPE FEAR RIVER 675, 683
CANKATUCKS CREEK 566
CARTERET COUNTY, N. C. 676
CARTERET PRECINCT 570, 572, 589,
   573, 678
CARTER'S CREEK (Va.) 696
CAROLINA RIVER 564, 566
CARTHAGE, N. C. 685
CASHEY RIVER 594, 596, 675
CASWELL COUNTY, N. C. 676
CATAWBA, N. C. 660
CATAWBA COUNTY, N. C. 660, 661,
   676, 682

CATAWBA RIVER 676, 683, 685
CATHERINE'S CREEK 562, 593, 594
"CEDAR WALK" (home) 611
CHAPEL HILL, N. C. 676, 693
CHARLESTON, S. C. 661
CHARLOTTE, N. C. 659, 660, 683
CHARLOTTE MINT 659
CHARLOTTESVILLE, VA. 661
CHARLES CITY CO. Va. 613, 638
CHATHAM COUNTY, N. C. 565, 676,
   677, 682, 684, 685
CHEEK'S MILL CREEK 648
CHERAW, S. C. 660
CHEROKEE COUNTY, N. C. 676,
   677, 680
CHEROKEE INDIANS 642, 644, 646,
   647, 676, 685
CHEROKEE NATION 642, 647
CHICKAHOMINY RIVER (Va.) 609,
   622
CHILESBURG, N. C. 684
CHINQUAPIN CREEK 593
CHIPOKES, CREEK (Va.) 613
CHOWAN COUNTY, N. C. 561, 566,
   635, 636, 645, 667, 676,
   677, 679, 682
CHOWAN PRECINCT 562, 564, 572,
   581, 589, 590, 593, 594,
   597, 619, 639, 673, 677,
   687
CHOWAN RIVER 559, 570, 588,
   593, 679, 681
CHOWANOKE RIVER 564, 567, 607,
   614.
CHRIST'S CHURCH, NEW BERN, N. C.
   656.
CHUCKATUCK SETTLEMENT (Va.)
   618, 612
CLAIREMORE, OKLAHOMA 647
CLARENDON PRECINCT 572, 673,
   677
CLAY COUNTY, N. C. 677
CLEVELAND COUNTY, N. C. 677,
   682
CLINTON, N. C. 684
COKESBURY CHURCH (NC) 685
COLONY OF TRANSYLVANIA 695
COLUMBIA, N. C. 687
COLUMBUS, MISS. 685
COLUMBUS, N. C. 686
COLUMBUS COUNTY, N. C. 677
CONCORD, N. C. 659, 676
CONOCANARO CREEK 648
CONTENTNEA CREEK 648
CONFEDERATE CONGRESS 659
COROTTOMAN RIVER (Va.) 612
CORRATUCKS CREEK 564, 567
COWAN'S FORD 676
COW ISLAND 593
CRAVEN CO. N. C. 656, 677,
   679, 682.

711

CRAVEN PRECINCT 673, 677, 680
CREEDMORE, N. C. 694
CROSS CREEK, N. C. 608, 677
CULPEPPER COUNTY, VA. 656
CULPEPPER REBELLION 563
CUMBERLAND COUNTY, N. C. 683, 687
CURLES, VA. 607
CURRITUCK COUNTY, N. C. 678
CURRITUCK INDIANS 676
CURRITUCK, N. C. 561, 678
CURRITUCK PRECINCT 572, 573, 575, 672
CYPRESS BRANCH 593
CYPRESS SWAMP 611

DANBURY, N. C. 686
DARE COUNTY? N. C. 573, 672, 678, 681
DALLAS, N. C. 660
DALLAS, TEXAS 626, 636, 637, 677
DARLEY, ENGLAND 694
DAVIDSON COUNTY, N. C. 660, 678
DAVIE COUNTY, N. C. 678
DEEP CREEK (RIVER) N. C. 682, 685
DEEP RUN 590, 594
DEMOPOLIS, ALA. 658
"DIANA" (Vessel) 655
DISMAL SWAMP 562, 676
DOBBS COUNTY, N. C. 649, 681, 682
DOBSON, N. C. 686
DOCTOR'S CREEK 567
DREWERY CHURCH 695
DREWERY, N. C. 694
DRUMMOND'S POINT 562
DUKE UNIVERSITY 678
DUMFRIES, SCOTLAND 693
DUPLIN COUNTY, N. C. 678, 686
DURANT'S NECK 568, 589

EASTERN VIRGINIA 656
EASTERN SHORE (Va.) 570, 617
EASTON, N. C. 660
EDENHOUSE POINT 561, 562
EDENTON, N. C. 561, 562, 597, 671, 677
EDENTON BAY 562, 593
EDGECOMBE COUNTY, N. C. 615, 620, 622, 627, 628, 630, 677, 678, 679, 680, 683, 686, 688
EDGECOMBE PRECINCT 648
EDGEFIELD DIST. S. C. 628
EGYPTIAN INTERNATIONAL COURT 660
ELBERT COUNTY, GA. 644
ELEVEN CREEK 694
ELIZABETH CITY, N. C. 561, 562, 563, 684
ELIZABETHTOWN, N. C. 575
ELIZABETHTOWN, N. J. 681
ELIZABETH CITY COUNTY, VA. 610, 612, 656
ENFIELD, N. C. 680
ESSEX COUNTY, VA. 617
EUTAW SPRINGS 693

FALLS OF TAR RIVER 649
FAYETTEVILLE? N. C. 659, 677
FILBERT CREEK 593
FLATTY CREEK 574
FLEMINGTON, N. C. 693
FLOWER DE HUNDRED (Va.) 613
FORK CREEK (Ga.) 644
FORKED SWAMP 593

FORT WORTH, TEXAS 635
FOURTH CREEK, N. C. 681
FRANKLIN, N. C. 682
FRANKLIN COUNTY, N. C. 622, 635, 679, 680
FULLER'S CHAPEL (NC) 695

GASTON COUNTY, N. C. 660, 679, 682
GATES COUNTY, N. C. 575, 590, 629, 630, 640, 641, 644, 672, 679, 684
GATESVILLE, N. C. 641
"GEORGE" (Vessel) 655
GEORGIA 615
GEORGETOWN, D. C. 660
GEORGIA LEGISLATURE 644
GEORGIA LAND BOARD 643
GLASGOW COUNTY, N. C. 680, 682
GLOUCESTER COUNTY, VA. 656
GOLDEN GROVE CREEK (Ga.) 644
GRAHAM COUNTY, N. C. 659, 680
GRANVILLE COUNTY, N. C. 611, 631, 637, 660, 677, 679, 680, 684, 687, 693, 694
GRAYSON COUNTY, VA. 674
GREENE COUNTY, N. C. 680, 681, 682, 685
GREENSBORO, N. C. 660, 661, 680
GREENSBORO FEMALE COLLEGE 660
GREEN HALL 594
GREENVILLE, N. C. 660, 685
GROVE HILL 696
GUILFORD COUNTY, N. C. 678, 685, 686
GUILFORD COURTHOUSE 680
"GUN POWDER PLOT" (NC) 676

HALIFAX, N. C. 659, 680, 684
HALIFAX COUNTY, N. C. 615, 618, 622, 659, 661, 677, 678, 679, 680, 682
HALIFAX COUNTY, VA. 646
HALL'S CREEK 570
HALL'S CREEK CHURCH 562
HALL'S POQUOSIN 594
HANCOCK COUNTY, GA. 628, 630, 637, 645
HANOVER COUNTY, VA. 693, 694, 695, 697
HARDY'S MILL 620
HARRIS CHAPEL 695
HARTFORD COUNTY 681
HARVEY'S CREEK 574
HARVEY'S NECK 561
HAW BRANCH 594
HAW RIVER 674, 682, 684, 697
HAYNESVILLE? N. C. 677
HAYWOOD COUNTY, N. C. 675, 680
HENDERSON, N. C. 687, 693, 695
HENDERSONVILLE, N. C. 660, 681
HENDERSON COUNTY, N. C. 681, 685, 687
HENDERSON MILL CREEK 693
HERTFORD, N. C. 684
HERTFORD COUNTY, N. C. 596, 679, 681, 684
HIBERNIA, N. C. 695
HICKORY CREEK (NC) 594
HIGH POINT, N. C. 678
HIGH POINT SEMINARY 661
HILLSBORO, N. C. 676, 684
HOKE COUNTY, N. C. 681
HOPKINS COUNTY, KY. 638
HORSE LANDING 594
HORSE POOL BRANCH 594
HUNGAR'S PARISH (Va.) 617
HYDE COUNTY, N. C. 678, 681.

HYDE PRECINCT, N. C. 587, 673, 681

INDIANS 676
INDIAN FIELD 566
INDIAN LANDS 594
INDIAN SWAMP 594
INDIAN TOWNS 641
INDIAN VILLAGES 679
IREDELL COUNTY, N. C. 659, 660, 681, 687
ISLAND CREEK, N. C. 695
ISLE OF WIGHT COUNTY, VA. 566, 567, 596, 610-613, 615-621, 623, 628, 629, 631, 634, 637, 639, 643, 645, 655, 657, 679, 697
ISLE OF WIGHT RECORDS (DEED BOOKS) Va. 629, 631

JACKSON, N. C. 684
JACKSON COUNTY, N. C. 681, 686, 687
JACKSONVILLE? N. C. 684
JAMES CITY COUNTY Va. 609
JAMES RIVER (Va.) 607, 694
JAMESTOWN, VA. 639
JOHNSTON COUNTY, N. C. 648, 677, 680, 681, 682, 686, 687
JONES COUNTY, N. C. 656, 682
JONESBORO, TENN. 685
JORDON'S JOURNEY (Va.) 607

KINOUGHTANEE RIVER 564
KENTUCKY 636
KIMSEY MOUNTAIN 677
KINGSTON, N. C. 682
KING'S MOUNTAIN 677, 679
KITTRELL, N. C. 695
KNOXVILLE, TENN. 659
KU KLUX KLAN 676

LANCASTER, S. C. 660
LANCASTER COUNTY, S. C. 678
LANCASTER COUNTY, VA. 619
LAURENBURG, N. C. 686
LAWNE'S CREEK (Va.) 620, 639
LEE COUNTY, N. C. 682, 684
LENOIR, N. C. 676
LENOIR COUNTY, N. C. 656, 661, 676, 680, 681, 682
LEXINGTON, N. C. 678
LEXINGTON, S. C. 659
LILLINGTON, N. C. 680
LINCOLN COUNTY, N. C. 611, 659, 660, 661, 676, 679, 681, 682, 686
LINCOLNTON, N. C. 659, 660
LINCOLN PAPER MILLS 660
LINCOLNTON PRESBYTERIAN CHURCH 660
LITTLE RIVER (N. C.)568, 574
LONG BRANCH 594
LONG CREEK (Ga.) 644
LOUISBURG, N. C. 679, 695
LOWER CHOWAN PRECINCT 597
LOWER NORFOLK CO. Va. 612, 613, 640, 685
LOWER PARISH ISLE OF WIGHT CO. VA. 630
LUMBERTON, N. C. 685
LYNHAVEN PARISH, VA. 612, 685

MACON COUNTY, N. C. 676, 682, 686
"MACPELAH" (home) 684
MADISON COUNTY, N. C. 682
MASSOCK'S MILL (NC) 674

712

MAHARRIE (MEHERRIN) CREEK 562
MARION, N. C. 683
MARROW'S CHAPEL 695, 696
MARSHALL, N. C. 682
MATTACOMACK CREEK 564, 594,
    595, 629.
MARTIN COUNTY, N. C. 682, 687
MAURY COUNTY, TENN. 693
"MAYFLOWER" (Vessel) 639
MARYLAND 617
McDOWELL COUNTY, N. C. 683
MEADOW CREEK (NC) 676
MECKLENBURG COUNTY, VA. 611,
    696
MECKLENBURG COUNTY, N. C. 674,
    676, 678, 681, 682, 683,
    685, 686, 687
MECKLENBURG DECLARATION 671
MECKLENBURG CONVENTION 676
MECKLENBURG SIGNERS 683
MEDINA, TENN. 635
MEHERRIN CREEK 596
MEHERRIN INDIANS 641
MEHERRIN RIVER 596, 607, 681,
    684
MEMPHIS, TENN. 661
MEXICAN WAR 661
MIDDLEBURG, N. C. 695
MILL CREEK ON NEUSE 649
MISSISSIPPI 672
MISSISSIPPI RIVER 685
MOCKSVILLE, N. C. 678
MONROE COUNTY, TENN. 680
MONROE, N. C. 661, 687
MONTGOMERY COUNTY, N. C.683
MOUNT MITCHELL 683
MONTPELIER,NC. 693
MOORE COUNTY, N. C. 682, 683
MORATUCK RIVER 561, 562
MORAVIAN IMMIGRANTS 679, 686
MORGANTON, N. C. 660, 675
MOSELEY'S POINT 589
MOUNTAIN CREEK, NC. 670
MULBERRY HILL 594
MURFREESBORO, N. C. 681
MURFREESBORO, TENN 681

NACOGDOCHES, TEXAS 637
NANSEMOND COUNTY, VA. 607, 608
    611-614, 619-621, 623,
    625, 628-630, 637, 639
    640, 655, 658, 679
NANSEMOND COUNTY, VA. PATENT
    BOOK, 631
NANSEMOND RIVER (Va.) 610, 611,
    614, 615
NASH COUNTY, N. C. 622, 627,
    645, 679, 683
NASHVILLE? N. C. 683
NATIONAL GENEALOGICAL SOCIE-
    TY 649
NEUSE RIVER 570, 572, 607, 648
    682
NEW BEGUN CREEK 562, 564-557,
    574
NEW BERN, N. C. 659, 660, 677,
    686
NEW BETHEL CHURCH 695
NEW HANOVER COUNTY? N. C.674
    675, 680
NEW HANOVER PRECINCT 673, 675
    676, 677, 683, 684
NEW KENT COUNTY? VA. 694
NEW ORLEANS, LA. 660
NEW POQUOSIN (Va) 610
NEW SANDY CREEK CHURCH 695
NEWTON, N. C. 676
NEW TOWNE HAVEN 608, 610
N. Y. STOCK EXCHANGE 637

NIXONVILLE, N. C. 562
"NINE OAKS" (Home) 693, 695
NORFOLK, VA. 562
N. C. PRECINCTS 671
N. C. UNIVERSITY 660
NORTHAMPTON CO. VA. 616
NORTHAMPTON COUNTY? N. C. 596,618
    619, 621, 627, 643, 645,
    679, 681, 684
NORTHERN NECK, VA. 656
NORTHUMBERLAND COUNTY, VA. 609,
    612, 642
NUTBUSH CREEK (NC) 694, 696
NUTBUSH CHURCH 695

OAK RIDGE, N. C. 695
OBION COUNTY? TENN. 638
OGEECHEE RIVER (GA) 643
OKLAHOMA 687
OLD BATH TOWN 653
OLD TOWN CREEK 594
ONSLOW COUNTY, N. C. 684
ONSLOW PRECINCT 673, 683, 684
ORANGE COUNTY, N. C. 572, 674,
    676, 678, 680, 681, 683,
    684, 687, 694
OXFORD, N. C. 680, 694

PAMLICO RIVER 648, 653, 674, 684
    685
PAMLICO SOUND 684
PAMPTICOUGH PRECINCT 572, 653,
    673, 681
PAMPTICOUGH RIVER 607
PASQUOTANK COUNTY 562, 684
PASQUOTANK RIVER 564, 567, 573
PASQUOTANK CREEK 574
PASQUOTANK PRECINCT 565, 572,
    574, 575, 672, 676, 678,
    684, 687
PEE DEE RIVER 674, 685
PENDER COUNTY 684
PERSON COUNTY 679, 680, 684
PERQUIMANS COUNTY 568, 576, 672
    679, 684, 687
PERQUIMANS PRECINCT 562, 575,
    576, 589, 684
PERQUIMANS RIVER 566
PHELPS LAKE 597
PHILADELPHIA, PA. 659
PIG BASKETT CREEK 622, 627
PITT COUNTY 677, 685
PITTSBORO, N. C. 659, 676, 685
PLYMOUTH, N. C. 687
POLK COUNTY, N. C. 685
POLK COUNTY, TENN. 680
POTOMAC RIVER (VA.) 641
PUBLIC LIBRARY (the first) 674

QUAKERS 613, 614, 619, 684
QUAKER SETTLEMENT, N. C. 562
QUEEN ANNE'S CREEK 597
QUEEN ANNE'S TOWN 677
QUEEN'S CREEK (York Co. Va.)608
    609, 610, 611, 617, 618

RAEFORD, N. C. 681
RALEIGH, N. C. 660, 678, 687,
    693
RANDOLPH COUNTY, N. C. 680, 683,
    685
RAPPAHANNOCK RIVER (Va.)612,641
REEDY CREEK (Ga.) 643
REGULATORS 676, 684, 685
REVOLUTION 660
RICHMOND COUNTY, N. C. 685, 686
RIEDSVILLE, N. C. 685
ROANOKE ISLAND 678, 685
ROANOKE RIVER 559, 582, 589, 631
    675, 680, 694

ROANOKE SOUND 678, 681
ROBESON COUNTY, N.C.681, 685
ROBBINSVILLE, N. C. 680
ROCKINGHAM, N. C. 685
ROCKINGHAM COUNTY, N. C. 660,
    680, 681, 685, 695
ROCKYROCK CREEK 594, 595
ROCKYROCK NECK 595
ROGERS' BRANCH 589, 593
ROWAN COUNTY 659, 674, 675,676
    678, 679, 681, 683, 685
    686
ROXBOROUGH, N. C. 684
RUGBY, ENGLAND 694
RUTHERFORDTON, N. C. 659, 677,
    686
RUTHERFORD COUNTY, N. C. 675,
    682, 683, 685, 686

SAN ANTONIO, TEXAS 635, 637
ST. THOMAS CHURCH, BATH 674
SALEM, N. C. 679
SALISBURY, N. C. 659, 661,
    678, 693
SALMON CREEK 597
SAMPSON COUNTY, NC. 678, 686
SANDY CREEK 685
SANDY CREEK BAPTIST CHURCH 685
SANDY POINT 589, 595
SAREM CHAPEL 630, 641, 643
SAVANNAH RIVER 644
SCONE'S DAM (Va.) 610
SCOTCH HIGHLANDERS 677
SCOTLAND COUNTY 686
SCUPPERNONG RIVER 597
"SEA ADVENTURE" 607, 655
"SEA FLOWER" 655
SEWELL'S POINT (Va.) 612
SHAFTSBURY PRECINCT 570, 572,
    589, 590, 594, 677, 671
SHELBY, N. C. 660
SHOULDERBONE CREEK (Ga.)637
    645
SHOULDERBONE BAPTIST CHURCH
    628, 630
SIAMESE TWINS 674
SKINNER'S POINT 561, 562,
    589, 595
SNOWFIELD, N. C. 655
SOMERS ISLANDS 655
SOUTHAMPTON CO. VA. 622
SOUTH CAROLINA CONFERENCE 660
SOUTH CAROLINA 615, 637
SOUTH FORK CATAWBA 679
SPANISH ALARM 618
SPARTA, N. C. 674
SPOTTSYLVANIA CO. VA. 646,656
SPRING BRANCH 595
SPRING VALLEY CHURCH 695
SPRUCE PINE, N. C. 685, 688
STAFFORD COUNTY, VA. 655
STANLEY COUNTY, N. C.683,685
STONELAND, VA. 696
STOPPING CREEK (NC) 593
SUGGS CREEK ON TAR 649
SULLIVAN CO. TENN 681, 685
SUMNER CO. TENN 622, 635
SUPREME COURT N. C. 660
SURRY CO. VA. 629, 640, 655,
    657
SUTTON'S CREEK 575
SWAIN COUNTY, N. C. 686
SYLVIA, N. C. 681

TANNER'S CREEK, VA. 612
TANYARD BRANCH (NC) 595
TARBORO, N. C. 679, 697
TAR RIVER 522, 527, 628, 648,
    674, 679, 697

TAR RIVER BAPT. CHURCH 627,695
TAYLOR'S FERRY 694
TAYLORSVILLE, N. C. 674
TENNESSEE 615, 672
TEXAS 615, 626, 661
TEXAS CHEROKEE NATION 642
TEXAS REPUBLIC 661
TIMBER BRANCH 595
TOISNOT CREEK 628
TOTTERING BRIDGE SWAMP 595
TOWNSVILLE, N. C. 694
"TRANQUILITY" (home) 696
TRANSILVANIA CO. N. C. 687
TRINITY CHURCH VANCE CO 695
TROY, N. C. 683
TRYON COUNTY, N. C. 677, 678, 682, 683, 686
TRENTON, N. C. 682
TRENTON, TENN. 635
TULL'S CREEK 573
TURKEY ISLAND (Va.) 567
TUSCALOOSA, ALA. 676
TUSCARORA INDIANS 561, 675
TUSCARORA MASSACRE 674
TUSCARORA WAR 675
TYRRELL COUNTY, N. C. 570, 573 597, 678, 682, 684, 687
TYRRELL PRECINCT 672

UNION CHAPEL 695
UNION COUNTY, N. C. 683, 687
UNION CO. S. C. 660
UNITY CHURCH 661
UNIVERSITY OF N. C. 676, 678, 683
UPPER PAR. NANSEMOND CO VA 631

VANCE COUNTY, N. C. 679, 680, 687, 695
VANDERBILT UNIVERSITY 660
VANN'S CREEK (Ga.) 644
VANN'S CREEK CHURCH (Ga.) 644, 645
VANN'S OLD FIELD (Ga.) 644
VARINA (Va.) 607

WADESBORO, N. C. 660, 674
WAKE COUNTY, N. C. 677, 678, 679, 680, 681, 687
WAKE FOREST COLLEGE 679
WAINS 694
WARREN COUNTY, N.C. 659, 679, 680, 687, 695
WARWICK CO. VA. 613
WARWICK PLANTATION (Va) 556
WARWICK SWAMP (NC) 595
WASHINGTON D. C. 659, 661
WASHINGTON & LEE COLLEGE 562
WASHINGTON, N. C. 675, 685
WASHINGTON CO. GA. 643
WASHINGTON CO. N. C. 672, 687
WATAUGA CO. N. C. 677, 687
WATAUGA RIVER 687
WATAUGA SETTLEMENT (TENN) 685
WATAUGA VALLEY (TENN) 642
WAXHAW CHURCH SC. 678
WAYNE CO. N. C. 649, 686
WAYNESVILLE, N. C. 680
WEBSTER, N. C. 681
WENTWORTH, N. C. 685
"WESTERN DEMOCRAT" paper, 660
Western Branch NANSEMOND RIVER (Va.) 614, 615, 616, 630

631
WESTMORELAND CO. VA. 609, 617
WEST POINT, GA. 697

WHITESVILLE, N. C. 677
VICACCON CREEK 595
WICKHAM PRECINCT 567, 673, 681
WILKESBORO, N. C. 687
WILKES CO. N. C. 676, 687
WILKES CO. GA. 643, 644, 645
WILLIAMSBORO, N. C. 693, 695
WILLIAMSTON, N. C. 561, 675, 685
WILMINGTON, N. C. 675, 680, 685 695
WILSON, N. C. 688
WILSON COUNTY, N. C. 630, 646, 649, 688
WINCHESTER, VA. 686
WINDSOR, N. C. 561, 675
WINSTON-SALEM N. C. 660, 679,680
WINSTON, N. C. 681
WOFFORD COLLEGE 660
WRIGHTSBORO, GA. 644

YANKIN CO. N. C. 688
YADKINVILLE, N. C. 688
YADKIN RIVER 677, 678, 684, 688
YADKIN COUNTY NC. 682, 683, 687, 688
YANCEYVILLE N. C. 676
YEOPIM INDIANS 568
YEOPIM RIVER 590, 593
YORK CO. VA. 612, 616-619, 622, 623, 624, 626
YORK, S. C. 669
YORK COUNTY, S. C. 660

www.ingramcontent.com/pod-product-compliance
Lightning Source LLC
Chambersburg PA
CBHW070737230426
43669CB00014B/2481